# FAMILY PARADIGMS

# THE GUILFORD FAMILY THERAPY SERIES
## ALAN S. GURMAN, EDITOR

**Family Therapy in Schizophrenia**
William R. McFarlane, *Editor*

**Mastering Resistance: A Practical Guide to Family Therapy**
Carol M. Anderson and Susan Stewart

**Family Therapy and Family Medicine: Toward the Primary Care of Families**
William J. Doherty and Macaran A. Baird

**Ethnicity and Family Therapy**
Monica McGoldrick, John K. Pearce, and Joseph Giordano, *Editors*

**Patterns of Brief Family Therapy: An Ecosystemic Approach**
Steve de Shazer

**The Family Therapy of Drug Abuse and Addiction**
M. Duncan Stanton, Thomas C. Todd, and Associates

**From Psyche to System: The Evolving Therapy of Carl Whitaker**
John R. Neill and David P. Kniskern, *Editors*

**Normal Family Processes**
Froma Walsh, *Editor*

**Helping Couples Change: A Social Learning Approach to Marital Therapy**
Richard B. Stuart

# FAMILY PARADIGMS

## THE PRACTICE OF THEORY
## IN FAMILY THERAPY

**LARRY L. CONSTANTINE**
*LUK Crisis Center, Fitchburg, Massachusetts*
*University of Connecticut, Storrs*

*Foreword by Carlfred B. Broderick*

THE GUILFORD PRESS
*New York London*

*To my parents: to my mother, Loraine, and, in loving memory, to my father, Philip; and to Don, who much later became another father. They nurtured and challenged me and gave me not only love but issues to work on that would someday lead me to the work I love so much.*

© 1986 Larry L. Constantine
Published by The Guilford Press
A Division of Guilford Publications, Inc.
200 Park Avenue South, New York, N.Y. 10003

Printed in the United States of America

Library of Congress Cataloging-in-Publication Data

Constantine, Larry L.
   Family paradigms.

   (The Guilford family therapy series)
   Bibliography: p.
   Includes index.
   1. Family psychotherapy.   I. Title.   II. Series.
RC488.5.C678   1986        616.89'156        85-17217
ISBN 0-89862-053-8

# FOREWORD

The purposes of an invited foreword are ambigous and various. When Larry Constantine sent his manuscript to me with the invitation to write this one I myself was involved in the early stages of planning a book to be tentatively entitled (or, more probably, subtitled), "Toward an Integrated Theory of Family Process." As I have continued work on that project I have come to appreciate that Constantine's work in the present monograph must be assumed before further work can go forward. This is the highest compliment I can pay the book and having paid it, I should like to proceed to outline what, for me, are the major contributions of the book and then to expand on a couple of points in a critical or at least cautionary vein.

Until this point one of the most germinal works in the field has been the now classic monograph of Kantor and Lehr, *Inside the Family* (1975). The present volume is best viewed as volume two of that theoretical effort. Kantor and Lehr's concepts are expanded, elaborated, systematized, and illustrated. Six innovations merit particular mention.

1. *The Kantor and Lehr family typology (random, open, closed) is expanded to include a fourth type, synchronous.* This expansion to a four-fold typology is central to Constantine's theoretical development. In the tradition of Talcott Parsons, he is able to do wonderous things with this quadruplex model, not the least of which is to establish its topological compatibility with all of the other four-fold typologies such as Leary's Interpersonal Diagnosis Circumplex (1957), the Olson, Sprenkle, and Russell Marriage and Family Systems Circumplex (1979), the Beavers Centripetal/Centrifugal Model (1981), and, especially, Kantor and Lehr's (1975) own four-player model (mover/opposer/follower/bystander).

2. *The Kantor and Lehr position that there are enabled as well as disabled versions of each family type is more fully developed and documented.* Perhaps one of the most useful contributions of this monograph is its undermining of the common tendency of clinically based typologies to promote a single model of family health. There are well-functioning closed families as well as pathological ones (indeed,

only such an awareness could explain Olson *et al.*'s (1979) finding that the most satisfied category in their whole sample of 1000 midwestern families were at the extreme "enmeshed" end of the continuum). And there are pathological as well as well-functioning open families (as many of us who have done therapy with clinical colleagues committed to an open paradigm can testify).

3. *Constantine details the circumstances in which families may shift from one style of being to another, either as a function of normal developmental process or of stress and failure experiences.* Much of this material is handled quite abstractly in the monograph but there is independent evidence from Olson *et al.* (1983) (albeit based on cross-sectional data) that such paradigmatic shifts do occur over the life cycle.

4. *Attention is given to mixed and borderline cases, both as theoretical categories and as clinical realities.* Once of the troublesome verities that dogs every economical typology is that real-life cases refuse to be confined by their permitted parameters. In this instance, real families persist in manifesting mixed characteristics that straddle categories and defeat tidy typologies. Constantine incorporates this into his model with extensive treatment of mixed, borderline, and transitional families. Although this clutters his discussion, it helps it to conform with reality.

5. *The theoretical model is illustrated with and tested against clinical case materials.* When the same author both develops the theory and reports the therapy there can be much cause for skepticism about the independence of the test. However, in this case two things add to the credibility of the exercise. First, when the author finds that a case does not fit the model very well he responds by modifying, elaborating, and specifying the model rather than by reinterpreting the case. Second, every clinician reading the book can (and probably automatically does) compare the model with his own experience so that there is a built-in check against rampant rationalization and bias. In my own judgment the author's cross-checking between model and clinical reality is honestly and profitably pursued.

6. *Constantine refuses to hit and run with his typology; he proceeds to specify and illustrate its clinical utilities.* In the closing chapters of the book, Constantine tests the value of his theoretical work as a guide to differential intervention. Since the ultimate justification of any theory lies in its applicability, this is both the most challenging and the most crucial task of the book. For this reason I should like to comment at somewhat greater length on this aspect of the monograph.

The proverb says that one should provide new bottles for new wine, and ideally one would wish that the author could test his model using techniques of intervention that derive precisely from the theory and are isomorphic with it. This is, of course, too much to ask of any veteran clinician. Constantine had done what each of us would do in his place: he has adapted his own personalized bag of tried-and-true therapeutic tricks to the new task.

I would like to argue that this is a highly appropriate thing to do on more than pragmatic grounds. Family therapists have been remarkably creative and prolific in their generation of techniques and interventions. For over 30 years we have been testing, polishing, refining, and revising our tools. Collectively, we have tried most of them on thousands of families with problems. By now it is reasonable to assume that there is some correspondence between the reality of family structure and function, and the handles we have come to use to intervene in families. If there is any merit to the theoretical model that Constantine had constructed, it should fit comfortably with any reasonable subset of the tools of the trade that have independently been shaped and reshaped by the realities of family intervention. In short, the fact that the precise interventions used to test the model constituted a personalized and arbitrary selection of all possible interventions and that they have no tightly crafted correspondence to the constructs of the theory strengthens the credibility of the test, in my view.

I have one final point to make in this preface. Earlier I alluded to Constantine's four-fold model as being in the tradition of Talcott Parsons. Some readers of this book may not know very much about Parsons since he was a sociologist. Suffice it for our purpose here to note that he dominated the field of sociological theory for several decades with a paradigm of social structure and processes that had at its core a four-celled model of reality that came to be known as the AGIL model, after the initial letters of the four cells. Into that infinitely serviceable rectangular matrix he was able to fit the four stages of group process (going clockwise around the model), the four stages of socialization and of therapeutic intervention (going counterclockwise around the model), the four gender-generation roles in the family, the four basic functional prerequisites of every social system, and much else besides.

I was his student during the period when his model ruled the discipline, and eventually I began to figure out the secret of the apparently infinite flexibility and applicability of his magic matrix. It involves a certain sleight of hand. When you establish two (any two) basic dimensions of social life and dichotomize each, then set them at right angles to each other you get your basic quadruplex. That is the easy part. The challenging and enjoyable part comes when you crea-tively demonstrate that this matrix can be reinterpreted as an analogue of almost any other four-fold way of dividing up the universe.

For example, we have noted that Constantine had little trouble finding topological correspondence between his own model and both Leary's and Olson's. Yet in Leary's model the two definitional dimen-sions are *Love* and *Dominance* while in the Olson model they are *Cohesiveness* and *Adaptability*. It may be useful and provocative to play with whatever overlapping content these two sets of dimensions might show, but it seems to me to be counterproductive to impose an identity upon them and then to reify the identity.

As it happens I have been well acquainted personally with Par-sons, Olson, and Constantine and have also met Leary. Each man was subject to a kind of trance state when the spell of the quadruplex was upon them as though, at that moment, they were in touch with Transcendent Truth. My own view is that these models of reality deserve our attention not because they are consonant with some under-lying rectilinear substructure of the universe but because they offer a slightly more complex and thus more adequate picture of reality than the even simpler dichotomous views of the world that we are often presented (rich and poor, black and white, liberal and conservative, and so forth).

It is sufficient praise to say that I feel Constantine's two-by-two model of the family universe is a worthy successor to the earlier versions. The reader may find the going a little slow in the early chapters as the author systematically works his way through the var-ious conceptual distinctions and permutations of his model. Then, in the later chapters the pace picks up as he shifts his attention to its clinical applications. But whatever the pace (and despite these qualifi-ers), in my view this book marks a milestone in the development of family process theory.

CARLFRED B. BRODERICK
*University of Southern California*

# PREFACE

As I prepare this preface, the last of the book to be written, I am aware, more than anything else, of how long it has taken. I have been writing this book for more than 6 years. Over a decade has passed since I began the work that culminates in it. Its roots were in the very modest effort to refine, clarify, and interrelate some of the separate models originally developed by David Kantor. How quickly it branched out to touch on diverse models and theories from many parts of family research and therapy. But the harder work of pruning and trimming, giving shape and focus to the concepts, has taken much longer.

The approach developed in this book hovers, like my professional career itself, in the twilight region between theory and practice. Throughout my adult life I have been involved in theory building, first in the information sciences and then in the family field, yet I have never felt well-nourished by ungarnished theory. Only at the boundary of theory-becoming-action where practice crystalizes into theory can I sustain my energies. I suppose it fits, then, that I have always been a teacher as well as practitioner. And I have learned that it is harder to teach theory than to teach techniques, hardest of all to teach the use of theory to inform technique. Perhaps this is why the book has been so slow to germinate.

If there is a single, dominant theme, a leitmotiv that runs through this work, it is simply this, that there is more than one way in which families, organizations, and societies may be founded and coordinated, more than one way to succeed. More passionately than ever I believe that this fundamental awareness of diversity in human experience and interaction is essential for progress in our field, perhaps even for our species. In the small and specialized endeavors of family therapy, I hope this book helps bring new ideas and precision into our understanding of human diversity.

There are so many people—students, colleagues, friends, and clients—who played a part in the evolution of this book and the theory on which it is based that acknowledging them all would be impossible. That some are singled out for special mention should not detract from those unnamed but not unvalued.

David Kantor started it all with his extraordinary insight and whimsical genius and his willingness to become teacher and mentor. The influence of his innovative research, clinical inspiration, and theoretical grasp is so pervasive to my work and thinking, so crucial to the paradigmatic approach, that to credit him wherever needed would riddle the pages with his name.

Throughout the development of the theoretical base and its expression here, my friend and partner, Joan Constantine, has been as generous with her criticism and personal perspectives as with her unflagging support. There is not an idea, concept, term, or relationship within my work that has not been touched, reshaped, and enhanced by the magic of our morning discussions.

My friend and cotherapist, Judy Israel, has been unstinting in her encouragement through some of my most difficult professional trials. My work and talks with her have added many critical pieces to the puzzle.

In the late stages, Jim Iovino, a friend and skilled clinician, added some extra seasoning. I am indebted to him and Joan for letting me use case studies of some of their clients to illustrate certain points with greater clarity than I could from my own material.

From Ed Musselwhite, Lucy Gill, Anginette Jones, and Mike Mitchell, my colleagues in the Options Consortium, I received cheerful enthusiasm and playful challenges at just the right time. They believed in me and in the potential importance of the paradigmatic model for regions far beyond the boundaries of family therapy. More importantly, they demanded that I find simpler ways to talk about the theory, that I use easier words and clearer examples. Even though we never did write our book on management and organizational development, the process was immensely worthwhile.

A few people have sustained an extended correspondence with me that has been of immeasurable value. James Hawkins, a persistent believer, friend, and challenging colleague has frequently known just the right question to ask to jar me off "top dead center." Michael Nugent first made me aware of the importance of the work of Leary; in the years since it has been a pleasure to play with ideas together. And David Reiss, whose years of research on family paradigms is an immense resource for the family field, has opened a dialogue that has already made its mark on my work.

I owe a special debt to Carlfred Broderick who, at a critical turning point in my writing, gave me the most precious gift a professional colleague can give: the unvarnished truth. He had the courage to be appropriately pessimistic while insisting that I not give up; he recognized the intrinsic complexity of my undertaking and then convinced me to redouble my efforts to develop ideas with the greatest economy and focus I could muster. Because of his generous and pointed suggestions, one unpublishable paper was transformed into two published articles, and the log-jam was broken.

Some people played important parts in the early evolution of the theory and my thinking. Lou Rappaport helped kick the project off in the first place by building with me an early bridge between disparate theories. Tana Hyatt Plauger was there the night when things first came together and helped shape the earliest versions of the "unified process theory" with me. David Olson gave me my first professional opportunity to present the breadth of my theoretical explorations and then helped me to expand them still further. My many colleagues in the Theory Construction and Research Methodology Workshop of the National Council on Family Relations have helped me, again and again, to sharpen and refine my thinking. The Workshop has been and remains the very quintessence of what collegiality can and should be.

I also am indebted to my teachers at the Boston Family Institute and colleagues at Boston State Hospital who played important roles in my professional development and therefore in the processes leading to this book, among them, Jeremy Cobb, Bunny Duhl, Fred Duhl, Meredith Kantor, Sallyanne Roth, Ann Spitzer, and Carter Umbarger. Their influence is everywhere.

Lastly, I must thank some of the kids who, in sharing part of their journey into adulthood, have helped me learn so much more about families and about growing up in them; most especially among them are Beth and Randy, Melanie, and Julia. And most importantly of all, I am grateful beyond words to two of my brightest tutors and most open friends—my daughters, Heather and Joy.

LARRY L. CONSTANTINE

# LIST OF FIGURES

# LIST OF TABLES

# CONTENTS

xix

# THEORY AND PARADIGM

# 1

# THEORIES AND WORLDVIEWS
## Perspectives on Families
## and Family Theories

Looking around the house gives Mrs. Cole a warm feeling of pride. She works hard to make a good home for her husband and three children. Tidying up a bit for their arrival home, she glances at the clock. Time to start supper. She knows how important it is for young children to be able to depend on regular mealtimes. Dinners are special to the Coles, a time for peaceful relaxation and the quiet sharing of the events of the day.

Through the open window Mrs. Cole can hear the sound of the electric hedge trimmer; her husband likes to putter in the yard for a few minutes after coming home from the office. She can just make out children's voices, too. Peeking out the kitchen window, she sees her daughter and two sons singing as they come up the flower-bordered walk. Melinda, she knows, will be a proper young lady at table, but she hopes the boys won't have to be reminded tonight about how to behave during supper.

When Mrs. Cole looks across the ally to her neighbors' house she sees the antithesis of her own orderly home. The lawn, if one could call it that, is an uncut jungle of weeds. The Randall kids are screaming "like wild Indians" as they play in and on the pile of junk—old tires, boards, and ropes—that serves them as a jungle gym. Mrs. Cole shakes her head, wishing she had *real* neighbors next door, a proper family, one that went to church and kept their yard in shape. It's not as if they were poor, she thinks, after all, Mr. Randall does have work at that computer plant, though he seems to be home an awful lot.

Suddenly Mr. Randall comes running out of his house, hands tucked under an apron. As he nears the gym-set that he and the kids built together the summer before, he pulls his hands from hiding and begins to spray them with two squirt guns. They jump him with mock anger, wrestle the guns from him, and give him a thorough dowsing, then run, squealing, for the sanctuary of the house. As he strolls back, Tim Randall surveys the scene, their "island of sanity in a sea of paranoia," as he and Glyneth call it. He stands ankle-deep among the "weeds," grinning over their rich, lush green even now in the doldrums of August, while the nearby lawns, carefully manicured, fertilized, and watered, are turning brown. There is nothing like natural, wild grasses, he thinks.

As he enters the front door, he kicks two pairs of sneakers to one side, steps over the piebald cat sleeping on the stairs, and walks through the living room. Sasha is scattering a pile of newspapers and magazines, probably searching for the Sunday comics again; Tara is cutting paper dolls in front of the TV. Tim would describe their home as comfortable, lived in. Suddenly he dashes for the kitchen and turns down the heat under the goulash: almost in time to prevent it from scorching. Cursing quietly, he looks for the soup spoon he was using, then sticks his finger in instead, smiling as he licks it. He calls the kids, who make him explain for the *fifth* time (or so he says) just what a town meeting is and why Glyneth has to be there.

At the last minute, Tara suggests they eat out on the sun deck, so they noisily make the move. Tim notices Meg Cole peeking from behind her kitchen curtains. They are an uptight pair, Tim thinks, compulsive neatniks. Lawton Cole is always fussing over the lawn and the hedges; and Mrs. Cole has her clubs and charities. They certainly keep the kids in line, though. Tim is surprised that there's a spark of spirit left in those three.

The Coles and the Randalls are clearly very different families. It is quite apparent that these two families approach the everyday problems of family living in divergent ways. Their distinct approaches reflect equally distinct notions of what a family is, what a family can be, and what it ought to be. It is not just that they behave differently, they even *see* things differently. When each turns outward to look at the world, to look at other families, it sees things from its own particular perspective as a family. To the Coles, who see themselves as a stable, close family, the Randalls are disorganized and irresponsible; to the Randalls, who in their own eyes are a spontaneous and creative group, their neighbors are rigid and compulsive.

The Coles and the Randalls operate within different *paradigms*. A paradigm is a model, a model of both the actual and the ideal. But a paradigm is more than just a model or representation; it is a way of seeing and a way of knowing as well. A paradigm is really a model of the world, a worldview.

This book is about family paradigms, the paradigms by which families are and can be organized. The Coles and the Randalls do not understand each other; neither family can fathom how the other can live "that way." Their paradigms put boundaries around their understanding, shaping and limiting what they can see and do. People who work with families come to their work with their own paradigms of what families are, can be, and should be, and what family therapy is, can do, and ought to do. Our training, our theories, and, of course, our own family experiences shape what we see and how we see it.

## THEORY IN PRACTICE

Look around. What do you see? I look around and beyond my desk I see flowered drapes and a doorway leading to the living room. My view of much of the living room is obscured. Through a curtain of spider plants and English ivy, I can see a brass rubbing of a 13th-century lady hanging on a walnut-paneled wall. My younger daughter is watching television. I can see neither her nor the TV, but I can hear a "Star Trek" rerun, and Heather is the only real "trekkie" of the family.

I have already departed considerably from what I can actually see. I have drawn on a mental model of my family, a theory, to reach a conclusion about data otherwise inaccessible to me. I need not leave it at that, however; I can test my theory. When I do, I learn that it is Heather. She is making something out of paper, as she often does while she's watching television. Had I listened more carefully, I might have heard the rustle of paper or the sound of scissors and, using a more elaborate theory, made a prediction that sometime in the next hour Heather would come tentatively to the door of the study and ask to show me her latest creation. This theory now includes not only models of preference and behavior, but also of relationship.

By making use of theory, I have certainly extended my grasp of some aspects of my environment, but what might I have done had I put aside theories and dealt only with data? Let me return to what I see. As I said, I can see the drapes, but "drapes" is a category, a *classification* of what I see, not what I see. I see patterned cloth; the patterns resemble flowers. These are more categories and conclusions: patterns, flowers, cloth. What I see are patches of color shifting slightly, slowly, leading me to conclude, on the basis of my heretofore unconscious theory of elastic surfaces and atmospheric perturbations, that what I see is cloth draperies moving in a very slight breeze.

Such an exercise of "returning to the data" is useful, especially to make visible our implicit theories, models, and assumptions. But we cannot get away from the fact that *all* perception is based on categories and conclusions, on mental maps of the reality around us. This should not be seen solely in a negative light, however, because *theory is understanding*; without theory, we have only data, facts, knowledge without meaning. The trick, then, is not to try and eliminate theory (which cannot be done in any event), but to make it explicit, to use it rather than be used by it, and to broaden it to embrace the range of paradigms by which real people in real families organize their life together.

This book, though it will often cast wide its conceptual net, is really about a fairly narrow aspect of theory in human experience: the use of theory in family therapy. Family therapy, however, is itself a broad field with many varied approaches and quite a number of schools of theoretical thought. Nevertheless, all approaches claiming the name of family therapy have in common the founding assumption that the family is an essential unit for understanding and treating emotional or behavioral problems, whether these problems appear to be "in the individual" or not. So we are most concerned with the theory of individuals in, and in relation to, the family as a unit.

Even more specifically, the theories of special interest are those that distinguish different "types" of families from each other, and recognize that there is more than one basic way for families to accomplish what they need to as families. For this reason, the approach of this book may be called "paradigmatic family therapy." A central idea of this approach is that families have distinct, stable styles of functioning based on fundamentally different paradigms that need to be taken into account in working with them. In this perspective, theory is not a way of "homogenizing" families, not an excuse for applying one answer to every family problem that comes along. Instead, family therapy becomes "customized" by theory to fit each particular family.

## THEORY: AYES AND NAYS

Any theory is a model that organizes and classifies data. It is an attempt to explain something. Theory makes it possible to predict and, sometimes, to control or change things. Theories, whether conscious or not, accurate or completely ill-conceived, are an intrinsic part of the process of perceiving and dealing with the external world. This conceptualization of theory is considerably broader and less formal than the sort of definition most family sociologists would accept. Formal theory, as we shall refer to it, is especially important and useful for traditional research. A formal theory consists of a set of precisely stated basic assumptions and postulates, rigorously interdefined concepts, and formally derived concepts, from all of which specific, experimentally testable hypotheses are deduced.

## Objections and Reservations

Whether formal or not, a theory is often thought of as what you are left with when you don't really know what is happening. Theories are for scientists, for teachers and intellectuals, not for everyday, flesh-and-blood people, certainly not for those who really *do* things. After a theoretical discussion, however stimulating, don't we have to "return to the real world"? In therapy, theory is often regarded as a barrier between client and therapist, a barrier that interferes with an authentic encounter between them as persons. It is a crutch that can disable the therapist's intuition, or a preconception that can prevent direct experience of clients and clients' situations. It is, at best, a poor substitute for practical experience and skill.

The major objections to theory and the use of theory in clinical practice fall into two broad categories.

1. *Theory interferes with perceiving and experiencing real events and processes.* To some extent this is a valid objection, especially when the therapist is more invested in substantiating a theory than in seeing a family. This danger can be reduced, if not eliminated, by the therapist taking an active part in the search for counterevidence. It can be far more important to know where you are mistaken than where you are right, especially if you want to really know what is going on.

A potentially more serious problem arises when therapists do not make their working theories explicit. An explicit theory can be examined, discussed, debated, and deliberately revised. An implicit one too easily slips below the conscious mind to become a sink for prejudgments and miscellaneous misconceptions. Since you cannot ever get away from theory completely, it is much better to have your personal theories "out in the open" where they can be inspected, and where there is some hope of compensating for the distortions they introduce.

2. *Family theory is divorced from clinical reality.* This also has some truth, in part because of the isolation between everyday practice and academic research and theorizing. Clinicians who do not actively use theory in their work and who do not share their experiences and

insights are as much to blame as the academics who do not consult them. But this separation of the clinic from the lab is contrived in any case: Theory and application can be practiced under one roof without harmful side effects.

## Theory and Competence

Every therapy has its practitioners who eschew theory altogether, arguing for a completely personal, intuitive, and atheoretical role for the therapist. Among family therapists who subscribe to this view may be counted some of the most prominent names in the field; their objections cannot be dismissed casually. However, far more of the prominent family therapists do subscribe to some theoretical position. Indeed, many of them have concocted their own theories and founded new "schools" of family therapy based on these theories.

The position of this book is that, since theory is unavoidable, the only real choices for the family therapist are between conscious, articulate theory and its mute, unorganized alternative, between more effective and less effective theories, and between evolving, responsive theory and unresponsive orthodoxy.

It is undoubtedly true that good family therapy can be done without the aid of any formal or explicit theory. There are individuals whose interactions with others are almost naturally therapeutic and conducive to change, just as there are those whose abrasive, intrusive, or controlling personal styles makes encounters with them "psychonoxious." Occasionally one encounters those gifted therapists whose manifest skill and creativity in working with families almost assure that they will rise to positions of influence in the field. Many become family therapy "circuit riders," traveling from city to city, institute to institute, leading workshops and dazzling us with live demonstrations of their healing magic.

This book is not written for gifted therapists, however. It is written for those who certainly want to keep improving but are unlikely to ever be called "gifted." We can't all be Carl Whitakers or Milton Ericksons. Most family therapy, after all, must be done by rather ordinary therapists of modest abilities. As a downhill skier, I was recently described as being a "classic, improving intermediate." As a family therapist, I would be proud to wear a similar label.

Through theory and its systematic, albeit flexible application to practice, ordinary family therapists can be "improving intermediates" and be assured of doing more than ordinary therapy. At the same time, family theory can thereby be continuously elaborated and made more clinically relevant. In this way, the therapist becomes theorist.


## THE NATURE AND DEVELOPMENT OF THEORY

The nature of theory, its derivation, and its relationship to reality, are not matters of merely philosophical interest but are vital to a dynamic discipline of family therapy practice. Theory, to reiterate, is an organization of data by which the data are interpretable, by which they can be explained. Theoretical matters are, therefore, inextricably bound up with questions of how humans come to know and understand things, what philosophers call *epistemology*, a word much used and abused in the family sciences. In human sciences in general we can distinguish three major approaches to theory, three paradigms, each an epistemology, each a worldview in its own right. Here these will be distinguished by the terms *empiricism, relativism,* and *interactivism.*

Empiricism (also "logical empiricism" or "logical positivism") is essentially the established worldview of "hard" science. All truth and all knowing is established and verified empirically. Empiricism denies the meaningfulness of questions about absolute reality. Though it ultimately originates in a leap of faith, that there is an independent, objective reality to be apprehended, it then excludes all other conclusions based on faith. It is predominantly deductive: hypotheses are derived from general theory, then translated into operational terms, and, finally, tested. It is often preoccupied with the testing of these hypotheses. Verification of theory is by repetition; research must be rigorous, sound in design and statistical analysis; knowledge is based on facts and built by small increments.

Relativism (or the phenomenological approach) rejects empiricism and objectivity in favor of subjective reality. Reality, or at least the only reality of interest, is in the mind. Knowledge is built through appreciation of the unique experiences and perspectives of individuals and groups. Ethnomethodology and participant observation are examples of research approaches within relativistic science. What is correct is what is perceived or experienced by actual human beings. Theory is not verified by hypothesis testing, but by direct report from subjects.

Interactivism (or "critical theory") sees positivistic and relativistic science as merely alternative ways of looking at truth and the accumulation of knowledge (Paolucci & Bubolz, 1980). It has been called "critical theory" because it began with a critical reexamination of the underlying assumptions of earlier traditions and the impact of these on the choice of subjects to study, the design of research, and the interpretation of findings (Gergen, 1982). The critical perspective has progressed to develop its own concepts of verification and theory building. In this evolving view, the test of a theory is in *praxis* (Habermas, 1974) or its practical application to situations. If it works, if it leads to effective action, it is valid in some important sense. In the critical/interactivist tradition, theory is both derived and verified by one and the same process, by the on-going critical reevaluation of theory employed interactively in relation to specific situations.

The approach to family therapy argued in this book is probably closest to that of interactivism. Whether a theory works, whether it generates effective action in the conduct of family therapy, is more important than theoretical and empirical rigor (though these are by no means excluded). In the critical/interactive approach, the therapist is drawn into the theorizing and research enterprise as he/she employs explicit theories of family and modifies them to the end of more effective intervention.


### Beyond Eclecticism

There are so many theories of family and of family therapy that the family therapist is easily lost in the welter of alternative models. Often personality and personal experience appear to be the major deciding factors in determining whether a particular therapist hooks up with this school or that one. Unfortunately, many of the most prominent theories in the family field are rather limited in scope. One will focus on family power at the expense of values or feelings; another will deal with feelings but neglect power. Entire schools of family therapy have been founded on theories that are really only fragments of theory. Few of today's contenders seem adequate to the task of dealing with the whole of what happens in real families.

To avoid these limitations, many teachers of family therapy advocate an eclectic approach to family theory, presenting an assortment of family theories and theorists. They seldom address the question of which model to employ when. This is no trifling question; the therapist is left to choose intuitively, leaving an important ingredient for the conglomeration of theory inexplicit. To make matters worse, the theories of Minuchin, Kempler, and Bowen, for example, are not merely competing alternatives among which the therapist may freely select. At points the available theories are mutually exclusive and completely contradict each other. Thus, eclecticism leaves to the student and the practicing therapist the very task that the entire enterprise of family research and theory building has itself been unable to carry out, namely, pulling it all together.

The paradigmatic approach developed in this book is an attempt to overcome the limitations of parochialism without the burdens of eclecticism. An overarching framework is derived from general systems theory and its application to human systems. This framework is based on family paradigms and their realization by actual families. Many partial and more specialized theories can be placed within this framework and interrelated by means of it. By building conceptual bridges and a common vocabulary, a comprehensive picture can be constructed out of portions of other theories that may otherwise appear to be unrelated or incompatible. Whatever its other limitations, the result can cover the phenomena of family and remain self-consistent. More importantly, the paradigmatic framework does not supplant or replace established theories, but rather furnishes a way to view them that clarifies their interrelatedness.


## Good Theory, Bad Theory

What do we want of a theory? What is a good theory? Probably the first thing that comes to mind is that a good theory should be *right*. However, though there is no shortage of wrong theories, there is no such thing as a theory that is unqualifiedly correct. At best we can say that a certain theory works within desired limits of precision for some range of phenomena. In fact, certain kinds of theory that are invariably correct may be of no use at all, as we shall see.


### TRUTH AND CONSEQUENCES

No theory can ever be proved, at best we can add to the weight of accumulated evidence supporting the theory. There is always the possibility that the next experiment will uncover an important exception. For this reason, disconfirmation can be much more interesting than confirming cases. The more general and universal the theory, the less counterevidence is needed to bring it down. It is for this reason that the young Margaret Mead concentrated on certain supposed cultural universals; all she needed was a single counterexample to call into question accepted anthropological theories concerning sex roles, for example.

It is possible, even easy, to construct an unassailable theory that cannot be falsified. Unfortunately, this is all too common in the human sciences where completely closed, self-fulfilling theories abound. For an example in family therapy, consider the following concocted theory. Any resemblance to any actual contemporary theory is purely conceptual.

> *The Grief Resolution Theory of Family Distress: All family prob-*
> *lems are the result of unresolved grief in connection with a past*
> *loss, either in the current or some previous generation. Unre-*
> *solved grief ties up mental/emotional resources making the fam-*
> *ily less able to cope with stress, thus increasing the likelihood of*
> *failure to adapt functionally to normal and extraordinary de-*
> *mands of family life. In extreme cases, the original loss and*
> *unresolved grief may be so thoroughly repressed that they are*
> *inaccessible. Nevertheless, new circumstances resembling the orig-*
> *inal situation can trigger a renewed crisis and reduced coping*
> *abilities.*

It is easy to see how readily such a theory could evolve. After seeing a number of families in which some past loss is uncovered and finding that their distress is reduced when suppressed grief is permitted to be expressed fully, the therapist generalizes: all families are like that. Once formulated in the above form, all new cases will fit the theory. Surprise! This is very much like the fabled presentation by a psychoanalyst who announced the most extreme case of penis envy in the annals of psychiatry. After more than 10 years in analysis, the patient had shown no evidence whatsoever of penis envy. He concluded, therefore, that she must have an extraordinarily severe case to have repressed it so fully.

For a theory to be useful and to yield useful guidelines and predictions for the therapist, it must be falsifiable.

PARSIMONY

One of the most basic cornerstones of science and of human knowledge is Ockham's Razor. Given two otherwise equivalent explanations for a phenomenon, we choose the simpler. No belief in the ultimate simplicity of nature is required; it is enough to wish to keep our own task as simple as possible. This is especially important for the family therapist constructing a theory of a particular family, for it is often the more baroque models that yield the least guidance as to how to bring about change.

GENERALITY

We want the theories on which we base our practice to be broadly useful. Addenda or elaborations may be necessary concerning specific client populations, such as families with anorexic or chemically dependent members, but we should not have to carry around a headful of disconnected theories to be sorted through for every case and situation.

LEVERAGE

Some theories more than others give a good "handle" on what actually happens in family therapy; some are more productive of intervention tactics. This aspect of theory is called "heuristic value" and is probably a combination of many other factors. Sometimes the heuristic value of a theory may be more important than its accuracy. If the theory suggests useful questions for the therapist or for the family or directs intervention in a direction that precipitates positive change, then it may not be too important that it is wrong in its general conclusions about families.

## Big Theory, Little Theory

To achieve acceptability, a general theory of families or of family therapy has to cover a lot of ground. To do that parsimoniously, it must be couched in fairly general terms. Large, general theories tend to suffer a great deal in the translation to the specifics of one small family. In fact, as they look at a particular family, the interests of the theorist and the therapist may really be in opposition. The theorist is interested in the ways this family resembles others, what it has in common with all families. The therapist is (or should be) more interested in what makes this family unique, how it operates, and what its peculiar difficulties are.

These conflicting needs can be met through distinct forms of theory. Throughout this book we will distinguish two varieties of family theory. A *nomothetic theory* is a general theory of how families typically work or fail. An *idiographic theory* is a theory of how one specific family works or doesn't; it draws on nomothetic theory for a framework and is constructed using the concepts and vocabulary of some nomothetic theory or theories, but its primary focus is on what is unique and different, on what makes one particular family special.

An idiographic theory is a model of a family, not a theory of families. It is constructed by the therapist and specially tailored to guide the process of therapy directly. In this way many of the limitations of highly general theory can be circumvented and the benefits of theory can be brought to bear on the problems of real families.

CHAPTER

# 2

# IMAGE AND PARADIGM
## Paradigms of Family
## and Family Therapy

All families must solve the same basic set of problems: They must work out ways of dealing with the tremendous trifles of day-to-day living, and they must address the larger issues of growing up and growing old, births and deaths, leaving home and returning home—issues that mark the longer life history of families. Although every family must provide security, yet leave room for individuals to explore, and must endure, yet adapt, families differ in how they set their priorities as they attempt to provide for basic needs and resolve conflicts among these goals.

### PARADIGM, REGIME, AND PROCESS

Every family develops its own special style, its own strategies for dealing with family living. In doing so, the family operates as if it were guided by a *family paradigm*, a model of what the family is, can be, and should be. A family paradigm is an image (Boulding, 1956), a point of reference for checking the family's realization of its own concept of itself. This shared construction of family reality is not only a way in which the family views itself, but also a way in which the family perceives its environment (Reiss, 1981). The term "paradigm" appears to have first been used in this sense by David Reiss (1971), who developed laboratory methods for researching family paradigms. It has been elaborated upon by David Kantor (Kantor & Lehr, 1975; Kantor & Vickers, 1983) and others. The family paradigm appears to be a central and remarkably stable feature of a family.

Families differ most dramatically in the setting of their priorities concerning certain fundamental human issues and in how they decide between competing goals. There are, in these choices, many ways in which families may fail, but there is also more than one way to succeed. For some families, such as the Coles of the first chapter, the past looms large, and the means by which they meet the demands of daily life and cope with change are tried and true, a basically unchanging repertoire of well-established approaches. For others, such as the Randalls, experimentation and exploration constitute a way of life. Any research that sums into one single column findings from such different families can mask important information about how families work. Similarly, therapy that recognizes only a single ideal for family living may try to push families into becoming what they are not, rather than becoming better at what they are.

## The Origins of Paradigm

The role of culture in shaping family process, especially the significance of ethnic variation, is coming to be recognized as important for family therapy. The culture affects families by many means, including, of course, the mass media. Perhaps most significant for family therapy is the way in which the founders of each family system function as "culture carriers" to shape the family's image of itself and its maps of family reality.

Ethnicity is an important mediator of culture and a long-neglected variable in family therapy (McGoldrick, Giordano, & Pearce, 1983). Verbal aggression that might be normal in families of one ethnic community, such as among New York City Jews, may be rare, or even be a sign of family disablement, among the Lutheran families of suburban Minneapolis. Ethnicity contributes both paradigmatic preferences and a rich broth of nuances seasoning family interaction.

Although family systems may be guided by or conform to paradigms, these images or constructs do not exist magically apart from the individuals making up the family, like some reified "group psyche" or "family soul." Neither can they be said to consist merely of the sum of individual images. The family's distinct "image" of itself as a family emerges from the interaction of its members' individual images of reality and their behavior, this collective family image is formed over time, and crucial features of it will often be traceable to certain critical events in the family history.

One family had adopted a Cambodian girl when she was 12, although they had requested a much younger child. To this family, being alike, fitting in, and being in agreement were very important. But the adopted daughter came into the family with 12 years of experience in another culture and a completely different family setting. Her arrival became a polarizing event around which the family organized itself for years. Everyone, including the new daughter, wanted her to become "one of the family, just like the other kids." The tension between the reality of her different history and place in the family and this already-established family image continually challenged their claim of being a calm and agreeable family. The parents tried to get her to share her feelings and experiences with them, as the other children did, but had difficulty with the resulting challenge to the family image that derived from her different viewpoint. The family ended up dominated by deep ambivalence about similarities and differences.

As this example illustrates, although all family members contribute to and share in the generation of a family's detailed paradigm, not all contribute equally or share the same images in precisely the same way. Often a family's images are shaped more by some members' personal images than by others'. Such persons may be said to be "architects" of the family system; because the collective family images emerge in an historical process, the parents, as first on the scene, are the most likely to function as architects (Satir, 1972).

## From Paradigm to Process

Though family paradigms are important to the understanding of family process, we never see a paradigm. The image or images comprising a family paradigm are not themselves visible to us, and may not even be in the conscious awareness of family members. What we see are particular patterns of behavior that, by their redundancy, become recognizable as characteristic of a particular family's way of dealing with life. The paradigm is the template for the patterns we see, but it is not the process itself. The strategic style we observe or measure does not "just happen"; for it to become recognizable as a family's "pattern in process," some mechanism must assure its continuance. Family systems are not passively balanced in equilibrium but can only continue their patterned behavior through active processes.

A *regime* is the set of mechanisms by which a collective pattern in process is regulated (Jantsch, 1975). Paradigm, process, and regime are interrelated, as shown in Figure 2-1. These three levels of analysis have also been referred to as worldview, structure, and process ( Sluzki, 1983). *Paradigms* are reflected in *process* through *regimes*, the regulatory mechanisms that generate and sustain patterned collective be-

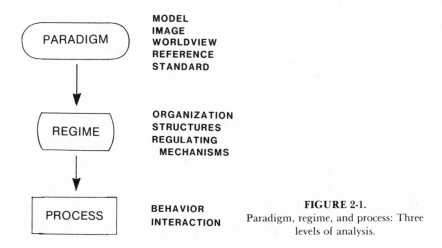

**FIGURE 2-1.**
Paradigm, regime, and process: Three
levels of analysis.

havior. The paradigm is the most abstract level and the most difficult to assess; process is the most concrete and most readily accessed. In the pivotal position is regime, which is the means by which paradigms, unobservable in themselves, can be translated into observable behavior.

In the most straightforward situation, a family's regime is successful in translating its paradigm into process. Figuratively, we might say the family succeeds at being itself. However, not all regimes are compatible with all paradigms, and it is possible for a family to be guided by one concept of family, yet be unable to put this into practice, either because its organization as a family is incompatible with its paradigm or simply because its organization is ineffective at generating the desired behavior.

In Chapter 4 we will see that there is only a limited variety of concrete mechanisms by which collective behavior in human systems can be regulated. The patterned behavior each type of regime generates is more compatible with some paradigms than others. A "mismatch" between a family's paradigm and its regime is not in itself a form of dysfunction, though the incongruence can compound stress in a family. Additional resources are consumed as the family strives to be or become something that is at odds with its methods or to behave in ways at odds with its image of family. Thus when paradigm, regime, and process fit together, less energy is demanded. Real families who have never heard of the niceties of our theories may mix and match behavior and ideals in seemingly endless variety and make these combinations work for them. Different members may hold competing paradigms and different subsystems may operate by distinct sets of rules. Nevertheless, the strengths and weaknesses of these combinations can be anticipated and understood from the same general perspective based on the simpler theoretical case where paradigm, regime, and process are all congruent.

## FOUR FAMILY PARADIGMS

There are many ways by which family paradigms can be distinguished; some of these will be explored in later chapters of this book. The approach developed here grows out of the pioneering work of David Kantor and his collaborators. Kantor and Lehr (1975) were among the first to recognize that fundamentally different types of families may be distinguished on the basis of what they called *typal goals*. From intensive direct observations of the daily routines of families they were able to distinguish and describe three basic "family stereotypes" that they termed *closed, random,* and *open.* Each "stereotype" represents a somewhat idealized description of one way a family might operate to regulate its boundaries and its processes to realize its own goals.

Kantor and Lehr's three family stereotypes, allowing for elaboration of the family's construal of reality as conceived by Reiss, are examples of family paradigms. For theoretical reasons, later supported by various researches (to be explored in later chapters), it became necessary to add a fourth basic paradigm, the synchronous paradigm. Thus, four basic paradigms, as represented in Figure 2-2, are closed, random, open, and synchronous. The rationale for the particular arrangement of Figure 2-2 will become clear as the fundamental nature of each of these four paradigms and their interrelationships are developed. At first the terminology may seem arbitrary and the definitions somewhat obscure, but with further exploration, the essential coherence of each paradigm will become evident.

All human systems may be understood in terms of paradigms and the regimes that translate paradigms into process. Whether they are families, business organizations, social clubs, or nations, all systems must define and maintain boundaries. All systems must deal with such fundamental dualities as individual versus group interests or change versus stability, but systems differ according to their paradigm in how these issues are dealt with and the priorities given to their resolution.

All four basic paradigms can form the basis for successful families; there is no single "best" formula for family living, no one "right

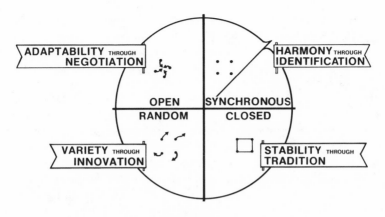

**FIGURE 2-2.**
Four family paradigms: A "map" of the "territory."

answer" in terms of family paradigm. Families guided by different paradigms will use different approaches to problem solving and be especially good at different things. Their divergent goals and methods will also mean they will be prone to somewhat different kinds of difficulties, but central to the paradigmatic approach is the principle that fundamentally different kinds of families can all succeed.

Real families are, of course, more variable than any such simple picture suggests. Their paradigms are distinguished by finer gradations and variations, intermixtures, and even combinations. Nevertheless, because the paradigmatic model rests on quite fundamental distinctions, it establishes the range of themes upon which variations can be built.

The four paradigms can be distinguished on the basis of their goal-directed behavior in time. All systems exist *in* time but differ in how they are oriented to the fundamental duality of continuity and change over time. The viability of all living systems is determined by the interplay of stability and adaptability; families that adapt too readily or resist too rigidly are disadvantaged. Within this requirement for survival and functioning, however, are many gradations and variants.

The "core image" of the closed paradigm is that of stability, security, and belonging. It is not that families guided by a closed paradigm never change, but that they prefer stability whenever possible. Closed families are primarily homeostatic, operating so as to correct deviations from established patterns. Because continuity and uniformity are given priority, the family as a group tends to be seen as more important than the individual. In a conflict of needs and interests, family comes first. The closed regime can be thought of as *continuity-oriented*, seeking to continue the past into the future. It is representative of the conventional, traditional families so well known to all of us. Its motto might be, "Stability Through Tradition and Loyalty."

The random regime, on the other hand, is *discontinuity-oriented*, maximizing change in a radical focus on the present. One of the most original contributions of the Kantor and Lehr (1975) team was to recognize that a particular kind of randomness in families is not the absence of pattern but a special kind of pattern in itself: the pattern of continual change. For the random paradigm, the guiding image is one of novelty, creativity, and individuality. Whenever possible, families guided by a random paradigm will opt for novelty and change rather than stable continuity. The individual is therefore paramount because individual creativity is the source of the family's variety. Though they are probably less common than closed families, random families are nevertheless often seen in therapy. The motto of a random paradigm family might be "Variety through Innovation and Individuality."

Many writers in the family field, among them Satir (1972), McGinnis and Ayer (1976) and Olson and colleagues (1979) have recognized a type of family distinguished from closed families by their openness of communication. Kantor and Lehr (1975) distinguish them by their collective goals. In *open* families, adaptiveness to the needs of both individual and system is the core goal; flexibility and balance are, therefore, emphasized.

The open paradigm is an image of adaptability, efficacy, and participation. The open regime may be said to be *consequence-oriented*, seeking to integrate past, present, and future in an adaptive mix of continuity and discontinuity that maximizes effectiveness. Both stability and change are valued because flexible choice between both is seen as necessary for maximal efficacy. Within the open paradigm, potential conflicts in need or interest between the individual and the group are seen as resolvable through a collective process of open negotiation and collaboration. The open paradigm is, therefore, above all else dedicated to communication, to open and authentic sharing in a search for joint solutions to the problems of family living. Its banner might read, "Adaptability through Negotiation and Collaboration."

The synchronous paradigm is based on images of harmony, tranquility, and mutual identification. The *synchronous* family depends on the extent to which its members "think alike" to avoid conflict and regulate its process. The synchronous regime may be said to be *coinci-*

*dence-oriented*, depending on a coincidence of goals and worldviews among its members. To the extent to which such coincidence exists, there are no conflicts between the individual and the group; neither comes first. It is aptly described by certain little-used words: it is based on *consentience*, a nonintellectual sense of unity, functioning *consentiently*, that is, acting in harmonious agreement and unanimity of mind. In their less well-functioning forms, synchronous regimes may appear as ossified or formless, depending on the extent of consentaneity, almost seeming to exist in a kind of stasis, outside of or untouched by time. The synchronous paradigm in its various manifestations tends to have a distinctly utopian, mystical, or magical flavor; not surprisingly, families guided by it are not well understood. Though uncommon, synchronous families do exist and have been described by both clinicians and researchers, without their theoretical significance becoming recognized. The motto of synchrony might be "Harmony through Perfection and Identification."

### Mixed Paradigms

Real families need not conform to our models and expectations, however sophisticated these may be. The four paradigms introduced in this chapter represent idealized types from a much greater range of paradigmatic variation to be elaborated upon in later chapters. The four fundamental paradigms are in a sense "polar" points that, as is represented in Figure 2-2, are as different as possible. In addition to the many possible "in between" variants, real families may also be guided by more than one paradigm, and these need not even be "compatible."

Nevertheless, families guided by competing paradigms will be prone to predictable problems based on the particular mixture of paradigms, the way in which these do or do not fit, the manner in which subsystems of the family interrelate, and the extent to which goals within one paradigm interfere with objectives important to another. These issues will be explored in greater detail in later chapters.

### PARADIGM AS WORLDVIEW

Each paradigm is itself a worldview, hence, from within any given paradigm, the view of families operating by any other paradigm is distinctively colored. From the perspective of any given paradigm, that paradigm seems better than the others. This accounts for some of the

difficulties faced when competing paradigms are brought together
into one family system.

From the perspective of a closed paradigm, there is only one way,
the "right" way, for a family to be; anything else is not a family. The
only alternative to a stable order is chaos and anarchy. To the closed
paradigm, both random and open families look this way, and synchrony, though not necessarily unattractive, is "utopian." From
within the random paradigm, there is more than one way to "do
family," but the alternative to the freedom and creativity of the random family is authoritarian oppression; both closed families with
their expectation of conformity and open families with their demands
for collaboration are seen as forms of tyranny over the individual.
Some random paradigm thinking, however, has postulated utopian
anarchies where "everything just happens to work out" in synchrony
(Constantine, 1984b), so it is also possible that the synchronous paradigm could look like utopia to the random paradigm, even as it may to
the closed paradigm.

To the open paradigm, closed and random regimes are merely
alternative strategies for solving problems, strategies that could even
be employed temporarily if the open regime chooses, but neither is
seen as quite as good as the more flexible and adaptive open regime.
The effortless harmony of synchrony, if it derives from long experience
with authentic collaboration, that is, from open process, would look
ideal to the open paradigm, but synchrony based on completely controlled socialization, on closed process, would not.

It is hard to say how the synchronous paradigm views the world,
but utopian literature gives some clues (Constantine, 1984b). The
synchronous paradigm would probably recognize the other three paradigms as distinct, but would consider itself above the "strivings" of
closed, random, and open regimes, which the synchronous regime
"transcends." The other paradigms are not tranquil enough, not sufficiently detached. As it is dedicated to sustained perfectionism, the
synchronous paradigm, though it may maintain a certain rational and
detached indifference to other worldviews, is likely to see them as
equally inferior.

## SUCCESS AND FAILURE IN FAMILIES

A family paradigm is like a floor plan, a family regime like a bare
house frame. The details of exterior finish and interior decoration may
vary considerably, but the floor plan and type of frame determine the
basic shape of the house, its fundamental strengths and weaknesses.

Once the basic distinctions in "construction" are drawn, many other aspects of family structure and process can be seen to follow accordingly, depending on a family's basic paradigm. How family boundaries are regulated, what values and attitudes dominate, and how information is exchanged and managed, all depend on the core goals stressed by the family paradigm. Detailed descriptions can be developed from research, such as that of Kantor and Lehr or David Reiss, from clinical observation, and from theoretical argument. Such descriptions are in remarkable agreement: it seems that the family paradigms embody real and important differences in the way families organize and operate.

In families that work as families, that succeed both as a unit and on behalf of their members, some realization of the typal goals of all four paradigms will be achieved. An effective closed family will have room for a certain amount of nonconformity and inventiveness and will allow for enough rebellion and individuation for adolescents to separate from the family successfully. Likewise, an effective random family will provide some degree of security and will not forcibly or prematurely spin its children off into the world. There will, however, be differences in degree and kind. The closed family will provide more security, the random family more opportunity for differentiation and self-discovery. Where security for the children of the closed family derives from dependable protection and rests primarily in the strength and wisdom of the older generation, in the open family, security derives from the on-going experience of successful collaboration and negotiation and rests in the mutual commitment of members to "hang in there" and "work it out."

In a similar vein, though all families are subject to shortcomings and possible failure, the particular kinds of problems and difficulties a family is most likely to fall heir to depend on its paradigm. The very stability and security of a closed family may make it somewhat boring and stultifying. By contrast, there is little danger of boredom in a random family, but it can become stressful if, for example, getting a square meal is left entirely to chance or individual initiative.

## A Paradigmatic Dilemma

To some extent, paradigms function like charters, setting limits on what a family can be and determining something of its probable fate. In remaining true to its charter, a family pays a price, even the family that successfully balances or integrates competing or alternative goals. The successful closed paradigm family, in maintaining tradition and sustaining loyalty will give to its members security and a sense of belonging, but not without sacrificing a certain amount of spontaneity and creative individuality. The random paradigm, of course, elevates these to primary importance, but as it succeeds it unavoidably foregoes some degree of stability and security. The open paradigm attempts to resolve the conflict between the first two paradigms by synthesizing competing goals through collaborative process. Open families can succeed in "having their cake and eating it too" by combining stability and variety into adaptability, and synthesizing individual and family needs through consensual decision making, but they too, pay a price. In its commitment to process and problem solving, the open paradigm gives up peace and tranquility; it is too busy "hassling things through."

The synchronous paradigm is the model dedicated to the perfection of peaceful and tranquil consentience. This is also, for the most part, an achievable goal. The successful synchronous family need not "hassle through" problems or "hash out" its differences, yet as a consequence of the difficult communication process it eschews, it misses out on a certain amount of intimacy, on authentic communication and contact between persons who are different.

## Therapy, Therapists, and Paradigms

Each paradigm seems to be limited in some fundamental and probably unavoidable way. For each, its existential flaw is the other side of its greatest strength. An understanding of family paradigms can be essential, therefore, for the family therapist wishing to capitalize on a family's strengths and trying to deal effectively with its weaknesses. These depend on the family's paradigm and the regime by which it operates, as do the most effective methods of intervention. Approaches developed for effective therapy with a population of mostly closed families, for example, might not be effective with an open family seeking therapy.

Families can live in all kinds of houses, from saltbox colonial, to Georgian revival and ranch-style duplex, but most people have their architectural preferences. The fact that all four family paradigms can work in practice does not mean that therapists don't have favorites. The family therapy field has had something of a romance with the open family paradigm (Constantine, 1983; Constantine, 1984a); though, as Kantor and Lehr (1975) have noted, since agencies and institutions tend to prefer working with closed families, which are more docile and predictable, many contemporary strategies of family therapy are really directed toward creating working versions of closed families.

The therapist should be aware of his or her preference for a particular paradigm or antipathy toward another. Personal values and value systems are an unavoidable feature of families and of family therapy (Trotzer, 1981; Zuk, 1979); however, it is not necessary to be *neutral* in order to recognize the inherent workability of all four paradigms. I may have a strong personal preference for living by an open paradigm, yet be ready to help others succeed in realizing their preferred family paradigms.

Theories of family, schools of family therapy, and individual therapists are often wedded to a particular paradigm. In many cases, this paradigmatic commitment and the bias it introduces is unstated and unacknowledged within the theory or by the therapists. The paradigm is implicit and must be deduced indirectly from the methods that are advocated and their supposed goals.

For example, structural (Minuchin, 1974) and problem-solving (Haley, 1976) family therapy both argue for the need to restore or reinforce an appropriate hierarchy with children subordinated to an effective parental executive subsystem. This concept of conventional parental authority and responsibility is absent or highly modified in the random and open paradigms. In an enabled open family, for example, parents do not "set" limits, but rather negotiate them with children in a collaborative process. Limits and rules regulating *parental* behavior are similarly open to such negotiation within an open family. Of course, this would itself be viewed as pathological or pathogenic from some therapeutic perspectives. How well an open regime might be working for a particular family could be missed altogether by the therapist intent on seeing anything unconventional as dysfunctional.

## Enabled and Disabled Systems

A broad definition of family function that applies equally well across paradigms is needed. Apart from its survival as a system, a family must enable the realization of the individual potential of its members. As collective and individual needs in all systems are apt to be in conflict, it is not surprising that the best functioning families somehow fuse or balance these needs.

Kantor and Lehr (1975) recognized this basic duality of the individual and the collectivity in distinguishing enabled and disabled family systems. In essence,

*An enabled family system is one which: (1) on the average, is able to meet most of its collective or jointly defined needs and goals; (2) on the average, enables most of its members to meet most of their individual needs and individually defined goals; (3) does not consistently and systematically disable any particular member(s) from meeting individual needs and goals.*

In other words, an enabled family is one that works on its own desired terms and in which no one is systematically left out. It must succeed not only as a unit, but on behalf of all its members as individuals. A family is disabled if it does not meet these criteria. Thus, for example, a family that works like a well-oiled team, but at the expense of the desired autonomy of its female members, is disabled; so is a family that cannot meet its own goals as an effective unit, even if everyone's separate ends are achieved.

This concept of enablement rests on a family's collective definition of itself and its purposes and on the individuals' definitions of their needs and interests. In this way, identification of a disabled system need not depend on an ethnocentric or culturally bound interpretation of the necessary functions of families. A family is disabled when it fails on its own terms or those of some of its members.

Because they balance or merge individual and family interests, all enabled families will resemble each other to a certain degree, carrying no mandate of their paradigms to a disabling extreme. The balance is struck, however, in fundamentally different ways within the four basic paradigms. Within the closed paradigm, individual needs are met *through* the family, which comes first. In the random paradigm, the group exists for the individual and its needs are met through their largely independent efforts. The open paradigm actively seeks to merge individual and group interests through dialogue and discussion. The synchronous paradigm relies on built-in similarity among members to assure that there is minimal conflict between individual and collective interests.

Returning to the example concerning parental authority, any enabled family will give its children a combination of freedom for exploration and self-discovery as well as protective limits that form part of a secure base from which to explore. In an enabled closed family, the extent and nature of both the freedom and the limits are determined, wisely, of course, by the parents. Freedom is granted when parents feel the child is ready and limits are set as the parents see these to be necessary. The best parents may, of course, listen carefully to what their children say and invite their contributions to the decision, but the rules are set by the parents and the final decisions are theirs.

In the open paradigm, freedom cannot be "granted" by anyone to anyone else, since it "belongs" to every individual. Limits are worked out cooperatively as needed for effective functioning within the family by drawing on the skills and experiences of children as well as parents. In the enabled open family, the children will be aware of and will feel free to draw on the store of knowledge and experience their parents possess, just as the parents will respect the value of the child's personal and immediate experience in many areas.

One might, for example, find a youngster from an open family and another from a closed family both taking part in the same overnight camping expedition. Both are permitted to be gone for the weekend and both call home when they get back to the staging area for the bus ride home. One child knows that kids must "check in"; it is a family rule set by parents and enforced through some penalty for nonconformance. The other child simply considers it part of a general pattern of being responsible and staying in touch with the family, something expected from parents as well as kids, just as had been discussed before the trip. The solutions may seem similar, yet may have been arrived at very differently.

For the family therapist the value of stepping outside a given paradigm is clear. By coming to understand and appreciate all family paradigms and the ways in which they differ yet are interrelated, the family therapist takes a significant step toward greater effectiveness in working with all families.

CHAPTER

# 3

# A PARADIGMATIC APPROACH
# TO FAMILY THERAPY
## The Interplay of
## Evaluation and Intervention

Paradigmatic family therapy is not a theory of family therapy or a body of family therapy technique, but a way of looking at families, theories, and therapies. It provides a way of organizing and making sense of the similarities and differences among families, theories about them, and ways to intervene with them.

Before beginning a road trip for the first time, it is useful to have some idea of the "lay of the land," the destination, and the route to be taken. Usually we consult a map or ask directions in planning the journey. Many years ago, when my wife and I first became interested in wilderness camping, we took a canoe trip into the beautiful lake country of Canada's Quetico Provincial Park. With our outfitters, we had pored over maps of the region and planned our trip carefully. When we set out from the outfitters' launch we checked the map one last time for good measure and paddled off up a wide, gentle stream, heading toward our first campsite. Three hours later we found ourselves in the cul-de-sac of a narrow neck of the lake. Pulling out the maps again we discovered we had paddled up the wrong bay. Had we checked our compasses before starting off, we would have learned immediately that we were heading in the wrong direction.

Family therapy can be like that. Some therapists do carry maps but then forget to get their bearings before setting out. Others fail to check the signposts as therapy moves along (or doesn't, as is also sometimes the case). Of course, family therapy may not always be like a trip by car or canoe; sometimes it is more like a magical mystery tour on a cross between a tortoise and a Brahma bull. But it can be made more systematic and reliable, possibly easier or even more fun, when the therapist uses a map, checks the compass, and frequently compares the map with the terrain.

The family paradigms introduced in the preceding chapter are a general map to a large territory. Recognizing the distinct regions of this territory leads to understanding the importance of knowing where a family is "coming from." If families differ in fundamental ways, they cannot all be approached from the same direction with the same old bag of tricks; large scale maps, however, are often wanting in detail. In working with an actual family the therapist must be something of an explorer, surveying and drawing new, more detailed maps of this family's unique realization of an abstract ideal. To use both kinds of maps effectively, the therapist must be acutely sensitive to the workings of particular families, always prepared to invoke an ever-evolving array of strategies and techniques.

The basic assumptions that distinguish the paradigmatic framework are relatively simple:

1. Families differ from each other in basic organization and in their images of family and family life. There is no *one* formula for family living. Many different kinds of families can be successful.
2. Families, like other human systems, function as if they were guided by overarching images—paradigms—which are reflected in family process through structure and organization—regimes.
3. Families vary widely in the regimes by which they are organized and the paradigms by which they are guided, but within this variability distinct primary forms can be identified.
4. Families that are guided by different paradigms and organized by differing regimes will tend to have different strengths and weaknesses as families.

From these four tenets, a paradigmatic approach to family therapy can be constructed:

1. As different primary forms of family differ in their strengths and weaknesses and in their probable direction of systemic failure, therapists need to identify and understand the unique paradigms by which families seen in therapy are guided and the special regimes that they have evolved.
2. Evaluation of the family system is essential for effective family therapy. A thorough assessment includes an understanding of a

family's problems as well as of the relationship between manifest problems and the family's regime and paradigm, not only of its disabled structures, but of its strengths and assets.

3. A unique, custom-tailored theory is constructed for each family, reflecting its particular paradigm and regime. This one-of-a-kind theory is made explicit as an overall map of the family.

4. Intervention is systematically related to evaluation, guided by the map of the family constructed by the therapist. Predictions and interventions derived from it are made explicit.

5. Theory—general theory as framework and special theory as map—is used actively and continually as a part of an interactive process in which theory guides therapy and is revised by feedback gained from its application in therapy.

6. The outcome of family therapy is assessed explicitly in terms of each family's own paradigm.

7. Therapists have a professional responsibility to become aware of their own personal family paradigms and the paradigmatic basis of the theories and techniques they employ. They have an ethical responsibility to distinguish their own paradigmatic preferences from those of the families with which they work.

Within the paradigmatic approach to family therapy two emphases emerge. First, evaluation becomes more important, especially evaluation of a family's paradigm and peculiar realization of it. Second, intervention is based on the active use of theory, of explicit models of families, to improve the fit between therapy and the practice of therapy with a particular family (cf. Argyris & Schön, 1974). These issues are not unique to one particular approach, but they assume a special importance in paradigmatic family therapy.

## THEORY-BASED THERAPY

Paradigmatic family therapy makes use of a discipline by which professionals can actively and continually improve their own skills and, at the same time, contribute to the advancement of the field of family therapy. The basic concept is that all parts of the therapeutic process be made explicit and subject to checks and counterchecks.

First, the therapist is explicit about the body of nomothetic (general) theory being employed and is aware of the limitations of the theory, especially its range of applicability and its assumptions. Second, the therapist studies the family in order to build an explicit idiographic (particular) theory that can be tested and revised. Third, the therapist uses an explicit idiographic theory to plan interventions. These designed interventions are, in effect, therapeutic experiments through which the working theory of the family can be revised, thereby leading to more effective interventions. Finally, the therapist formally assesses the outcome of therapy and uses the information gained to further check the idiographic theory and, in turn, the nomothetic theory on which it was based.

Stated this way, the whole concept may sound rather imposing and rigid. In practice, however, the therapist does not give up spontaneity just because a session has been planned or because the therapist has an overall strategy for the conduct of therapy. A good therapist is always prepared for a change of plans, ready for the interesting sidetrip that promises new vistas or holds the potential of an undiscovered shortcut. Changes and exceptions merely become part of the journey and are used to expand and elaborate understanding of the family and of family therapy. The change of practice demanded by the theory-based approach is in the superstructure in which therapy takes place, not in the therapy itself, which may be as creative, as playful, as inventive, or as glum as the therapist chooses to make it.

Still, to some readers and reviewers this approach to family therapy may sound mechanical or "engineered." Attention is likely to be drawn to my background, which includes an education in the information and management sciences. In truth, I do believe that family therapists can learn some things from engineers, not because people are machines or ought to be dealt with mechanically, but because both engineers and family therapists are professionals. To be a professional means to be invested in increasing competence and efficacy and to take an active part in the advancement of the profession as a whole. It is not enough to go to conferences and workshops and accumulate continuing education credits; without explicit and continual checks on performance, the family therapist remains, in some sense, an amateur rather than a professional.

An explicit theory of family and family change functions as an adaptable goal against which the conduct of therapy can be checked. The interactive use of theory is, therefore, at the core of family therapy rising above amateurism.


## FROM EVALUATION TO INTERVENTION

Family therapy is not a single process based on one set of skills. The therapist's intentions and focus of attention, as well as the techniques brought into play, shift with time, not only from moment to moment or from one session to the next, but also in an overall pattern over the duration of therapy. Ordinarily these are not phases or stages in the usual sense of the terms, but rather shifts in importance, as the salience or frequency of particular activities and concerns call on different cognitive and interpersonal abilities. Although the phases of family therapy may be familiar territory to the experienced family therapist, it is worthwhile to reexamine them within a paradigmatic framework. As the schematic representation in Figure 3-1 suggests, they do not neatly sort themselves out sequentially, but overlap.

Evaluation is the process of determining what's happening in a family and how that family works; intervention draws on the results of an evaluation to bring about change in the family; assessment reevaluates the family to ascertain the effects of intervention. These activities not only overlap in time but in function as well. A group drawing task, employed by the therapist to gain a better understanding of a family, impacts on the family and therefore is also an intervention. Maneuvers to shift the balance of power between the spouses may yield new information about the rigidity of the family system. The very process of assessing outcome gives the family new information, possibly altering it still further. The most useful distinction is that the flow of information of primary interest to the therapist differs depending on the process: in evaluation and assessment, the direction of main interest is from the family to the therapist; in intervention the reverse is true.

There is also a difference between evaluation and intervention in the way the therapist deals with novel information originating in therapy. David Kantor once said to a supervision group that novel

**FIGURE 3-1.**
Phases and relative emphases of therapy process.

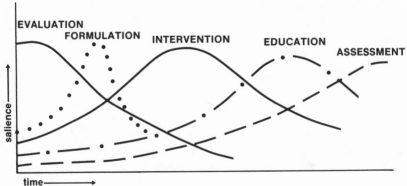

information is like a rabbit suddenly hopping onto the scene. The normal temptation is to chase the rabbit, even to follow it down its hole, but during evaluation, when the therapist is still mapping out the family territory, this urge must be resisted. Instead, the therapist merely notes the size and color of the rabbit, where it appeared and where it disappeared. An inadequate evaluation is frequently the result of "chasing rabbits"; if the therapist is busy chasing rabbits, he/she may never learn what the total population of rabbits is and may miss prairie dogs entirely. Furthermore, the rabbits that scurry across the scene early in therapy may only be decoys. Therapists who are particularly atuned to certain themes—incest, alcoholism, or male oppression, for example—can be especially vulnerable to being led down a rabbit hole by a family decoy.

Whether or not the therapist engages in a conscious, intentional family evaluation, and whether or not evaluation is considered a distinct phase to be punctuated and distinguished from later therapy, evaluation does take place. From the moment of first contact with a family, the therapist is building a mental picture of the family, the problem, and what to do about it. The arrangement of phases in Figure 3-1 is not a prescription but a description—we cannot assess outcome until we have done something; we cannot choose among an infinitude of therapeutic interventions without knowing what is needed for a particular family. The choice, then, is not whether to evaluate a family, but rather whether to do so consciously and by design.

Regardless of how thorough and carefully planned it may be, evaluation limited to the earliest part of therapy is not enough. Unavoidably, the family therapist continually evaluates and assesses as therapy continues, gauging the impact of interventions and revising the map of the family. Evaluation is both a phase and a process. This must be kept in mind even when the discussion, for convenience, focuses primarily on evaluation as a phase.

## Evaluation versus Diagnosis

With the popularity of television medical dramas everyone has heard of diagnosis. Diagnosing the disease *is* the drama in many shows. The greying medical genius pours over angiograms, ponders the minute clues, and peruses old medical texts to figure out just what rare ailment has stricken the handsome rock star. Hackneyed though these plots often are, they point to important aspects of diagnosis.

Diagnosis depends on nosology, the systematic classification of diseases. It presumes that a set of distinct diseases exists, each with distinctive symptoms, each with its specific etiology or course of development from a specific cause or causes. Diagnosis, aside from the interesting detective work it may on rare occasion entail, is really a matter of figuring out into which predefined box a particular patient fits.

Family therapy does not yet have an adequate listing of "diseases" and their "symptoms" into which families may be classified. Instead, the afflictions of "identified patients" are pressed into service. Thus one hears of the "anorexic family" or of "alcoholic families." Even if it were possible to develop a nosology of family system "ailments," many family therapists and theorists would question whether it would be desirable. Family systems are extremely complicated entities. Each family develops unique, convoluted strategies for its continued emotional and physical functioning. What is adaptive under some circumstances is maladaptive under others; what is functional in one form is dysfunctional carried to the limit; a useful strategy becomes disabling when it is the only strategy available.

Families that work do not necessarily differ markedly from those that do not. Rarely, if ever, does the difference result from some specific, identifiable "pathogen" or disease-causing agent. Differences in degree and in context rather than in kind distinguish "healthy" families from those in need of help and change.

In family therapy, therefore, diagnosis in its established medical sense is not appropriate. This does not mean that the family therapist should simply begin "treatment" without a careful and systematic evaluation of the current circumstances of the client family; it only means that a somewhat different process is in order. Of particular importance is the identification of a family's basic paradigm, its style and strategy for solving problems. This will be seen in later chapters to be related not only to the kind of problems it is likely to experience but also to the likelihood of success with various approaches and techniques of therapy.

## Assets, Liabilities, and Pathology

Even within the "disease model," it is not sufficient merely to identify the disease; the treatment may depend on the severity of the affliction and other specifics of the patient's health. A patient might not be strong enough for surgery, or, instead of a powerful drug resorted to only in extreme cases, a slower, safer intervention may be used where general good health permits.

In family therapy, it is as essential to understand the strengths of a family as to catalog its weaknesses. The therapist who does not take these into account only makes the therapy more difficult. Often this is a therapist who is trying to cure the family rather than facilitating the family to draw on and build its own resources for change.

For example, in one single-parent family, the mother and three oldest children loved to talk; their communication channels were open and functioning well. Taking account of this, the therapist would save up certain comments until the end of each session, when there was no time left to deal with them, knowing that these would become topics of discussion in the car on the way home. The family would reliably "do their homework" concerning the issue raised, usually reporting their progress the following week.

A complete evaluation results in a thorough cataloguing of the family's assets and liabilities in areas of interest to the family therapist. The headings under which this catalog will be organized will depend on the nomothetic theory being employed by the therapist. Using the paradigmatic framework, it is fairly easy to determine whether an evaluation "touches all bases" needed to proceed with therapy, because the framework includes a complete "catalog" of the dimensions in which family process takes place. It can never be *guaranteed* that an evaluation has not missed significant features of the family system's operation; however, once the basics of how a family operates in each dimension are identified, the evaluation has at least covered the territory overall.

Some family therapists, even some schools of family therapy, focus on pathology, on the dysfunctional or malfunctioning aspects of a family. Too often the therapist is thereby tempted to think that evaluation is complete once some central pathology is identified. Worse, there is a tendency, especially among beginning therapists, for this focus to degenerate into "pathology hunting."

The problem, as it was once colorfully expressed to me, is that a family is like an old barn—it has been around a long time. Over the generations a great deal of shit accumulates. It's not hard to find; almost any place you probe will turn up a shovelful. And the more you dig the more you will uncover. Even enabled families will prove to have their "buried shit" if the therapist digs for it. The therapist's questions should always be: What is working and what is not? Why and how does it work? Why and how does it not?

## The Results of Evaluation

The purpose of evaluation is to develop a clear and comprehensive picture of how a particular family works in its present context. In the specific nomothetic language or format with which the therapist is most comfortable, a theory is constructed of how the family works, its strengths and weaknesses, how it became what it is, and how it might change to work better as a unit, as well as on behalf of its individual members.

Evaluation creates the first draft of the detailed map by which the therapist's work will be guided through the unfamiliar territory of the family's system. Without such a map the therapist is handicapped in several respects. The result of evaluation, the map,

1. identifies the basic type of terrain: a family's basic paradigm and the regime by which it is regulated;
2. indicates points of entry or access to the family's territory, starting points for therapy;
3. outlines unknown territory to be explored further;
4. highlights areas of special interest as well as ones to be avoided or approached in a special way;
5. marks checkpoints against which progress in therapy can be measured;
6. furnishes the means for verifying both the map, the idiographic theory of this one family, and the nomothetic theory from which it was derived; and
7. facilitates monitoring of the effectiveness of the therapist's attempts to help the family change itself.

The specific content of an evaluation depends on the nomothetic framework in which it is expressed. In all cases, however, it must identify characteristic features of individuals and of the family as a system and describe their interrelationships. Of particular importance are the interrelationships between individual symptoms and systemic disablement. This subject will be covered in greater detail in Chapter 10.


Formulation: Bridge to Intervention

Sometimes a family therapist will complete a well-conceived and well-executed family evaluation, then plunge into a therapeutic process that seems to bear little relation to the results of evaluation. This often occurs with an experienced individual therapist who has "learned family therapy" but has yet to adopt a comfortable personal style for dealing with whole families.

The link between evaluation and intervention is formulation. In this process the therapist formulates what are considered to be the key disabled features of the family system and plans the intervention strategy by which these will be reenabled. The planning aspects of formulation deal with both short-term tactics and long-term strategy. Although the latter is always recognized as more tentative and subject to revision, the long-term view is essential to provide the therapist with signposts against which progress can be checked.

It has often been argued that the "science" of family therapy is still so limited and inadequate that formulation of long-term intervention strategy is a mere exercise, since actual and planned therapy will differ so completely. What is important is not how closely the therapist adheres to the plan, but that, when a different tack is taken, the therapist be aware of it and be able to explain or justify the departure. If it is true that the therapist's planning and predictive abilities are limited, or the theoretical bases for planned interventions are inadequate, this will become apparent as each exception or revision is made. Even more importantly, the therapist will begin to build a base of knowledge from which to improve theory and strategic skills alike.

In this connection I would like to introduce Mackenzie's First Law, a principle borrowed from another field but applicable here.

*Mackenzies's First Law: If it isn't written down, it doesn't exist.*[1]

Human memory is too selective and malleable to be reliable over the long haul of family therapy. This is not a plea for formal written records for agency files; these are, admittedly, an often onerous part of the work of the therapist and may be organized in ways that make them of limited use to the systems-oriented family therapist. Formulations should be kept in whatever way is most useful to the therapist and adds the least clerical burden, otherwise they will simply not be kept. Thus therapists develop idiosyncratic ways of recording formulations, which are nevertheless better than *no* records. Though some standardization may be desirable for comparative purposes, it is difficult to imagine instituting any guidelines without first resolving conflicts among different schools of therapy or risking alienating the proponents of these schools.

Effective formulation must derive from the evaluation, not merely spring full-blown from some intuitive wellspring of the gifted therapist. From the evaluation the therapist extracts particular aspects of the family's disablement that become the focus of intervention. The focal issues do not exclude other aspects of the family's operation from consideration, but merely provide a starting point and a handle on the whole of the system's workings. If the therapist is pulled toward some

---

1. In an ironic twist, K. D. Mackenzie never wrote down his first law; however, since it has been quoted in the written works of others, it does exist.

formulation that does not exactly follow from the evaluation, it may be a sign that the evaluation was incomplete; neither the formulation nor the evaluation need be abandoned completely under those circumstances, but the therapist should be prepared for further evaluation to complete the link.

The strategy and initial tactics of intervention should derive from the formulation of the focal issue and from the overall map of the family produced by the evaluation. An example of such a map is shown in Figure 3-2. ("Mapmaking" will be covered further in Chapter 12.) A school-aged child, Brett, is pictured as central in the map of the family, virtually running the show, while the mother and father are, in effect, at opposite "edges" of the family. Brett has little to do with his sister and brother, except to "parent" them. The therapist has concluded that both the mother's frequent threats to leave and Brett's whining dependency at school are symptoms of this arrangement. The ultimate aim is to move the parents closer together and toward the center, freeing the parentalized child from the burdens of his role while simultaneously substituting some of the rewards of dependency for those of dominance. (This does not imply that these changes would necessarily be desirable in all similar cases; the family paradigm must

**FIGURE 3-2.**
Map of Brett's family.

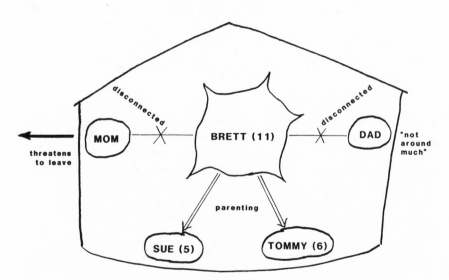

be taken into account. This simplified example merely illustrates the formulation process.)

The strategy is first outlined in terms of the idiographic theory, "on the map" as it were. The plan might first bring the parents closer together at the periphery, then bring them toward the center *with* Brett, focusing on nurturing him, then move Brett outward. These moves might be translated into a concrete treatment plan in which the parents are seen in couple's therapy directed toward increasing affection between them without invalidating the emerging differentiation on the part of the mother. During this phase, Brett's "parental" activities are indirectly encouraged. Next, he is seen with his parents, allowing him to keep "center stage," but in the context of a more united parental subsystem. Finally, he is seen with his siblings with the focus on enabling natural alliances with his brother and sister.

The advantage of formulating strategy first in terms of the idiographic theory developed in evaluation and then translating into concrete, "real world" terms, is that it assures that interventions and theory will be related. The formulation can then be used to check the progress of therapy, and interventions serve to check the validity of the formulation.

## ASSESSMENT OF OUTCOME

If a family does not leave therapy "prematurely," therapy is usually terminated in one of two ways: by mutual agreement that it "feels finished," at least for the present (which may mean that the presenting symptoms have been alleviated), or by completion of a contracted number of sessions. Too few therapists terminate on the basis of an assessment of the results of therapy and even fewer do follow-up assessments. It is very difficult, therefore, to tell whether anything good is really happening. Outcome research demonstrating the efficacy of family therapy may be reassuring to those of us with the temerity to charge money for what we do, but the research literature is silent on the question that should be most important to each therapist: Does the therapy *I* do have any real positive effects? (Of course, the answer may not be pleasant to learn; this could be part of the reason why so few therapists assess results and why the field as a whole has preferred arbitrary educational standards to performance criteria for licensing.)

In assessing outcome, therapists get information about changes in the family and feedback about their own performance. Frequently, the feedback itself suggests ways to improve therapeutic effectiveness, especially when less "successful" cases are compared with the more spectacular outcomes. In effect, therapists become their own supervisors and instructors, by drawing the family into the process with an explicit provision for outcome assessment.

Each therapist, whether in private practice or working in an institution or agency, also has a chance to contribute to the general knowledge of family therapy. The field of family therapy needs frontline field reports from clinicians to test the armchair philosophizing of theorists and the laboratory generalizations of researchers. It would be of immense value if, for example, an experienced therapist were to report on a series of families with an anorexic identified patient, all doggedly treated according to a popular model, all with less than ideal outcomes. The value of such findings would hinge on the availability of documentation showing careful evaluation, reasonable formulation and intervention, and disappointing results.

This is not to say that only negative findings are important. I chose this type of example because the literature is crammed with success stories and is sadly deficient in interesting failures. Sound theory depends on both.

## A PARADIGMATIC VIEW OF THEORIES AND THERAPIES

Underlying any approach to family therapy is a model of what a family is, can be, and ought to be, in essence, a picture of the desired outcome from therapy (Fisher, Giblin, & Hoopes, 1982). In many schools of family therapy, as well as some theories, this model remains partially implicit. These paradigms nevertheless guide therapists and the process of therapy, steering them and the families they treat toward certain outcomes and not others (Kantor & Neal, 1985). The paradigmatic framework can be used to understand these therapeutic paradigms and the interrelationships between the various schools of therapy.

Two distinct issues emerge, the paradigm for "the healthy family" and the paradigm for the process of therapy itself. These need not be the same or even closely related. Both may affect the ability of a given therapy to deal with families of different paradigms. Virginia Satir and her followers are very clear, for example, about the model they see as healthy: a family based on the open paradigm. But Satir's writing (e.g., Satir, 1972) actually only contrasts an enabled form of an open paradigm family with a disabled version of a closed paradigm family.

Research-based models can show similar paradigmatic preferences because of inadvertent selection biases or more subtle factors in the interpretation of the data or construction of the model. Frequently one particular paradigm will be identified as healthy or functional and contrasted with disabled versions of some or all of the other paradigms. Of the theories that make fairly clear typal distinctions, nearly all have "favored" either the open or the closed paradigm. In a review of 18 family typologies, Leonard (1981) found that 13 equated forms of the open paradigm with normality or healthy functioning.

Some therapists' preferred family paradigm may have to be inferred. For example, numerous therapists and theorists consider it important for families to have clear intergenerational boundaries, with a well-established "parental subsystem" having "executive authority" over the family. This model characterizes the regimes of enabled, effectively functioning forms of closed paradigm families, but is not necessarily typical of successful open paradigm or random paradigm families, which are more likely to reflect a commitment to a more egalitarian structure.

To the therapist using the closed paradigm construct of "parental hierarchy," the radically egalitarian individuality of a working random paradigm family may look like neglect or "parental abdication," and the cross-generational role flexibility of an open paradigm family may look like "parentalization of children" or "blurred parent–child roles." What might be a definite sign of breakdown within a closed paradigm family can be perfectly normal and functional in another form.

Family therapy itself may be conducted within different paradigms. In some, the therapist is the expert who is in charge, using power and superior knowledge to manipulate and bring about change. Other schools stress therapy as an open communication process in which the therapist models authentic communication and participates with family members in a growth and learning experience.

As with family functioning, there is no one way to conduct therapy, but the paradigmatic framework should help the family therapist to become more aware of the range of options available and of the fit between theoretical assumptions, style of therapy, and family paradigms. When these are grossly mismatched, therapists may inadvertently undermine their own effectiveness.

The paradigmatic framework does not supplant established theories of families and family therapy, rather it augments them by mapping out the boundaries of theories and the interconnections among them. A therapist schooled in a form of therapy wedded to a particular paradigm may, for example, supplement it with concepts and techniques borrowed from another approach based on a different paradigm in order to be more effective with families not well covered by the original school of thinking. The routes by which such linkages can be affected will be made clearer in later chapters.

# SYSTEMS IN THEORY

# 4

# SYSTEMS IN GENERAL
## Basic General Systems Theory

Most contemporary works on family therapy acknowledge some debt to general systems theory. A book on family therapy that does not include an obligatory reference to von Bertalanffy (1968), the father of general systems theory, would be suspect. Yet the amount of genuine general systems theory that finds its way into family therapy theory and practice is actually quite limited. The vocabulary is freely borrowed, much as English borrows from French or German: with a certain amount of disregard for nuance and derivation. The concepts of general systems theory are freely, even loosely employed in describing families or interventions. The terms *homeostasis, feedback, open system*, and *morphogenesis*, all borrowed from general systems theory, are virtual coin of the realm in family therapy. Yet on close examination these are often revealed as mere tokens, for they are not used with the same precision and rigor with which they were originally formulated. Moreover, such terms and concepts are used in isolation from the larger body of general theory in which they are properly imbedded. A substantial body of this systematic, in some places even rigorous, theory remains largely untouched by family therapists and theorists.

The sloppy use of terms, the use of "systems theory as metaphor" (Constantine, 1980a), handicaps the field of family therapy. There are interesting and powerful implications of systems theory that become evident only when the material is approached with care. I will not attempt to condense the greater body of general systems theory into a single chapter. Instead, I want to lay the foundation for the remainder of the text by developing some solid definitions and by selecting among general principles of systems theory those that have the most immediate applicability to family therapy.

## BASIC GENERAL SYSTEMS THEORY

General systems theory (sometimes called "general system theory") has many origins, for it grew from the spreading recognition on the part of scientists in numerous disciplines that there were common threads in their work, that rules and relationships in one field had counterparts in others, and that general principles could be extracted from these points of coincidence to form a generalized theory transcending the specialization of separate disciplines.

At many points, general systems theory exposes its roots in biology, cybernetics, and information theory, but it is intrinsically multidisciplinary, looking for patterns in theories and uniformities across different fields, seeking to unify science by developing theories that are applicable to systems of all or many kinds, be they biological systems, electromechanical systems, or social systems among primates. This is an ambitious goal, some would even say an impossible one. It would certainly be quixotic were it only the effort of a few, but there are many scientists, mathematicians, and philosophers involved in the effort and many tools at their disposal.

### Analogy, Isomorphism, and Metaphor

Some might question the validity of generalizations from biology or electronics when applied to the family. The human family is, after all, a living, vital entity made up of real human beings with complex personalities and modes of behavior. Social Darwinism in the last century taught us of the dangers and limitations of analogy. It was once fashionable among social scientists to identify parts of society with organs or functions of the body (Buckley, 1967): the industrial and political leaders with the brain, the garbage collectors with the excretory system, and so forth. However, one looks in vain for the bile duct of society, and which comprises the brains and which the gluteus maximus turns out to depend on who is drawing the analogy.

Analogy is based on similarity; its effectiveness as an analytical tool depends on whether the similarities being noted are essential or superficial with respect to the conclusions drawn and whether similarity extends beyond merely those noted aspects. But there are more powerful forms of association that can be used to generalize across disciplines.

An isomorphism is a much more exact form of correspondence and supports more secure generalizations. *Isomorphic*, which means "same structure," is borrowed from mathematics.

*Two things are isomorphic if all the parts of one thing can be placed in one-to-one correspondence with the parts of the other such that the relationships between parts in the one can be matched up with those between the corresponding parts of the other.*

Figure 4-1A illustrates two "things" that are isomorphic. Though they look very different, they have identical structures, consisting of corresponding chains of objects. The light lines show how the objects of the system on the left can be matched up with those of the system on the right with each of the heavy connecting lines on the left corresponding to one of the circular "links" on the right. On the other hand, the systems in Figure 4-1B appear to be visually similar but are *not* iso-

**FIGURE 4-1.**
Isomorphy and anisomorphy.

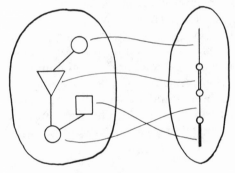

(A)  isomorphic systems

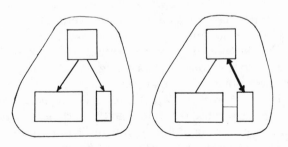

(B)  anisomorphic systems

morphic, since their parts and interrelationships cannot be put into one-to-one correspondence.

General theories can be developed from two sorts of isomorphisms. One might notice, for instance, that the parts of a cell can be placed in one-to-one correspondence with the parts of some human social institution and therefore take a principle of cell biology and map it into an equivalent rule or principle that is applicable to the social institution. Or one might note that two or more *theories* in different fields are isomorphic and thereby realize a generalized form of the theory that is based on the common structure. The paradigmatic framework for family theory underlying this book rests on a great many isomorphisms of this latter form, isomorphisms between theories or models.

Metaphor has not played a great role in general systems theory but it will in our use of idiographic theories of families. A metaphor is a symbolic representation that captures essential features of an object or phenomenon by using description in terms of a completely different class of objects or phenomena. A metaphor can make visible or bring into the fore aspects of a phenomenon that might be missed in more direct view. A metaphor is also a compact representation that can convey a multitude of facets of and implications about its object. In a sense, a metaphor conveys more information than it contains because it is accurate or appropriate to many levels of implications. When a good metaphor has been found for a family, for instance, we are likely to hear, "That's them, all right!" The right metaphor is really a compact theory or model of a particular family.

### The Systems View

Systems theory also reflects a point of view (Laszlo, 1972). Its viewpoint may seem at times to contradict ordinary experience; this stems, in part, from the fact that it deals with areas where traditional science and mathematics have not succeeded too well. The two best-established approaches to understanding our world are mechanics and statistics. The mechanical approach—exhaustive, detailed, linear analysis and modeling—works well as long as what we are trying to understand does not have too many parts and the parts do not interact too strongly. If there are many parts, however, we usually resort to the statistical approach, which assumes that the parts are independent, not organized, and behave randomly. Thus mechanics deals with organized simplicity while statistics deals with *dis*organized complexity.

What these views lack is a means for dealing with *organized complexity*; this is the domain of systems theory (Weinberg, 1975). It covers a great deal of territory of interest to human beings, for it deals with phenomena that are complex and highly organized and where there are strong interactions among parts. The family is a good example of the organized complexity for which the systems view is most appropriate. Until general systems theory and its various constituent specialties evolved, organized complexity remained little understood.

The general systems view is also characterized by its concern with wholes, rather than, or in addition to, an attention to parts. Although sometimes rigorous and often analytical, the systems view is not reductionist. It does not attempt to explain wholes by reduction to simpler parts; rather, it understands parts by the functions they serve in the whole. In looking at phenomena in their entirety, the systems view attempts to comprehend behavior and performance in their full complexity. Instead of a precise analysis of a single aspect or dimension of a phenomenon, the systems view seeks a global, if less punctilious, comprehension.

The systems view of the world departs most radically from traditional notions (often dubbed commonsense) concerning the notion of causality. In the nonsystems view, every event has its cause or causes in preceding events—one seeks *the* cause or the *real* reason. In this linear or "Newtonian" view, ultimate causes are sought by tracing back through proximate causes. This kind of causal chain is represented in Figure 4-2A. However, many phenomena do not yield to such a linear analysis of causality.

Consider, for example, this simple question, that bane of countless unsuspecting parents: "Okay, who started this?" In rapid succession one hears something like this.

"He started it; he hit me!"
"She did; she took my truck!"
"Well, he spit at me first!"
"That's because you wouldn't give me the pail."
"Well, I wouldn't give it to you because you're so mean!"
"I was only telling you what was right."
"Well, you got up on the wrong side of the bed."
"Oh, yeah? You were crabby when you *went* to bed!"

And so on. Any search for ultimate or "real" causes here could well lead back to the birth of the younger child—or earlier.

Often it appears that A does not cause B, nor does B cause A, but rather that A and B are the cause of each other, as in Figure 4-2B. Mutual or circular causality is sometimes called "Gibbsian" after the mathematical physicist, Josiah Willard Gibbs, who used the idea of

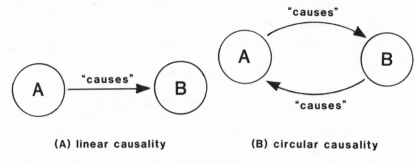

**(A) linear causality**          **(B) circular causality**

FIGURE 4-2.
Newtonian (A) and Gibbsian (B) notions of causality.

simultaneous mutual causality to understand certain problems in physical chemistry and thermodynamics. It is not the little boy's antagonistic behavior that causes the little girl's antagonism, or vice versa; they
cause each other. Put another way, explanation is not in the actions of
the parts, but in the system as a whole. The system *is* the explanation.
The two fight because it is in the nature of their mutual relationship—
what relates each to the other and what passes between is the cause of
the fight. Although circular causality may seem strange to the "natural" mind, conventional wisdom has, in many instances, incorporated
it. After all, "it takes two to fight."

## Basic Definitions

Many common misapplications of general systems theory can be
traced to careless definition of terms. This is more than a matter of
academic pedantry versus informality; well-developed definitions can,
in themselves, lead to useful insights.

### SYSTEM

How many times has it been said that a family is a system or behaves as
a system. But what are we talking about? Just what is a system?

*A system is a bounded set of interrelated elements exhibiting
coherent behavior as a unit.*

A number of important aspects of systems and systems theory can be
derived from this definition.

### BOUNDARY

A boundary separates the internal parts of a system from its *environment*. Because the set is bounded, not everything is in the system; what is inside can be distinguished from what is outside. In this sense, the boundary may only be conceptual, a definition of membership in a group, for example. As we shall see, however, such "merely" conceptual boundaries can be as real as the masonry walls that enclose a fortress.

### SUBSYSTEMS AND SUPRASYSTEMS

The boundaries one perceives depend on where one is standing. Inside the citadel wall, the castle within looms as the system. From a far hill, the peasant huts beyond the walls, together with the fortifications, are seen to form a still larger system. Every system has *subsystems* enclosed by it, and for every system there is a *suprasystem* enclosing it—down to the quarks comprised by subatomic particles and out to the farthest reaches of the universe. Over the more modest ranges surrounding the family, the choice of what is system, subsystem, and suprasystem, is still wide. Family therapy may focus on the nuclear family unit or include the uncle who lives over the garage. Therapy can be directed at the marital subsystem or, as in the "ecological approach," may include school teachers, neighbors, and other involved parts of the social suprasystem in which a family is imbedded.

### OPEN SYSTEMS AND CLOSED SYSTEMS

A system that affects and is affected by its environment is called an *open system*. A *closed system* is completely isolated from its environment and, therefore, can be analyzed as a limited and self-contained entity. All living systems, including all human social systems, are open systems.

In physics and chemistry, theory and experimentation are based on assumptions of closed systems. Yet even here the closed system is only a mathematical abstraction; no real physical system is or can be completely isolated from all aspects of its environment. Interactions are sometimes reduced to where they seem to be unimportant relative to internal processes or effects of interest. Although approximations can be made, for example, that ignore losses to the environment or inputs from outside radiation, the truth is that the closed system is always only a convenient fiction. The modern chemical plant, designed on the assumptions of closed models of chemical processes, provides an illustration. As the process water raises the temperature of a lake near the plant and fish begin to die, picketing consumer activists provide input proving that chemical equations do not account for the entire system. Thus, whenever the term "system" is used here, it should always be taken to mean *open* system in this thermodynamic sense, that is, a system in significant interaction with its environment.

### STRUCTURE AND PROCESS

A system consists of *interrelated* elements and has *structure*. (An unstructured or chance collection of objects is known to systems theorists as a *heap*.) Structure is one of the most important aspects of systems and one of the most abused words in contemporary jargon.

In recent decades many fields have undergone some form of a "structural revolution" (Lane, 1970). In mathematics we find the theory of structures, in the information sciences "structured design" and "structured programming." Structuralists abound in developmental psychology and linguistics; structuralism thrives in philosophy and structure/functionalism hangs on in sociology. And we must not forget structural family therapy. At times it has seemed that to get a paper published or a dissertation accepted one needed to work some variant of the word "structure" into the title. "Structural" and "structured" have become equivalent to "good," "effective," or the latest and greatest. But the word "structure" really only refers to a technical aspect or feature of all systems.

> *Structure is the sum total of the interrelationships among elements of a system, including membership in the system and the boundary between the system and its environment.*

The structure of a system comprises aspects of the system that are relatively static or enduring. The relationship of father to son, for example, can be an aspect of the structure of a family. However, nothing in any living system is truly static or fixed. Though some people say, "Once a son, always a son," fathers have been heard to pronounce, "He is no son of mine anymore." Changes in even such enduring aspects of family relationships can occur and are given varying forms of social and legal recognition in different cultures. In our culture one can, for example, by adoption become the legal son of someone else. The definitions and experience of the relationship after an adoption will depend on the people involved. An adopted child may never feel like "one of the family," or a mother may feel that the adopted child is "just like one of my own."

This suggests an important structural concept, that there is no one "true" structure of a given family. Structure depends on what is of interest and on point of view. The family may look very different to the youngest child than to a visiting social worker, and it may have one structure for purposes of the U.S. Census and quite another for its own members. This can be especially important for the family therapist to keep in mind when working with "variant" family forms like cohabiting couples, families reconstituted after divorce, and communal families based on voluntary association. The legal and social definitions may be at odds with the structure of the family in its own terms. This clarifies why a broad definition of structure is essential for the therapist, whose needs may go far beyond those of the family sociologist who can be contented with formal structure and hardly touch on the inner meanings of families and family members.

*Process* is likely the second most abused word in the contemporary lexicon. Process in a system is the behavior of the system as such. Process refers to those relatively dynamic or transient aspects of a system that are observable by virtue of change or instability, whereas structure becomes observable and is of interest because of its comparatively stable and unchanging nature. Though some theorists and therapists would attempt to make a hard and fast distinction between the two, even in the physical world such distinctions ultimately dissolve, proving to be matters of degree. The physical structure of a machine, for example, changes with decay and maintenance, breakdown and repair, improvement and modification. Viewed on a geological time scale, the "structure" of the machinery in a factory is seen as short-lived transients.

What is process or dynamics and what is structure or statics in a family depends no less on the chosen scale of time. A brother and sister may fight over use of the bathroom one minute, then race amicably for the school bus the next: this is process. If we observe the same process on successive school days, we are dealing with pattern in process. If the pattern is found to be stable over many weeks, we are justified in referring to this pattern as part of the structure of their sibling relationship.

Structure can also be said to be "pattern in process," which leads to one of the popular aphorisms of family therapy:

*Everything is process.*

The vase on the shelf has a graceful form, the shape of a slender pear, but it was once formless clay and someday it may be dropped, discarded, crushed in a landfill, and reduced to clay once more. The children who are today part of our daily patterns, will tomorrow be our infrequent guests, and one day play other roles in a family yet unborn.

## SOME BASIC PRINCIPLES OF SYSTEMS

Some principles of systems are so universally useful or so centrally important that it is fair to call them laws. Among these, the best known to family therapists and theorists is the Composition Law (sometimes known as the nonsummativity principle).

> *The Composition Law: The whole is more than the sum of its parts.*

This law of systems contradicts the wisdom of mathematics and mechanics. It says that for each level of composition comprising a system, that is, where there is sufficiently complex organization and sufficiently organized complexity, new properties or characteristics emerge that are not present in the component parts but are functions of the organization. These new properties are called *emergents*.

In a sense, the whole of family therapy rests on this principle. When there are problems among or within its members, the family is the preferable unit of analysis and intervention because the strength of its interactions guarantees that important aspects emerge at this level. Family therapists look at the whole because the parts do not add up to the entire picture. In fact, the Composition Law has a simple corollary:

> *No system can be comprehended merely by an examination of its parts or subsystems.*

A family cannot be thoroughly understood through separate interviews with each of its members, nor through meetings with the parents and then the children. This is not to say that evaluation and treatment with individuals or subgroups are never useful or appropriate, only that what can be learned from these processes cannot add up to the functioning of the family as a system.

Another closely related general systems law has been given far less attention by family therapists.

> *The Decomposition Law: The part is more than a fraction of the whole.*

There are aspects of the part that can be said to become submerged in the system. Therefore, the individual can never be fully understood solely within the context of some particular system. I am more than who I am in my family, more than who I am in the classroom. Some aspects of "me" are "submergents" in each of the many systems in which I function.

The Decomposition Law is important for family therapists to remember, though it may be hard to come to terms with the reality that what you see in family therapy is not what *is*, but only what is emergent at that level of system composition. For a truly comprehensive understanding, individual and family must both be studied.

The task of the serious analyst of families is complicated indeed. The Composition and Decomposition Laws indicate that the complexities are in the nature of the beast and not dispensable additions. As if this were not enough, we can draw on one more very useful general law—the Generalized Law of Complementarity (Weinberg, 1975)—or what might be called "everyone's Heisenberg" (after Heisenberg's Complementarity Principle in physics).

> *The Generalized Law of Complementarity: To the extent that there is a "graininess" or limit to resolution in measurement (which there always is) or the process of observing affects the observed (which it always does), then, within the limits of resolution or interaction, any two measurements or observations will be* complementary, *that is, interdependent but not reducible to each other.*

This means that looking at something from one place precludes seeing something else. It also means that observations by two therapists can never be made to agree fully.

The family literally does not look the same from different sides of the room. The therapist sitting between Mom and her youngest is likely to miss significant aspects of the facial expressions or gestures of one or the other. If the family is rearranged so that all face the therapist, the system becomes different; the observer has changed the observed. We can never get "all the data" or construct a "true picture" of the family.

All is not lost, however, for the three laws just introduced also suggest how their effects may be minimized. A useful understanding of the family system can be constructed by combining multiple views of the family as a unit with ones of its subsystems and constituents.

## LIVING SYSTEMS

Human beings, as well as systems made up of them, are examples of living systems. A special branch or school of thought within general systems theory dealing with all such systems was pioneered by James Grier Miller (1978) and is known as General Living Systems Theory (GLST). The basic concept underlying GLST is that certain facilities or functions are necessary for the survival and viability of living systems at all levels, from the isolated cell, to organs, organisms, and, ultimately, to supranational human social systems. The basic principle on which GLST is based is that of "shred-out."

> *The Shred-out Principle: Subsystems and functions critical for the survival of a living system at one level of evolution "shred out" into more complex equivalents at successively higher levels, increasing in differentiation and integration.*

This principle establishes an isomorphism between living systems at different levels. The facilities for certain kinds of processing of information, matter, and energy have evolved at every level because natural selection would favor living systems that were *totipotential*, that is, that included the full complement of these critical facilities. Critical subsystems may be dispersed downward into subsystems, upward into suprasystems, or laterally into other living or nonliving systems, but they remain essential. Evolution favors increasing complexity because greater degrees of freedom for adaptability improves the odds for long-term survival.

Miller identifies 19 critical subsystems found in living systems: eight that process matter and energy, nine that process information, and two that process both. Matter, energy, and information all must be processed by two subsystems: (1) the *reproducer* and (2) the *boundary*. The subsystems that process only matter and energy are (3) the *ingester* (which takes in matter and energy), (4) the *distributor* (which distributes it throughout the system), (5) the *convertor* (which changes the form of some input), (6) the *producer* (which synthesizes new, enduring forms), (7) the *matter and energy storage*, (8) the *extruder* (which outputs matter and energy as projects or waste), (9) the *motor* (which moves the system), and (10) the *supporter* (which maintains components in their proper spatial relationships).

The subsystems that process only information correspond approximately to those above: (11) the *input transducer* (which inputs sensory messages) and (12) the *internal transducer* (which changes the form of internal messages), (13) the *channel and net* (which distributes data), (14) the *decoder* (which converts messages into "private," internal code), (15) the *associator* (which establishes associations between data), (16) the *memory*, (17) the *decider* (or executive subsystem), (18) the *encoder* (which converts from "private" to "public" code), and (19) the *output transducer*.

The somewhat unusual vocabulary was devised by Miller to apply to equivalent functions at all levels. It is certainly not sacred, though it might facilitate communication about the functions of living systems between different disciplines. Nor is 19 a magic number; although this list appears to be complete, it is possible that some hitherto undiscovered requirement of life will necessitate expanding the list, and it is conceivable that other arrangements or groupings could be more useful and meaningful.

GLST also incorporates other broadly useful vocabulary. *Artifacts* are nonliving objects incorporated by living systems. Artifacts serving as critical subsystems are, appropriately, called *prostheses*. Artifacts are actually a part of living systems. A house is, legitimately, a component of a family system. It is a prosthesis functioning as part of the boundary and supporter subsystems. The spatial arrangement of a family's artifacts do not merely reflect aspects of the family's values and process, or do they simply shape or influence these, they are literally part of the family system.

The layers of a hierarchical system whose decider function is distributed over multiple levels are called *echelons*. A *group* is a multiple organism living system without echelons. An *organization* is a system with echelons. Miller (1978) considers families to be groups, claiming they lack formal echelons. In fact, however, it depends on the type of family, its basic paradigm and regime for regulating itself. More will be said about this in Chapter 6.

The GLST approach supplies the theorist and therapist with an exhaustive categorization of elements of the family system within one broadly useful framework. The 19 critical subsystems can serve as a checklist against which the therapist matches data about a family, or elements of the idiographic theory of that family, to verify that a thorough assessment has been done or to identify missing information. Similarly, the theorist must account for phenomena associated with all critical subsystems before calling a theory comprehensive.

By virtue of the isomorphism established by the Shred-out Principle, theories, models, and empirical relationships established for living systems at one level can be transformed into equivalents at another level. Miller (1978) tabulates more than 150 "cross-level hypotheses," principles that apply at two or more levels. An example of one such generalized principle is Miller's number 5.1-1:

> As the information input . . . increases, the information output increases . . . but gradually falls behind as it approaches . . . the channel capacity. . . . The output then levels off . . . and finally, as the information input rate continues to go up, decreases gradually toward zero as break-down or the confusional state occurs under overload. (p. 122)

This hypothesis has been verified for living systems ranging from cells to human groups.

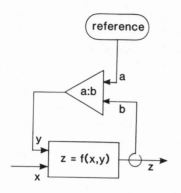

**FIGURE 4-3.**
A generalized example of a feedback
loop.

## FEEDBACK AND CONTROL

The link between structure and process, the way in which structure determines process, is found in the concept of *feedback loops*, named because they are circular interrelationships that feed information from output back to input. The two kinds are usually called positive and negative feedback, however, we will not use these terms because they have so many different, often conflicting, meanings. "Positive feedback" sounds good, and when someone criticizes our performance, we are likely to call it "negative feedback." Such usage conflicts with the systems theory meanings. The terms we will use are more suggestive of what each type of loop does.

The general case of a feedback loop is represented in Figure 4-3. Some portion of the output of a system is compared to some standard of reference, generating information that becomes part of the input again. In families, paradigms are the ultimate standards of reference against which family process is compared. The output of the family system is its behavior, and the regime is the control structure regulating it.

### Attenuating Feedback Loops

The function of attenuating feedback loops (called "negative feedback" by other writers) is to maintain aspects of system performance or behavior within certain limits. This is accomplished by feedback that attenuates deviation from prescribed limits representing the "desired" behavior of the system. An example of how such loops attenuate deviation can be found in the nearest bathroom.

In the tank at the back of nearly every modern toilet is a mechanism that insures that there will always be just the right amount of water for the next flush. It operates as shown in Figure 4-4. A valve attached to a float controls the flow of in-coming water: the higher the water level in the tank, the less water is admitted; the lower the level, the more flows in. The loop is from water level to float to valve to water inflow to water level. (You can pick any starting point.) The feature that defines it as an attenuating loop is that there is some quantity for which an increase ultimately results in a compensating decrease of that same thing. Going once around the loop, the direction of change gets reversed. In this example, less water in the tank results in more water coming in, which results in more water in the tank. Whether we use it once a day or many times, the float-valve feedback loop functions to keep the tank, on the average, full but not too full. Deviations from the desired level are not eliminated (there is a large *transient* each time we flush), but deviations are attenuated.

If we were to introduce a leak in the tank, we would observe some interesting "behavior." With water pouring steadily out, the float would drop, letting more water in. If the leak isn't too big, eventually the valve will be letting enough water in to equal the outflow and the float will not drop any further. This is the *steady state* or *homeostasis*. It is not static, but a dynamic balance maintained by an attenuating feedback loop. Whatever the size of the leak (within the limits of how

**FIGURE 4-4.**
A deviation attenuating feedback loop.

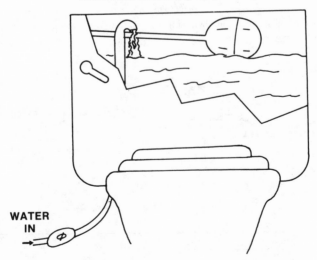

**WATER
IN**

fast water can enter), the float-valve will adjust the system so that inflow will tend to equal outflow. Note that to accomplish this there must be a continuous inflow of water and constant monitoring or regulation by the attenuating feedback loop. All homeostatic mechanisms require energy; they depend on continual input and regulation by active feedback. Thus it can be seen that for something to stay more or less the same in a family takes work; there must be a mechanism that maintains it that way.

Looking very closely at the action of the float-valve feedback loop we can discover another general feature of attenuating loops. The valve cannot keep up exactly with the level of the float: The arm attaching the float to the valve can bend some and the valve will always stick at least a tiny bit. Therefore, the float drops just a little too far before the valve opens wider. Water is then flowing in faster than it is flowing out, and the level in the tank will rise until the arm is bent enough to start to close the valve a bit. Thus, the "steady state" isn't truly steady; the water level and the flow rate will fluctuate up and down, as shown in Figure 4-5. This *hunting* behavior is characteristic of all systems behaviors controlled by attenuating loops. The amount of the swing about the desired level can be reduced by "taking up the slack" in the loop so that the feedback takes place faster, but hunting can never be eliminated in any real system.

Wide swings in behavior can be indicative of control by attenuating feedback that is too slow; tiny, rapid oscillations are characteristic of very fast, "tight" feedback. These indicators can be very important

**FIGURE 4-5.**
Illustration of "hunting" behavior in deviation attenuating feedback.

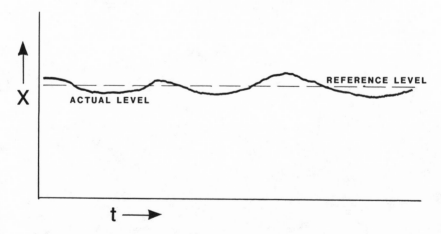

to the family therapist seeking to understand what makes a family function the way it does.

Deviation attenuating loops regulate many behaviors in families. For example, when the therapist is interviewing a couple in their home, the woman says, "Dear, the boys are getting awfully noisy down there."

The man goes to the doorway leading to the basement and hollers down, "Okay, you guys! Keep it down to a dull roar." The level of noise drifting up from the basement diminishes somewhat, and the interview continues. A bit later, the woman interrupts her husband.

"Things are pretty quiet down there," she comments. "I wonder what the boys are up to?" Once more he goes to the basement door.

"What are you two doing?" he bellows. "I don't hear the electric train anymore."

"Aw, we're not doing anything, Dad," comes the reply, followed by giggles and the simulated sound of a steam locomotive.

The loop involves (1) the mother, who monitors the level of noise from her sons and signals their father, (2) the father, who takes action intended to reverse deviation from the norm, and (3) the sons, who make the noise. Note that this system reduces deviation in either direction from the desired reference level; it exercises bidirectional control. The mother is not comfortable if the boys are either too quiet or too noisy.

It is tempting to say that the mother governs the behavior of the system, but that is not strictly true—the entire loop does. If any one of the players were to change their part or if any one of the channels were to be blocked, the overall behavior would change. The loop may be interrupted and the pattern it controls altered at any point in the loop. Consider, for example, what the effects would be of the following changes to the loop: (1) the woman becomes partially deaf; (2) the boys play in the same room as the interview; (3) the therapist involves the mother in another activity so she tends not to notice the boys' noise level.

## Amplifying Feedback Loops

An amplifying feedback loop functions so as to increase deviation from some point of reference. A small input is amplified into a large effect. For our example let us take a dual-control electric blanket, that is, one equipped with separate temperature controls for each sleeper in a double bed. However, in this case the blanket has inadvertently been turned over so that the control on the right regulates the temperature on the left, and the control on the left controls the temperature on the right. The system is represented in Figure 4-6. The loop goes from Barb, to the left control, to Bob's side of the blanket, to Bob, to the right control, to Barb's side of the blanket, and back to Barb.

Everything is fine as long as both Barb and Bob are comfortable, say, with a middle setting on the temperature control. But what if Barb finds she is just a tad cool? She reaches over and turns up her control a little bit. Bob's side gets warmer, so he turns his control down some. Barb is now more than a tad too cool, so she jacks up her control still further. Now Bob is *much* too warm. And so it continues until by morning Barb is bundled up like a mummy, and Bob has only the barest corner over him. The amplifying feedback relationship causes the actions of one part of the system to escalate the actions of the behavior controlled by the loop. What makes this an amplifying rather than an attenuating loop is that an increase in something, traced through one cycle of the loop, ends up in a still greater increase.

No system parameter can increase without limit. In this case, eventually Bob's control is turned off and Barb's is set as high as it can go. In every case of escalation caused by an amplifying feedback loop, some other process ultimately limits the extent of escalation. There are three principle ways in which this can happen.

1. *System or subsystem breakdown.* All or part of the system can break down as a consequence of the runaway behavior. (If the blanket overheated and burned out, for example.)
2. *An attenuating loop in some suprasystem intervenes.* (For example, the room thermostat might cause the heat to come on, warming Barb enough so that she lowers her control.)
3. *The "program" of some part of the system can change.* (For example, Barb, instead of continuing to reach for the control, might give up and get some blankets for herself.)

This example clearly illustrates how the behavior of the system is determined by the structure—the sum of the interrelationships—not by the behavior of the component parts in themselves. This system differs from the "better behaved" ordinary system involving a dual-control blanket *only* by a change in relationship between blanket and sleepers. All the parts "behave" the same in both cases. Indeed, any attenuating loop becomes an amplifying loop merely by introducing an inversion at some point in the loop so that deviation is *not* reversed in one cycle around the loop.

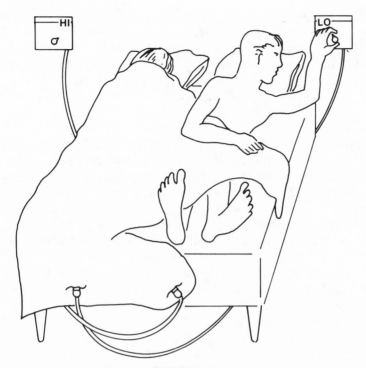

**FIGURE 4-6.**
A deviation amplifying feedback loop.

### AN AMPLIFYING LOOP IN A FAMILY

Let us do a follow-up interview on the family that was introduced to illustrate attenuating feedback loops. It is years later. The mother, who has turned her hearing aid up to take part in the interview, notices noise coming from the garage. She tells her husband to go tell the boys to cut it out. He does, but the banging and scraping continue. She tells him to get tough.

> "Now I told you to be quieter, boys!" he shouts.
> "Damn it, Dad, we got to get this damned dent out of the Ford," comes the reply.
> "Now don't you talk that way, Fred!" the father says.
> "Oh, shove it!"
> "I will not stand for that kind of talk!" the father shouts.
> "Oh, yeah? I don't give a diddly what you can't stand," Fred shouts back.

What happens next? The fight could continue to escalate from shouting to pushing to fisticuffs. Eventually one of the components could break down. (Father could lose his voice or Fred could get knocked out.) An attenuating loop could supervene. (The neighbors, fed up with the fighting, could call the cops.) Or one of the internal programs could change. (Father might realize that his sons can't be bossed around anymore and instead go turn his wife's hearing aid down.)

From these examples it might be easy to conclude that attenuating loops are desirable and amplifying loops undesirable. This would be a mistake on several counts. Real families, even though they may exhibit one form of feedback more predominantly than the other, are actually regulated by complex networks of intertwined attenuating and amplifying loops. The attenuating loops limit change and variety in the behavior of the family; the amplifying loops increase it. Amplifying feedback allows a family to pick up on the small triumph of their youngest child's first bike ride and turn it into a party full of joy for everyone. Then again, amplifying feedback can turn a small setback into a collective depression. Conversely, attenuating loops can keep a family on an even keel or lead to a stultifying sameness.

## Morphostasis and Morphogenesis

Attenuating and amplifying loops regulate the levels or values of aspects of a system's behavior. Feedback loops regulating process, that is, system dynamics, do not themselves regulate or determine system structure; they are, in fact, aspects of structure. The attenuating loop of our bathroom feedback system—the float valve, water inlet, tank, and bowl—are stable, enduring features of the system. Neither the loop as a whole nor any of its component parts has any control over this structure, either to maintain or to alter it. To find a mechanism that affects the structure of the system, not merely the values of some behavioral parameters, we must look to a higher level.

Observe young Clarise, one family's budding engineer, as she rigs a wire from the flush handle to the faucet handle on the sink. The system now has a different structure. When she turns on the water to wash her hands, the toilet automatically flushes. This is *morphogenesis*, a change in the structure of the system. Mom enters, removes the wire, and paints some porcelain enamel over the spot where the wire scratched the tank. This is *morphostasis*, maintenance of an existing systemic structure.

Morphostatic mechanisms function with respect to system structure in the same way that attenuating feedback (homeostatic mechanisms) function with respect to system process—both diminish deviation from existing values or established goals. It is essential to note that the mechanisms that monitor and maintain behaviors within specified range do not, in themselves, involve mechanisms for maintaining the structure of the feedback mechanisms; these must be at another level in the system. This distinction is not often clearly made by family therapists and theorists, who use homeostasis (behavioral constancy) and morphostasis (structural constancy) interchangeably.

Morphogenic mechanisms generate new form by amplifying deviation from established structure, just as amplifying feedback brings the values of behavioral variables into new ranges. (There is no term like homeostasis corresponding to morphogenesis. "Homeogenesis" would be nonsense, meaning "sameness changing" or "sameness creating.")

If we return to the principle that all is process and that the distinction between process and structure is a matter of time scale, then attenuating feedback and morphostasis, amplifying feedback and morphogenesis, collapse into single concepts. However, structure changing–maintaining feedback loops are, nevertheless, distinct from the loops they conserve or alter. The furnace, ductwork, room, thermostat, and connecting wiring compose an attenuating feedback loop maintaining temperature within a set range. Nothing in this thermostatic system either maintains or modifies the structure of the feedback loop. No thermostat has ever repaired itself or reversed its wires. These functions are exogenous. They depend on mechanisms that can examine and influence structures, which amplify or attenuate deviation in the long period phenomena that, in turn, control short period dynamics.


## BOUNDARIES AND INTERFACES

The boundary of a system is what separates it from its environment, from all that is nonsystem. More profoundly, it is the boundary that *defines* the system as an entity. Spencer Brown (1972) has demonstrated that, logically, the very act of indication is equivalent to drawing a boundary around something. When it comes to systems that, like the extended family, are conceptual, definition and boundary will be seen even more clearly to be equivalent constructs. This does not mean that the boundaries of human systems are not "real," for they possess all the characteristics of and are every bit as real as the boundaries of physical systems.

Figure 4-7 shows two systems, a forest and a meadow. Where is the boundary between them? The middle of the forest is obviously and easily distinguished from the middle of the meadow, yet where does forest cease to be forest? At point A? Point C? We may be able to construct objective definitions of both systems, yet we will always find a region of uncertainty where we are unsure inside which system we stand. This is the boundary. Its fuzziness is not a property of "forest" or "meadow" as human constructs, but of boundaries per se. Examine the pond in the figure. Surely there is a clear physical boundary between the water of the pond and the air above it. Or is there? As we examine this sharp boundary ever more closely we reach a point, at the molecular level, where we find no sharp line, only a region where one may find water molecules and one may find air molecules with varying but roughly equal probability. Far below this region any molecule selected at random is almost certain to be water; far above, it will most surely be air. But in the region of the boundary, air and water mix and interpenetrate exactly as do grass and trees where meadow meets forest.

**FIGURE 4-7.**
Boundary between forest and meadow subsystems.

The region of the boundary where two systems meet is called an *interface*. It is always represented by a gradient in some phenomena, such as "density of trees" of "likelihood of finding a member of the Smith clan." Boundaries of human systems may be complex in total, yet they can often be described adequately by a few salient characteristics: *permeability, selectivity,* and *variability*.

All boundaries are semipermeable; no boundary can block all matter, energy, or information. Grass creeps under the hemlocks; pinecones fall into the meadow and grow into trees. Even solid steel has a finite permeability to the passage of gases. Nevertheless, all boundaries resist the passage of material, energy, or information to some greater or lesser extent.

Except at identifiable openings, such as the road into the wood or the gateless walkway into a yard, it always requires extra energy to cross the boundary of a system. Almost without exception it is easier to cross in one direction than the other, and the direction of easier travel can depend on the traveler. The vacuum cleaner salesperson is likely to find it much harder to enter the home than to leave it; exit may even be assisted. The teenage daughter may find, to the contrary, that it is leaving that presents the difficulty.

The boundary is necessary for the existence of the system. Without it, system and environment become indistinguishable and the system ceases to exist per se. However, systems may vary enormously in the permeability of their boundaries and the selectivity of their boundaries as filters of material, energic, and informational input and output. One organization may accept as members anyone who pays the initiation fee, whereas another might be restricted to third generation Macedonian immigrants who serve a two-year apprenticeship. In human systems, permeability may depend on many complex factors. What is completely acceptable at one time may be blocked at another; what is legitimate in one modality of communication may not be in another. Uncle Henry is welcome for a weekend visit, but he may not be if he shows up some Wednesday at 3 A.M. It may be all right to express my liking for your friend by verbal compliments but not by passionate embraces.

The boundaries of some human systems are highly variable as a function of time and of place; others vary little and are highly uniform. Usually one finds that families have prescribed routes of entry. Family members may use the side entrance, guests and strangers the front, and tradespeople the back, for example. In others it hardly matters, and on occasion one might find a household where climbing over the garden fence is responded to no differently than walking up the driveway. The same variations can be found in variability as a function of time. Certain times of the year or of the day may find the boundaries more open than others.

   Understanding system boundaries is essential for family therapy, as the therapist must meet and interact with the family at the boundary, crossing and recrossing it, entering to evaluate and intervene with the family, exiting on termination. It is, of course, a tautology, but "everything happens at the interface." Because family boundaries and how they are managed depend on family paradigm, a knowledge of family paradigms makes what happens at the interface more manageable by the therapist.

# 5

# HUMAN SYSTEMS
## Communication and
## Control in Human Systems

Although human groups, families, and societies are all examples of systems and, therefore, obey the same basic laws of systems as developed in Chapter 4, this does not mean that there are no emergent properties of systems at this level. Indeed, when the components of systems are human beings, a number of new aspects become salient. Human individuals have individual memories, personal models of reality, and enduring patterns of behavior and perception. They are, or like to believe they are, intentioned in their behavior and motivated by self-defined goals that may or may not fit with systemic objectives. They are complex information processing systems that communicate.

Some of the material in this chapter may seem elementary or "old hat." Ground already well covered by others is retraced here not only for applicability to the rest of the paradigmatic approach to family therapy, but also, in some cases, to set the record straight where what is generally believed in the family field about important systems theory and communications concepts is misleading.

The individual and individual behavior are often slighted in family systems theory. As the Decomposition Law demands, a genuine systemic analysis must include an understanding of system components; for the human family and its immediate subsystems, the principal components are, of course, human individuals. It would not be too difficult to force a Procrustean fit of systems theory into the bed of conventional psychological or psychodynamic models of the individual, but neither would it be much in the spirit of the present approach to theory. We will, therefore, take on the somewhat greater and more rewarding challenge of constructing a more genuinely systems theory view of the individual as the human component. Attention will be limited to those aspects of the individual as system that are most important for understanding families as systems of individuals.

As Figure 5-1 suggests, when the components of a system are human individuals, we are interested in the special characteristics of two aspects of their participation in the system. First we are interested in what passes *between* the human members, the exchanges of material, energy, and information taking place in the system, that is, in human communication. This may be the more obvious aspect of human systems and some schools of family therapy do not go beyond a consideration of interpersonal communication.

The second human element of interest is what goes on *inside* the individuals. This is probably less obvious a consideration and certainly more difficult to access. It has been argued by some that whatever resides inside the individual is irrelevant to effective family therapy. Radical behaviorism even maintains that there is nothing inside. My position is that I require of any theory that it at *least* explain *me*. And I know that there is something inside me that is looking out right now, watching the flickering characters generated by the fingers I

**FIGURE 5-1.**
Internal and interpersonal aspects of human systems.

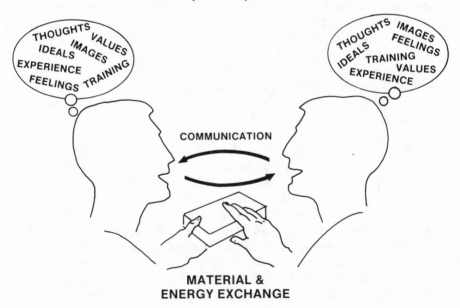

dance over the keyboard of my word processor. Some may argue that they have no person, no freedom, no dignity, but I assert that I have these and more.

## THE HUMAN COMPONENT

Humans belong to a class of systems that process information in complex, highly sophisticated ways. Although certain computer programs now represent the most complex systems ever constructed by humankind, the greatest of these remains many orders of magnitude less complex than the human brain. Nevertheless, humans share some characteristics with computers. Both are programmed yet adaptive. The fact that every instruction to the computer was written out in advance does not prevent a computer program from responding to inputs and behaving in ways that vary with and depend upon not only the immediate input, but also the history of all previous inputs.

### Pattern and Programs

The behavior of human individuals varies considerably in its flexibility and responsiveness to varying circumstances. At one extreme we have stereotyped responses that seem almost wholly independent of the situation, that take little or no account of new incoming information. At the other is behavior that is finely tuned to the current situation, continually evolving and expanding as it incorporates and adapts to detailed aspects of the immediate context. But far more human behavior is programmed than we would always like to admit. Especially in our own therapy and training as therapists, we come to learn that much of what we do, though it may seem at the time to be unique, spontaneous, and freely chosen, is really part of enduring patterns in our lives that repeat again and again with only small variations. In the disabling extreme, maladaptive patterns may become automatic and habitual (Mahoney, 1980). Far from resisting regularity and regimentation, humans seem to seek it. Too much choice generates anxiety, and often we run from freedom (Fromm, 1965).

It is as if there were a drive for pattern that shows up, not only in the regularities in our behavior, but in our interpretations of reality itself. This propensity for pattern has two sides: we search for pattern and we create it. We strive to make sense of things, to build models that fit and explain, even sometimes at the expense of accuracy. We find or make in our lives themes and focal images, discovering and searching for purpose. We invent religions to define direction and explain the unexplained; we look to the constellations for the comfort of destiny or choose the guarantees of pseudoscience over the insecurities of inexact and frightfully limited science.

All too easily we create or see pattern even where there is none. I once walked into a laboratory where a computerized television display was generating beautiful kaleidoscopic patterns in perfect synchrony with the music coming over a transistor radio. I was transfixed by the beauty of the display and impressed by the ability of the computer program to interpret the music so perfectly. But there was no connection whatsoever between the radio and the display! The computer was generating colored shapes completely at random. So strong was the illusion of pattern that even knowing there was none did not destroy it. Organized motion and shapes are even perceived in the random flickers of "snow" when a television is not tuned to a channel.

There is, of course, an adaptive side to this seemingly misguided drive for pattern. It leads us through the complexities of corporate politics; it pushes us to learn the secrets of our environment; and it enables us to negotiate the interpersonal intricacies of everyday family life.

## Maps and Mind

How does the human component process information communicated within a family system and generate new behavior and "messages"? Even though we are far from being able to answer such a question in detail, we can construct useful models of major aspects. Figure 5-2 shows one such model. The human individual is viewed in terms of the cognitive maps by which incoming data are perceived and interpreted, and the collection of behavioral options available for response. These two components will be referred to as the "map" and the

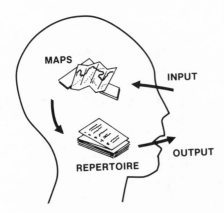

**FIGURE 5-2.**
Individual maps and repertoire.

"repertoire." Each is a complex and highly organized system in itself. Whether they are in fact distinct subsystems in the human individual is not important here, only that we can consider participation of the individual in human systems in terms of these two aspects of internal organization.

The patterns in our behavior are not so much a function of direct "programming," of "wired-in" sequences of responses connected with specific sets of stimuli, but a function of another property of humans as information processing systems: we are mapmakers. We build, through our integration of experiences, internal maps of the external territory. Not only do these personal maps of external reality guide us in our travels through the territory, but they determine how we transform and interpret new information.

A map is a representation, in different media and form, of a territory, in this case, external reality. Although schools of thought have evolved around more restricted views, the evidence suggests that our personal maps have both linguistic and spatial components or forms. We each function as if we had a private vocabulary and grammar that determine how we interpret incoming messages from other people and from the rest of our environment (Bandler & Grinder, 1975). Our construal of interpersonal reality can be represented as a hierarchical collection of rules that express what input counts as what message and permit, demand, or prohibit specific responses in a given context (Cronen, Johnson, & Lannamann, 1982). But we also operate as if we carry spatial maps, metaphorical images that summarize, in succinct form, crucial aspects of our selves and our relationships with others. It is these images that are tapped into so effectively by family sculpture (Constantine, 1978; Duhl, Kantor, & Duhl, 1973). Certain of these metaphors, critical images, may assume transcendent importance to us in our personal relationships (Kantor, 1980).

## Learning, Change, and Therapy

Our actions, including, of course, our verbal statements, are shaped by our personal maps and repertoires. Thus, when someone says, "I've tried everything!" we are inclined to argue rather than to take the statement as true within the framework of the speaker's map of reality. As Bandler and Grinder (1975) put it:

*The map is not the territory.*

Personal maps of interpersonal reality vary considerably in their accuracy, complexity, and utility. Provided it is not substantively distorted, a more articulated and detailed personal map permits finer discrimination and greater latitude in response and interpretation.

One's repertoire, the total range of behavioral options available to the individual, also shapes interpersonal effectiveness in participating in human systems. A person's repertoire can include responses that are unlikely or highly conditional. An individual may be *capable* of physical violence in self-defense, yet never become violent, exercising a wide range of alternative options before resorting to force. Another person might not even have a physical response to threat in his/her repertoire. Just as your personal maps determine what you can see, hear, think, or feel, your repertoire determines what you can do about it.

*One can take in only what is in one's personal map; one can do only what is in one's repertoire.*

If a situation calls for taking in truly novel information or seeing something in a new way or demands a new order of response, then the map and/or repertoire must be expanded.

Messages are interpreted within the context of a person's maps or rules, but they can also form the context for a reinterpretation of rules or revision of maps (Cronen *et al.*, 1982). Which becomes context for the other, map or message, will depend on both. When the tendency for the map to be the context predominates, the relationship of the person to the interpersonal world will be highly stable; when messages tend more often to become the context for reinterpreting the map, the relationship of person to system will be very fluid. These are, with respect to the context for construal of interpersonal reality, feedback loops that attenuate or amplify deviation from the reference established by the existing maps. Therapy seeks a fit between message (the intervention) and map that will permit productive revision of the map to facilitate easier and more wide-ranging travels.

The limiting case of map as context is one that is absolutely complete and therefore closed to all novel input that could become the context for revision. Such a map need not be very large or sophisticated. One example would be a map that places all unexpected and otherwise unexplained events in a region marked "Actions of the gods, who are a mystery." As everything will fit, nothing challenges the map or calls for its redrawing. At the other extreme would be a view of all events as unique, all messages as exceptions to existing rules that, therefore, must be forever revised and expanded.

Relying on the best evidence available about human learning and memory, we have to conclude that the person's map grows additively, that, aside from slow deterioration, nothing is lost. One does not "unlearn" anything, but only learns something new to add to and modify or mediate the effects of what was learned before. Matters that were once major issues only become less important as new interpretations, new behaviors accrue. Old ways of relating remain like insensitive guests at a party, hanging around long after their presence is needed or desired. These responses and interpretations only await a sufficiently powerful context to become reactivated. The more the edges of the map expand, the less likely we are to fall back on earlier rough sketches, but these are not erased. Personal growth is, therefore, a matter of elaborating our maps and retracing the elaborations so that they may stand out against older traces.

The goals of family therapy with respect to the individual may be thought of in terms of the impact on individual maps and repertoires. The short-term goals of family therapy may be concerned only with an adaptive shift to reenable a family system within the family's existing worldviews and behavioral options. Crisis intervention or the early phases of therapy may work predominantly in this mode. The result, when successful, is a better working system, but one with no new capabilities; little or nothing has been learned!

Effective family therapy aimed at growth, enhancement, and prevention seeks also to enhance and elaborate people's understanding of their family and human behavior in general, and to provide them with increased options for the future. Members are left with larger, more accurate maps of reality and with larger, more effective behavioral repertoires. In this way, less of the behavior of the individual and the family system is determined by past programming and more of it can be immediate and adaptive to present circumstances. This is clearly related to the goals of many schools of therapy that seek to help the individual function in a more rational, adult mode (Berne, 1964), to remain in the here-and-now, or to maximize the "free attention" available for response and action in "present time" (Evison & Horobin, 1982).

## Feelings and Meaning

To put this into a more distinctly human and less mechanical context, we must take into account what has been argued to be the special province of our species. "Birds fly, fish swim, and," we are told, "people feel." People have feelings about their own and others' behavior and about their interpretations of the world.

Perhaps because feelings are so real and so demanding a part of our experience, they have long been a major focus of therapy; some therapies deal almost exclusively with emotions. The portions of our maps and repertoires that are associated with the strongest feelings can be especially important in shaping our interpretation of and response to any situation. Failure to take into account the emotional investment, or *cathexis*, an individual has in something can hinder the therapist or lead to unexpected outcomes. Emotionally charged patterns may be especially easily called into play, and it is possible that completion of an interrupted sequence of emotional expression may be therapeutic (Evison & Horobin, 1982; Mahoney, 1980). On the other hand, exclusive focus on emotion, even if it can lead to change in families and individuals, is clearly at odds with the full complexities of human experience and an unnecessary restriction of the attention of the therapist. Although feelings do not seem to exist apart from either our thoughts about them, our interpretations of events that trigger them, or our prior or subsequent actions, it is the exceptional therapist who addresses thought, feeling, and action in balance (Mahoney, 1980).

To have feelings about something we must have interpreted it in some way, however primitively. We cannot experience fear of something that we have not interpreted (in the broadest sense) as a threat, for instance.[1] Feelings themselves may be fairly simple things, but they become, in turn, input for our cognitive processes. Depending on the context, the same physiological response may be labeled as many different emotions. Thus there is a feedback loop interconnecting our "emotional apparatus" and our "interpretive apparatus," as shown in Figure 5-3. This feedback loop may play a major role in sustaining feelings over a protracted period and is a primary focus of rational-emotive therapy (Ellis & Grieger, 1977).

A central feature of every person's map of interpersonal reality is the self-image. Certain features of the self-image may play particularly important parts in shaping a person's behavior; these may be considered to be "core images" or "critical images" (Kantor, 1980). Often a person's core images are formed around certain critical events in the past. Because of the role the family plays in the nurturance and

---

1. This view refers to the accepted concept of the primacy of cognition over affect (Lazarus, 1984). Zajonc (1984) has argued that, under some conditions, emotion can be autonomous from cognition, but this rests on a particularly broad interpretation of affect.

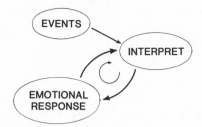

**FIGURE 5-3.**
Relationship of cognitive and
emotional components of emotional
experience.

development of the individual, family experiences are among the most likely to be involved in the formation of critical images.

## HUMAN COMMUNICATION

Human systems are communication systems. Everything that a person does conveys some message. The mother who merely sits reading the newspaper while her husband argues with the kids over which TV program to watch is communicating. She may be saying a great deal about her priorities and her feelings. That each family member may interpret her behavior differently does not make this noncommunication. She may be angry; or she may believe that by staying out of it she is showing acceptance of disagreement and trust in her family's abilities to resolve them. The family, in turn, may see her as uncaring— whatever she does, some message will be received.

The first axiom of human communication (Watzlawick, Beavin, & Jackson, 1967) is simply:

*All behavior is communication.*

This has a simple, profoundly important corollary:

*One cannot not communicate.*

The consequences of this axiom and its corollary are many. If I have good reason not to communicate, perhaps because whatever I communicate will get me into trouble or because all that I communicate is used against me, I am likely to resort to varied tactics, from the merely ineffective to the bizarre to the ridiculous, in my attempt not to communicate anything. However, even if I leave, assuming I am able to do that, my leaving is itself a message.

## Dysfunctional Communication

Many disturbed patterns of communication can be viewed as futile attempts not to communicate. The following are among the most commonly observed forms of noncommunication:

1.  The constant message. When the same message or messages is repeated endlessly, the content diminishes toward zero and begins to be ignored. This might happen to someone whose communication is limited to a set of stock aphorisms and clichés delivered with uniform ennui.

2.  The self-cancelling message. Some people become adept at delivering messages that are self-contradictory or that invalidate themselves. "But, of course, I don't know anything about this," invalidates whatever precedes or follows it. The contradiction or invalidation may be either implicit or explicit.

3.  Tangential communication. Seeming nonsense and continuing irrelevance and distraction are common forms of attempts not to send any message.

4.  Hyperbolic communication. The regular use of hyperbole and exaggeration can lead to messages being discounted by others. This may be used as a form of self-cancellation, as when someone says, "It is all my fault! Everything in the *world* is my fault." The hyperbole cancels the literal content of the message.

5.  Echoing. A device that always and reliably only repeats the message delivered to it sends no message of its own. Human beings can only approximate the perfect telephonic repeater and, in the process, are likely to convey many implicit messages, such as, "I am scared," or "I have no opinions of my own," or "you are the only one who counts." This form of noncommunication is sometimes employed by the therapist who wants to fade into the background as a personality or who wants to keep the client alone as the focus of interaction; it is the mainstay of Rogerians.

6.  Symptomatic communication. Symptoms of physical, emotional, or mental disability can substitute for other communications and lead to the discounting of one's communication. This tactic may permit the individual to say many things not

otherwise permitted. "Oh, don't pay attention to him, he's crazy."

Although most forms of attempted noncommunication are primarily functions of the form of message *transmission*, two clinically important patterns represent efforts at noncommunication through the way in which *incoming* messages are processed.

7. Literal–figurative crossing. Figurative language abounds in human communication. By taking literally what is, by consensus, clearly meant figuratively, or, conversely, by taking literal messages as figurative, subsequent communicational behavior can be caused to be discounted.

8. Imperviousness. The more complete one's apparent imperviousness to the content and intent of other's communications, the less one is called upon for messages and the more one's messages are likely to be discounted.

## Forms of Communication

The first axiom of human communication also focuses our attention on forms of communication that are not verbal. Many such forms can be identified; all are important to the family therapist. Verbal behavior, communication in words, received much of the focus of early psychotherapists, and today we still find many family therapists who interact with the families primarily in a verbal modality. In recent decades, especially among family analysts and therapists, nonverbal behavior has been attended to more closely.

Nonverbal communication can be subdivided further in many ways. *Paralinguistic* communication includes all vocal but nonlinguistic components of communication, such as tone, inflexion, pace, and so forth. *Proxemics* deals with the spatial relationships between communicators, like body position or distance. *Haptic* communication involves touch or direct contact, while *kinesics* deals with body motion. *Strepitic* communication covers the rather specialized area of audible but nonverbal communication: finger snaps, whistles, knee slaps, and the like.

It is essential that the family therapist be aware of the full range of modalities over which human communication takes place, even if all nonverbal behavior be lumped under "body language." Understanding a family requires understanding the communication patterns in all modalities. In addition, effective family therapists remain cognizant of their own communication in multiple modalities. The therapist must know and choose what message is being sent nonverbally as well as verbally. This is important not only to avoid having an unintended impact on a family, but for maximum use of the therapist's resources.

Many therapists, though aware of nonverbal communication, do not fully realize that they can, by effective use of all channels, serve multiple ends in a single transaction. For example, a therapist may want to agree with a husband's basic argument with his wife while communicating emotional support to their young son, who is anxious over the parents' growing disagreement. While placing his hand gently on the boy's back, the therapist says, "Your father has some important things to say." By using proxemic and kinesic channels to carry one message and verbal channels for another, the therapist accomplishes two things at once.

## Syntax and Semantics, Structure and Content

In all communication, but most clearly in written and spoken language, there is evident an important distinction between the *form* of the message and its *meaning*. The term *syntax* refers to the arrangement of elements of a message, the word order and structural interrelationships between types or classes of words. In English, for example, adjectives generally precede the nouns they modify, while in Spanish, adjectives follow the noun. These are matters of syntax. The *semantics* of communication refers to the meaning or interpretation associated with a message. "The royal road" in English and "*el camino real*" in Spanish have the same semantic content, though they differ in syntax.

A related distinction of greater importance to understanding human systems is that between structure and content. The *structure* of human communications refers to the regularities of interactions, which may occur in any aspect of communication, not only the actual *content* of messages. In fact, most of the important patterns in family process are unlikely to be at the level of content. A couple may talk about many different subjects, yet follow identical scenarios in every case. It might be that the subject is always raised by her; he follows with a dissenting or critical comment; they engage in an intense but largely intellectual debate; and, finally, after expressing regret at having raised the subject in the first place, she withdraws in sullen silence.

To see such patterns in communication often requires that the family therapist ignore the content of communication. New therapists easily become caught up in the drama of family process, the content of a family's interactions, thereby missing the regularities that appear when content is allowed to fade into the background.

## Digital and Analogic Communication

In human communication, as in all information processing, information may be represented or encoded in either of two different basic schemes. *Analogic* communication is representational; the encoded message is an analog, symbolic representation, or metaphor for what is being communicated. Encoding is accomplished through use of a medium that is continuously varying. The strength of a blow in a fight could, in the retelling, be communicated analogically by the loudness of a grunt or the speed of a swing. In digital encoding, the message is composed of discrete packets or units that are associated arbitrarily with intended meaning. A hieroglyph for a tree resembles the tree, but there is no relationship whatsoever between any actual tree and the letters of the written English word or the phonemes of the spoken word "tree."

This distinction is important because of intrinsic limitations of each mode. In analogic communication, it is impossible to express the absence or negation of something.

> *Gedanken Experiment: Imagine that you cannot speak and are with a stranger whose native tongue is different from yours. How would you communicate that you are not going to threaten the other person? Imagine yourself on the receiving end of such attempts. How do you interpret them?*

Animals, which may only possess analogic communication, have developed elaborate rituals for essential communication of negatives. For example, to communicate, "I will *not* kill you," an animal may launch an attack, then suddenly break it off, repeating it several times. To communicate, *"Don't* kill me," one tiger will expose its neck to the jaws of another. If the message is received, the other tiger closes its jaws gently but firmly around the neck. If the first tiger pulls away, the second one will turn the ritual bite into a savage attack. This process is exquisitely paradoxical; the form for "do not kill me" is essentially what the message, "I give up; kill me," would be.

In addition, analogic communication lacks or has degenerate forms of syntax. Without benefit of the subtleties made possible by sequence of elements, analogic communication lacks the precision of digital communication. It can, however, be more efficient and compact, conveying huge amounts of data with few representations. A child's drawing of a family or a single plaintive cry may convey almost instantly what it would take many minutes to explain in words. Yet while more may be communicated faster via analogic communication channels, ambiguity is also correspondingly higher.

As in so many distinctions we have looked at, there is here a certain fuzziness and overlap. Even in terms of electronic signals, digital communication is achieved by representation in an analog medium, such as changing voltage or frequency. And verbal communication does not come in truly discrete packets; we do not hear words or even phonemes, but rather a continuous stream of continuously varying sound. Our brains must parse this stream into phonemes and map phonemes into words.

Some important writers in this field (e.g., Watzlawick *et al.*, 1967) have equated analogic with nonverbal and digital with verbal communication, but this is not necessarily the case. Ameslan, the North American sign language widely used by the deaf and hearing-impaired (Riekehof, 1978), is an important and interesting special case. Ameslan is entirely nonverbal, yet it is digital in consisting of strings of discrete symbols, called signs. Many, but not all, signs are analogic, having representational value. Ameslan does have a grammar, a prescribed syntactical form, but word order is substantially less important than in spoken English. In general, however, nonverbal communication is analogic, and verbal can be regarded as digital.


## CONTROL IN HUMAN SYSTEMS

An outstanding feature of human systems is that their components are concerned with control. "Who's in charge here?" is a frequent, crucial, and typically human question. The perception of being in control or of being controlled by others and external events is a central dimension of human experience (Lefcourt, 1976). Most people believe that at least some of their behavior is deliberate and intentioned and arises from their individual motivations.

A classic view of human behavior places control over behavior *inside* each individual. But we have already shown that the behavior of a system is determined by the structure of the system taken as a whole and not by its components taken separately. We might, therefore, ask, "Is anyone in charge?"

With the introduction of general systems thinking into the behavioral sciences has come a shift in views. In a paper that has become one of the classics of the field, Gregory Bateson (1971) argued that control over behavior of a system can only be said to reside in the system as a whole. For his analysis Bateson took a system comprising a steam engine with a flywheel and governor attached. Such a system is represented in Figure 5-4. As the speed of the reciprocating piston increases, the flywheel and governor rotate faster. The weights attached to the governor swing out under centrifugal force, causing the steam valve to

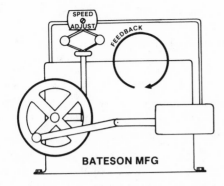

**FIGURE 5-4.**
Steam engine feedback loop.

close somewhat, thereby slowing the engine. As it slows down, the governor admits more steam.

We have in this system a simple attenuating loop that will tend to keep the speed approximately constant, hunting around some mean value. Control over the behavior of the system as a whole cannot correctly be attributed to any one component, such as the governor, for it is the interconnection of components that results in the observed steadiness of speed. It is as illegitimate to argue that the governor controls the piston as to say the piston controls the governor, so Bateson reasons.

Although it is correct to assert that no one component controls the behavior of the system as a whole, it does not follow, as Bateson argued, that control can *only* be said to reside in the whole. A more sophisticated analysis leads to conclusions that are more complete and useful for the conduct of family therapy.

Consider, for example, a series of experiments that tamper with various components of Bateson's system. We discover, for instance, that turning one of the bolts holding the machinery to the floor has no effect on the behavior of interest. (Although, if we remove all the anchoring bolts we might discover some interesting new behavior!) Thus it is possible to assert that some components have *no* control over some behaviors.

Other parts are found to have only limited control. The tie rod connecting the piston to the flywheel may be bent and distorted to varying degrees, but unless it is broken altogether, the speed will change little. Eventually we find that one particular component, the adjusting screw on the governor, allows us to vary the speed very finely and precisely and to set the level around which it fluctuates. Thus some subsystems can legitimately be said to have more control over behavior than others, even though no one, in itself, controls the behavior in total.

After many such experiments with many different systems we would find a general rule.

> *The greatest potential control over system behavior is associated with those subsystems that are the most highly articulated, in particular, that have the most articulated model or mapping of the system as a whole.*

In families, then, as in other human systems, no one controls the whole system. The observed behavior is a function of the structure of the system, the totality of interrelationships among the participants. But some persons may have or be able to exercise more control over collective behavior than others.

## Collaboration and Responsibility

No pattern in human interaction can repeat without the collaboration of all participants. Even though some family members may control more of the family's process than others, anything that is part of a characteristic pattern requires the collaboration of all. Just as the behavior of a feedback loop may be changed by altering the loop *at any point* in the cycle, so a pattern in family behavior can potentially be altered by changes in the behavior of any member. This is not to say that *any* change will alter behavior of the system—some changes will be inconsequential—only that change is possible from any point.

Here is another of the marvelous dualities that characterizes the individual in human systems. Since no one person controls the system, no one person can be blamed for what happens in a family. However, since collaboration is required for repetition and, since any person can potentially alter the pattern, each one is responsible for his or her part in the process.

## The Driven System

Anomolous situations of control over systemic behavior can occur. One such anomaly is the *driven system*, a phenomenon of considerable theoretical importance that also arises in therapy. A driven system is one in which some aspects of system behavior seem to be completely determined by the behavior of one member.

Driven systems were discovered accidentally and first investigated in family therapy training programs at the Boston Family Institute and Boston State Hospital. In a role-playing exercise, families were set up in which trainees were told to select their own roles and relationships and then to enact a common family scene, such as a dinner time. No other instructions were given openly, but one participant was secretly given special directions. These secret directions varied in specifics, but always were of the form: "Whatever happens, always do _____." For example, "Whatever is said to you, respond with something that completely changes the subject or direction."

Under these conditions, certain aspects of the roleplaying became completely predictable. For example, families in which one member had been given the above instruction to "be irrelevant" were invariably very high in energy. The system as a whole seemed to be largely governed by the behavior of a single member. This seemed to defy the notion of systemic process as a collaborative outcome of all relationships in a system. For some time the anomolous behavior of driven systems was difficult to explain.

What makes these systems exceptional is that there are aspects of the behavior of one member that are in no way affected by the behavior of others in the system. Instead of being responsive to input from other parts of the system, some fixed "programming" originating outside the system governs that member's behavior. For a feedback loop to be completed, the output of a component must be some function of its input. In the driven system, the loop is broken, as represented in Figure 5-5. With respect to the family system, the "driver" has become strictly a transmitter of behavior. Of course, there remains the element of collaboration with the external agent.

The key elements of the driven system are: (1) an external agent that serves as a source of (2) directives or instructions that are in some manner independent of context or input from other members of the system, and (3) an internal "driver" collaborating with the agent to carry out the program in the system.

Structures of this form can occur in real life whenever one member is being directed by some agent (system or individual, real or imagined) outside a family in such a way that their responses to communication are no longer dependent on input from others in the family. The "external programming" is fixed, overriding, and dictates specific responses that are in some way unresponsive to context. Clear examples can be found where a family member has undergone religious conversion and has joined with a cult that absolutely prescribes specific behaviors and relationships in families. Thereafter, some por-

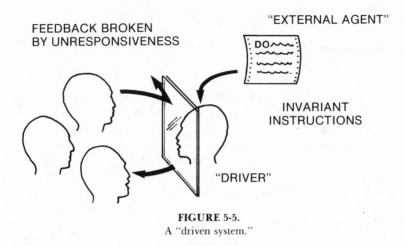

FEEDBACK BROKEN
BY UNRESPONSIVENESS

"EXTERNAL AGENT"

INVARIANT
INSTRUCTIONS

"DRIVER"

**FIGURE 5-5.**
A "driven system."

tion of the family's collective process is predictable and determined by the external programming.


### Punctuation and Relationship

From the perspective of the therapist or other observer of the system, control is generally dispersed throughout the system. This does not prevent the participants from perceiving the situation differently, nor do they have to agree among themselves.

Consider this story of a married couple in a small village in Dahomey. The wife has approached the local shaman: her husband almost completely ignores her; whenever they do talk they always end up fighting. She explains, "The problem is that he ignores me." The shaman, being a budding family therapist, seeks out the husband. The husband says, "The problem is that she won't leave me alone. She pesters me incessantly with trivia." When she won't leave him alone, he yells at her until she cries; then he leaves to work on the garden or to meet with other village men.

"Ah, but," the woman now explains to the shaman, "that's not it at all. I try to talk with him about various things because I want him to pay attention to me. I only do that because he is always so busy with other things, like work in the garden."

Each clearly sees his or her own behavior as "caused" by the other; each feels "not in control." Now if the shaman is interested in "what is really going on" he may ask, "Well, how did this start? Has it been going on long?" But it has been going on as long as they can remember and, not surprisingly, each sees the other as the prime mover. Neither expresses much hope for the future.

Their communication may be represented as in Figure 5-6. Husband and wife are each "punctuating" the communication differently. The basic "sentence" as the husband sees it is: "She pesters, therefore I retreat." To the wife it is: "He ignores me, so I try to make conversation." There is no beginning or ultimate cause for the sequence, although there may be an end.

The shaman goes privately to the man and gives him a large bead. It is used to ward off pestering wives. All he needs to do whenever his wife begins to pester him with nonsense is to place it in his mouth and suck on it continuously while nodding his head and looking directly into his wife's eyes. It does not work instantly, but eventually it will make her stop. When she does, he can take it out and resume whatever he was doing. To the wife, the shaman gives his consolations. He says he does not think she can talk well enough to interest her husband, but she is free to go on trying.

In a few weeks the woman returns to report that her efforts to be more interesting have succeeded, that her husband has become very attentive. In the village lodge, the husband thanks the shaman for the magic bead that has stopped his wife from arguing with him. Of course, the shaman could have altered the feedback loop in any number of ways at several different points to have achieved the same results.

**FIGURE 5-6.**
Discrepant punctuation of an interaction.

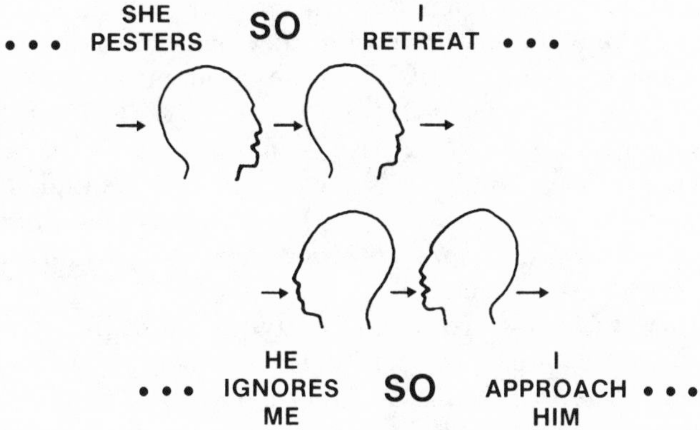

### Report and Command, Data and Control

All information processing systems deal with two basic kinds of information. In "hard systems" these are termed data and control. Data comprise information to be processed or dealt with by a component in a system; control says what to do with data or how to process them. Communications with (and between) computers make, for example, a distinction between instructions and data or between operators and operands, as in the statement:

$$a := b * c$$

which is a direction to replace the data known as "a" with what you get when the data known as "b" are multiplied by the data known as "c." The symbols ":=" and "*" are control (operators or commands) specifying what to do with the data (the operands).

Ordinary language communication between people also contains data and control elements. Consider the message:

Write down "A bird in the hand."

The first two words direct the reader to do something with the remaining words of the sentence. In addition, note that the control part of the message also establishes or specifies a relationship between the persons communicating. The originator of this message is asserting control over the receiver. Of course, the receiver may punctuate things differently, denying such a relationship or asserting a different one. (Did you, the reader, write down anything?)

In most writing in this field these two elements of human communications are termed "report" and "command" (Bateson, 1972; Watzlawick *et al.*, 1967). As generally used, the "command" component of communication refers to anything that communicates something about the relationship between the communicators, although Watzlawick states that punctuation of the communication is the most important thing communicated. The concept of "control" used here is narrower than is implied by the term "command," for it refers only to the matter of punctuation in the sense of assertions about that central human question, "Who's in charge?" There are other important components of messages that can be distinguished, but a detailed analysis will be deferred until Chapter 8.

Another reason for avoiding the more usual distinction of "report" and "command" is that these terms have been equated by Watzlawick and others with verbal and nonverbal modes of communication, respectively. While there is a loose correlation, both "report" and "command" aspects of a message may be communicated either verbally or nonverbally. I may say to you, in a perfectly flat tone, "Take out the garbage." The use of the imperative form communicates *verbally* the control message that I am in charge. If you say nothing at all, but sit there scowling at me, nonverbally you have made a different control assertion.

There are only a limited number of possible assertions about control (Constantine, 1976a). An assertion may be made about oneself or about another and may either claim or deny control. In ordinary language this means that control messages, whether implicit or explicit, verbal or nonverbal, take one of four forms:

"I'm in charge."
"I'm not in charge."
"You're in charge."
"You're not in charge."

When these are combined in various ways the results may be either congruent (in agreement) or discrepant. When I directed you to write a phrase above, I asserted, "I'm in charge." If you slammed the book down at that point, you would have been asserting, "You're not in charge." Or perhaps you went blithely on, claiming to be in charge of the learning process and demonstrating it by just reading the text.

## PARADOX AND METACOMMUNICATION

It is not only possible for humans to communicate, but also to communicate about their communications. Were this not so, this chapter would not exist. Metacommunication makes reference to communications, for example, "This paragraph introduces the concept of metacommunication." Metalanguage is the language used to accomplish metacommunication. The prefix "meta" designates something beyond, outside of, or at another level.

Many prominent writers in the family field have used these terms in ways that are at odds with accepted technical definitions. Nonverbal communication is not "meta" to verbal communication. Both are simply components of messages communicated via different channels. I may use a shrill voice when saying, "You are my son." My tone of voice is not "about" my sentence any more than the typeface in which this sentence is set is "about" the sentence. My tone does not refer to that sentence; it is merely an added component of the whole message. If I said, "I should not have said 'You are my son,'" then I would be metacommunicating, making a metastatement.

By the same token, the command components of communication

are not necessarily "meta" to the report aspects; it depends on how the command is communicated. I could say, "Take out the garbage. That's an order!" There I have communicated the control (command) component in a metacommunication; my second sentence refers to my first.

Paradoxes, self-contradictions, may arise whenever a statement refers to itself, when a message is both communication and metacommunication (Hofstadter, 1979). These can be perverse as well as delightful. Ponder these examples:

> This sentence incomplete.
> I am not the person reading this sentence.
> This sentence says nothing.
> Do what this sentence says.

Such paradoxes and twists arise from self-reference. An earlier view in both mathematics and family therapy was to consider paradoxes and self-referential structures as undesirable and to be eliminated. More recently, paradox has been seen to have both normal and "perverse" forms and to be a significant component of ordinary human communication (Cronen et al., 1982). A mathematics has even been constructed in which self-reference and paradox are legitimate both in statements and as values of expressions (Varela, 1975). In this formalism, a statement may be true, false, or autonomous (literally, "self-naming," that is, defines itself circularly and, therefore, paradoxical).

# A FRAMEWORK
# FOR FAMILY WORK

# 6

# FAMILY REGIMES
## Family Systems in Operation

Although families are particular examples of human systems in general, they also possess unique characteristics that distinguish them from other forms of human systems. For one thing, experience in or with the family represents a very high proportion of most persons' life experience. Feelings attached to these experiences are apt to be especially strong, increasing their salience. For young children, an even greater proportion of life experience is connected with the family.

The family also has an extended lifespan—there are not many human systems of which one is so long a member. School ends eventually, and jobs may be changed many times, but it is rare for anyone to have been a member of more than a couple of families or lived with more than a few in a lifetime.

The family probably provides the majority, though not by any means all, of the key experiences that contribute to a person's core images. It is not merely that the family provides such an abundance of early interpersonal experiences, but also that these are the most likely to be highly cathected.

## FAMILY FUNCTION

The family, especially within family sociology, has most generally been distinguished from other social institutions by its special role in society and the critical functions that have been delegated to it. Using the concepts and definitions of systems introduced in Chapters 4 and 5, the family can be defined in terms of its functions as a system:

*A family is (thermodynamically) an open system defined by the norms of the culture of which it is a subsystem, or by reference to those norms, as having unique status and special functions for fulfilling the needs of its members, who are persons related by culturally and personally defined ties, including the* expectations *of indefinite continuity and reciprocal obligations.*

Among the special functions most commonly delegated solely or especially to the family are procreation, sexual satisfaction for marital partners, and socialization of children. In contemporary society, however, none of these remains the exclusive or necessary province of the family. It is essential for the therapist to recognize this and hold to the broadest possible definition of family and family functioning because of the wide array of family lifestyles encountered in contemporary practice. The broad definition above covers single-parent families, communal families, gay couples, or traditional nuclear families—all important variants on the contemporary family scene.

Although "functional" families may sometimes be distinguishable from "dysfunctional" ones, the necessary or even desirable functions of the family are today not as clear as they once might have been. Moreover, even the most dysfunctional family usually continues to work in significant ways. Pejorative labels such as "sick," "unhealthy," or "pathological" often only barely disguise biased, ethnocentric assumptions of what families *should* be like.

Families that present themselves or are referred for therapy or counseling are often called "problem families." Yet *all* families have problems and some families never seen in therapy have greater problems than those that do seek help. What distinguishes families in need of outside help is neither the number nor the severity of their problems but their responses to the problems life presents them, in short, whether their problems disable them or not. One family may become stalled by the smallest setback, while their neighbors seem to eat up crises and conflicts as if they were between-meal snacks.

Most attempts in the family sciences to define function or dysfunction are hopelessly intertwined with assumptions, explicit or implicit, of certain lifestyles and particular paradigms. Alternatives, however successful or satisfying to their participants, become *defined* as dysfunctional or illegitimate. For one example, the notion that "healthy" families must have clear intergenerational boundaries and a well-defined, hierarchical power structure is applicable to the closed paradigm, as introduced in Chapter 2, but may be less useful when applied to other kinds of families.

To *define* the family in terms of a procreational function, for example, could rightly be called "pronatalism." *If* a family has children, however, then it incurs an extra functional burden, for it then carries the primary responsibility for their care and for assuring that they realize their potential for independent functioning as individuals and as the nuclei for new families. To succeed, the family with children must put itself out of a job by making itself expendable to them. Thus all families, like all living things, have a finite lifespan.[1]

## Enablement in Families

In order to understand disabled or dysfunctional forms of family regimes, it is useful first to develop a more thorough grounding in the basis and operation of enabled, functional, "successful" forms of each regime. The paradigmatic approach to family requires an especially broad, elemental concept of family functioning, one that is independent of variations in both lifestyle and paradigm. Such a conceptualization must be grounded in the most basic requirements of human systems.

Is there a bare minimum of what a human family must do to be a family? What are the necessary functions of a family system? Every living system must maintain the integrity of its boundary, its definition as a system, to survive. Families do not have to be totipotential (fulfilling all the functional requirements of living systems) so long as they are imbedded in a social suprasystem that is; they must, however, continue their existence as systems.

Thus, a family must succeed *as a system* in realizing its own paradigmatic goals, meeting the demands of its environment, overcoming the difficulties it encounters, and sustaining itself over time. On the other hand, it is not acceptable for the family as a system to accomplish all this at the expense of its members or it will still, in some other paramount sense, have failed. Thus, for a family to "succeed," it must also enable the realization of its members' goals and satisfaction of their needs as individuals. It must be kept in mind, however, that in the real world it is not possible for all needs and objectives of all individuals and the system as a whole to be met at all times. As the needs and interests of the group and of individual members in the group are often in conflict, the need to resolve these forms the basis of distinct paradigms and regimes. Although they

1. In theory, a clan is a family with a potentially indefinite lifespan, but it is a conceptual rather than real system. Heinlein's science fiction classic, *The Moon is a Harsh Mistress*, produced a speculative candidate for a marital system of indefinite lifespan: the "line marriage," in which new partners periodically enter a group marriage.

differ in the methods chosen to achieve this balance or integration, all enabled families have in common their relative success in dealing with this core dilemma of human existence.

## FROM FAMILY PARADIGM TO FAMILY REGIME

Family paradigms were first introduced (in Chapter 2) without a full theoretical justification or a systematic derivation. While Kantor and Lehr's (1975) model was grounded in their direct observations of families, the expanded model can be developed from a strictly theoretical derivation. Proceeding from theoretical first-principles has some advantages. For one, it clarifies the reasons certain family features tend to be found together. Without this understanding, descriptions of family paradigms and regimes can sound like mere catalogs to be memorized. Another advantage of a theoretical derivation is that it highlights the need for *four* distinct paradigms to account for the full range of phenomena in human systems.

To develop a systematic theoretical understanding of the possible variations in families as systems, we must again return to fundamentals. A system was defined in Chapter 4 as exhibiting coherent collective behavior. Collective pattern in process must be maintained by some mechanisms. Family systems are not at passive equilibrium but can only continue patterned behavior through active processes. To reiterate:

> *A family's* regime *is that set of mechanisms by which collective pattern in process is regulated. A family's* paradigm *is the image or set of images that models what a family is, can be, and ought to be, thus serving as a point of reference for the family regime.*

It is now appropriate to focus on regimes as more concrete and visibly manifest features of family systems. As we learned in Chapters 4 and 5, there are only a limited number of distinct concrete mechanisms by which collective behavior in any human system can be regulated. Families, as with other human systems, can be regulated by interpersonal communication forming feedback loops and by the internal "programming" of members. Thus four fundamentally different *regimes* can be distinguished. Coherent behavior in human systems may be regulated (determined, maintained) by attenuating or amplifying feedback communication, or, in the absence of feedback communication, by a coincidence of the internal "programming" of the individuals in the system. The four logically possible basic regimes are, then, (1) closed regimes regulated by a predominance of deviation attenuating (morphostatic) feedback, (2) random regimes regulated by a predominance of deviation amplifying (morphogenic) feedback, (3) open regimes regulated by a complexly integrated mix of amplifying and attenuating (mixed morphostatic and morphogenic) feedback, and (4) synchronous regimes (Constantine & Israel, 1985) regulated more by coincidence in the maps shared by members than by feedback. The basis of such "coordination without communication" has been established in general systems theory as "channelless communication" (Conant, 1979). Table 6-1 tabulates the key defining characteristics of the four possible regimes. These features and their relationship to the characteristics of the four basic paradigms outlined in Table 6-2 will be discussed in subsequent sections.

There is a logical pattern in the interrelationships among the four regimes as defined above. If A and B are conceptually interrelated as a duality, then the closed, random, open, and synchronous regimes are, successively, characterized by (1) A but not B, (2) B but not A, (3) A and B, and (4) neither A nor B. Once this logical structure is recognized, many details pertaining to the four paradigms and their realization through specific regimes are much more easily remembered.

This logic may be recognized as an extended form of a *dialectic*: one form, a *thesis*, is succeeded by its *antithesis*, then, in turn, by a *synthesis* of those forms, to be followed ultimately by an *antisynthesis*, which is antithetical to synthesis, that is, a negation of the dialectic. As Figure 6-1 represents, the extended dialectic orders and interrelates the paradigms and regimes of the four primary forms. Thinking in these terms may be useful to the reader; it will also play an important role in Chapter 9 when developmental issues are considered.

In an equivalent manner the four possible paradigms can be distinguished on the basis of their goal-directed behavior in time without reference to the regulatory mechanisms governing that behavior. All systems exist *in* time but differ in how they are oriented to the fundamental duality of continuity and change *over* time. The closed paradigm is essentially *continuity-oriented*, seeking to continue the past into the future. The random paradigm, on the other hand, is essentially *discontinuity-oriented*, maximizing change from the past in a radical focus on the present. The open paradigm may be said to be *consequence-oriented*, seeking to integrate past, present, and future in an adaptive mix of continuity and discontinuity that maximizes effectiveness. The synchronous paradigm may be said to be *coincidence-oriented*, depending on coincidence of the maps that organize the behavior of its members. As it does not depend on process, on interaction, for its regulation, there is a timeless, atemporal quality to a synchronous system; it is *neither* continuity- nor discontinuity-oriented.

**TABLE 6-1.**
Primary Features of Four Regimes

| | Closed | Random | Open | Synchronous |
|---|---|---|---|---|
| *Control mechanisms* | | | | |
| | Deviation attenuating feedback communication, continuity-oriented | Deviation amplifying feedback communication, discontinuity-oriented | Attenuation and amplifying feedback communication, consequence-oriented | "Programming," not feedback communication, consentaneity or coincidence-oriented |
| *Boundaries* | | | | |
| | Closed, controlled, fixed | Open, uncontrolled, erratic | Defined but permeable, flexibly managed | Rigidly defined, but not actively controlled |
| | New information filtered, censored | New information imported but not shared well | New information freely imported, shared | New information denied or ignored, not shared |
| | Insiders/outsiders distinct, limited ingress and egress | Insiders/outsiders not sharply distinct, free ingress and egress | Insiders/outsiders distinct but flexible, monitored ingress, easy egress | Insiders/outsiders distinguished by worldview, ways of thinking, coming and going unclear |
| *Structure* | | | | |
| | Fixed, hierarchical, authoritarian | Changing, anarchical, egalitarian | Adaptive, heterarchical, teleocratic | Nonadaptive, amorphous |
| *Roles* | | | | |
| | Assigned, differentiated | Unassigned, not differentiated | Alternated, notated, shared | Static but reflecting "programming history" |

**TABLE 6-2.**
Defining Features of Four Paradigms

| | Closed | Random | Open | Synchronous |
|---|---|---|---|---|
| *Time* | | | | |
| Stability | Stability | Change | Stability and change | Neither change nor stability |
| | Past-oriented, continue past into future | Present-oriented, discontinue past | Integrate past, present, and future, all is process | Atemporal, enduring timelessness |
| *Individual versus group* | Loyalty, family comes first, dependence | Freedom, individual comes first, counterdependence | Mutuality, individual *and* group, interdependence | Transcendent identification of individual with group |
| *Truth* | By tradition | By innovation | By negotiation | By perfection |
| | Absolute, permanent, tried and true, proven | Relative, transient, personal | Pragmatic, relative and absolute, proof in praxis | Ultimate, eternal, invariant, "what is, is," |
| *Environment* | A dangerous jungle | A playground for adventure | A challenge for mastery | A formless sea |
| *Other systems* | Only alternative to order and rule is chaos | Only alternative to freedom is oppression | Many alternatives, take best of all | Alternatives "imperfect," to be transcended |

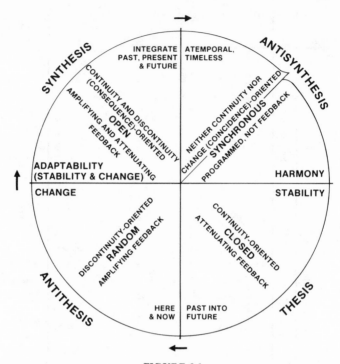

**FIGURE 6-1.**
Extended dialectical relationships among paradigms and regimes.


## FOUR PARADIGMS, FOUR REGIMES

In actual families, certain features are likely to cluster together and to
be more characteristic of one particular regime than another because
they are more compatible with its paradigmatic goals and regulating
mechanisms. For a system to be organized by a regime incongruent
with its paradigm or to sustain process incongruent with its regime
wastes energy. On the average, then, a functioning system will tend
toward structures and patterns of behavior consistent with its paradigmatic goals and mechanisms of regulation. Thus the primary forms,
the theoretical family "types" or "stereotypes" in which paradigm,
regime, and process are all congruent, represent local energy minima,
configurations that take somewhat less energy to sustain a given level
of functioning than would families with somewhat less perfect "alignment." Families with conflicting mixtures of paradigms or an incompatibility of regime and paradigm can, nevertheless, succeed, but they
are prone to unique problems associated with these admixtures. These
complexities will be saved for later chapters.

All human systems may be understood in terms of paradigms and regimes whether they are families, business organizations, social clubs, or nations. All must define and maintain boundaries, and all must deal with such fundamental dualities as individual versus group interests or change and stability. But systems differ according to their paradigms in how these issues are dealt with and the priorities given to their resolution.

## Closed Regimes and the Closed Paradigm

To reiterate, a closed regime operates as if its principal goal in time were continuity (stability); its processes are predominantly homeostatic, regulated predominantly by feedback that attentuates deviation from established goals. The closed regime is a traditional family because, in giving priority to stability and continuity, it relies on tradition.

### INDIVIDUAL AND GROUP

In the closed paradigm, when the needs or interests of the individual conflict with those of the family, the family must take priority. In this way, stability is served, since the family itself is the larger and more stable entity. This does not mean that individuals always come out on the short end of things, but only that, in a crunch, on the average, collective needs are given priority. "The family comes first."

If the family is an enabled system that works for its members as well as for itself as a family, then the resolution of conflicting interests will give the family a stable way of doing things but not at the expense of any particular members. Members will have to sacrifice for the family but, in the process or in exchange, will get most of their important needs met. The needs of the individual are met *through* the group, however, and the relationship of most individuals to the group will be one of dependence. The closed regime demands loyalty and self-sacrifice of its members and depends on these for its continued success. Its primary injunction to its children could be, "Be loyal."

### TIME

All enabled families adapt to changing external conditions and the evolving needs of their members. The closed paradigm, however, prefers stability to change. Whenever possible, the closed regime attempts to solve problems in ways that minimize change. The closed regime does things "the way things have always been done," which is "the right way." ("If it was good enough for my father, it's good enough for you.") Actions in the present serve primarily to preserve the patterns of the past and build the future. The past and future are thereby often elevated at the expense of here-and-now concerns. The past was "the good old days" of "basic values," while the future is "a brighter day tomorrow" or "the better life to come." Planning for the future is an essential aspect of closed regimes, as this contributes to predictability and continuity over time.

### INFORMATION AND COMMUNICATION

Systems manage information in different ways. Information itself can be disruptive of established patterns, consequently, in closed regimes, information is carefully controlled and regulated, and communication is channeled and restricted. For instance, traditional families, guided by a closed paradigm, are more likely to have secrets, to keep information about finances or about sex from the kids, to have certain topics that are "just not discussed at the dinner table," and to separate "man talk" from "girl talk."

In service of stability and continuity, closed regimes attempt to restrict the influx of "newfangled ideas." Access to information generally conforms to the hierarchical structure, and those who are older, more experienced, more thoroughly socialized and committed to the status quo are granted access to more information. The old teach the young; wisdom flows downward from those who have acquired it, but always selectively. Managers in closed regimes gather information from all subordinates but regulate who is told what. Parents in traditional families expect their children to report their activities, but do not necessarily share plans and ideas with children. Though the flow of information differs in each direction, each echelon in closed companies, as well as closed families, keeps information from both lower and higher echelons. Children keep things from parents as much as parents keep them from children.

Like all valued resources, hard-won information is also hoarded and protected by members of families with closed regimes. But information per se is not valued by closed regimes and some information is definitely unwanted. ("I don't want to hear it." "If you can't say something nice, don't say anything at all." "Tell me it isn't true.") Thus restricted exchange is reinforced, and the closed regime has less access to certain kinds of information than others. Usually it is negative or critical information that is less accessible.

The more closed a system, the more dedicated to stability, the more likely it is to block or deny communication that challenges the paradigm or calls the regime into question. Information that implies that the regime's tried-and-true ways aren't working could necessitate a change. This is ironic, of course, because information about the failures in a closed regime may be precisely what is needed to preserve and continue the family; but the closed paradigm does not permit questioning its basic assumptions, therefore, new information that challenges these is filtered out or blocked by the closed regime.

In the purest case, truth is absolute, immutable, and permanent within the closed paradigm. What is right and true has already been established, and it is everyone's job to discover it and/or preserve it. There is little room for subjectivity and relativism, and tolerance for diverse viewpoints can be very limited.

BOUNDARIES

The boundaries of families with closed regimes tend to be clearly marked, closely watched, and well maintained. The yard is likely to have a fence, a hedge, or a border of flowers around it. Strangers will be carefully "checked out." There never is much difficulty telling the insiders from the outsiders. Blood ties are very important; if someone is "family" they are treated markedly differently from "just friends."

The family is a protected, well-bounded haven, an island of order in a sea of chaos. Outside is dangerous, threatening, or at least difficult. The alternative to the proven, tried-and-true ways of the closed order is chaos or anarchy, hence other regimes and alternative lifestyles are likely to be perceived as part of a difficult and dangerous environment against which the family must protect itself to maintain its stability.

ROLES AND STRUCTURE

In the closed paradigm, roles are sharply distinguished and internal boundaries are as clearly delineated as the external boundary. The intergenerational boundary is solid; some things are for children, some for adults.

Hierarchy is a system's arrangement in echelons (layers) based on responsibility or control. In closed regimes, structure is always to a greater or lesser degree hierarchical. Hierarchy is necessary if continuity is to rule. In fact, so much of both general systems theory and family systems theory is imbedded within the closed paradigm that many theorists consider hierarchy to be an intrinsic and necessary feature of all systems. This is not true, of course, and neither random nor open families depend on hierarchy for their regulation.

Families with children tend to express their paradigm most clearly in their parenting. In the closed paradigm, parenting is authoritarian and restrictive. Parents are apt to view children as needing to be molded and shaped to conform to parental expectations. Parental wishes dominate; they tend to promote dependence and insist on obedience. The aggressive and sexual impulses of children are especially likely to be controlled and suppressed, as these are most disruptive of established process. Punishment is likely to be used, but not in all closed families; children will be encouraged to seek parental approval in any case.

In enabled closed families, these aspects of parenting will not be extreme or distorted. Parents will "rule with a firm but loving hand." Children will be "taught right from wrong," and parents will "set limits" to "guide their children in the right direction."

### AN ENABLED CLOSED FAMILY

To understand the Maxwells one must understand Jim Maxwell. He is a "winner" and sees himself that way, a success in nearly every aspect of his life. Intelligent, sensitive, and caring, he seems to be equally at ease with both people and things. A Catholic, he always wanted a large family; he and wife Jeanie have nearly raised five children. Jeanie probably would have preferred to stop at three or four, but has been a devoted and competent mother nevertheless.

Jim started out as an engineer. At the age of 26 he plotted out his career and decided there was no reason he could not become a division president of a major corporation by 36; he slipped by only one year, but did it having to change jobs only once.

When he changed jobs, the family moved to a new city. There, with Jeanie's help, Jim designed a house for the family. It is an unusual structure of three stories plus a basement. The top story consists solely of the large master bedroom suite, decorated in white and gold. On the second floor are the children's bedrooms: girls on one side of the hall, boys on the other. These rooms are predominantly done in greens and blues. On the ground level are the living room, kitchen, and so forth, where earth-tones predominate. The family is well aware of the metaphor in the decor. The basement houses Jim's shop and expensive HO-gauge model railroad. Elaborate plans for completion of the huge layout are posted on one wall; it's a 25-year job.

It would be a mistake to think that Jim "has it all" at the expense of others. If he is a dictator, he is a thoroughly benevolent one who understands his wife and children as unique persons, taking their needs and wishes into account when making a decision. The family seems to have fun together and would be described by most observers as "warm and close."

On one occasion, Jim took the arrival of guests from another state to reveal a surprise present for the family: a trampoline. After making sure that everyone understood the function of the "spotters" around the edge, Jim helped each person in turn try out the trampoline. His approach was tailored to each child. With one he teased and gently provoked; with another, he was lavish with support and encouragement. Each got just what was needed to bring out their best. Finally, when everyone except one of the guests had taken a turn, Jim turned to her and said quietly, "So, I suppose you'll want a try, too." It was so matter of fact that, before she could protest or explain her shyness, she was already happily bouncing on the trampoline.

## Random Regimes and the Random Paradigm

The easiest way to think of the random paradigm is as the antithesis of the closed paradigm. While the closed paradigm is centered around continuity and stability, the random paradigm is centered around discontinuity and change. The random regime operates primarily by morphogenic processes that induce or promote change by amplifying deviation from existing patterns.

### INDIVIDUAL AND GROUP

In the random paradigm, individuality reigns supreme. In fact, anything that limits or restricts the individual is anathema. Thus when conflicts arise between self-interest and group priorities, self-interest is considered more important and the group must give way. The relationship between the individual and the collectivity is thus one of radical independence or even counterdependence. This rugged and radical individualism best contributes to the paradigmatic goal of change and variety, for it draws most directly on the creative and innovative potential of individual uniqueness. Of course, from the viewpoint of a closed paradigm, this looks like unworkable anarchy, a formula for chaos.

In actual fact, enabled random regimes do strike a balance between the group and the individual, but in a drastically different manner than closed regimes do. The closed regime imposes order and, in preserving and protecting the group, leaves enough room for self-expression and individual priorities. The random regime exalts the individual and, in promoting creativity and innovation, creates enough opportunities for spontaneous cooperation.

Random families do not always do things independently, nor are they always flying off in separate directions. But they depend on *spontaneous* cooperation and general individual good will for collaborative ventures. This may seem like a precarious basis on which to rest the stability of a group, but stability is not the primary goal in the random paradigm.

The primary injunction given by the random family is "Be creative." Its success as a family depends on the inventive abilities of its members as fostered by the family.

TIME

The term "random" denotes absence of pattern, but, paradoxically, in its avoidance of pattern the random paradigm generates in its own distinctive one. The pattern in process one observes in random regimes is one of rapid flux; change itself is the constancy. The random paradigm is committed to the maximum exciting variety possible while still surviving as a system. In a sense, the catch phrase is, "Wait a minute, things will change."

The willingness and ability of the random regime to experiment with and alter its tactics is the key to its viability. Though it is unlikely to stick with any particular strategy, however successful that may be, through rapid and wide-ranging exploration its chances may still be good for finding some approach that works for any given problem.

INFORMATION AND COMMUNICATION

If you phone a random regime family and leave a message for someone who is not there, the message may never get through, not because of censorship or filtering, but because information is easily lost or ignored in the rapid pace of change. ("Uncle Sedwick is turning up the driveway? Oh, yeah! I meant to tell you, Mom. He called and left a message last week sometime. It's here someplace. I think I wrote it above the 'Doonesbury' strip I was reading.")

Input from the outside is valued. Visitors from afar, new fads, new games, gadgets, or gimmicks are all most compatible with the random paradigm, as these are sources of the variety and excitement it values. Because of the emphasis on individual creativity, there tends to be a certain amount of competition for new input, as well as some territoriality about ideas. ("Figure out your own way.") New input is apt to be of short-lived value. What occupied and fascinated them one week may be all but forgotten the next.

Truth in the random paradigm is always relative, always subjective. What is real is determined by the individual, and no two realities need to match. This serves the random paradigm's orientation to communication and decision making. Any difficult discussion is readily terminated without having to reach a conclusion or successfully convey an idea. ("You see it your way and I see it mine. We don't have to agree or even understand each other.")

BOUNDARIES

Random regimes maintain the most open boundaries of any system. Little distinction is drawn between inside and outside, nor between insiders and outsiders. A constant flux of visitors and quasi-family members is typical. On the one hand, this may make it difficult for a therapist to settle on an appropriate unit of treatment; on the other, it may not be as important to have all the significant people involved, as the family itself may not consider the distinction important.

The environment may be seen as an extension of the family, a playground for further games and adventures, or a proving-ground for tests and individual challenges. On the other hand, authority and hierarchy that may limit the independence and creativity of the individual are seen as oppression.

ROLES AND STRUCTURE

The random paradigm does not legitimate roles, hence random regimes tend to blur or even obliterate them. Of all families, they tend to be the most radically egalitarian, at least in values.

During role plays in training workshops, families whose members were preselected by a preference for the random paradigm frequently end up with the most bizarrely egalitarian family structures. Often they elect to be a communal family or a cooperative household, but on two separate occasions workshop participants have formed families consisting solely of children; in one they had "done in" their parents!

Role can be important in the random paradigm in a certain way: it is important to be different, to distinguish oneself as unique. It is no more legitimate to follow someone else, to "conform," than it is to impose one's style on another. The sixties' expressions, "Do your own thing," and "Don't lay your trip on me," were particularly pointed ways of expressing the random paradigm's viewpoint on roles and relationships.

Random regimes are essentially anarchic in that they resist and avoid formal structure, organization, and governance. The commitment to anarchy does not prevent a random regime from functioning altogether, but an enabled random family will only have the absolute minimum organization necessary. Any collective decision making is likely to be chaotic and disorganized and to be characterized by a considerable amount of competition. The random paradigm does not require consensus, and conflicting individual needs or interests need not be resolved. More often than not, decisions are made independently by individuals, and the family simply accepts the results. This is easier to do under the random paradigm, since "dissenters" are always free to do as they wish in any event.

### AN ENABLED RANDOM REGIME

The Russells live in a small southern California community known for its appeal to artists, craftsmen, psychotherapists, and ex-movie stars. Sue Anne Russell lives with her son and three daughters in a converted stable and greenhouse precariously perched on a hillside. One end of the greenhouse is walled off to form a kitchen, common room, and one bedroom. Officially the kids sleep on bunks in the former stable, but in fact, on any given night you may find them sprawled almost anywhere. Visitors, of which there are many, are as likely to be offered the one "real" bedroom as to get a sleeping bag in one corner of the common room. In either case, a sleepy child may plunk down in the spot before you get there.

Becca (Rebecca), at 14 is the oldest and is seldom around. When she shows up, she often brings a friend or two to sleep over. Todd is a quiet 12 year old who last year suddenly decided to become a vegetarian; the family adjusted easily and almost without comment to his distinction. Linni (Jacqueline), who is 11, earns extra money doing TV commercials. Randi (Miranda), at 10, dreams and schemes to get a horse, even offering to give up her portion of the stable to house it.

On one particular night, Sue Anne has invited her boyfriend, Tajio, to stay over. The kids are in the kitchen area excitedly experimenting with 37 ways to serve the new vegetable they just discovered: jicama. Randi groans, "I thought I could get the big bed tonight. You two sweety-sweethearts will pro'ly push me out. Why can't Tajio sleep in one of the bunks?" Everyone giggles.

Todd suddenly remembers an all-night horror spectacular at a nearby drive-in movie. "Let's go to that," he proposes. Sue Anne asks how he plans to get there. The kids start talking over various schemes until one of them proposes they "hit on" Barry, a family friend who lives about a mile down the road. In a flash all four are gone. Within a few minutes Linni returns (she "doesn't want to miss anything") and pitches in to help her mother feed the ducks and chickens they keep in a penned area of the yard. When they finish, they find Tajio has started a stew cooking on the stove and is now peering over the horoscope he has just cast for Sue Anne.

Visiting the Russells one is never sure how or when things will happen, but somehow they do. Despite apparent unpredictability the work gets done, the children advance in school, and the bills get paid. There is never great surplus except in fun, which seems to be abundant.

## Open Regimes and the Open Paradigm

In the open paradigm, adaptability to the needs of both individuals and group is paramount. Adaptability implies change, but it also implies fit or purpose. Thus the open paradigm does not value change in itself, as the random paradigm may, but only insofar as change can improve effectiveness for some purpose or end. Similarly, the open paradigm values continuity, but not as an end in itself, only as the means to achieve specific goals. Effectiveness or *efficacy*, as Kantor called it, is therefore a central goal.

### INDIVIDUAL AND GROUP

In the open paradigm, both the individual and the group are equally important, and the needs of one are not to be subordinated to those of the other. In keeping with its dialectical position, the open paradigm is dominated by "both/and" thinking, in contrast to the "either/or" logic of the closed and random paradigms. The open paradigm is based on the belief that it is always possible to work out a creative integration or synthesis of competing interests which will meet the needs of all. Open regimes, therefore, operate by dialogue, discussion, and negotiation as the means to uncover, understand, and finally integrate divergent needs and interests. The belief that this is possible helps sustain the process; success in working things out reinforces the belief, leading to a very typical kind of "faith in process." ("We can work it out." "Hang in there, we'll figure something out.")

An open regime fosters interdependence. Real interdependence, as opposed to mutual dependency, requires the flexibility to shift between dependent and independent behaviors. Group process is the foundry in which joint solutions to problems are forged through collaboration.

As group process is so essential to the success of the open regime, its primary injunction might be, "Be authentic." Authenticity carries with it the notion of a commitment to full and honest sharing of feelings as well as ideas.

## TIME

Open regimes seek to integrate past, present, and future effectively; their orientation might be termed "pantemporal." The open paradigm values history as a source of knowledge without being bound to it; it values the present moment as the center of existence, experience, and action connecting past and future; it is future-oriented in dedication to long-term effectiveness through adaptability. In open regimes one finds side by side both the experiential, here-and-now orientation of the random paradigm *and* the "investment," "stewardship" orientation of the closed paradigm. The future is not merely an extension of the past, but is to be built, created, and defined by choices and action in the present. There is an intrinsically proactive element to the open paradigm. The family is more than "the living realization of a tradition," more than simply "whatever happens"; the family is what it chooses and decides to be.

## INFORMATION AND COMMUNICATION

The effective integration of family needs with the diverse needs and interests of members requires communication. The open paradigm considers good communication to be absolutely essential, and it considers knowledge and information to be valuable in and of itself.

Members are expected to disclose fully to each other and to contribute freely to family discussions and negotiations. As individuals and as a family they actively seek out information that might be of use in problem solving. Authentic expression of feelings is considered to be as important as sharing of thoughts and ideas because feelings are also valued as input for working things out consensually. Neither discussions within the family nor information coming from outside are filtered or censored. Children are not shielded from "harsh realities." Reality and realism are positive, since the environment is seen by the open paradigm as masterable and as the source of information useful for problem solving. There are usually no taboo topics, consequently, family discussions may be freewheeling and colorful.

Where the closed regime may tend to block the flow of information and the random regime may tend to lose it, the open regime is more likely to become inundated in information as it collects, sorts, and shares whatever it can find.

Truth within the open paradigm is mutable yet solidly anchored in the masterable reality. The establishment of what is correct is not based on reference to repositories of truth, such as religious teachings or technical authority, on which the closed paradigm might rely, nor is it merely a matter of finding one's own way, as it would be under the random paradigm. Within the open paradigm, truth emerges from process, and the correctness of an idea is a function of its effectiveness in practice. ("Try it out." "The proof is in the pudding.")

## BOUNDARIES

The boundaries of families governed by an open regime are usually fluid and flexible, yet clear. Here again, they integrate aspects of closed and random regimes, combining the clarity of closed boundaries with the flexibility of random ones. In relation to outsiders and the environment, they are not nearly as open as random systems. Although extremely open to the import of new information, they are selective about who they let in and are apt to be more "protective" about information going out of the family.

Internally, open regimes promote clear but open boundaries between individuals. Individuality and personal boundaries are respected but, at the same time, the expectation is one of easy passage. A closed door requires a knock, but it would be rare for a person to be denied entrance. Members are also free to come and go. As a rule they would tell the others where they were going and what they were doing, but no one would demand this information of another.

The open paradigm perceives the environment as presenting a challenge that can be mastered. Outside is distinct and separate but a source of enrichment. Other regimes are perceived as simply other choices. They are not prejudged but are evaluated by the same criteria the open family applies to itself, "how well it works."

## ROLES AND STRUCTURE

Roles are not seen as the property or proper place of specific individuals, but as part of the common functions of the family, tasks or assignments to be shared or rotated. As in all things, the watchwords are flexibility and adaptability. Members are expected to be able to fill many different roles and these may be exchanged quite frequently. As a result, in open regimes there is a strong egalitarian ethic that includes both the right of the individual to take on a variety of roles and the responsibility to learn to do whatever is required. Individuals may show special abilities or interests in certain areas, but these are not used as an excuse for "permanent assignment" to that role.

Generally the egalitarian role structure applies not only between the sexes but also across generations. Open families with children will favor verbal skills and early socialization to collaborative problem solving. Children are seen as full members of the family and are encouraged to take on responsibilities commensurate with their developing abilities.

The open regime, like the random one, is not hierarchical. It is *heterarchical*, in contrast with the more anarchical structure of random regimes. This contrast is particularly sharp when it comes to childrearing: While the random regime tends to permissiveness, leaving children free to do much as they please, the open regime accords children much the same rights as the parents but places comparable expectations on them ( Constantine, 1977a).

### AN ENABLED OPEN REGIME

On the Simaks' refrigerator door is a sign reading "Gripe of the Week." There is a fresh entry signed "Pam": "Helly's smelly sneakers. Barf out." Heloise and Pamela are twins, but they have never dressed alike. "Helly," lean, intellectual, and athletic at 13, wants to be a journalist or an Olympic medalist in track and field. Pamela, who fills her fashionable clothes well, wants a new boyfriend or a trip to Spain. Older brother, Mark, thinks they're both fun, even though neither one will listen to him drone on about his passion for ham radio. Only 6-year-old Timmy will put up with that; he doesn't understand much, but at least he gets to be with his big brother.

At the supper table, Ward Simak asks whether there really is a problem about smelly sneakers or if Pam is just baiting her sister again. The discussion shifts to Nancy's complaint to Timmy that when it's his week to gather laundry, he puts it off until 5 minutes before the week ends. "But Nancy," he says to his mother, indignantly, "It's not my week now. This week I have to honcho. So, Helly, better get your sneakers and your dirty underwear into the laundry before we all have to evactuate." Everyone laughs. Nancy tells him that the word is "evacuate." Ward reminds him that being "honcho" for the week, which everyone does in turn, does not mean bossing people around.

Nancy says she has a more serious question to raise. The health maintenance organization where she works wants to interview families about their health concerns and habits for research they are piloting. The discussion at the table becomes lively, with the twins expressing the strongest reservations. Mark suggests that maybe they are at that stage when they feel more private about many things. He suggests they table the discussion until Nancy can find out more about just what sort of things they will be asked. Everyone agrees.

Mark asks if the interviews have anything to do with Nancy's friend, Gary. Nancy complains about the emphasis he put on the word "friend." Ward looks crestfallen. He is unhappy about what appears to be a growing intimacy between his wife and her co-worker. He and Nancy begin to argue about his "jealousy" as the kids, seeing that it is not their fight, begin to clear the dishes. The argument does not seem to resolve how Nancy should behave toward Gary, but Ward seems reassured that Nancy takes his anxiety seriously. They hug before going to the living room to join the kids who have put on a new record album. Soon they all are dancing.

### Synchronous Regimes and the Synchronous Paradigm

In the synchronous paradigm, peace, harmony, and tranquility are of transcendent importance. The synchronous regime is based on consentaneity, an essential agreement or singularity of mind among family members. The system is regulated more by the extent of existing agreement among members than by feedback processes of interpersonal communication. This permits it to maintain closely coordinated family activity without having to go through the protracted processes in which the open regime indulges.

Many aspects of the synchronous paradigm may sound utopian (Constantine, 1984b): it is cooperation without conflict, continuity without process. It is quite possible that the paradigm is intrinsically paradoxical. The paradox appears to arise from a systemic goal to *be* synchronous as distinguished from *becoming* synchronous. The question is how great harmony and unity are to be achieved and maintained without interpersonal processes that unavoidably involve a certain amount of disharmony and disunity. Consistent with the intrinsic paradox of synchrony, synchronous regimes that become disabled may take on either of two apparently distinct forms that are, in fact, closely related: they may appear to be amorphous, with the kind of formless sameness an amorphous fluid exhibits, or they may be better described as ossified, with a dry, brittle deadness (Constantine & Israel, 1985).

The utopian aspects of the synchronous regime are embodied and reflected in its commitment to perfection, whether rational or mystical/magical. Its expectations for itself as a family and for its children as individuals are equally high, and some would say, unrealistic. The demands are often implicit and unarticulated, identifiable mostly by a vague awareness that nothing seems quite good enough. Perfection is, obviously, related to the synchronous regime's need for agreement to function with a minimum of interaction.

INDIVIDUAL AND GROUP

In the synchronous paradigm, the issue of the individual versus the group does not exist; there can be no conflict when everyone is "of one mind." With complete agreement, individual interests and collective interests coincide. In a sense, the individual is called on to transcend self to achieve a complete identification with the group. This, of course, is the ideal of the paradigm; at best, real systems will show varying degrees of approximation of complete coincidence.

In any case, the synchronous regime seeks harmonious and conflict-free cooperation through complete agreement. Differences, since they could lead to disharmony, will tend to be minimized, denied, disallowed, or avoided by reduced interaction. Thus the primary injunction might be, "Be alike." To the extent that the injunction succeeds, the regime can operate as a synchronous one.

TIME

There is a certain timeless quality to any system that can sustain coordinated action with little or no communication. This atemporal quality is apparent in descriptions of utopian societies and communal groups based on the synchronous paradigm (Constantine, 1984b). The ability of the synchronous regime to keep functioning on its store of shared knowledge also depends on an essentially unchanging environment.

In clinical work with families, the timelessness of the synchronous regime shows up as a quality of sameness that in its extreme forms may be described by observers or even family members as deadness. In a sense, this is just an exaggerated form of the peace or tranquility of synchrony.

Change, like individual differences, may tend to be denied or ignored. Unlike the closed regime, which actively counters the forces of change, the synchronous regime may merely pretend they don't exist, ignore them, or wish them away.

INFORMATION AND COMMUNICATION

Communication is unnecessary, or at least relatively less essential, for coordinated action in a synchronous regime (Conant, 1979). It is likely to be minimal and to carry maximal meaning for family members. In principle, if two people know almost the same things and perceive things nearly identically, communication need only deal with exceptions. People who have lived together for many decades may show reduced communication, yet high levels of mutual understanding.

Of course, one cannot not communicate. Even were they not to speak, members of a synchronous family would still be communicating nonverbally. Synchronous families may converse less than others, but they do talk; they just aren't as likely to really express much. Actual communication can be minimized by reducing both meaning and emotional significance, thus conversations in synchronous families tend to be highly rational and conventionalized.

Members of a synchronous family are expected to "just know" what is expected, needed, and appropriate, to understand without asking what each other wants or feels. Something akin to "mind reading" is expected. In successful synchronous families, family members very often will be able to interpret for one another and to start or finish each other's statements with astonishing accuracy and insight. Where the open regime emphasizes the processes of acquiring and sharing knowledge, the synchronous one is more interested in knowing per se.

Truth, therefore, is also timeless. This resembles the closed regime's reliance on eternal verities, but with a distinctive "flavor" related to the synchronous paradigm and its perfectionistic or utopian commitment. There is often a zen-like quality that may smack of mysticism but with an appeal to "ultimate reality." ("What is, is; what is not, is not.") The exact nature of truth and reality are not specified, truth is implicit, and it must be apprehended by each one individually. As there is only the one truth, however, all true seekers must eventually find their way to the same conclusion.

BOUNDARIES

The boundaries of synchronous regimes are clearly delineated by the required similarity and agreement of members: someone who agrees and is like us is one of us; someone who does not think like we do is not one of us. On the one hand, this formulation extends the system boundary beyond the normal physical and relational boundaries of families. The physical dispersal or concentration of members does not affect its sense of unity (or lack thereof) as a family.[2] On the other, it may exclude someone who is "actually" a family member because they

2. This aspect of synchronous systems is made especially clear by a literary construction in Kurt Vonnegut's novel, *Cat's Cradle*. The term "karass" is introduced, meaning a team of people who, scattered though they may be, are working on one common piece of "God's work." They may not be in communication, or even know each other, yet they are joined, mystically, by their collaboration on a common problem. On meeting each other, members of the same karass instantly recognize their consentience, the bond or sense of unity rooted in their common effort. A karass is a synchronous system.

do not think like one of the family. The boundary is thus implicit, like so many aspects of the synchronous regime. Members may physically disperse themselves within the community, yet remain aloof and disconnected from it.

The synchronous regime does not "patrol" its boundaries as a closed or open one might, but it may require occasional confirmation of its constituency. Thus members may be called on to demonstrate that they are indeed one of the group by revealing that their true innermost thoughts and feelings are quintessentially congruent with the collective definition of the family.

An enabled synchronous family's relationship with the environment is apt to resemble a closed family's. In more disabled forms, the failure of synchrony and the relative isolation of individuals can lead family members to feel adrift at sea alone. Other regimes and lifestyles may be seen as distinct and potentially workable, but as distinctly inferior to the perfected ideal of transcendent identification.

ROLES AND STRUCTURE

Some clinical descriptions of families that seem to be synchronous regimes have characterized them as amorphous or formless. In a sense, synchronous regimes are "understructured," but, although they can exhibit the separateness and independence of random regimes, they lack the energy and excitement of disorder. When enabled, synchronous regimes are smoothly and closely coordinated.

Because of the identity of the family members' mental maps, in principle, roles are interchangeable, and anyone may take on any role or task. In practice, this does not result in flexibility, as the members of a synchronous regime are disinclined to introduce change. Some degree of structure may reflect a residue from the history that gave rise to the group's synchrony. Synchrony resulting from strict regimentation may be quite different from that resulting from extended communication.

AN ENABLED SYNCHRONOUS REGIME

Tabor House is a religious communal family. Started by Franklin Tabor and his two grown sons, Marshall and Edwin, it has grown slowly and without active recruitment to eight members who regard themselves as members of a real family. It is united by a shared interest in meditation, a special variant of Transcendental Meditation developed by Franklin, and a dedication to bringing peace to the world by a personal example of harmonious living.

As members return at the end of the day from their jobs and volunteer work, they greet each other with right hand on the other's left shoulder, holding each others' eyes for a long moment. Otherwise there is little contact, as each retreats to a separate room to meditate for an hour before dinner. At supper, conversation is polite and quietly friendly, mostly centering on events of the day. There are frequent silences and no interruptions. The meal regimen is well established. When everyone is finished, they all rise and clear the table. All pitch in with the clean-up and the dishes. After dinner, while others are quietly meditating or listening to music, Marshall and Lynette, who are still students, study at the big kitchen table. No one disturbs them.

Adam enters and looks in the refrigerator for a snack. Finding no apples, he checks on the status of other fruit before deciding to make a trip to the nearby co-op store. Lynette, finished with her homework, glances up at Adam with a look of inquiry. He smiles and says, "Sure." They walk out the back door together. Although they are good friends, there is an unwritten house rule against getting too involved in potentially disruptive relationships. They are content for the present with a pleasant but casual friendship.

Members of the household seem adjusted to this tranquil experience. Each at one time came to visit the group for awhile and simply stayed on, without formal invitation or commitment. Others, who found the somewhat monastic style too stultifying, moved on. Franklin Tabor calls this, "natural selection." It works for the Tabor House.

## PARADIGM AND PAYOFF

Each kind of family regime is a strategy for dealing with certain central and unavoidable dilemmas of life, and each paradigm is an image of what is most important to keep in mind as these dilemmas are faced. Some of the most critical distinguishing features of family paradigms and regimes were outlined in Table 6-1 and 6-2.

Certain observable aspects of family regimes are more distinctive and more closely related to paradigmatic commitments than others. The way the family socializes and deals with children is not only an aspect of routine functioning, but also a means for the transmission of paradigm from one generation to the next. Since the resolution of problems is at the heart of a family's continued existence and success, the style in which problems are solved and decisions made is a distinctive manifestation of regime and underlying paradigm (Reiss, 1981). Regimes are compared in Table 6-3, which outlines styles of parenting and childrearing and strategies of problem solving and decision mak-

**TABLE 6-3.**

Characteristic Processes in Four Family Regimes

| | Closed (hierarchical, "consensus sensitive") | Random (anarchical, "achievement sensitive") | Open (consensual, heterarchical, "environment sensitive") | Synchronous (coincidental, automatic, "distance sensitive") |
|---|---|---|---|---|
| **Coping and problem solving** | High investment in closure, low tolerance for ambiguity leads to | Low investment in closure, high tolerance for ambiguity leads to | High investment in closure, high tolerance for ambiguity leads to | Low investment in closure, low tolerance for ambiguity leads to |
| | need for agreement, rapid closure without dissent more important than quality | lack of closure on common solution, individualistic and competitive process | deferred closure, maximum information accumulation, common solution | erratic, early closure on little information or accumulation without closure |
| | Conservative, rapid solution; best under scarcity or marginal conditions, stable environment | Inventive novelty; best with abundant resources, periods of rapid change | Optimal integration of new and old, merging group and individual needs; best with ample time, skilled members | Automatic, effortless solutions, quality depends on form of consentaneity; assumes changelessness |
| **Information and communication** | Controlled, (maintains agreement, continuity) | Information not controlled but not shared | Information and communication valued, free sharing | Information understood, communication minimal, implicit |
| | values internal data over external, prone to censor or distort data | Values external data over internal, prone to lose or ignore data | Values internal and external data, prone to inundation, excess accumulation | Relatively insensitive to internal and external data, prone to obscure or mystify |
| **Children and parenting** | Restrictive: child is blank slate to imprint; parents impress own expectations, dominate, set limits | Permissive: child is potential to set free; parents impose no expectations, abdicate, set no limits | Democratic: child is partner to be helped to discover own expectations; parents and child collaborate, negotiate limits | Perfectionistic: child is extension or projection; strong but implicit expectations, invisible limits |
| | Discipline, punishment and reprimands; encourage child to seek approval, promote dependence and obedience | Lax, little supervision, may be inconsistent, neglectful; discourage dependence and promote disobedience | Freedom without license, support for autonomy with dependency allowed; promote cooperation, responsibility | Indirect control by parents who deny responsibility; promote identification and appearance of agreement. |

*Note.* Adapted from Constantine and Israel (1985).

ing. Problem solving is differentiated on the basis of the family's collective need for proceeding to closure on a common solution and their ability to tolerate ambiguity. These conform to the familiar dialectical relationship: closed regimes have a high need for closure and low tolerance for ambiguity, random regimes have little need for closure but high tolerance for ambiguity, and so forth.

In any side-by-side comparison it readily becomes evident that each regime has certain advantages, particular things it does better or more easily compared with other regimes. Each offers its members specific payoffs in return for their membership.

The closed regime, when it succeeds in maintaining stability and conserving and accumulating resources, provides a secure refuge, a solid basis for a sense of belonging. But the closed regime is not as good at helping the individual to differentiate and develop unique personal talents. It does little to foster creativity and inventiveness, unless these fall within narrow, predefined limits. But creativity and individuality are the special province of random regimes, which offer excitement, discovery, and self-expression far more than security and belonging.

Open regimes combine goals and advantages of closed and random regimes, providing both belonging and individuation. But the forte of open regimes is really what Kantor and Lehr (1975) called efficacy, secured through the smooth integration of individual and group goals. Since the open regime seeks to overcome conflicts between group and individual interests, individuals have a better chance of achieving their ends. The open regime encourages the fullest development of individual and collective problem-solving skills. This integration does not come without price, however. The open regime must expend considerable energy in intense negotiations. Its members must participate fully and authentically in these interactions for their diverse perceptions, interests, and creative contributions to be incorporated into the whole.

Such intensity is anything but peaceful. The synchronous family is best at offering tranquility and harmony. When synchrony succeeds, the member is given a sense of unity and transcendent identification of self and whole without the intense and anxious striving of the open system or the authoritarian control of the closed. The perfected result is an efficient, almost effortless governance.

The systemic advantages and individual payoffs of each regime are summarized in Table 6-4. These can be seen to follow simply and directly from the basic principles of each underlying paradigm.

The dilemma that results from a family's commitment to a particular paradigm was introduced in Chapter 2. The heart of this dilemma

**TABLE 6-4.**
Principal Systemic Advantages and Individual Payoffs of Four Regimes

| | Closed | Random | Open | Synchronous |
|---|---|---|---|---|
| *Systemic Advantage* | Stability, accumulation of assets, wealth, "material excess" | Change, generation of new approaches, rapid adaptation | Overall adaptability, effectiveness, optimal fit in short and long term | Harmonious functioning, effortless efficiency, avoids needless adaptation |
| *Individual Payoff* | Security, sense of belonging, certainty and familiarity | Self-discovery of personal identity, sense of uniqueness and excitement | Actualization, sense of effectiveness and authentic involvement | Peace, tranquility, sense of "transcendent unity," "detached identification" |
| *Problem Solving and Decision Making* | Conserves past learning; quick single decision; good with scarce resources, marginal but stable and familiar conditions | Inventive, creative; quick new alternatives; good when resources abundant, periods of rapid change | Best at merging novel and proven ways, individual and group needs; best with ample time and skilled members | Rapid and efficiently "automatic" decisions; quality varies, assumes unchanging problems in shared repertoire |

can be restated quite succinctly: The closed family achieves stability and offers security but, in doing so, tends to sacrifice excitement and individual creativity. The random family promotes individuality and novelty, but at the expense of some degree of stability. The open family seeks to integrate the benefits of closed and random paradigms, getting both stability and excitement, creativity and security, but to achieve these it relies on an on-going struggle for consensus through intense, authentic communication. It, too, pays a price, sacrificing peace and tranquility in its commitment to process. In turn, the synchronous system, in elevating tranquil harmony to a transcendent goal, faces reduced authenticity and intimacy.

It should now be abundantly evident that, although each paradigm's adherents may claim its superiority or essential rightness, no regime has any clear and universal advantage in all circumstances and for all ends. The closed and synchronous regimes, though well-suited to the dependable conditions of a relatively unchanging environment, are less well adapted to periods of rapid social flux. The open and random regimes, which may be highly effective at encouraging individuation and originality, are likely to be less effective than closed and synchronous systems at promoting group identity and efficient decision making.

It is incumbent upon the family therapist to appreciate these differences, taking into account the special strengths and peculiar weaknesses of each family seen. It is not necessary to advocate a paradigm to appreciate its benefits, or to denigrate one to be cognizant of its costs; but understanding the differences may make a great deal of difference in the conduct of therapy.

CHAPTER

# 7

# PROCESS AND COMMUNICATION
## Interpersonal Behavior in Families

As the family is, in the final analysis, composed of real, flesh-and-blood persons, family process is ultimately generated out of individual behaviors. Although these behaviors may be intricately interdependent and may manifest emergent organization and pattern at the level of the family system, nevertheless, interaction arises from individual action.

It is possible to look at individual behavior and communication within the framework of family paradigms and the regimes by which they are implemented. In this way, we will see that a practical model of individual behavior can be assembled without adding any essentially new constructs to the general model introduced in Chapter 2 and elaborated in Chapter 6.


## PSYCHOPOLITICS

Ideally, we would like to be able to organize and understand individual behavior in a way as fundamental as paradigm and regime are for collective behavior. Kantor and Lehr (1975) make this possible through their contribution, "psychopolitics" or the "four-player model."

Kantor and Lehr found that the families in their study had worked out distinctive collective strategies, interpersonal sequences for working toward both joint and disparate goals, in which particular members took particular positions in relation to each other and to the collective action taking place. The researchers identified four distinct positions that a person could assume in relation to the collective action: moving, following, opposing, bystanding.

Psychopolitics is concerned with the behavioral options of individuals, the operations, styles, and strategies through which individuals seek personally important ends through interpersonal process. In the psychopolitical model, behavior is categorized by *position* on the basis of the relationship of an act to collective action or joint activity. *Moving* originates or defines some specific collective action; *Following* continues or cooperates with an established action; *Opposing* alters or blocks an established action; *Bystanding* consists of remaining outside or neutral with respect to an established action. This is an elementary and logically exhaustive list of the possible relationships between individual acts and collective actions. Although it describes individual behavior it is intrinsically a systems-oriented model since it classifies individual acts by reference to their relationship to collective action.

The scope and simplicity of this model can be appreciated in the following analysis:

Half a dozen people are standing around in silence in a nearly empty room, passing time, waiting for something to happen, for someone to start something. One of those present notices some folding chairs against a wall and begins to unfold and arrange these in a circle. She is, in the sequence that has just begun, a Mover. Her relationship to the current action is that she initiated it and defined what it would be. Almost immediately, three others start taking chairs away from the wall and add them to the growing circle. Their position is Following, supporting and continuing the action. One of those left starts to rearrange the chairs into rows. With respect to this sequence, which is still incomplete, she is Opposing, as her action blocks or alters the already established collective action. The last person stays out of the way, neither helping nor hindering the action. By Bystanding, he is in a position to see the entire pattern of action as none of those involved in setting up or rearranging chairs can.

All four positions are functional, despite the fact that most people and most families will express preferences and value judgments concerning different positions. Following is often perceived as weak, but the Follower who is careful and selective about Following has as much chance of achieving individual goals as one who more consistently initiates action. Systems need Following; without Following, everything that happens must be completed independently or else it will be at risk of being blocked. Oppositional behavior is sometimes seen only as detrimental, but the family in which no one can ever Oppose is handicapped, having difficulty stopping or changing directions even when this is necessary. Bystanding is necessary if a family is to learn about its own workings; and if nobody ever Bystands, then the stage of action may tend to get unnecessarily crowded and heated.


## Psychopolitical Flexibility and "Stuck" Players

The ability to operate in any of the four positions is an elementary form of interpersonal flexibility. The person who can, at any time, freely elect to take any relationship to an established action has a greater likelihood of effectiveness than one whose options are more limited or less flexible. A family that collectively shows such flexibility has more ways of getting to any desired end than one that divides up psychopolitical positions more rigidly. In the extreme, some families show patterns of interaction in which members positions and responses to the positions of others are remarkably predictable. Each person is, in effect, stuck in one psychopolitical position or a narrowly defined combination. The richer and more flexible the psychopolitical repertoire of a family, the more likely it is to be enabled. Research based on coding of psychopolitics from transcripts (Covey & Tannen, 1976) and videotapes (Koch & Hattem, 1983) has confirmed the relationship between psychopolitics and enablement. Psychopolitics are more rigid in clinical than nonclinical families, for example.

Individuals apart from their families show varying degrees of psychopolitical flexibility. Stuck players who have rigid and persistent preferences for one position are more common than might be imagined. They can have a strong impact on the systems in which they participate.


## Moving and Movers

The position of Moving defines a collective action that may or may not be carried to completion whether in its initial form or in some altered form. Moving creates a focus, defining a center of action. The Mover is spatially and metaphorically *central.*

In a given sequence the Mover is not always obvious. In one family, for example, the mother was almost invariably the first to speak, yet careful observation revealed that, just before she spoke, her husband would almost inaudibly clear his throat. He was a covert Mover for whom his wife acted as "mouthpiece."

A Mover is a "starter" but not necessarily a "doer." Initiation or definition of an action may occur openly or covertly. Specific Moves by particular Movers may be carried to completion, blocked, or simply abandoned. Although Moving may often be done with substantial energy, this is not necessarily the case, as the preceding example illustrates.

A Stuck Mover tends to seek most or all goals by starting and defining action. Stuck Movers often have problematical effects on the systems in which they participate. In the extreme, a Stuck Mover may be unable to stay out and may not know how to be "in" except when defining "the name of the game" or "running the show." Stuck Movers are often better starters than finishers and may have difficulty following through on the many things they start. If the nature of the situation precludes such a person from initiating or defining the action, then he or she is likely either to start a separate action elsewhere, or to engage in a struggle for control of the system.

## Following and Followers

Following is defined by the act of supporting, continuing, confirming, agreeing with, or otherwise facilitating an existing definition of action. In affirming a spatial locus of action as defined by a Move, Following constitutes or promotes motion toward a center of action; metaphorically, Following is *centripetal*.

Following is not a passive relationship to collective action, though some Followers, like some Movers, may act comparatively weakly or with low energy. Effective Following requires interpersonal skill and perceptiveness no less than effective action in any other position. The Follower achieves personal ends in large part by selecting when to Follow and whom to Follow. Thus a Stuck Follower is likely to be disabled; he/she is likely to be docile, dependent, and conforming. Some Following is essential if a system is to be able to carry collective action to completion, but a system having predominantly Stuck Followers may have difficulty getting things started and changing directions once they are going.

## Opposing and Opposers

The position of Opposing is defined by the act of countering an expressed action. Opposition may involve blocking, stopping, or interfering, or it may involve altering, modifying, or amending. Opposition enables a system to change directions or to cease an ineffective action. In its enabled, effective versions, Opposing is the source of novelty and creativity. Opposition amounts to "taking off on a tangent." Just as the tangential momentum of a rock pulls outward on a whirling sling, so Opposing establishes a *centrifugal* force in relation to the action.

Excessive Opposing wastes energy. Stuck Opposers, individuals who are the most persistently and consistently oppositional, are often labeled as the "bad guys" and may be scapegoated by some systems. The most elementary form of Opposing is simply to say, "No!"— possibly the most primitive form of self-assertion and differentiation. Strong Opposers are often seen as negative and rebellious. When they are more effective and less extreme in their opposition, they tend to be described as creative and unconventional. The family systems that foster Opposing are those that foster independence and differentiation.


Bystanding and Bystanders

Kantor and Lehr's brilliant insight that the apparent nonparticipants are an essential part of any process is of immense importance to understanding family process. This is tantamount to recognizing that the audience is a part of the theater.

The position of the Bystander is intrinsically paradoxical, in that Bystanders are at once "outside" the system of action they are Bystanding, and yet they have an impact on the system and are, therefore, "inside" it. This is a specific application of the complementarity principle introduced in Chapter 4. The act of observing affects the system, hence it is a different system with and without the observer and different observers will report different systems.

Bystanders, however, are in a better position to see and understand the process than any other players, although that system they can observe is of necessity the system *sans* Bystander. They often act as repositories of a family's images of itself as a family because they are in the best position to be aware of the totality of these images and their realization in process. They may in turn articulate or act out the family's images, thus giving others access to them.

An "active Bystander" is one who addresses process, who contributes or comments on it in explicit verbal or nonverbal form. There is, thus, a logical connection between metacommunication (introduced in Chapter 5) and Bystanding. The Bystander retains this privileged or "meta" position in relation to family process by communicating speculatively or neutrally. In this way, a Bystander can participate yet remain "outside," as neutral comment and speculation do not, in themselves, constitute either facilitation or modification of the action, nor do they define new action.

The Bystander is in a powerful position, both because of the knowledge to be gained from the position and from attributions of power by other participants. The statements of a "person of few words" are often accorded exceptional weight. Families and other groups frequently work to draw in Bystanders whose potential knowledge may generate anxiety and discomfort as long as it is unshared.

Bystanding thus fulfills an important function for the system as a whole. Without active and effective Bystanding, the system cannot fully understand itself. Without such understanding, a system cannot reliably initiate and effect purposeful changes in its own structures.

Bystanders do not *necessarily* understand what is going on. They may be asleep, confused, looking the wrong way, subjectively caught up in the action, or otherwise disabled as Bystanders. A Stuck Bystander is unable to participate in process, and characteristically remains on the periphery. The person whose repertoire is limited in this way is not only closed out of the active emotional life of the family, but cannot even benefit from the accrued power from Bystanding.

Strong Bystanders are often perceived as dominant but aloof, or as cold and detached. On the other hand, the neutrality of more effective Bystanders can also communicate a broad and general acceptance.

## PSYCHOPOLITICS, PARADIGM, AND REGIME

Each of the family paradigms subsumes basic attitudes about the relative merit of different individual behaviors. The closed paradigm, for example, favors Following, which, as it continues established collective action, is most compatible with the closed paradigm's interest in preserving tradition and continuing the past into the future. The closed paradigm looks least favorably on Opposing, which is apt to be disruptive and to promote discontinuity. In contrast, the random paradigm values behavior that "alters, changes, or blocks established action." It is less sanguine about individual attempts to take charge, especially those made with the expectation of being Followed. Thus the random paradigm values Opposing but finds Moving to be problematic.

The pattern implied in the preceding paragraph carries over for all paradigms. There is, consequently, a simple, direct relationship (an isomorphism) between the systemic model of paradigms (and regimes) and the psychopolitical model of individual action. This relationship is represented in Figure 7-1. Each paradigm will tend to promote one particular psychopolitical position relatively more than the other paradigms: the closed paradigm promotes Following, the random para-

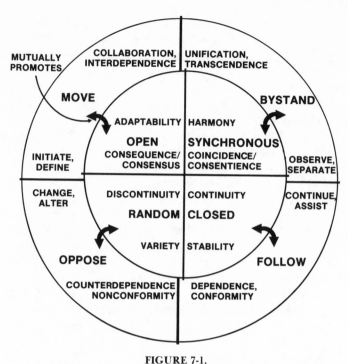

**FIGURE 7-1.**
Interrelationship of systemic regime and individual psychopolitics.

digm promotes Opposing, the open paradigm promotes Moving, and the synchronous paradigm promotes Bystanding.

In all but the most severely crippled actual regimes, all positions will be represented at one time or another. Moving, in particular, which initiates and defines action, must occur in all regimes. What varies is the expected frequency of each position, and, especially, the most common response to Moving. In the closed regime, Moving itself will be relatively uncommon, restricted by the hierarchy, and prescribed roles to certain members in certain contexts. The most probable response to any Move will be Following. In the random regime, the more probable response to a Move is an act of Opposition that changes or redirects it. In the synchronous regime, which does not depend as much on interaction to sustain coordinated action, Bystanding, remaining neutral or outside the action, will be a more frequent response to a Move than it would be in the other regimes. Action in these cases is independent but parallel.

The connection between the open paradigm and Moving is somewhat less obvious than the others. The open paradigm values individual initiative and responsibility but seeks collaborative solutions to problems. As the open regime synthesizes elements of random and closed regimes, it accepts Following and Opposing as equally valid responses. However, its egalitarian style and heterarchical structure permit relatively more Moving than either the closed or the random regime. The hierarchy of the closed regime coupled with the importance of Following assures that Moving is restricted and limited. The predominance of Opposition in the random regime tends to prevent Moves from being effective through interpersonal action—most Moves will be blocked or altered rather than assisted toward completion. The random paradigm, correspondingly, discourages attempts to dominate or "lay one's trip" on someone else. All things considered, Moves are relatively more permitted within the open paradigm and are more likely to be met by other Moves in open regimes than in other regimes.

The connection between psychopolitical behavior and regime works both ways. If you gather a number of people with strongly Oppositional styles and put them into a group, the system they are most likely to implement will be distinctly random. Likewise, a group with preferences for the quiet detachment of Bystanding will tend to form a synchronous regime, if they do anything at all.[1]

That different paradigms have different preferences regarding psychopolitical positions is very important for the family therapist to understand, especially as these preferences are likely to affect children most strongly.

### Psychopolitics in Closed Families

Closed regimes generally prefer children to Follow, at least within the family and toward parents and parental figures. When successful in socializing their children, the result will be individuals with more experience in Following than in other positions, thus when these offspring form their own families, they are most likely to create

1. This connection has been informally confirmed in numerous training workshops by the author. A brief behavior sample (described in Constantine, 1980b) was used to identify the probable psychopolitical preferences of workshop participants who were then, without knowledge of the theory or the intent of the sample, assigned to role-play families. The workshop as a whole later assessed the regimes represented by brief "snapshot" role plays. Groups presumed to be dominated by Opposers were universally identified as random, groups comprising mostly putative Followers were usually clearly identifiable as closed, and groups of Movers were most frequently, though less than half the time, described as open regimes. The case of Bystanders and synchronous process was not tested in these experiments.

another closed regime. All systems require a certain amount of Moving; in closed regimes, this will be largely the job of parents. The well-socialized offspring of closed families will have only limited direct experience of this sort upon which to draw. They must instead rely on behaviors modeled by their parents. This constitutes a specific mechanism, therefore, favoring the perpetuation of the closed paradigm from generation to generation.

The closed paradigm definitely does *not* value Opposing, at least not within the family. Opposition can pose a threat to the established order. The closed family's response to Opposition, especially consistent dissidence or deviance, is characteristic: control it, contain it, or cut it off. Initially, parents will Move, attempting to control Opposition by stronger assertion of authority. Failing this, they will try to contain it, limiting its impact by isolating the dissenter. In this way a scapegoat may be created; closed families are most likely to select a dedicated Opposer for this role. If necessary, the family will ultimately cut off the Opposition by ejecting the Opposer. ("As long as you choose to act that way, you are no son of mine. Get out!") Many variant strategies are possible, including the extremes of placement with agencies of the more powerful systems of the larger society, as when a family files a writ or certificate resulting in state custody of an incorrigible child.

Opposition beyond family boundaries is treated differently by the family. The child is expected to Oppose processes and regimes that are incongruent with the family's paradigm but to Follow those that are congruent. Children would be expected to Oppose peer suggestions to use disapproved drugs or to Oppose proselytizing efforts by competing religious groups, for example, but not to Oppose "legitimate, established" authority, such as school officials. One problem, of course, is that the closed regime does not provide many opportunities to learn effective Opposing. Thus a psychopolitical position on which the continuation of the paradigm is very dependent, is not facilitated by closed regimes.

Bystanding may or may not pose a problem for the closed family. In the final analysis, Bystanding is conservative; in itself it poses no threat to the established order, though, of course, it does not contribute much to it either. The Bystander, however, is in a potentially powerful position. Bystanders are in a better position to see the system as a whole and to understand its weaknesses as well as its strengths. Should Bystanding be left for another position, the Bystander is armed with greater knowledge or insight and, therefore, the possibility of greater effectiveness. The power accumulated by the Bystander can be a latent threat to the family.

It is also sometimes difficult to tell Bystanding from Opposing, since Opposition can be expressed by withholding or withdrawing. Most Bystanding has an element of this in the quality of nonparticipation or of being "above it all." On key issues, the closed paradigm denies the possibility of the kind of neutrality claimed by the Bystander. ("You're either for us or against us.")

Moving in closed families is carefully circumscribed, something to be entrusted only to those who are the least likely to take the family in a new or undesired direction. If anyone other than the "family head" is allowed to Move, it is under clearly defined circumstances often dictated by the leader. ("While I'm away, Tommy is in charge. Understand? I want you to do what he says.") Outside the family, however, independent initiative may be strongly valued by the closed family. The fact that the closed family may have two distinct sets of psychopolitical preferences for behavior within and without the family is simply another example of the sharply defined external boundary it maintains.

## Psychopolitics in Random Regimes

The random regime thrives on Opposition. If it is an enabled regime, Opposition will be creative, inventive, and will serve the family well; in a disabled regime, the high rate of Opposition will do little more than contribute to chaos. In either case, where the characteristic response to a Move is Opposing, the energy level is elevated.

The random paradigm has a complex relationship with Moving. On the one hand, its commitment to independence would seem to favor Moving; on the other, it rejects authority or attempted domination. The independence of random regimes is actually better described as counterdependent, thus Moving is acceptable only as long as it does not include the expectation of Following: as long as it is, in effect, isolated rather than relational. ("Do your thing, but don't lay your trip on me.") Since the characteristic response to a Move is Opposing, a Move is less likely to be carried through to completion through facilitation by others. Thus Moving may be effectively disabled by the high incidence of Opposing in random regimes.

Members of random families, however, frequently perceive what they are doing as Moving, as defining new action. A close examination of the actual sequences of psychopolitical acts in such systems reveals that there is an ambiguous character to many acts. It is difficult to distinguish "defining" from "redefining." In context, however, any attempted Move that would define a new direction before the established action is completed (or abandoned) by the system *functions* as Opposing. In other words, "Moves" that come while "a motion is still on the floor," having been neither passed or clearly defeated, function in part as Opposition and are often perceived that way by others.

Bystanding is not intrinsically a problem for the random regime, as Bystanders fit with the norms of independence. Consistent Bystanders may, however, be seen as not sufficiently creative.

### Psychopolitics in Open Regimes

The synthesizing tendencies of the open regime also carry into psychopolitics. For its consensual problem-solving processes to be effective, *both* Following and Opposing are equally needed as possible responses to a Move. All members must be able to Follow and Oppose in congruence with their authentic feelings and stance on any matter. In addition, the egalitarian, collaborative norms of the open paradigm also require that each be able to take charge as appropriate for effective problem resolution.

The relationship of the open regime to Bystanding, however, is conflictual. On the one hand, the open regime seeks to evaluate and rearrange its structures, to define itself in the most effective way. This requires Bystanding on its own process in order to understand it and alter or reinforce it effectively. However, the open paradigm is based on active involvement and communication. Hanging back and "just watching" violates the norm of "getting in there and working it out." All members must contribute their ideas and authentically share their feelings, not remain neutral or uninvolved. Bystanding is required by their problem-solving approach but tends to be blocked by it.

### Psychopolitics and Synchronous Regimes

The synchronous paradigm is most compatible with Bystanding. Its commitment to "coordination without communication" favors detachment and rational neutrality. Members are, in effect, Bystanders to each other's actions. Moving is acceptable, in fact, independent initiative is valued, but Opposing is not, since Opposing would carry the regime away from synchrony.

Synchronous regimes have an ambivalent relationship with Following. Following would assure close coordination, but only if there is explicit definition of the action and declaration of expectations. Not only would that violate the communication norms of the synchronous paradigm, but it risks being met with Opposition, which would destroy any apparent synchrony. Furthermore, Following should be unnecessary if there is real synchrony; members should already know what to do and not have to Follow each other. Moreover, the paradigm favors separateness and independence, which would be denied by dependency and Following. Bystanding, "staying out" is compatible with the detachment of synchrony, while Following is clearly a form of involvement, "being in," something the closed paradigm values instead.

## A Psychopolitical Paradox

It should now be abundantly clear that there is a pattern in the relationship of each regime to the psychopolitics of the next adjacent regime. The relationship is conflicted, one of ambivalence. The closed paradigm wants members to be able to resist forces that might distract them from the tried-and-true ways, but it does not allow them to learn this by Opposing within the family. The random paradigm values true independence and initiative but the random regime tends to disable effective Moving. The open paradigm is based on self-reflection and planned changes in its own structures, yet its very mode of problem solving makes it difficult to Bystand. The synchronous paradigm is based on close agreement and identification, yet the synchronous regime makes it difficult to Follow, since expectations remain implicit because the system limits communication.

This ambivalent, paradoxical relationship is presented in Figure 7-2. Like the existential dilemma introduced in Chapters 2 and 6, this also appears to be a flaw or limitation built into every paradigm. Enabled regimes will find ways to minimize the effects or to compromise the tendency to disable crucial psychopolitics, but the dilemma will remain.

## DEFENDED COMMUNICATION STYLE

When family members become invested in an interaction in such a way that their self-esteem is at stake, they tend to fall back on certain, somewhat extreme, defended styles of communication. From clinical and workshop experience, Satir (1972) identified four basic variations of defended communication that people employ when their self-esteem "pot" is "hooked," that is, when they fear judgment, rejection, or exposure of weakness. These were called *Blaming, Placating, Distract-*

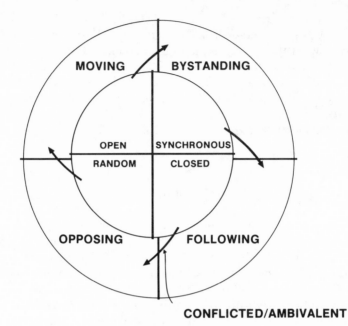

**FIGURE 7-2.**
Relationship of paradigm/regime to "next" psychopolitical position.

*ing,* and *Computing* (or "superreasonableness"). The function of all four of these styles of communication is defensive.

*Placating* involves compliance, blind obedience, and self-abnegation. The Placater surrenders, gives in, denying the self, saying in effect, "Whatever you want is okay. I feel like nothing. I am worthless. You know best." The Placater is ingratiating, apologetic, agreeable, and always seeking approval from others.

*Distracting* is characterized by irrelevance, the denial of meaning of significance, and changing the subject. It is, in effect, tangential communication. Whatever is said is irrelevant, hence meaningless. Distracters effectively cancel communication that leaves them relatively invulnerable to outright attack.

*Blaming* defines the problem as being in others. The Blamer is an accuser, "a fault-finder, a dictator, a boss who acts superior and seems to be saying, 'If it weren't for you, everything would be all right'" (Satir, 1972, p. 66). This style is aggressive and dominating; it denies the other person.

*Computing* involves dispassionate rationalization and detached intellectual analysis. The Computer is cold and aloof, claiming neutrality and denying feelings about the subject. Computing is a style characterized by calm, cool, and collected "objectivity." Satir uses the term "disassociated."

Most people can identify among these four communication styles the one they most readily fall into. Many therapists have found that problematic interactions in families can be understood in terms of the way defended communication styles appear to fit (or not to fit) together. Work by Grinder and Bandler (1975) and Bryson (1978) has supported both the validity of the concept of defended style and its utility in therapy.

### Psychopolitics and Defended Communication

This picture of defended communication is not, however, a new and entirely independent model to be learned by the family therapist. Examination of the descriptions of each style reveals them to be specialized examples of psychopolitical positions. Placating is a defensive form of Following: compliant, accommodating, and self-effacing. Distracting is a defensive form of Opposing: indirect and tangential, hence less vulnerable to attack than more open and direct Opposition. Blaming is predicated on taking the initiative, on the premise that the best defense is a good offense, clearly a Mover's style of defense. Computing is an exaggerated, well-defended form of Bystanding: neutral, detached, unswervingly rational.

The link between psychopolitical position and the defensive communication style of particular individuals is at best probabilistic, a statistical correlation, but it has been well supported by clinical experience and preliminary research (Constantine, 1980b). The relationship between the two models includes some subtleties. Blaming, which has been described by Satir as including "disagreeing," seems to border on a form of Opposition. Superreasonable communication often carries overtones of superiority, which suggests the characteristics of Movers. In Figure 7-3, each of the four forms of defensive communication is pictured as an exaggerated form of a psychopolitical position, which is considered to fall near the border between quadrants. Previous studies (Constantine, 1980b; Bryson, 1978) lend credence to this interpretation.

### Defended Communication, Regime, and Paradigm

If defensive communication is related to psychopolitical position, it must, in turn, be interrelated with family style, with regime and paradigm. This relationship is fairly straightforward, but one must

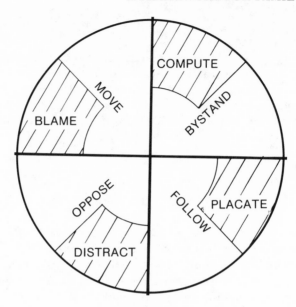

**FIGURE 7-3.**
Defended communication as exaggerated psychopolitics.

keep in mind that defensive communication is likely to be a sign of family dysfunction and disablement. Defensive communication will not, therefore, match up with the best of what each regime is capable.

A tendency for Placating under stress or threat will assure continuity of established processes and reinforce any established hierarchy, thus, the closed paradigm is more likely to engender Placating than any other defensive style. Note well, however, that a closed regime marked by a substantial amount of Placating will almost certainly be a disabled one; individual needs are almost assured of being sacrificed to continuity of the regime.

Similarly, a preference for Distracting will certainly contribute to random process, though not likely a very effective one. The random paradigm's ideal of continuous change and preference for independent behavior will mitigate against Blaming, Computing, and Placating. Individuals with skill at changing or altering the action, with experience in "being different," are not likely to have trouble Distracting.

The calm and detached neutrality of Computing is highly compatible with synchronous norms of harmony and tranquility. Communication is reduced and restricted by the superreasonable commitment to what is rational and objective and to the avoidance of feelings and all that is personal and subjective.

Least apparent is the relationship of Blaming to the open regime and open paradigm. Of the defensive styles it is the most intense, the most confrontive, hence more compatible with that aspect of the open regime. A group of Blamers may not make an effective open system, but the process they get caught up in will certainly be characterized by the high level of intense, direct communication characteristic of open regimes. The connection between *Blaming* and open regimes is not easily reached from Satir's original formulation, though it follows from the unified approach of this book. Much of the difficulty stems from Satir's position that open families are desirable and closed ones are not. Her model does not recognize the potential for disablement in open families; instead, Satir associates a fifth, undefended communication style with open family process.

A thorough understanding of the relationship of defensive communication to family paradigm and regime depends on a more elaborate picture of dysfunction and disablement in families; the relationship should become clearer when these are taken up in Chapter 10.

## Defended Communication and Evaluation

Understanding individual communication style in relation to family regime and psychopolitics can be useful to the family therapist in a number of ways, but especially for evaluation. The behavior of individuals and systems under stress is often more stereotyped or exaggerated, as well as being less variable than under more "normal" conditions. Thus defensive style may be more obvious and more easily categorized than behavior taken more broadly. The tendency to fall back on one particular style of defensive communication may be indicative of a more general but less narrowly defined preference for the corresponding psychopolitical position. Conversely, a clear preference for one position, say, Bystanding, may be used as the basis for a tentative hypothesis that, under stress, that person will be likely to rely on Computing for defensive communication.

The predominance of one particular style of defended communication among several members of a family may be an important clue to the family's regime and its underlying paradigm. In any event, such a predominance will generate a process characteristic of a disabled form of the corresponding family style.

## PSYCHOPOLITICS AND INTERPERSONAL STYLE

Many therapists who have made extensive use of the psychopolitical model are eventually drawn into the use of its terms as descriptions of stable traits of individuals as if they were personality characteristics or character traits. A family member might be described as a "real Stuck Mover, dominating and controlling, very quick to jump in." Such an interpretation, though appealing as a metaphor, diverges from Kantor and Lehr's original intention to describe the behavioral redundancies in interactive sequences. In the final analysis, however, recognition of individual interpersonal style is not fundamentally different from recognizing family regime as a summary of collective family style. These are, as argued above, actually interrelated to the extent that there is greater compatibility between certain regimes and certain psychopolitical styles than between others.

### Psychopolitical Style

Psychopolitical position is not only a description of action but also of the style in which action takes place. Many individuals, not only clients, seem to have a strong preference for or tendency toward acting from certain psychopolitical positions at the expense of others. This skew from a completely balanced intermix in psychopolitical positions is one factor contributing to an individual's interpersonal style. Each distinct position also comprises a distinctive style. The style of a person's "favorite" position may color their behavior even when acting from another position. For example, Moving, taking the initiative, is often perceived as dominant and active; a person with a strong tendency for Moving may retain these traits even when merely watching, by pacing around and making remarks about what is happening.

### Psychopolitics and Interpersonal Circumplex Models

Working from an extensive clinical data base, Leary (1957) developed an interpersonal model of personality based on a circumplex or circular fan of interpersonal styles of adaptation. There has been extensive subsequent use of the model in research and clinical practice, including marriage and family therapy (Nugent, 1978; Nugent, Rouanzoin, Asmann, & Lighty, 1976). This model provides a bridge between family theory and personality theory.[2]

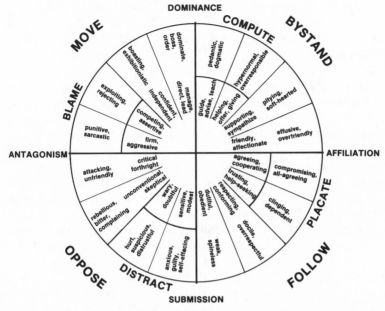

**FIGURE 7-4.**

Interrelationships of Leary, Satir, and Kantor models of interpersonal behavior. Adapted by permission from T. Leary, *Interpersonal diagnosis of personality.* New York: Roland, 1957, p. 65. Shown aligned by *computed* axes.

The interpersonal diagnosis model is based on the principal dimensions of affection–hostility, dominance–subordination. These are intrinsically interpersonal rather than characterizing isolated individuals, as they refer to the relationship between individuals. A condensed version of the model is presented in Figure 7-4. Modes of interpersonal adaptation vary continuously around the circumplex. Adjacent modes are more similar than more distant ones, and polar opposites are also functionally opposite. More extreme, less adaptive behavior is represented further from the center. Although it has been formulated and interpreted in various ways, something akin to this underlying struc-

2. This bridge of multiple spans was achieved through a complex collaborative process. The relationship between defended communication and psychopolitics was worked out with the help of Lou Rappaport. This subsequently made possible relating those two models to a model of existential positions used in transactional analysis (Ernst, 1971), which had, in turn, been related to Leary's interpersonal model by Michael Nugent. L'Abate (1976) also made an initial attempt to map the Leary model directly into the Satir model, but was, by his own assessment, somewhat less successful.

ture for interpersonal attribution and behavior has been repeatedly identified in research and has formed the basis for both elaborations and refinements (Benjamin, 1974; Wiggins, 1980). Although criticism and extensions of the model are relevant here, we will first consider the interpersonal circumplex in its original form.

With relatively few exceptions, the terms are consistent with the psychopolitical model as arranged in Figure 7-3. Note especially the fine distinctions made on either side of the boundary between one quadrant and another. For example, the style of Moving adjacent to Bystanding is also the most clearly dominant in a nearly neutral manner ("manage, direct, lead"). Just over the border into the next quadrant, Bystanding characteristics begin to appear (from "advise, teach" to "pedantic"). Superimposing the Satir models, as has been done in Figure 7-4, clarifies how these are examples of psychopolitical position; the best fit places these on the border with the next anticlockwise position. Just "over the border" from Opposing into Moving introduces a "superior" character relating to Blaming (e.g., "punitive") not present on the other side. The compatibility of Superreasonableness with "hypernormal" and "pedantic" behavior is clear, as is that of Blaming with "punitive" and "exploiting," and Placating with "clinging" and "always agreeing." Less clear is Distracting as "anxious" or "suspicious," and so forth. The upper right quadrant is the most problematic, as the Leary model considers only active behavior; inactive forms of Bystanding are not represented. Instead, neutrality is represented only in the form of universal comfort or acceptance. In its original form, any sense of aloofness or detachment is generally absent from the Leary circumplex.

Interestingly, empirical research attempting to confirm the circular distribution of variables has often found a "gap" in the upper right quadrant of the circumplex (Lorr & McNair, 1965; Stern, 1970; Wiggins, 1979). Through careful scale construction considering only bipolar pairs (e.g., gregarious–extraverted versus aloof–introverted), Wiggins (1979, 1980) was able to construct a more mathematically sound circumplex that included cold, calculating, and aloof attributions, but in the lower left quadrant; it completely lacks the "hot" opposition present in that quadrant of the Leary model. Like a number of other formulations, it concentrates the positive traits on one half of the circle, with the most positive (gregarious–extraverted) in the upper right.

The Structural Analysis of Social Behavior (Benjamin, 1974) is a more complex, multiplanar circumplex model that has come into some use in the study of families. It explicitly introduces a dimension implying involvement or engagement (control versus autonomy), but the language of its variables does not lend itself to interpretation in relation to Bystanding or its disabled variants. A detailed analysis of the potential contributions and shortcomings of this model are, however, beyond the scope of the current discussion.

Even without solving the problem of the upper right quadrant (which, as we have seen, seems always to involve some paradox or seeming contradiction) the interpersonal circumplex model is useful in filling in some of the finer distinctions in behavioral style that are identified more broadly by the categories of the psychopolitical model. It provides additional detail useful for understanding the characteristic style of different regimes, such as implying rebellious and unconventional style for random regimes and a hypernormal character for synchronous ones. It also suggests directions for the refinement of Satir's conceptualization of defended communication, filling in the gaps between Distracting and Blaming, Blaming and Bystanding, and so forth.

### Principal Dimensions of Interpersonal and Family Process

The isomorphism between interpersonal behavior and systemic organization suggested in this chapter would superimpose the axes of these two models. In the Leary circumplex, the axes were originally labeled as dominance–submission and love–hate, although these are also often referred to as superordination and affiliation (Triandis, 1978)—but the axes of the two models in Figures 7-1 and 7-2 were not labeled. Is there a way to make sense of these axes and their juxtaposition?

On the map of individual behaviors, below the axis are Following and Opposing, behaviors that are reactive, implying an external locus of control; above them are nonreactive behaviors, implying an internal locus of control. Both Moving and Bystanding have also been characterized as "dominant." Thus the vertical axis may be thought of in terms of superordination–subordination, proactive–reactive, and internal–external locus of control. Looking to the horizontal axis, Moving and Opposing are not hostile or even necessarily disaffiliatative, but they both involve differentiation from prior collective action. Thus, the horizontal axis may best be thought of as representing identification–differentiation. These axes are not the *same* as those of the Leary circumplex, but they are obviously similar and stand in comparable relation with the elements of their respective models.

Something similar may be satisfactory for the map of systemic process. Closed and random regimes are *reactive*, defining themselves in relation to past action, either continuing it or discontinuing it. The open regime, by contrast, defines its process out of internally planned and negotiated adaptation to present problems without the need to react to the past, whether in submission to it or in struggle against it. The synchronous regime has its own way of being nonreactive, standing apart from time and relying on internalized identification. And, while both closed and synchronous regimes clearly depend on and promote similarity, random and open regimes need and encourage greater differentiation.

The rather unexpected association of locus of control with family style established by this theory has received empirical support from the work of Bloom (1985). In two separate samples, a scale measuring external locus of control of family process correlated negatively ($-.59$ and $-.32$) with a measure of open family organization ("Democratic Family Style"), but positively (.40 and .35) with a measure of random family organization ("Laissez-faire Family Style") and positively (.36 and .13) with a measure of closed family organization ("Authoritarian Family Style").

CHAPTER

# 8

# THE DIMENSIONS OF PROCESS
## Dimensional Analysis of Family Process

One of the major tasks the family therapist faces is to meaningfully organize the overwhelmingly complex data from the family. Here, good theory has much to offer the therapist by providing a systematic framework into which data may be cast and understood. There are numerous theoretical frameworks that analyze family interaction or family functioning into distinct factors or aspects. Some of these theories refer to the factors as dimensions (e.g., Howells, 1975). Although many of these may be valid factorings of family process, not all are equally useful for family therapy.

One of the best reasoned of the dimensional models is that of Kantor and Lehr (1975), who identified six independent dimensions in which family interaction takes place. The analysis in this chapter builds on their work. This component of the paradigmatic framework has three significant advantages over competing frameworks: (1) It follows directly from elementary, observable aspects of transacting systems in general and human families in particular. (2) It is a complete, exhaustive formulation that covers all aspects of family process, thereby serving as a valuable check on the completeness of any formulation of a family. (3) It is easily related to clinical concerns in evaluating and intervening into family systems.

## THE EIGHT DIMENSIONS

The office where I write is a 16- by 20-foot room in which I also do most of my private practice therapy. This is the space in which much of my working life is spent, and its dimensions are the physical dimensions within which interactions will take place. A married couple talking here can only be so distant: Ralph cannot get more than about 25 feet away from Gena. The closet offers other possibilities, and there are three exits: one is a sliding door leading to a 10-foot drop where a deck will someday be. (The latter aspect of the space can give pause for thought when working with seriously depressed clients.) Physical space shapes, and is shaped by, interpersonal process. Try carrying on an intimate conversation with someone at the opposite end of a long table, for example; or watch the slow rearrangement of furniture as a good party progresses.

In my office, interactions with and between clients are also bounded by another dimension, the 90 minutes that a session usually lasts. The dimension of time is as basic as that of space. When I can, I prefer to see clients in longer sessions because these fit the pacing of my style of therapy better than the 50-minute hour. It takes time to work up to some things, and I like plenty of time to process thoroughly the work that we do in a session.

*Space* and *time* are the basic dimensions in which human interaction, indeed all action in the physical universe, can take place. We move about *in* space and communicate *through* space *over* time. What moves in or is communicated through space over time are *matter* and *energy*. We cannot interact within the physical universe, at least so far as that is generally understood, except through movement of gross matter or transmission of energy through space over time.

The material, energic, spatial, and temporal components of interaction constitute the *physical dimensions of human process*. As all physical action takes place in terms of these same dimensions, they are not unique to human interaction. Human interaction in space over time also serves functions not shared by all other systems of objects. We are, as Chapter 5 made clear, communicating beings; the matter and energy we exchange serve to communicate messages; what is communicated may itself be differentiated into "dimensions" (Sweeney, Tinling, & Schmale, 1970). Messages have not only literal *content*, but also implications for the *control* of the process. I can tell my daughter that I don't *like* reruns of "The Brady Bunch" in a tone that asserts authority. She can then tell me that she doesn't like John Chancellor in a tone that makes clear that she regards it as a matter of opinions of equal value. We have just had a transaction in both the dimensions of content and control.

Messages between persons also carry significance or *meaning* and emotion or *affect*. The news, I explain patiently to her, is more important because it concerns things that affect our lives. She scowls at me, and I get the feeling that the meaning of "important" is very different for her and that she resents being lectured. Then we both laugh at Mike Brady's attempts to appear to be the reasonable, democratic father while expecting his children to share all his values.

Content, control, meaning, and affect are the *informational dimensions of human process.* The exchange of literal meaning and control messages is a capacity we share with other information processing systems, but only for humans (and possibly other intelligent, sentient beings) can messages carry significance and feeling.

Kantor and Lehr identified only six dimensions of family process: space, time, and energy (which they called *access dimensions*), and power, meaning, and affect (which they refer to as *target dimensions*). The analysis here adds the dimensions of matter and content to make a complete set. These additions may often be of lesser importance to the therapist, but they cannot be ignored altogether. For theoretical completeness, both matter and content are necessary and will, as shown below, sometimes emerge as salient for therapy. Kantor would include material transactions with the spatial dimension and cover content under meaning. There is, however, an evident distinction between energy in space and matter in space. There is also empirical evidence in studies of communication and attribution that content or immediate, literal interpretation, is a distinct dimension of human interaction (Weiner & Mehrabian, 1968).

The complete dimensional model is represented schematically in Figure 8-1. The dimensions are interrelated. Matter and energy, moving through space in time, communicate content and control, which serve to convey meaning and affect. The central dimensions in the figure (matter, energy, content, and control) are the more concrete; the outer ones (space, time, meaning, and affect) are more abstract. There is also a difference between the dimensions represented in the left and right columns; the latter have a quality of greater dynamism compared with the dimensions in the left column.

The physical dimensions of process (space, time, matter, and energy) are "access" dimensions in that they serve as the media by which desired targets in content, control, meaning, and affect are communicated; they give access to dimensions of particular human interest. In turn, each target dimension has an ultimate end, what I will call its *functional target*. The functional target of a dimension is its effective purpose and normally the primary reason why persons will use it for transactions (or, at least, what they stand to gain from operating successfully in that dimension). The functional target of content transactions is knowledge, for example. These will be discussed as each dimension is introduced in detail.

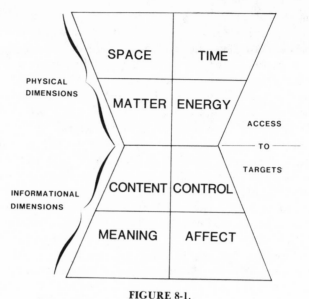

**FIGURE 8-1.**
The eight dimensions of human interactional process.

## PHYSICAL DIMENSIONS

### Space

Spatial relationships constitute one of the earliest and most important modes of human interaction. It is all but certain that some of the meanings we today attribute to approach and withdrawal, closeness and distance, were held even by the Neanderthalers. The management of space and the use of space as a metaphor is so intrinsic and pervasive in the human experience that it often passes unnoticed. In families we are interested in both the employment of actual physical space and the spatial metaphorization of transactions in other dimensions.

#### LITERAL OR PHYSICAL SPACE

For survival, individuals and groups must be able to manage space, to execute coordinated movement in space, and to manage their spatial boundaries. We tend to take this capacity for granted, yet its development is one of the major tasks of the infant.

The impact of people on their physical space is often more obvious than the impact of space upon individuals and interaction, but many disciplines, including architecture, have been attaching increasing importance to the way the immediate physical environment affects interaction. Whatever its rationale in protocol or family tradition, the seating at the dinner table at the very least affects who may communicate with whom more readily. A room that is too small for the number of occupants or for the intended use can lead to a constriction of process, but it can also lead to a heightened intensity of interaction. One of the most memorable parties I ever attended packed 120 boisterous German exchange students into a three-room apartment. We could barely move and scarcely hear each other above the endless verses of *"Varum ist es am Rhine so Schön,"* but we sure had a great time! That night we returned to our apartment, which was in a building with narrow, unlighted halls and a miniscule entry way—not surprisingly, hardly anyone in that building knew each other; there was no way to meet accidentally.

In family process we are interested in how a family arranges space and how it arranges itself in space as these mirror aspects of their functioning and structure and are, in turn, reflected in them. The layout of their home, the placement of furniture, and their seating in the therapy setting are all among the important aspects of the spatial dimension we want to note.

THE SPATIAL METAPHOR

Spatial terms and spatial metaphors are extremely common elements of everyday language, but especially as applied to interpersonal relationships. Consider these:

"that went over my head"          "she went above him with the
"you seem distant"                    matter"
"I turned my back on him"        "up in the air"
"meet me half way"                  "at her side"
"you're getting close"              "touched by the gift"
"she turned the meeting            "he's pushing his son away"
  around"                              "where are you?"
"I feel close to him"               "I've been there"
"I'm behind you in this"           "drifting apart"

Spatial metaphor comprises a rich, largely nonconscious, partially forgotten language. Its elements are proximation (distance), position, posture, and gesture. It is operative as a communication medium at almost all times, whether or not the messages it carries are intentional or congruent with other communication. Even without comment, sliding your chair closer to someone can communicate

warmth, caring, and support, for example. The messages communicated by spatial metaphor are frequently among the most powerful
exchanged in families, as with the Meyers:

> The first floor of the house is an ell formed by a long living room and the
> dining room (see Figure 8-2). When the cotherapists are admitted by
> the mother, the father is seated in a large, heavy armchair at the apex of
> the ell. He does not rise when she ushers the therapists into the room.
> From his chair he can survey the entire downstairs with the exception of
> the bathroom and kitchen lying inside the ell. He can see every entrance
> to the house and all ingress and egress for the downstairs, including both
> entries to the kitchen and the stairs leading to the upstairs and to the
> basement. In the archway between living room and the dining area is a
> portable TV, facing away from him. On the far side, his adult son eats
> alone while watching TV. At intervals, the father will rise with his drink
> in hand, cross to the TV, set the glass upon it, lower the volume, pick up
> the glass, take a drink, and then return to his chair. Moments later the son
> will rise and turn the volume back up, starting the whole cycle again.
> When in the same room, father and son maintain maximal possible
> distance or keep the TV or some other physical barrier between them.

The initial tableau proved to be a rich and highly significant
description of the family system. Superficially, the mother regulated
access to the family, and it was she who held a job and maintained
contact with relatives; but all comings and goings were monitored by
the father who controlled the patterns. He dominated much of the
family interaction and kept the focus on himself as the apex of the
triangle, yet blunted his control with drinking. Mother would not
intercede between father and son, even when violence was threatened,
which was not infrequent. The son managed the boundary between

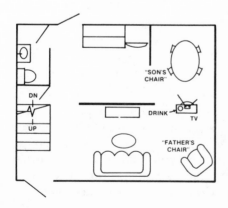

**FIGURE 8-2.**
Floor plan of the Meyer house.

himself and his father primarily through the television: it was a family "prosthesis," a mechanical device substituting for a vital function in the family. The interface between father and son was defective and required the TV. Later in therapy, when it was suggested that father and son sit back to back, they couldn't manage it and the son retreated upstairs in a panic.

Even as the spatial metaphor manifests aspects of family process, it can be manipulated to alter them. Placing the mother in the armchair between father and son changed the interaction dramatically. Much later, when the therapists were called to intervene in a crisis, they arrived to find the mother and son watching TV. When father returned from his "cooling off" walk, he seated himself beside them on the sofa and started watching, too. With the original function of the TV as interface in mind, the therapists considered this spatial metaphor highly significant, especially as the father and son ordinarily remained far apart. Rather than opposing this structure, the therapists made use of it, encouraging comments about the show. Soon the family was involved in a lively interaction about themselves and their relationship with the TV as a symbolic intermediary, taking a step toward more effective communication.

Humans build and preserve understandings of complex interpersonal relationships at least in part as spatial, pictorial "maps" that capture and represent large volumes of data in comparatively compact metaphors. Such imagery is an essential component of dreaming, the principal function of which is to consolidate understandings of the external world (Hartmann, 1973). The importance of the right hemisphere in visual interpretation of nonverbal behavior has also been established (Ornstein, 1972). This would account for the facility with which most people are able to act out and arrange quite elaborate spatial representations of family relationships and strategies, as in such family therapy techniques as family sculpture (Constantine, 1978; Duhl et al., 1973).

## Time

Phillip Wylie (1968) called *Homo sapiens* "the magic animal" because of its faculty of "time binding," transcending time by perceiving it, fixing it through memory, bending it through understanding, and moving backward and forward through it freely in thought. Time is the truest, most inexorable reality, more immutable than the material world. It is time that is certain: only through it do death and taxes qualify. We must live in time, but we cannot move freely through it as

we can through space. Using and accepting time's passage is a fundamental task for all humans.

The essential quality of human time is that it is "bound" by its
rhythmicity; or, as Eric Berne (1964) put it, we "structure" time by
introducing regularities in it, even if these patterns, like the social
pastimes by which we "pass time" with strangers, have no other
meaning or significance. At the biological level we are immense clock-
works of cycles, counterpoised and multiphased rhythms that range
from sleep and wakefulness to sodium ion concentration. Research has
confirmed the importance of these rhythms as they influence behavior.
Our behavior and lifestyle, in turn, close the loop and influence
biochemical rhythms. Hartmann (1973) found that a person's lifestyle,
more than other factors, correlated with patterns of dream episodes as
well as the total time spent in dreaming.

Cycles at the psychological–behavioral, personal–interpersonal
levels are also abundantly evident, though the relationships—if any—
with biochemical rhythms are not yet known. Each individual has
characteristic cycles of effectiveness. Some people are at their best on
rising, others peak later in the day, and still others are not in best form
until far into the night. Family process is affected by the meshing of
such individual rhythms and by the extent to which they are in or out
of phase.

In families, certain times of day emerge as more crucial than
others, both as good representatives of family process and as periods
more likely for conflict. Dinner time often provides an ideal sample of
a family's basic organization and patterns of interaction. Morning,
when the entire family is competing for limited facilities under the
pressure of external time demands, is another critical period in most
families' daily lives. Bedtime is yet another, when parents and children
are likely to struggle for control over their own and each other's lives
and when sexual tensions between parents (or the absence of these) are
apt to color the proceedings.

In addition to these circadian or daily rhythms, other, longer
cycles have been observed. Erik Erikson (1950) argues that human
development over the lifespan follows large-scale cycles. Personal
growth also seems to follow cycles in which comfort and satisfaction
slowly become anomie, which may give way to depression; a creative
crisis is precipitated, triggering a new spurt of insight, then consolida-
tion, and a return to a plateau of satisfaction. Many of us are aware of
our own long cycles of productivity and fallow periods, especially
when it comes to creative work.

The progress of a family's development as a system is another
important aspect of time in families. Families that are just beginning

as systems have different issues in the fore than families that have already seen the exit of all the grown children. Cyclic and stagewise patterns in family development will be explored in depth in Chapter 9.

The time dimension has its own boundaries; that is, people regulate access in time as much as in space. Appointments, visiting hours, quiet periods, and taboos on 2:00 A.M. phone calls are all examples of time boundaries. The salience of time as a dimension and the importance of its boundaries vary from family to family. Some people and families that do not effectively regulate spatial boundaries may rely heavily on temporal patterning for boundary maintenance.

> In the Rustin family, time was of preeminent importance, serving as the principal access dimension and even substituting for other dimensions. Mrs. Rustin habitually took longer than everyone else to get ready for a family event or outing, thereby getting attention and gaining control over the process. Eventually, after being repeatedly pressured to hurry, she would announce that she was not going and tell the others to go on without her. Mr. Rustin would then reassure her that they would wait for her, whereupon she would begin, at last, to move somewhat faster. Others in the family had their own variants of the strategy. One gained *control* by delay; to her, love was proved by the willingness of others to wait. Not only did time substitute for control and affect, but for spatial boundaries as well. For years, Mr. and Mrs. Rustin went to bed and rose at very different times, thus reducing the intimate contact between them. Fittingly, their eldest child spent a great deal of time in the hospital where visiting hours sharply delineated the contact with her parents. Her mother also had the habit of showing up just before the end of that allowed time, further reducing contact.

The use of time can be carried to even greater extremes, as in the Meyer family in which a young adult and his father were able to minimize overt conflict by adopting mirror-image schedules. The son would sleep all day, rising at supper time. The father, who would usually be drunk within an hour or two of dinner, went to bed early. The son then stayed up all night, going to bed at dawn before his father got up.

In family process we are also interested in the family's basic orientation to time. Are they primarily oriented to the past, to the present, or to the future? Are these seen as meaningfully connected or unrelated? Are "the good times" now or something only remembered or hoped for in the future? As we saw in Chapter 6, orientation to time will tend to vary with the family's regime. Closed regimes tend to underplay the present while random regimes attach little importance to past or future. Open regimes seek a synthesis of past, present, and future, while synchronous regimes seem to stand apart from time, consider time to be irrelevant, or see all times as equivalent.

## Material Transactions

People give, receive, accept, reject, and exchange many material objects every day. Some of these are significant primarily for what they are physically (a sweater, a pencil), and others (money, a set of car keys, for example) are more significant as tokens representing or giving access to other objects. Material transactions are of interest both for their substance and for their interplay with transactions in other dimensions. Both aspects must be taken into account by the therapist. Forgetting the simple material content of transactions can lead to a kind of psychologizing that can leave people feeling misunderstood or unappreciated, and can even be dangerous. A gun is more than a symbol when it is pointed at you. The clients' irregularity in paying may not be "resistance" at all, but simply a direct consequence of limitations in their material resources.

On the other hand, ignoring the personal meanings and family attributions associated with material transactions or their use to carry messages from other dimensions can lead to a poverty of understanding, missing the richness with which simple transactions are often endowed. The sweater might be the laboriously created message of love and caring; a sharpened pencil carefully laid on the desk by a writer's spouse may communicate support and encouragement. Money could be access to power or a substitute for affection someone is unable to express otherwise. The car keys given by Dad with a barely perceptible hesitance communicate his trust in his daughter as well as his worry, while to her the keys could mean escape and freedom.

Gift exchange and commerce, sharing of food and implements, are ancient and still operative forms of social cement. They are no less important within families than between families who are neighbors or kin. Noting the process in material transactions is essential to understanding a family.

Consider the matter of allowances, which in some families can be a sophisticated ritual of great significance and in others may be merely a matter of fact. Who gets an allowance? All children? Children over a certain age? Wife and children? What kind of statement does this make about the status of members, about power, dependence, and freedom? Who actually gives the allowance? Is it given regularly or more sporadically? Are the amounts excessive? Inadequate? Does the allowance truly belong to the recipient? Can he or she spend it on anything, including "frivolities"? Is the allowance a right, an automatic division of the family wealth, or is it contingent on performance of certain labor? To what extent is giving the allowance purely a material transaction, to what extent a transaction in power, a mechanism for transmitting values, or a substitute for affection or attention?

The answers to these questions not only reflect unique features of particular families but also will vary in general with family paradigm. Closed families are more likely to make allowances contingent on behavior, for instance, while open ones are more likely to have some single standard for allowances applicable to all members.

### Energy

Aaron does everything with intensity. Carol's style is calm and reserved. Energy—intensity, or forcefulness with which actions are performed—has an effect on others. Imagine a stranger advancing slowly toward you with manifest deliberateness, muscles tensed, each step executed with force and precision. His expression is unreadable. What is your impulse? Imagine another stranger coming toward you at the same speed, with the same ambiguous facial expression, only casually, relaxed, and at ease. How would it feel different?

As with other physical dimensions, every individual and family must learn strategies for managing their own energy and the energy of others, for building it up, using it, conserving it, and countering it. A family must have reserves or sources of energy sufficient to meet task demands. If energy in the family comes mostly from one person, the family is less viable, more fragile than if all members can vary their contributions, supplying most of the energy at times, sharing the load equally at others, or drawing on the resources of other members as best fits the situation.

Individuals whose consistent style is very high or very low in energy can have a substantial, often problematical, impact on the systems in which they participate. The high energy person's impact is often most immediate, while the effects of very low energy can be slower and more subtle in becoming manifest. Extremes of energy affect process irrespective of the position being played. Consider a group leader who occupies the physical center of a group, Moving and directing it, but with little energy. This tends either to encourage a low-energy group or to draw out excessive energy in response to the energy vacuum created. In contrast, a person of great energy who "merely watches," but with intensity and great energy, can drown out any other action taking place and draw the center of activity outward.

The following are key questions about energy in connection with a family: Is this a high energy or a low energy family? How widely does the energy level range? Where does the energy come from? Who has an abundance and who lacks energy? How is energy stored, and how is it mobilized and channeled to fill needs? Does it flow easily, or are there blocks in its distribution? How do individuals and the family "refuel"?

## INFORMATIONAL DIMENSIONS

### Content

Hugh Samson is a hard driving engineer who often takes his work home with him. When he is under the pressure of excessive demands, he can be counted on to display a certain pattern of irritability. Should he have trouble getting down to work or make a serious mistake in his calculations, he may launch into a tirade at everyone, from his wife to the family cat. When he needs something and can't find it, the general mess is at fault and everyone is to blame for the mess. He catalogs their many failings and demands the immediate restoration of order and correctness to his world.

But his family knows what is happening: Hugh is pressured. He has slipped behind at a time when he can ill afford to slip. He is angry at himself for failing and is panicked that he will be unable to meet all the demands on him. He turns his anger and fear outward. Hugh's image of himself is also at stake. He believes he can succeed if only he has a stable and ordered environment on which to depend. Thus the key dimensions are meaning and affect. His family has learned that he is not angry at them, but when they try to ignore or downplay his outbursts, these only seem to escalate.

However, their adaptational response fails to alter the pattern because it ignores the literal message in Hugh's tirade. The piles of magazines and toys left in his office by others do make his work more difficult, perhaps enough to make the difference between meeting his deadlines or missing them. Dismissing his behavior as merely the fallout from outside pressures is a mistake. For his part, Hugh would be more successful in communicating with the rest of the family if he could separate the content from the meaning and affect in his messages.

Family therapists, trained to observe pattern and dig for underlying meaning and motivation, can be especially vulnerable to missing the literal content of what family members say to each other. Therapists do need to learn the underlying patterns in control, meaning, and affect, but not to the exclusion of direct and obvious content. In exchanges between clients and therapists, ignoring content can lead to anger toward the therapist, since the clients will feel unheard and misunderstood; attending to content can serve important therapeutic functions. All descriptions of family process in terms of control, meaning, and affect are abstracted from the actual data of the families transactions. Therapists tend to remember the abstractions ("he was angry at them") more readily than the content ("his brow creased"). Returning to the data, the content of communication, can often reveal the possibility of alternative interpretations; trying a literal, even naïve, reading of exchanges can expose new dimensions of what is taking place.

The content dimension is important in connection with a family's problem-solving ability. Effective problem solving and decision making requires the ability to process content, factual information, and the ability to separate content from other dimensions. A family that hears nearly every attempt to convey information as a move to dominate or an expression of superiority will have difficulty arriving at competent solutions to its problems. Families that habitually ignore content and give supremacy to feelings will also be less effective; so will families that deny that there is anything but content, as they will miss the personal and emotional significance of their conclusions as well as of the input to their decision making.

The functional target of transactions in content is knowledge; by exchanging information we stand to become knowledgeable. Teaching and learning are characteristic processes in content transactions, but content is also the dimension of choice for passing time, as in talking about the weather, for example, since content involves the least personal investment. It is the informational dimension that is neutral, concrete, factual, objective, and detached. (Not surprisingly, it is the preferred dimension of process in synchronous families.)

## Control

The subject of control in human systems was explored in depth in Chapter 5. Control is the actual regulation or determination of process by any component or part of a system or by the system as a whole. Transactions in this dimension are messages that control or attempt to control process, or that make assertions about control. These assertions may be communicated by any medium and may be explicit or implicit. Often, but not always, control assertions are communicated nonverbally and are left implicit. The act of asserting control or not does not make the assertion true. There may be agreement among family members as to control over their collective process, in which case the interaction is said to be "punctuated congruently," otherwise the punctuation is discrepant.

Family theory, in the social sciences as well as family therapy, more often considers power; psychology more often considers dominance. Dominance and power are aspects of the control dimension. For some purposes these terms and their uses may be interchangeable, but some careful discrimination can be useful.

The functional target in the control dimension is personal efficacy; successful transactions in control ultimately serve to bring about the personal goals of individuals. The goal, unless perverted or exaggerated, is not control of the system per se. A person is effective if he/she is usually able to bring about conclusions to process that meet his/her needs or serve to further personal ends. To be powerless or have little power is to be unable to bring about conclusions that meet personal needs or serve personal ends.

Power in this sense, efficacy, need not be very obvious. A quiet and self-effacing husband may be very powerful, every effective in getting what he wants; and it is common for very young children to be powerful and aware of their power in this sense. *Dominant* or *dominating* are better terms for a family member who vigorously, openly, and frequently asserts control in a family.

Another use of the term, power, is to refer to *clout* or the ability to determine the contingencies, the rewards and punishments, associated with another's behaviors. Parents generally have more clout than children; they are stronger and have more material resources at their disposal. They may use their clout or not depending on the family's style and the parents' attitudes about power in this sense. Having clout does not necessarily mean being powerful; in some families, parents with a great deal of clout may be dominated by a child with little.

POWER AND PSYCHOPOLITICS

There is a tendency for Movers to be seen as powerful and dominant, Followers as weak and submissive. Opposers are not perceived as powerful, though they are seen as seeking power and are thereby in competition with collective process; Bystanders are generally experienced as powerful and yet not seeking power, therefore not in competition with the process. It is possible to be effective from any position, of course, but the attribution of power to Movers and Bystanders more than Followers and Opposers has an underlying basis.

As the previous chapter argued, both Following and Opposing are reactive to an external definition of the process. While it would sound strange to refer to both Moving and Bystanding as active or proactive, they have in common that they are not *reactive*. It is this internalization of control over action that is perceived by others as powerful. As shown in Figure 8-3, the attribution of power is consistent with the dimensions of interpersonal adaptation formulated by Leary (1957) as related to the psychopolitical model (compare Figure 7-4).

As mentioned earlier, there are four basic assertions with respect to control in an interaction between self and other: I'm in charge; I'm not in charge; you're in charge; you're not in charge. These correspond, respectively, to Moving, Bystanding, Following, and Opposing, respectively, as shown in Figure 8-3. To initiate or define action, Moving, is—in the control dimension—to assert control; to Follow an established action is to acknowledge control by another; to Oppose is to deny or object to control by another; to Bystand in the control dimension is to remain outside or neutral with respect to control, saying, "I'm not a part of this." These connections become especially clear in instances of defended communication. The superreasonable Bystander does not direct others in the family to perform a particular action, but invokes reason rather than authority. ("It's not a matter of

**FIGURE 8-3.**
Relationship of psychopolitical position to power and reference for control.

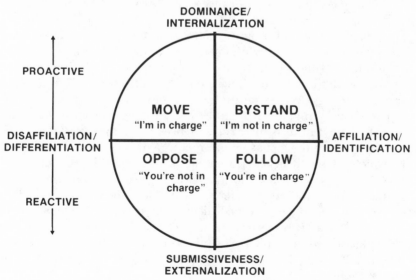

what I think is best but one of what can be shown, logically, to be the most reasonable course. Let us consider, for example, the merits of . . .")

A form of communication that could be called *psychopolitical incongruence* results when the psychopolitical position in the content and control dimensions do not coincide. For example, a person may superficially Follow while covertly undermining the intent of the Mover. This Following while denying an assertion by the Mover that he/she is in charge is "Following in the style of an Opposer." Psychopolitical incongruence results whenever control and content levels do not correspond as in Figure 8-3. For example, early in family therapy training a head nurse was asked to observe an interview role-played by two other students. The nurse sat on the floor only a foot or so away from them and leaned forward so that her head swiveled almost constantly from one to the other. She, rather than the interviewers, was the center of the action—she was Bystanding in the style of a Mover, communicating that she was in charge, as she almost always was in her personal and professional life.

## Meaning

Meaning refers to the human *significance* of communications. What an interaction means to participants or to an observer goes beyond the literal content of the messages exchanged. Words and gestures have personal and familial significance that grows out of the totality of individual and group experience, as well as culture and history.

The dimension of meaning is the medium of symbol, metaphor, and image. Its concern is with the interpretation of messages, however communicated and whatever they might be "about" at the surface level of content. In the meaning dimension the family therapist is interested in many things. Values, attitudes, ideology, and worldview are all aspects of meaning. What are the family's images of itself and how does it see the world? Is there convergence among the views of various members or are these sharply divergent? What are their self-images? How do they see themselves? Imagine themselves? What are the family's "private codes" and "local dialects," their internal consensual meanings for common experiences? How does the family deal with differences? Are these admitted, denied, or ignored? Do they value difference or sameness? Are meanings clear or ambiguous? How are meanings shared, if at all? Do members validate each other as unique persons? Meaning is such a rich ore that many therapists mine it almost exclusively.

In the rush to interpret, the therapist must also be sensitive to private meanings and the differences between his/her interpretations and those of the family. When a couple speaks repeatedly of their "raging battle" at home, but shows only the coolest and most rational discussion in sessions, the therapist is likely to wonder what they "really mean." It may turn out that, to this couple, a "raging battle" is an argument in which one of them quietly says, "Well, I'm not satisfied. I'm really angry at you."

### THEMATIC MATERIAL AND FAMILY MEANINGS

Observing someone else's family can sometimes result in the feeling that something important has happened that escapes your grasp—to find out what's happening and what it means, you have to enter into a family's own meanings. To some extent families develop their own language. From the larger language they select a more personalized vocabulary that becomes invested with special significance or importance. When certain words are used with unexpected frequency, they often turn out to be signs of important family themes.

In one family, words having to do with equality and fairness were used repeatedly, especially by the parents. ("We try to treat them all alike." "We agree about that." "They all feel the same way." "She's just like her sister. They do things the same way.") Of course, words like "agree" and "same" are perfectly ordinary and useful words, but ones that most people do not find as many occasions for using. Discovering this personalized vocabulary was another clue that this family did, indeed, have a preoccupation with issues of agreement and disagreement and attempted to deny or suppress differences among the children.

Family themes may also be identifiable by their absence; however, the avoidance of particular words or themes is hard for the therapist to recognize unless there are other reasons to expect it. In one family with a terminally ill parent, nothing was ever said about health, sickness, or death, which were, in fact, central themes for the family.

### METAPHOR AND FAMILY IMAGES

Metaphor is a powerful mode of communication because it conveys meaning far beyond the complexity of the symbols used to communicate. A metaphor is often the most compact description possible of a person, family, or situation. Consider, for example, "This family is a bowl of rising bread dough." This metaphor conjures up many images: the dough is sticky and it would be hard to climb out of it; it is warm and it would be wonderful if it weren't so raw; it is slowly growing; it has a smooth white exterior, but you can't tell what's underneath the surface; it's full of air, but you could suffocate in there. For the family being represented by the metaphor, these are all apt descriptions.

The therapist may ask family members for short, symbolic pictures of what their family is really like. Often family members volunteer metaphors without being asked. A disappointed mother, whose college-age sons are totally lacking in any sense of life direction, describes her random paradigm family as "a circus that can't get its act together." The single parent of a strongly closed paradigm family, who is caught in a struggle with his four teenagers, one a heavy marijuana user, says, "It's a zoo. Only I wish that little animal over there were in a cage."

The therapist can set up structures that encourage metaphorical expression of personal and family meanings by, for example, asking family members to introduce each other as if each person were some kind of animal; the choices are often very significant and can provide input for very fruitful interaction. Expressive techniques, such as ones discussed in Chapter 13, are useful in drawing out the richness of family metaphors.

ICONS AND ICONIC PRESENCE

In a family of three children whose father was declared "missing in action" during the Vietnam conflict, a photograph of the missing father figures prominently on the mantelpiece. When she is at a loss for what to do, the mother glances toward her husband's picture; before he goes to bed, the oldest boy, who still dimly remembers his father, usually pauses for a moment at the fireplace and looks at the picture. The picture is an icon, a symbol or image evoking and standing in for an absent or departed person. It is not uncommon for MIA families to have an iconic presence that plays a meaningful part in their daily interaction.

In another family, a single mother kept a belt belonging to her former husband on a hook in the kitchen. "The Belt" was referred to so many times in sessions that the therapist finally concluded that it served as more than an instrument of the mother's attempt at discipline, but as an icon for the children's father.

MEANING AND IDENTITY

People express and share images as part of the process of finding out who they are. The functional target in the meaning dimension is identity: personal identity and family identity. From the symbolic, metaphorical, and analogic exchanges of interaction in meaning, pictures of the self and of the family are built.

## Affect

In families the dimension of affect is very important; we are interested in how feelings are expressed and how they are received. Are family members able to separate and distinguish affect from content, control, and meaning?

Just as there are themes in a family's transactions in meaning, there is often a dominant affect or mood. Do people feel good or bad? The dominant affect may be fear, warmth, hate, even apathy. Affect may be rock steady or highly variable, even volatile. It may be intense or controlled.

### THERAPY AND AFFECT

There seems to be some tendency for therapists to adopt extremes of style in the dimension of affect. Some therapists "go for the affect," striving for gut-spilling emotional breakthroughs; to them, any session that is not intensely emotional is unsuccessful. At the other extreme are therapists who value rationality above all, who consider "emotional display" and "catharsis" as irrelevant to growth and change.

In between is an approach that strives for an accurate sensitivity to people's feelings and an awareness of legitimate differences in how affect is handled by families and individuals. The therapist needs to consider paradigmatic variation in how families manage affect and be prepared to deal with the emotional expression that emerges, yet not feel the need to create it in all cases without regard to the specifics of a family.

### FUNCTIONAL TARGETS IN AFFECT

Kantor and Lehr (1975) originally argued that the functional target in affect was intimacy; however, this has proven to be a slippery term with many definitions. To some, intimacy means sharing feelings, but to others, the sharing of meanings—personal images—is more important. Some families will regard some affect as intimate and not others; expressions of warmth may be regarded as intimate, but not hostility. Some families aim for comfort, security, and acceptance, rather than what is usually taken to be intimacy. A family that describes itself as "very close" may be intimate by its own definition, yet share either feelings or meanings very little.

Perhaps another clearer and more universal formulation of the functional target in affect is possible, but it has eluded those working in this area. "Warmth," "closeness," or "engagedness" may be a better expression of it than "intimacy."

## PROCESS DIMENSIONS AS FUNCTION OF PARADIGM AND REGIME

There are two senses in which process dimensions, regime, and paradigm are interrelated. First, differences among regimes may be identified in every dimension of process—each primary form of family has its own style of transaction in each dimension. These are summarized in Table 8-1, which may be read as a compact description of the four primary forms of family regime/paradigm, their similarities, and their differences. The entries in the table are elaborated upon in succeeding sections. Each regime also has a particular association with one dimension, which may be viewed as a primary or key dimension of that regime. In this area, some of the connections are not well understood and may appear to be somewhat more obscure than other aspects of the paradigmatic framework.

### Meaning and Identity

The random paradigm with its norms of exploration, individuality, and uniqueness places a special emphasis on personal identity, the functional target in the dimension of meaning. The random regime is well suited to "doing your own thing" and "finding yourself." Although the random paradigm has a special commitment to meaning and the processes building personal identity, all paradigms form the foundation for identity and all effective regimes contribute to the creation of identity. Each paradigm and regime, however, bases personal identity in different areas and contributes in different ways to its acquisition.

In the closed paradigm, personal identity is derived from group identity. An individual is identified with the primary groups to which he/she belongs. ("I am an Italian–American." "You are a true Blackfoot, son." "She's a McDowall, all right.") In the past, and to a lesser extent today, the greatest part of personal identity was rooted in one's occupational group, the social role one played. ("I am a mechanic,"

**TABLE 8-1.**
Dimensional Analysis of Family Regimes

| Content | Control | Meaning | Affect |
|---|---|---|---|
| *Closed* | | | |
| Necessary; learning, acquisition | Authority, rules, discipline, preparation | Permanent tradition, tried-and-true, shared certainty | Regulated, prescribed, formal |
| *Random* | | | |
| Unimportant | Anarchic, personal, freedom, choice, competition, challenge | Relative, intuitive, phenomenological; creative inspiration | Spontaneous, whimsical, passionate, intense |
| *Open* | | | |
| Useful; testing, experiment | Equality, cooperation, participation, persuasion, consensus | Contextual, pragmatic; relevance, tolerance; dialogue, diversity | Authentic, responsive, expressive |
| *Synchronous* | | | |
| All important; knowing | Implicit, understood, indirect; consentience | Universal, timeless, rational, correct | Limited, reserved; denied or avoided |

rather than "I do mechanics.") The individual is as dependent on the group in the area of identity as in any other. The group is the first point of reference; identity is rooted in belonging. To know yourself in this paradigm is therefore based in the past, in knowing your ethnic, cultural, linguistic, and family heritage. In the best of closed regimes these are stable and dependably communicated; in the worst, they are denied and obscured.

An essential aspect of the meaning dimension is the meaning of truth, which varies from paradigm to paradigm. In the closed family, truth is fixed and immutable, already known and anchored in permanent tradition. The true meaning is determined by authority and by the past. ("Your father knows what's right.")

In the random paradigm, identity is rooted in the individual and comes from self-exploration and personal discovery. The past is not as important in this process as experience—experiencing in the here-and-now. Trying many things and having different experiences is part of the process. One expresses oneself; one studies oneself. In the more extreme cases the random paradigm is translated into self-centered preoccupation with "me-ness." When they work well, random regimes are good places to discover one's unique identity.

Truth is relative in the random paradigm. Its epistemology is phenomenological: your truth is unique to you. Differences between your truth and my truth are to be expected, and there is no need to resolve or even necessarily to understand the differences. ("How you see it is how you see it." "What's true for me is what's true for me.")

To the open paradigm, identity is an inseparable admixture of self and context, hammered out through interaction with others. It is associated with what one does and how, not as a role but as a manifestation of personal competency. Identity is not stable but emerging or evolving. Like all meaning in the open regime, personal identity emerges through process.

The epistemology of the open paradigm is based on "proof in praxis," on what works out. Truth is something that emerges from interaction, a common truth emerging out of the distinct truths of the participants in process. Thus, again, the open paradigm synthesizes elements of closed and random paradigms.

In the synchronous paradigm, a person is who a person is; identity does not "emerge" but rather "exists." As the group and the individual are not fundamentally distinct, personal identity and family identity are, in essence, the same. The fact that this may sound somewhat magical to those who do not identify with the synchronous paradigm is consistent with the paradigm. The process that children growing up in synchronous families seem to go through to form their personal identity is one of internalizing the identity of others. If this "works," they are sufficiently like the others to sustain synchrony in the family.

Truth in synchronous paradigms is implicit. There is one truth, though there may be many paths to it. Truth is apprehended by the individual, but it must match the one preexisting reality of the family. Truth may be based in "direct knowing" of "what is" or on "rational, logical discussion" of "objective reality." The appeal of logic to the synchronous regime is its perfectness and the faith that correct reasoning can only lead to the one correct answer. Nonrational faith in one ultimate reality may obviously serve the same function.

## Content and Knowledge

The synchronous regime has a special affinity for the content dimension, which is related to its conception of truth. The neutral, objective character of the content dimension is consistent with its need for a single shared reality. ("The facts are obvious. Only one conclusion is possible.") Its commitment to coordination through identification rather than communication also contributes. Transaction in neutral content reduces the strength of interconnection (the coupling) between communicating members, thus members of a synchronous family stay with content as much as possible to maximize the likelihood of agreement and minimize the significance of any disagreement that might materialize. ("Interesting weather we're having.")

This affinity for content and dispassionate consideration is completely consistent with the psychopolitical propensities of the synchronous regime. Bystanding is a neutral position with respect to action; the corresponding defended communication style is "computing" or superreasonableness.

Content is important to the open regime, but only as input to the consensual negotiation, only as it is needed for efficacy. The importance of content to the closed regime is in its need for preparation, a method for assuring stability. Knowledge is valued, but within limits; much learning and knowledge is perceived as threatening and disruptive of the established order. Random regimes are likely to see content as distinctly less important than other dimensions.

## Control and Efficacy

The special relationship between the control dimension and the open paradigm arises from the latter's investment in consequences and its commitment to efficacy through adaptability. The consensual decision-making process requires all members to take responsibility for holding up their own end of the dialogue and assertively seeing to it that the consensual resolution meets their individual needs. As the open regime permits a disproportionate amount of Moving, the characteristic transaction in control is likely to be "I'm in charge." The open process permits a multiplicity of definitions of the action because it uses these as the basis for synthesis. In its typical "both/and" logic, the open paradigm accepts that more than one person can be "in charge" simultaneously. Consistent with its paradigmatic commitment, bids for control in an enabled open regime tend to be explicit, direct, and purposeful.

The closed paradigm restricts and regulates control as it does all process dimensions. Consistent with its investment in a hierarchy, most of the time most members are expected to acknowledge control by authority, to Follow in the dimension of control. The closed paradigm assumes only one person can be "in charge" at a time.

The random regime resists control, rebels against authority, and denies dominance. As Opposition is the modal psychopolitical position, members of a random family are most likely to assert, "You're not in charge."

## Affect and Closeness

Kantor and Lehr originally characterized the affect ideal of closed families as "caring with reserve," but questions have since emerged about whether this is the most universal and fundamental formulation. Arguments based on ethnic differences were first advanced by Leonard (1981), who pointed out that typical Middle Eastern families are clearly closed in every respect except that emotions are expressed intensely and frequently. In American families, the closed paradigm is reflected in attempts to modulate affect carefully; at a funeral, for instance, the bereaved may attempt to remain calm and collected, struggling to maintain control in public, keeping the full expression of grief private. In Lebanese families, however, the closed paradigm is reflected differently in affect, and the bereaved are *expected* to wail loudly and publicly.

Various interpretations of this difference are possible. The paradigmatic framework might be intrinsically culture-bound, like most previous approaches to family process, but this seems unlikely since it rests on such fundamental principles of human systems and has been built specifically to bridge between different worldviews. It is also possible that the Lebanese and American cultures simply favor particular, distinct forms of mixed regime, but then this admixture would itself have to be explained. Another explanation seems more likely.

The closed paradigm seeks to maximize continuity by relying on tradition. It is not the content of the traditions that define the closed family, but its relationship to them, thus the closed family is, by its definition, culture-bound. The variability between closed families in different cultures may be considerable, though the latitude within a specific culture or a specific family in that culture is much narrower. What the North American and Middle Eastern closed family have in common in terms of their handling of affect is that both *prescribe* what, when, and how feelings are to be expressed—to remain true to the tradition, the Lebanese widow *must* wail, the American must not.

Thus, the general quality of affect in closed families is that it is controlled, regulated, and prescribed, not that it is necessarily reserved. The particular sense of intimacy or closeness that results from the sharing of affect in prescribed ways will thus vary from culture to culture. It is important for closed regimes to regulate affect because it is otherwise unpredictable and disruptive.

In random families, affect is expressed more idiosyncratically and with greater spontaneity and variability. Although random families are the antithesis of closed ones, it is not in the content of transactions but in their style and process that they are the opposite. They reject continuity itself, not necessarily the specific traditions continued by their culture. Cultural specificity is less likely in random families because they reject controlled, regulated expression of affect in general, not some particular prescription for feelings.

In open families, the expression of feelings is important because of the need of the system to have the fullest access to every member's viewpoints, needs, and interests. But feelings are just more grist for the mill. The demand for authenticity includes, but is not limited to feelings, as open regimes seek to integrate the emotional and the rational.

The synchronous paradigm tends to deny feelings rather than regulate them, and individuals are normally unexpressive of feelings. The synchronous paradigm may validate direct knowing or connate knowledge, or emphasize the path of reason and rationality, but it avoids or denies the base passions and the world of emotion with the possible exception of "transcendent" feelings of oneness, unity, and ultimate calm.

By process of elimination, the key dimension of process in closed families should be affect, but this is not an entirely satisfactory correspondence. The fit is marginal even if one is prepared to see a connection, via the systemic payoff of closed regimes, between affect and warmth or closeness. It is difficult to interpret what it means to say that feelings are the key dimension of process in families that so carefully control and regulate them.

### Functional Targets and Regime Payoffs

Table 8-2 relates the principal payoffs of closed, random, open, and synchronous regimes to the functional targets in each target dimension of process. The "best fit" is consistent with the interpretation of

**TABLE 8-2.**
Identification of Key Target Dimension by Regime

| Regime | Payoff | Dimension | Functional target |
|---|---|---|---|
| Closed | Security, belonging, stable nurturance | Affect | "Affirmative intimacy," closeness, nurturance |
| Random | Identity, differentiation, self-discovery | Meaning | "Purposeful identity," self-awareness |
| Open | Practical effectiveness, constructive adaptability | Control/power | "Constructive efficacy," mastery |
| Synchronous | Harmony, universal identification | Content | "Complete knowledge," wisdom(?) |

the key dimensions of process outlined above. More speculative is the possibility that different regimes may have preferred dimensions in access, or physical dimensions. The focus of closed families on material security is fairly evident, as is the concern with energy in the high energy, demanding environment of the open family. An association of space and time as key dimensions for random and synchronous regimes is only weakly supported by clinical experience. Taken together, Tables 8-1 and 8-2 provide a rather detailed map of the dimensions of family process as these vary among different family paradigms, further highlighting the distinctiveness of each paradigm.

# 9

# CYCLE AND CHANGE
## Processes in Family and
## Individual Development

The circle of folding chairs fills slowly, as latecomers trickle in. A fog of anxious silence blankets the group; though they wish to break it, they do not, save in hushed brevity. Little is said beyond ritual greeting and stereotyped inquiry. They do not know what to expect nor what is expected of them. Nothing is defined except that they are here—the group has no structure of its own. What patterned behavior we see comes from the elements of the common cultural heritage carried into the group within each member. They wait for the arrival or emergence of leadership, for direction, for structure. Even left completely alone, they will not wait long in this amorphous limbo, for the need to structure time (Berne, 1963) is strong in the human animal. Soon they will be passing time with "pastimes," conventional conversation about the weather, transacting in the "tremendous trifles" of the content dimension. External and previously defined norms predominate over ones created from within the group during this amorphous period of pastimes before the formal beginning of the group (Berne, 1963).

An experiential training group provides a convenient laboratory for understanding the universals of the development of systems. The group we will "watch" has been set up carefully. It is the first such experience for its members, a varied group who have never met before. They have been told only that they will be taking part in a group experience. They are, therefore, far from any equilibrium as a system and have many degrees of freedom. Their options are many and far from settled. They are quite different from a group that meets to play bridge or to become a chapter in the League of Women Voters. This choice of a starting point makes the changes the group will experience stand out more sharply and occur more rapidly than in a club or task-oriented group, but does not otherwise change the order and focus.

In a short time someone Moves, suggesting direction for the group. This may be a previously designated leader, or a spontaneous "volunteer" whose need to Move is greatest. In any case, a leadership structure begins to emerge. Having leaders and direction relieves anxiety and helps members feel secure. The leader or leaders increasingly become the focus of the group and their leadership the center of its life. Other members are dependent on them and on the hierarchical structure that emerges. For the most part they are cooperative and Follow as the group collectively goes through a process of orienting itself to its tasks and its member to each other. Roles begin to be defined and assigned, and a group structure emerges.

But dissatisfaction with the structure also begins to grow, and deification of the leaders gives way to discontent. Discontent and dissent grow, as dependence is slowly replaced by counterdependence. The ordered and stable structure of the earlier history gives way to rivalry and competition, even open revolt against the authority of leadership. The primary concern shifts from tasks and "things" to people and feelings. Anger and hostility dominate as the members go through an almost "adolescent" rebellion.

As the group persists, however, the focus shifts from leaders to other members. They stop looking to leadership to solve problems and begin to work out differences among themselves. Effective communication becomes more important as the group seeks to negotiate and establish its own goals and norms. Emotions and the work of the group are more integrated as they once more focus on being productive, without pushing down the feelings that their activities may generate.

Sooner or later the work of the group will end. As this time approaches, themes of separation and termination emerge. Members of the group look back and evaluate its work and their relationships, appraising the gains and the shortcomings of their experience together. Increasingly they may fall back on latent patterns and habits for coordinating their activities. A sense of integrated identification prevails, and universal themes of death and endings become manifest in their discussions as they prepare for withdrawal.

As a system, the terminated group exists only in the minds of its former members. It is only definable by their separate but common memories of their shared experiences and by the effect of these on their independent actions.

## THE MORPHOGENETIC SEQUENCE

In the brief group history presented above, a steady succession of regimes can be perceived, with corresponding shifts in individual behaviors and in relationships between the individual and the group. The group began as an amorphous synchronous regime with little real interaction. As leadership structure emerged, a closed regime was established with pronounced dependency. This gave way to an increasingly random regime as individuals became more Oppositional and counterdependent. Eventually a more open regime based on collaboration, communication, and interdependence was forged. As it approached termination, more Bystanding occurred and the regime became more synchronous. The progression represented in Figure 9-1 reflects the developmental history of small systems observed over their lifespan.

### Small Groups and Development

The description introducing this chapter was constructed to clarify the special focus of each stage or phase in group development and to sharpen the differences. In real groups, the phases overlap and blur into each other, as represented in Figure 9-2. Nevertheless, the succession of distinct orientations, themes, and structures is clear enough in many kinds of groups so that numerous researchers, group leaders, and clinicians have all observed and reported very similar, highly compatible accounts of the group life cycle. The convergence of many models and research findings in this area has been argued in reviews by Tuckman (1965; Tuckman & Jensen, 1977) and in an empirical and theoretical synthesis by Lacoursiere (1980). The support for the consistency of these developmental sequences is extensive. (Lacoursiere, for example, bases his group development stages on parallels in 28 studies involving more than 108 training groups, four studies of 38 problem-solving groups, 27 studies of more than 100 therapy groups, six studies involving more than 75 encounter groups, and 20 studies of more than 60 "naturalistic" student groups.)

The essential compatibility of so many findings rests in fundamental aspects of the paradigmatic framework. Such a progression in regimes has been anticipated by work on the thermodynamics of open systems. Prigogine (1965) developed a mathematical framework called nonequilibrium thermodynamics for understanding all such systems. As proved mathematically by Prigogine (1965; Glansdorff & Prigo-

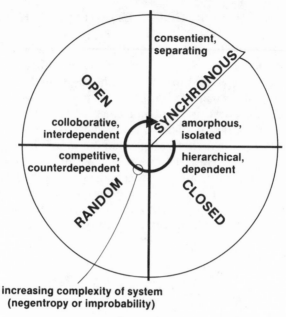

increasing complexity of system
(negentropy or improbability)

**FIGURE 9-1.**
Morphogenetic sequence of systemic regimes.

gine, 1972) and empirically verified, provided a system has many degrees of freedom and remains far from equilibrium, then, as long as it continues to import free energy, it will inevitably evolve through a succession of increasingly complex regimes.

The order in which regimes emerge will be called the morphogenetic sequence; it is the same as that defined by the dialectical relationships among them. In evolving from closed, through random and open, to synchronous, the system is carried through the logical dialectic first introduced in Chapter 2: thesis, antithesis, synthesis, and antisynthesis. The amorphous precursor stage is, for this purpose, "nonsystem"; the closed regime is the thesis impressed upon this *tabula rasa*. This sequence places the regimes in order of increasing unlikelihood or increasing complexity. The simplest and easiest structure to define and maintain is the straightforward hierarchy of the closed regime. The close coordination of the "utopian" or "perfected" synchronous regime depends on the vastly more improbable close identity of members' internal "maps." The sequence is, therefore, one of increasing *negentropy*, a measure of information or improbability.

There is also a functional relationship among the regimes arranged in this order (Constantine, 1984b). A "successful" closed regime supplies a base of security and stability from which independent exploration can be launched, a base that can survive a period of randomness. It also provides the authority against which counterdependence and rebellion can be directed. The open regime depends on already established differentiation among members who can assertively hold their position, yet who can cooperate with the collective process. The open regime cannot synthesize what does not exist, therefore it depends on experience in closed *and* random regimes and the ability to Oppose *and* Follow. The positive identification of the group in the termination phase of perfected synchrony does not occur spontaneously, but emerges from a prolonged process of communication and shared experiences.

There does not seem to be any set timetable for the morphogenetic sequence. Research (cited above) has reported essentially similar phases in groups as short-lived as 2½ hours and as long as 4 years. The clarity or strength of each regime is often less in the shorter-lived systems, suggesting smaller cycles within larger cycles. The thematic shifts are often superimposed on an underlying paradigmatic basis that remains more constant. A task-oriented group in business may superimpose relative shifts in regime on an organization that is always to a greater or lesser degree formed around the closed paradigm. An

**FIGURE 9-2.**
Schematic representation of overlapping phases in group/system development.

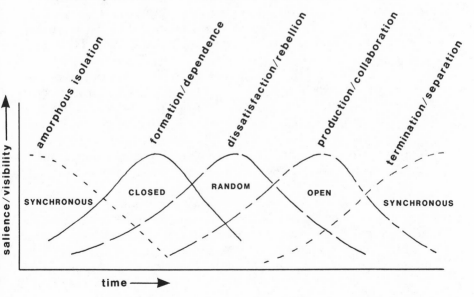

informal discussion group may adhere to an essentially open paradigm while going through phases when it is more closed, more random, and so forth. As always, paradigm is more stable than regime, which is more stable than process. In particularly strong closed regimes reflecting closed paradigms, the succession may take place *only* at the process level.

## Morphogenetic Sequence in Families

The connection between the developmental dynamics of small groups and family process may not be completely obvious. The morphogenetic sequence itself does not simply rest on small-group research, although that is the largest empirical data base supporting it. The sequence is a function of fundamental relationships between regimes that favor the early emergence of closed regimes and their succession by random and then open regimes, ending in synchrony. Empirical research on families is lacking, but the parallels are clear and the metaphor is appealing.

When children are young, they are more dependent and more in need of clear leadership. As they develop and begin to assert themselves this authority is challenged and the family becomes more random. Parents either relax their leadership or find themselves with open rebellion. As it succeeds, the family brings its children to adulthood and to a collaborative relationship between equals. Eventually, a smooth synchrony emerges out of the long renegotiation of the family's basis. The quiet, unspoken closeness and high level of agreement between successful old married couples is another example of the late phases of this sequence.

This ordering of regimes can also be understood in terms of the dimensional foci of each regime and the payoffs each provides. The closed regime fulfills the most basic needs: security, a sense of belonging, material needs. The random regime addresses "higher" needs for differentiation and self-expression. The open regime addresses still "higher" goals of generativity and actualization of fullest potential. Finally, the synchronous regime focuses on "transcendent unity," and development of wisdom and perspective.

The same succession may be found on still longer time scales, when the unit of analysis is a system much larger than the family. DeMause (1974) summarized the succession of childrearing styles over recorded history in a model that is essentially compatible with the morphogenetic sequence of Figures 9-1 and 9-2. McGinnis and Ayer (1976) describe the succession of family styles as proceeding from closed, through "directionless" (on close analysis, a disabled form of random regime), to open. As the morphogenetic sequence is an extended dialetic, it is not surprising to find isomorphic sequences in the other models of paradigmatic succession, for example in psychotherapeutic paradigms (Levenson, 1972) and scientific paradigms (Weinberg, 1975). Societal and cultural implications of paradigmatic succession have also been considered (Constantine, 1984b), but go beyond the scope of this discussion.

## INDIVIDUAL DEVELOPMENT AND PARADIGM

The group development models make clear the connection between individual behavior and group dynamics posited within the paradigmatic framework (see Chapter 7). Figure 9-3 represents the sequential ordering of individual behaviors implied by this relationship. Within the paradigmatic framework, clues to this relationship first emerged from family therapy with families in which certain members were "stuck" in one psychopolitical position. Experience showed that it was difficult to teach a Stuck Follower to Move unless he/she was first helped to learn how to Oppose. In other words, learning how to take

**FIGURE 9-3.**
Ordering of psychopolitical position in the acquisition cycle.

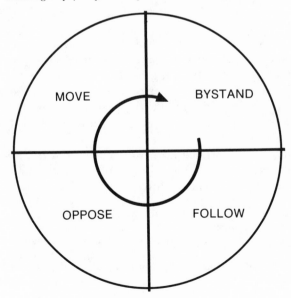

charge begins with learning how to say no. This is at the heart of most assertiveness training. Similarly, it proved very difficult for Stuck Movers to learn how to Follow before they got the hang of Bystanding; not until they had learned how to slow down, stay out, and watch could they then learn to Follow effectively. This implies an order of acquisition (Constantine, 1976a) that corresponds to the order in which psychopolitical positions emerge in group development.

Indeed, individual development appears to parallel the morphogenetic sequence in systems completely. The young preschooler, almost completely dependent on his parents, soon learns to say no and to resist, but this, in turn, is transformed into cooperative responsibility for self. Skynner (1976) was among those to note this isomorphism and its dialectical nature, referring to the neo-Freudian synthesis of psychosexual development that recognizes an oral–dependent stage, an anal–resistant stage, and a genital–cooperative stage. These are clearly related to Following, Opposing, and Moving as well as to closed, random, and open. This leaves Bystanding to be matched with latency, which is theoretically a detachment from the sexual process in terms of zonal focus.[1]

Of course, others have formulated individual development models with more categories, for example, interposing a stage of "independence" between "counterdependence" and "interdependence," but the essential ordering is the same.

## Moving as Synthesis

The parallels between regime and psychopolitical position are weakest when it comes to the dialectic relationship between successive quadrants. It is easy to see Opposing as the antithesis of Following. If Moving, which defines the center of action, is a synthesis, then Bystanding, which is outside or at the periphery, is evidently the antisynthesis. But in what sense is Moving a synthesis of Following and Opposing?

Chapter 7 demonstrated how Moving that did not allow for the completion of established action functioned, at leaste in part, as Opposing. Research experience involving the coding of psychopolitical

---

1. In a dramatic recent presentation at the World Congress on Sexology, Borneman (1983), on the basis of extensive new research on child sexual development, argued for an earlier preoral phase, the cutaneous stage, characterized by an amorphous or diffuse erotic focus throughout the skin. Still more intriguingly, he claims that the ultimate postadult stage of psychosexual development is also so characterized.

sequences (Constantine, 1984c; Covey & Tannen, 1976) suggests that an act functions as a pure Move only if it (1) occurs at a natural point of "punctuation" in the sequence and (2) introduces a new image or definition of action. A natural point of punctuation is one where a previously defined action has been dropped, successfully stopped, or successfully completed. If the actor cannot cooperate (Follow) to the point of reaching such a punctuation point, the act will have some character of an Oppose. If the actor cannot introduce something new and different (Oppose), the act will function as a Follow. Thus, an effective pure Move synthesizes skills or behaviors relating to both Following and Opposing.

## THERAPEUTIC IMPLICATIONS

The morphogenetic sequence is an unusual view of family development. Family development is more commonly concerned with actual and physical events—births, deaths, entering school, leaving home, and the like (e.g., Liddle, 1983). Such matters are, of course, essential issues in family development, but the framework here suggests they occur in a context that includes not only the family's paradigm but also its place in the morphogenetic sequence. The impact of critical life events will depend on the current regime of the family. The birth of a "bonus baby," for example, may be relatively easy for a closed family to deal with, even though the other children might be teenagers. On the other hand, a random family that has already taken on characteristics of a synchronous regime may have great difficulty with the change itself and with the dependency needs it creates.

One of the most important implications of this integrated developmental model is that, regardless of paradigm, the healthiest, most adaptive and enabled families will exhibit a process that slowly changes over time, progressing from more closed, through random, to more open and synchronous patterns. This aids and is driven by the individual development of family members. In less adaptable and more rigidly committed families changes may only appear at the level of process, but in the most successful ones, actual shifts in regime are to be expected.

For example, an enabled closed family might adhere quite closely to its closed paradigm and yet, when its children are teenagers it will have, in comparison with when the children were toddlers, a more random or open regime. In keeping with its multigenerational traditions, it will cautiously and appropriately relax its strictures and permit the individuation processes of adolescence to proceed. Limits will still be set within the authority structure of the family, but those limits will become increasingly generous and will allow for increasing input from the older children. It is, thus, a developmental failure for families not to exhibit some progression in their regime and manifest processes.

The morphogenetic sequence of regimes in healthy families is likely to reflect the unique quality of the overarching family paradigm at all stages. Consider, for example, a family guided by a deep commitment to an open paradigm. When their children are very young, it is necessary for the parents to set certain rules or establish standard procedures, but the rules they set during this more closed phase will be different from those that would be established by a closed paradigm family. The open paradigm family in an early closed regime would establish rules that reflect an underlying belief in the collaborative nature of family process, that respect the personhood and separateness of the child, and that enhance the opportunities for learning and accepting responsibility.

To take one such area, almost all families have rules about eating at mealtime. These serve to avoid waste, to assure an adequate diet for children, and possibly to teach nutrition. In the open family going through an early, more closed phase, the parents might set a rule like, "You must eat everything you put on your plate." This is subtly but importantly different from, "You must eat everything on your plate." (What is on the plate may have been put there by someone else.) It is in sharp contrast with a purely closed rule, "You eat what I tell you." The open paradigm rationale for their variant is that it helps children learn about their own nutritional needs, respects the integrity of their own bodies, and makes them responsible for the consequences of their own behavior. In the purely open paradigm family, the rule would be a family rule, applying to adults as well, even though the exigencies of the closed phase may have led the parents to impose the rule on behalf of the children.

Open paradigm parents who fail to set some such rule can be left in the energy-wasting position of negotiating what their two preschoolers will eat each night. Not making accommodations in regime to the developmental needs of family members or the developmental stages of the family as a whole is a developmental failure that consumes resources and may disable a family. On the other hand, accommodations that are fundamentally inconsistent with the family's paradigm also waste energy and may reduce a family's ability to cope with other stresses and crises.

To help families adopt necessary strategies from other regimes, the therapist needs to bear in mind the bidirectional interaction between individual behaviors and regimes. New interpersonal behaviors are enabled or promoted by a transition from one regime to another, a transition that requires and is facilitated by new behaviors. For example, a closed family motivated to adopt a more open regime needs to pass through a period of some randomness as new skills and individual perspectives emerge.

## INDIVIDUAL AND SYSTEM: AN ISOMORPHISM

The psychopolitical model and the model of "family stereotypes" were originally distinct and separate theoretical constructions by Kantor and Lehr, but it is now clear that these two models are strongly and systematically interrelated. This connection is made possible by the recognition of a synchronous mode of systemic regulation, by a detailed analysis of interpersonal behavior and focal themes within each paradigm, and by identification of the extended dialectic by which interpersonal and systemic behavior may be ordered. With this chapter, the isomorphism, the equivalence of structure, between the map of individual process and the map of systemic process is completed.

To say that these two pictures are isomorphic does not mean that they are one and the same, it only means that they have the same basic structure. The elements of each model are ordered by an extended dialectical relationship and can be differentiated in terms of compatible principal dimensions. A single set of structural relationships thus serves as a model for both individual and systemic process.

The connections between the models should be recognized as circular and probabilistic, not as causal and deterministic. Following does not "cause" a closed regime; transition to a random regime does not "cause" the emergence of Opposition. Family development is a phenomenon emergent at the level of family system. Although some have viewed family development as "driven" by individual development, the Composition Law assures us that the succession of regimes and observable process in families as a whole cannot be understood merely as the sum of individual development. Individuals and families each go through their own developmental processes, which exhibit similar structure but are not identical. Although each may influence the other, neither *determines* the other. The fact that structurally similar development can occur over the lifespan of a family and within a group of young adults over the course of a weekend "marathon" group demonstrates that the morphogenetic sequence functions, at least in part, as an autonomous phenomena at the systemic level.[2]

An understanding of the close correspondence between these two models is a powerful tool for understanding and intervening with families. It allows one to move conceptually back and forth between different levels of analysis without having to invoke an entirely new or unrelated model. The connections between the two models will be used in numerous ways throughout the rest of this book.

---

2. It is tempting to formulate this general correspondence in the form of another general systems principle: "Morphogeny recapitulates ontogeny." Systemic development follows the same general outlines as individual development (Constantine, 1977b).

CHAPTER

# 10

# FUNCTION AND DYSFUNCTION
## Enabled and Disabled Regimes

As there are different types of families, there are different ways that families can fail. All four regimes—closed, random, open, and synchronous—can succeed, although differing systemic goals assure that various aspects of family life will receive different levels of attention and reach varying degrees of optimality. What is judged optimal by one regime may be serious dysfunction to another. Each regime has its own weaknesses and is prone to particular modes of failure more than others.

An understanding of the different modes of failure for each type of family regime is important for the family therapist because each mode of failure requires somewhat different overall strategies of intervention. There is no substitute for genuine sensitivity to a particular family's specific problems, but the task of the therapist can be simplified and some substantial errors avoided by a general notion of the class of problems and required class of interventions.

To define family disablement in the family's own terms does not mean that disabled families have no common features. An enabled family system must balance its needs as a system and the interests of its members, and the competing individual interests of members. It is not surprising, therefore, that enabled families share common traits or similar strategies for balancing conflicting variables. Regardless of regime, enabled family systems resemble each other within limits; this is not true of disabled families. In a sense, the ways to fail are more distinct than the ways to succeed as a family.

Each family regime is particularly prone to fail in certain ways. Numerous researchers, theorists, and therapists have concluded that certain dimensions of family functioning are key and that disabled or "unhealthy" families can be differentiated in terms of these dimensions. The paradigmatic framework simplifies the task of interrelating these various theoretical and therapeutic models.

## THE PARADIGMATIC BASIS OF DISABLEMENT

The basic principle behind the paradigmatic view of disablement is very simple, although its implications are myriad and complex. Confronted by problems, families do whatever they do best, each regime applying its own version of problem solving. When this doesn't work, they try harder. "Trying harder" is itself defined paradigmatically: families try harder by doing more of the same. Thus, by using the resources of its regime and remaining true to its paradigm, each family under stress has a natural tendency toward exaggeration of its own special character.

A family paradigm represents a commitment to certain priorities that incline a family in one direction or another as it seeks to overcome difficulties. For this reason, as families of different types become overstressed, they are prone to basically distinct modes of failure. A family's regime consists of its essentially stable structures maintaining coordinated family process. The regime is resilient and not likely to change fundamentally in response to stress, especially as it is guided by the family's paradigm. Paradigms are regarded as even more invariant features of a family and are, therefore, quite unlikely to change under even severe stress.

The stability of paradigm can be appreciated if it is remembered that a family paradigm is the family's way of perceiving the world, including their problems, as well as their way of approaching and solving problems. Thus, the most likely response to any challenge from within or without is for a family to respond in a manner consistent with its paradigm and organization. The more difficult and intractable the situation, the more extreme are the measures that will be taken, extreme, that is, in a way consistent with the family paradigm. The longer an impasse is sustained, the greater the degree of typal exaggeration.

The closed family confronted by problems relies on tradition, authority, and loyalty to solve them. The more difficult the problem proves to be, the stronger are the attempts to control, to pull the family into line, and to maintain consistency against a threatening world. Thus closed families tend to become more isolated from the world, more strongly and intensely connected internally, and more rigid as they become increasingly disabled. The rallying cry is essentially "Fall in! Toe the line!"

The random family relies on spontaneity and creative individuality to find solutions to problems. As members work with increasing independence to find more creative solutions, family process becomes more chaotic, less coordinated. The random family tends toward greater separateness and chaos as it becomes more disabled. In the random family, the appeal is, "Be more creative! Find something new!" (which, it must be noted, does not imply a change of basic tactics; finding something new is what the random family does normally).

When initial attempts fail, the open family hangs in there, trying to hammer out a consensual solution. They gather more and more information and try harder to communicate. They become inundated with information and overwhelmed by hashing things through. As they question more and more of their basic rules, less and less is clearly known. They go around in circles. If problems remain insoluble they become more and more enmeshed in a process that generates chaos. Their rallying cry is "We've got to work this out. We'll talk it through again and consider it more thoroughly!"

The synchronous family relies on its essential agreement to enable it to solve problems in a coordinated way while acting independently. When this consentaneity breaks down, the family moves toward greater separateness. To remain coordinated and true to its paradigm, it narrows its scope and restricts its actions to those on which there is the closest agreement. Thus it becomes more rigid and stereotyped in its behavior while also becoming less connected. As synchronous families are based on similarity and do not deal as well with difference, which would contradict their synchrony, it becomes increasingly necessary to deny differences and problems, hiding these under a veneer of agreement and competence. As it becomes disabled, the synchronous family attempts to continue "business as usual" and insists, "There is no real problem. As always, we are really in agreement about this." Less and less happens as they become increasingly "dead" as a family or increasingly disconnected from their real problems.

## A Simplified Model of Disablement

The patterns of disablement described briefly above can be integrated into a simple model of disablement as a function of regime and paradigm. This is shown in Figure 10-1. More extreme forms of each regime are further from the center with the probability of disablement correspondingly increasing. The systemic characteristics of disabled regimes—rigidity, chaos, enmeshment, and disengagement—are con-

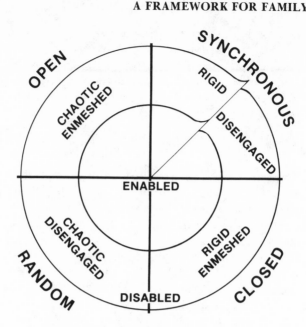

**FIGURE 10-1.**
Basic model of systemic disablement as a function of regime.

sistent with the dialectical relationships among regimes. Disabled random regimes—chaotic and disengaged—are the antithesis of disabled closed regimes—rigid and enmeshed. Disabled open regimes synthesize these into chaotic enmeshment; disabled synchronous regimes are the antisynthesis, neither enmeshed nor chaotic. It is important to realize that it is a family *regime* that becomes disabled or "dysfunctional," not the family paradigm. Although it is conceivable for a family to have a fundamentally defective and inadequate model of family and the world, the primary forms of paradigm are, in themselves, basically workable.

## MODELS OF FAMILY DYSFUNCTION

Using the outline of a paradigmatic view of family disablement it is possible to interconnect other theories and models. A number of these models provide distinctly useful perspectives and supply detail for an integrated understanding of disablement from a paradigmatic standpoint. These details will be filled in by Chapters 15 through 18.

Structural Family Therapy

The primary focus of structural family therapy (Aponte & Hoffman, 1973; Camp, 1973; Minuchin, 1974) is on boundaries internal to the family: those between members and between subsystems in the family. Evaluation and intervention emphasize the structure of alliances and subsystems. Boundaries are considered to range from rigid and impermeable to diffuse and transparent. Boundaries of intermediate permeability, called "clear," permit subsystem functioning without interference from other parts of the system but allow contact and access to resources across boundaries. Clear boundaries are ones that are readily identifiable but are not rigidly drawn.

Minuchin identifies two basic types of disablement: enmeshment and disengagement. An enmeshed family has overly diffuse boundaries; a disengaged family has boundaries that are too rigid. Other concepts are clustered around these defining features to form two syndromes.

In the disengaged family, communication across subsystem boundaries is difficult, handicapping the family's protective functions. Requesting support is difficult. Stress must be very high to be communicated across a subsystem boundary, and even then the response may be slow or inadequate. The family system tolerates wide individual variation, but the sense of independence is so extreme that there is a lack of loyalty and little sense of belonging.

The enmeshed family is a rigid microcosm where diminished interpersonal distance and blurred boundaries are coupled with excessive communication to produce a systemic overload. The system's resources become inadequate to adapt and change under stress. There is a heightened sense of belonging, but this is achieved at the expense of autonomy and independent exploration.

Conceptually, the disengaged family is a clear description of a disabled random regime. The tendency of the random regime to maximize independence is carried to an extreme, almost paradoxically resulting in the failure of the family to meet individual needs while also failing to maintain its integrity as a system.

The enmeshed family is, in most respects, a disabled closed regime. The fit is improved if "blurred boundaries" is interpreted as referring to overinvolvement and to relatively low levels of individuation. While closed regimes characteristically have substantially closed interpersonal boundaries, especially as regards authentic intimacy, they are, nevertheless, strongly connected systems.

A closely related set of concepts is that of centrifugal and centripetal families (Stierlin, 1972). The centrifugal family maintains interpersonal distance, is more oriented to outside than inside, and has a tendency to expel its offspring. The centripetal family is inward turning, tightly bound, and views the outside as frightening or threatening.

## Circumplex Model of Family Functioning

Based on a comprehensive review of family research and theory, Olson and colleagues (1979) expanded on the Minuchin model by distinguishing a second dimension. In the *circumplex model*[1] there are two principal dimensions of family functioning, *adaptability* and *cohesion*. This model is shown in its original form, in Figure 10-2. Under various rubrics the dimensions of cohesion and adaptability have been postulated by many writers and found by many researchers to be of central importance to family functioning.

Adaptability is the ability of a system to change its structure in response to situational and developmental stress. In the circumplex model it ranges from the extreme of chaotic morphogenesis to that of rigid morphostasis. Olson argues that optimal functioning requires an intermediate range of adaptability corresponding to a balance of morphostasis and morphogenesis. The more extreme a family's adaptability, whether high or low, the less well it will function. Excessive adaptability implies that a family is overly ready to change in response to too small a stimulus. It should be kept in mind that Olson and colleagues use "adaptability" in a limited technical sense defined within their model and not in the colloquial sense in which more adaptability is always better.

The other dimension of the circumplex model is cohesion, which is the emotional bonding or sense of identification members feel toward each other and the family, ranging from enmeshed at one extreme to disengaged at the other. Again, an intermediate range of cohesion is assumed to be the most functional.

The circumplex model separates variables that are merged within the structural family therapy model. Disabled systems are characterized by extremes on either of two dimensions, leading to four extremes of

1. Olson and colleagues use the term "circumplex" in a nonmathematical sense. Technically, a circumplex is a circular fan of variables having two principal components (Wiggins, 1979, 1980). Olson's model has the requisite two dimensions but lacks the fan of constituent variables. The circumplex models of interpersonal behavior and attribution introduced in Chapter 7 are true circumplexes in the technical sense.

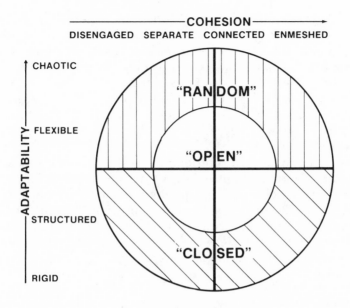

**FIGURE 10-2.**
Olson and colleagues' original "circumplex" model of family function–dysfunction.

system failure: rigid disengagement, chaotic disengagement, rigid enmeshment, and chaotic enmeshment.

Rigid enmeshment characterizes an extreme form of a closed regime, wherein excessive feedback via attenuating loops assures rigidity. It is this form of enmeshment that is described by Minuchin (1974). Chaotic disengagement describes a random regime of excessively differentiated individuals. (The structural family therapy model does not stress the chaotic aspects.) Were an open regime to become excessively connected, its process would aptly be described as chaotic enmeshment, brought about by excessive feedback via its complex mixture of attenuating and amplifying loops.

At first glance, the concept of a rigidly disengaged family would appear to present some theoretical problems. If the family is disengaged, what maintains the rigidity? If separateness is excessive and interaction low, how can process be constant? Once again, we would have to invent the synchronous regime had we not already done so. The rigidly disengaged family is, as a family, essentially "dead," a failed synchronous system.

This analysis requires a revision of Olson and colleagues' original circumplex model wherein all healthy systems were designated "open." It is common in current clinical practice and in popular theories of family to equate open regimes with enabled systems (Constantine, 1983, 1984a). It is easy to see how this conflation comes about, since the paradigmatic goals of an open regime give priority to the synthesis of individual and collective interests. This does not mean that paradigmatic goals will be met, only that the creative integration of competing needs will be emphasized. It is possible that open regimes have an advantage in this respect, but they are not guaranteed success.

One of the important contributions of the circumplex model is that, in revised form, it supplies the necessary theoretical constructs for characterizing disabled families with open regimes and with synchronous regimes. Chaotic enmeshment, what might be called highly differentiated overinvolvement, is the probable mode of failure for open regimes; rigid disengagement, unvarying underinvolvement, characterizes the disabled extreme for synchronous systems.


### The Wertheim Typology

Wertheim (1973) developed a typology based on several aspects of family morphogenesis and morphostasis. Her original terminology and definitions of variables may be somewhat confusing in this context, so some restatement is necessary. Essentially, two kinds of morphostatic mechanism were distinguished: forced and consensual. In Wertheim's terms, "forced morphostasis" is maintained by an imbalance of power in the absence of consensual validation. It leads only to "apparent stability." "Consensual morphostasis" achieves "genuine stability" consensually validated by all members through an appropriately balanced distribution of power. Although families high in both consensual *and* forced morphostasis are postulated by Wertheim, this appears to be a logical contradiction, unlikely under any interpretation. Thus family morphostasis may be consensual, forced, or minimal.

The second factor in this typology is "induced morphogenesis," the ability of the family to respond to exogenous demands for change. It is really a feature of the external boundary: its openness to certain forms of new information.

The typology (without the two self-contradictory types) is presented in Table 10-1. It is evident that the "closed–pseudointegrated" family is rigidly enmeshed. The "closed–disintegrated" type most closely resembles a rigidly disengaged family, and the "externally open–unintegrated" appears to be chaotically disengaged. The "open–

**TABLE 10-1.**
Principal Aspects of Wertheim's Typology of Families

| Type[a] | External boundary | Morphostasis | Description |
|---------|-------------------|--------------|-------------|
| 1. Open–integrated | Open | Consensual | Cohesive, adaptable |
| 3. Externally open–unintegrated | Open | Minimal | Little internal cohesion, regulated by external influences, internally allienated, attachments to outside figures, unregulated, antisocial behavior |
| 4. Externally open–pseudointegrated | Open | Forced | Ordinarily homeostatic potential for change in therapy, residual "ego strength," relative internal rigidity |
| 5. Internally open–integrated | Closed | Consensual | Adapt spontaneously to external reality and internal differences; cohesive, strong yet flexible; adaptation through creative internal process, not by confronting demands; considerable "ego resources" |
| 7. Closed–disintegrated | Closed | Minimal | Little structure, few resources for change, breaking up, lack motivation |
| 8. Closed–pseudointegrated | Closed | Forced | Rigid rules of interaction, defensive, intolerant of spontaneous transactions |

[a]Wertheim's self-contradictory types 2 and 6, which would have both forced and consensual morphostasis, have been excluded.

integrated" and "internally open–integrated" types are variants of enabled open regimes. Only the "externally open–pseudointegrated" seems to have no equivalent in the extremes of the circumplex model; it appears to be a milder form of rigid enmeshment.

## The Consensual Experience Model

On the basis of extensive laboratory research into family problem solving, Reiss (1971, 1981) and colleagues identified key dimensions of problem-solving style. Two of these (configuration, or solution enrichment through cooperation, and coordination, or degree of synchronization of member solutions) differentiated four family paradigms. These are defined abstractly in terms of the manner in which a family perceives and explains its environment and its own operations. These are *consensus-sensitive, distance-sensitive, achievement-sensitive,* and *environment-sensitive* families. Fairly detailed clinical descriptions of these families have been reported (Costell & Reiss, 1982).

## CONSENSUS-SENSITIVE FAMILIES

Consensus-sensitive families are high on coordination but low on configuration, members producing highly similar solutions that are lacking in subtlety. In these families, a sense of order is derived from the predictability of responses from other members. Though the exchange of information is high, agreement must be maintained at all times; dissent is not tolerated. Little information is taken in from the environment, which is perceived as threatening, chaotic, and unknowable. Consensus is achieved quickly because dissent is disallowed and little consideration is given to environmental information unless it is distorted or oversimplified.

Clinically, these families have been described (Costell & Reiss, 1982) as doggedly united, often maintaining marriages despite major conflict and adversity. They are embroiled and preoccupied with each other. Hostility tends to be covert; disruptive feelings are denied and repressed. The sharing of information is blunted and inhibited, maintaining a facade of consensus and conformity. Adolescent identified patients from such families are characterized as "happy-go-lucky," but covertly manipulative and hostile, and at times self-dramatizing.

## ACHIEVEMENT-SENSITIVE FAMILIES

Achievement-sensitive families are the opposite of consensus-sensitive ones, high on configuration but low on coordination, producing complex solutions through competition rather than cooperation. Members make use of information from the environment and are sensitive to cues from each other but operate in an individualistic, competitive mode, in opposition to each other. They can creatively generate solutions to their problems but work independently.

Clinically, achievement-sensitive families have been described as cynical, hostile, and angry. Adolescent identified patients from these families have been characterized as rebellious, obstructionistic, and adept at opposition in the family and at being provocative with others. The families maintain a posture of deviance and estrangement, holding views that are deviant and cynical. They are competitive, mutually defeating, and distrustful, with a "dog-eat-dog" view of other's motivations. They thus resemble Kantor's description of the breakdown of a random family as individualism degenerates into competition for scarce resources in a struggle for survival.

## ENVIRONMENT-SENSITIVE FAMILIES

High in coordination *and* configuration, environment-sensitive families closely coordinate their solutions toward mutual enrichment. Closure on a consensually agreed upon solution is very important in the environment-sensitive family, although it may be much delayed because as much information as possible is gathered and objectively evaluated. Information is freely taken in from the environment and openly exchanged among members. The environment is perceived as masterable and trustworthy.

When clinically involved, these families have been described as gregarious, direct and honest in confronting their problems, and confident in their abilities to master them. They were open and involved with other families and quick to incorporate new information, rapidly disseminating it among themselves. Fathers were exceptionally involved with their children compared with other groups of families. Adolescent identified patients were open, assertive, and aggressive, well integrated with peers and often chosen to be leaders. They were described as showing self-confident aggression but forming intense, warm therapeutic alliances.

## DISTANCE-SENSITIVE FAMILIES

Distance-sensitive families are *low* in both coordination and configuration, producing simplified solutions with little cooperation. Although information from the environment is taken in by the interpersonal distance-sensitive family, it is not exchanged freely among members. They use little information from each other and offer little assistance. Each member appears to be expected to demonstrate mastery individually; information sharing is seen as a weakness. Problem solving is highly variable: solutions may be selected quickly on the basis of little information, or information may accumulate indefinitely without resolution. Distance-sensitive families are disengaged but are described as having a quality of deadness that is clearly not chaotic.

These families tend to be perplexed and overwhelmed. Parents have been described as incompetent and literal-minded. The views of the family lack subtlety and complexity; members tend to think in concrete, superficial terms, rather than psychologically. Adolescent identified patients from distance-sensitive families seem to be pseudo-mature, covering their vulnerability and low self-esteem with a veneer of competence. Family members are separate and unengaged with each other and with therapy.

Research reported by Reiss[2] confirms a relationship between this model and the Olson circumplex model, though not with the Kantor typology. However, clinical descriptions of families and the problem-solving styles and worldviews abstracted from experience with families scoring in each quadrant of the Reiss model convey a fairly consistent relationship.

The consensus-sensitive family most closely resembles a disabled closed regime. This is especially apparent in terms of its orientation to dissent (opposition), its control over incoming information, and its definition of itself as struggling against external chaos. A few clinical features could also characterize a synchronous regime, for example, inhibited information sharing and denial of feelings. The achievement-sensitive family resembles a form of random regime whose independence and differentiation has degenerated into internal competition. Although members of these families have been described as embroiled with one another, this appears to be limited primarily to competitive, antagonistic interactions; in other senses they are estranged, distrustful, and isolated. The environment-sensitive family, especially in its problem-solving approaches, appears to have a form of open regime, enabled or mildly disabled. The distance-sensitive family is the least clear, but appears to operate under a form of synchronous regime, definitely disengaged, apparently not chaotically. This correspondence is also supported indirectly by the dialectical relationships among types based on coordination and configuration. The consensus-sensitive (closed) family is high in coordination, low in configuration; the achievement-sensitive (random) family is the opposite; the environment-sensitive (open) family is high on both coordination and configuration; and the distance-sensitive (synchronous) is low on both.

2. This work (Sigafoos, Reiss, Rich, & Douglas, 1985), done in collaboration with David Olson and David Kantor, was reported at the Theory Construction Workshop, 1983 National Council on Family Relations annual meeting. Family configuration, closure, and coordination, the basis of Reiss's typology, were assessed by the standard laboratory problem-solving task and the Olson circumplex model was assessed by a paper-and-pencil instrument (FACES II). A family's paradigmatic commitment within the Kantor and Lehr typology was assessed by an ad hoc paper-and-pencil measure.

## Family Casework Diagnosis

From an early study of nearly 900 family casework files, Voiland (1962) developed a typology of disordered families: *perfectionistic, inadequate, egocentric,* and *unsocial.* These are described briefly in Table 10-2. In some respects, all four classes of families can be seen to resemble closed regimes but with enough differences to suggest distinctly different modes of disablement. A relationship to family regimes and paradigms seems probable, but establishing the best corre-

**TABLE 10-2.**

Summary of Salient Features of Families within Voiland's Social Casework Model in Relation to the Paradigmatic Framework

| Voiland's typology | Paradigmatic framework |
| --- | --- |
| *Inadequate family* <br> Reliance on external help, parental neglect, haphazard physical care; helpless, perplexed, and overwhelmed; children inactive, overcompliant, or ingratiating; things work out, like "magic"; "pseudoindependence"; parents as "spectator," rules not actively taught | *Amorphous synchronous* <br> Disabled; possibly collapsed *closed* regime with some *random* elements |
| *Unsocial family* <br> Disrapport with environment, deviant, disrespectful of social authority; haphazard care, no adherence to schedules, irregularity of household management; inconsistent, undecisive, "kaleidoscopic" parenting; runaways, intense sibling rivalries, jealousy | *Random* <br> Disabled *random* regime |
| *Egocentric family* <br> Self-centered, overbearing, opportunistic; mutual blame, antagonism; sexual "deviance" or "promiscuity"; eroticized overinvolvement, excessive demands with overprotection; accelerated self-reliance, children as adult surrogates | *Open* <br> Disabled *open* regime with some elements of *closed* regime |
| *Perfectionistic family* <br> Required faultlessness, avoidance of open friction; children anxious, unable to measure up to implied demands, criticized if not functioning to "maximum capacity"; perfection expected in responsibility, self-criticism, achievement, and social conformity; hostility or aggression not acceptable, social success is being "nonhostile"; parental choice dominates | *Perfectionistic synchronous* <br> Disabled; possibly with elements of *closed* regime |

spondence is difficult. Voiland's labels carry connotations that do not always represent the families they identify, and her rich clinical discussions do not always make clear the boundaries between categories. Two previous attempts have been made to link the casework diagnosis categories with other clinical and theoretical work, leading to only partial success.

L'Abate (1976) attempted to make connections by way of the Satir (1972) model of defended communication, introduced in Chapter 7 as isomorphic to the psychopolitical model, hence to family paradigms. L'Abate was led to associate the "inadequate family" with "placating," the "egocentric family" with "distracting," the "unsocial family" with "blaming," and the "perfectionistic family" with "computing." The logic of pairing the "egocentric family" with "distracting" is particularly opaque, especially since Voiland singles out blaming as characteristic of the egocentric family. There remains some room for interpretation, but close examination reveals Voiland's "unsocial family" to be chaotically *disengaged* compared with the chaotically *enmeshed* pattern displayed by the "egocentric family" (Constantine, 1983, 1984a). The "perfectionistic family" is more ambiguous, having characteristics of both closed and synchronous regimes, although L'Abate's reasoning would make it a synchronous regime. The "inadequate family" is even more an ambiguous case, with features resembling closed and amorphous synchronous systems.

From the summaries of Voiland's typology in Table 10-2, both general trends and important inconsistencies may be noted. Fortunately this model is not the sole source of clinical descriptions of disabled regimes. Cross-checked by other sources and theoretical arguments, Voiland's close attention to childrearing and marital functioning adds very useful details to clinical composites.

## The Distance-Regulation Model

The distance-regulation model of Kantor and Lehr (1975) is the most closely related to the paradigmatic framework and was the original point of departure for derivation of the framework. The distance-regulation model identified three paradigms—open, closed, and random. Theirs was perhaps the first theoretical model of family to recognize apparent "randomness" in families as a distinct pattern rather than the absence of pattern. It also was the first to describe in some detail the possible disablement of open families. Their description of disablement in the three regimes is summarized here.

CLOSED-TYPE DISABLEMENT

The flawed closed family was described by Kantor and Lehr as "sealed off from the world" in "insular purity." In trying to "forestall evolution and change" its "traditional standards become isolated and parochial." Its members, "overly inbred and undifferentiated," must give "absolute obedience." Affection deterioriates into "hollow echoes" while authoritarian power goes unchallenged. "Dogmatism and conformity dominate"; "creativity and originality may be punished as unwarranted deviations."

Eventually, rebellion is fomented against the "absurdity and unenforceability" of its authoritarian demands. In its public disagreement and turbulence, these runaway families may resemble random or open regimes.

RANDOM-TYPE DISABLEMENT

As it becomes disabled, the random family becomes "truly chaotic." Members act as "totally independent entities, making no vital connections" until life is "careless, scattered, and incomplete," with only "frequent and furious fights" and "spasms of hostility" for interaction. "Nothing is allowed to remain constant," as a "pervading lack of discipline and an unwillingness to cooperate" take over. Feelings become exaggerated but remain unrecognized and unvalidated in the chaos of "egregious nonsense" and incomprehensibility. No one in pain can "compel the attention and support of others." "Survival of the fittest" becomes the rule as self-centered competition for resources escalates. This runaway continues until "a new authoritarian closed-type system is established" by supremacy of one competitor or by submission to outside authority. Otherwise, the system is torn apart "emotionally if not physically."

OPEN-TYPE DISABLEMENT

In the disabled open regime, "the core purpose of adaptation through consensus" leads to "eternal wrangling and disagreements." The family perimeter is expanded, drawing outsiders into the conflicts, assuring containment of members, or obscuring conflicts. Conflicts remain unresolved leading to "indeterminacy," "ambiguity, incongruity, and internal contradiction." "The desire for synthesis results in" mere "halfway measures" and "a middle way, which goes nowhere." "Emotional authenticity" degenerates into "a burlesque of exuberance" or "dispassionate resignation." Thus, the open regime's tolerance for ambiguity permits ambiguity and confusion to mount, while its commitment to pursue closure keeps it locked in a chaotic process of never-ending negotiation.

Breakdown follows when "latitude, allowance, and tolerance," become a form of individual tyranny countered by pressure to surrender autonomy. Exhausted, members withdraw emotionally or splinter into separate units. In the most severe case, "mindless destruction" ensues, as the system gives up on consensus and attempts to eject its dissidents altogether, even as they "try to explode it from within."

## A SYSTEMS THEORY OF DISABLEMENT

Many previous models of family dysfunction and disablement have tended to focus more narrowly on specific aspects at the expense of others, have lacked clarity in identifying elementary phenomena, or have been paradigmatically incomplete. The composite they form is rich but lacking somewhat in coherence. What is needed is an integration around basic principles of system operation.

### Coupling, Coping, Breakdown, and Decay

Families and their human subsystems are, of course, living systems. Miller (1978) has shown that, across all levels of organization, living systems are subject to much the same kinds of failures. Since families are information processing systems that communicate, an important class of failures arises from too much information or information that arrives too rapidly (overload) or from too little information (deprivation). Stimulus deprivation research supports the hypothesis that the human organism has a need for information. Extensive research by Miller and colleagues has established one of the most important cross-level hypotheses of general living systems theory, the information overload hypothesis:

> As the rate of input to a system rises, the system will process and output information at an increasing rate. Eventually the channels of the system become saturated and the processing and output of the system fall behind. Finally, if the overload continues, the system breaks down or fails altogether. (p. 122)

This rather abstract hypothesis is important because it can be related to an essential aspect of family systems: coupling. Coupling is the amount and intensity of feedback between and among components in a system. In highly coupled systems, the behavior of any one component is highly influenced by, and influences the behavior of, all other components. In human families, this is not merely a function of the amount of interaction or the information exchanged, but its significance (meaning) and emotional impact (affect). A married couple can be highly coupled even though they don't talk much if their every exchange is fraught with great personal significance and overflowing with deep feeling. Conversely, a family that talks all the time can be quite weakly coupled if they always stick to facts and conventional, everyday matters with no important metamessages.

Families can become either too strongly or too weakly coupled. Which they are likely to do depends upon which regime is operant— open and closed regimes are most likely to become excessively coupled, random and synchronous regimes insufficiently coupled. These tendencies arise from each regime's response to problems.

## Coupling and Cohesion

The nature of cohesion in family systems depends on the regime. Both open and closed families are quite highly cohesive, yet they achieve cohesion in very different ways. In the closed system cohesion arises from imposed structure and indoctrinated values; it is manifest in family loyalty and overt agreement. Cohesion in an open regime arises from personal commitment and from experienced success in process; it is manifest in "hanging in there" and open sharing of disagreement. Random systems rely on commitment to the excitement of the shared experience in the here-and-now, a common willingness to "seize the moment" and "go with the flow." Synchronous regimes have their own form of cohesion resting on their shared sense of identity, their "consentience."

A closer examination of the phenomena of system stress and breakdown indicates that coupling, rather than cohesion, is the key variable for understanding systemic dysfunction. It is, at any rate, more fundamental and concrete. A simple analysis suggests that the optimal coupling is neither too great nor too small. Excessive coupling in a family causes stress and symptomatic behavior, leading eventually to some form of breakdown in the family system structure; inadequate coupling leads to degeneration and entropic decay.

What is optimal is a function of the system's complexity and regime. Whereas there are intrinsic differences in the expected degree of coupling in different regimes, typal exaggeration leads to errors in different directions. More complex, more articulated systems can also tolerate greater variation. Thus, without becoming dysfunctional, open systems can be more strongly coupled than can closed ones, and synchronous (perfectionistic) ones can be less coupled than random regimes without dispersing. Furthermore, changes in coupling may have one effect in families with one regime, and quite the opposite in families with another. The effect of increases or decreases may even depend on the exact developmental phase of a family, having different effects for families of the same regime but at different points in development.

## Regime Responses to System Challenges

Families are never absolutely enabled or disabled, but only relative to a context. A family may function well because it has never been seriously challenged. Many closed families move quite successfully through life until children become adolescents whose sexuality and independent minds can no longer be suppressed or denied. And a family experiencing serious distress may be confronting problems of a scope surpassing what a family might reasonably be expected to surmount. The element of luck in family health and development cannot be ignored.

A challenge to a system is a situation requiring some response from the system. Challenges may be great, such as the death of a parent, or small, such as a late meal. They can come from within (a child starting school) or from without (a burglary). Challenges can be normal (the onset of menopause) or highly unusual (the inheritance of a million dollars). For some families, ordinary daily existence can present numerous serious challenges; for others, nothing short of a bomb will seriously challenge them.

A challenge becomes a crisis or a chronic stressor when it surpasses a family's coping resources. On the average, then, the greater the individual and collective repertoires of the family, the more likely it is that it will find some means of resolving, overcoming, or circumventing some problem. For families, other things being comparable, flexibility and richness of interpersonal resources are what succeed.

Economic and social resources are important in this context, too, but here we are concentrating on the emotional and behavioral resources of the family itself. This should not be taken as justifying precisely what many therapists tend to do in practice, slighting the role of the larger context in both problems and potential solutions. The purpose here is to simplify and highlight the general issue of function and dysfunction before returning to the ecological perspective, which includes the environment and suprasystems.

A family system becomes disabled *relative* to the challenges presented it. When a family's coping mechanisms fail, however, the family does not ordinarily try new mechanisms. They may initiate a search for solutions, or seek advice, or run around in circles, or give up, but whatever they do it will come from their existing repertoire and will, at least at first, consist of variations on the established family themes. Initially, then, families retain the same regime. Random regimes continue to seek novel solutions through creative, spontaneous individuality; closed systems stay closed, trying to use accepted solutions and methods of problem solving within their hierarchical structure; open families go right on discussing, elaborating, and negotiating toward consensus. Indeed, within their own paradigmatic interpretations, all families behave alike when confronted by a failure of their methods—they try more of the same.

### TYPAL EXAGGERATION AND BREAKDOWN

The first principal form of family disablement is, therefore, typal exaggeration, extremal versions of the four functional regimes. Kantor and Lehr (1975) refer to this exaggeration of typal goals as an "error of substantiation." Although it is possible for a family system to be intrinsically disabled in this sense, flawed by design, so to speak, it is more likely that typal exaggeration is the result of the failure of the family's normal coping mechanisms against some challenge to the system.

A typal extreme continued long enough becomes what Kantor and Lehr (1975) called a runaway system. Should this continue long enough, the system undergoes breakdown. The form of the breakdown depends on the regime and the details depend on the family, but all breakdown entails a necessary loss of structure. The simpler structure will, in some sense, relieve the stress of the unresolvable challenge, but at a cost. A brick chimney that collapses under the stress of a tremor, becomes a shorter structure amidst a rubble heap; it is then stable and may withstand further quakes, but its entropy is greater, that is, it is simpler and more probable. And, quite clearly, there has been a loss of function.

Precisely as the developmental perspective in the last chapter would predict, as regimes break down they fall back to "simpler" regimes. Thus open regimes break down into random regimes, random ones into closed, and closed into synchronous. While the regressed system may thereby survive the immediate challenge, like the collapsed chimney, it remains handicapped. Breakdown to an earlier regime is, thus, to disabled forms. The resulting combined model of the generation of disablement in family systems is shown in Figure 10-3.

In addition to typal exaggeration (runaway) and breakdown, family systems can regress (decay entropically) because of insufficient informational and energic input. Family systems can also suffer from an "incommensurability" between regimes of different subsystems or between the family's paradigm and its actual structure and process in practice. Elaboration of these more complex and specialized modes of dysfunction will be taken up in later chapters.

### Repertoire, Complexity, and Disablement

Figure 10-3 simplifies family regime for the sake of clarity; in actuality, a family regime is characterized also by its complexity, by the total repertoire the family brings to the challenges it experiences. The indicated points for "prototypical" families of each regime shown in

**FIGURE 10-3.**

Typal exaggeration and collapse as a function of initial regime of a family: Most probable paths.

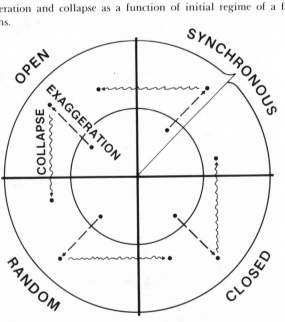

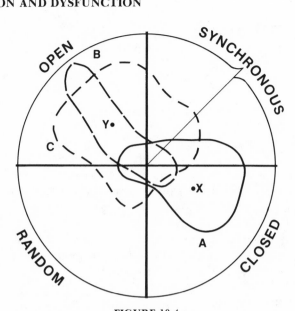

**FIGURE 10-4.**
Representation of systemic repertoires of three families.

Figure 10-3 are a condensation of a more complex representation that would show the complete range of behaviors of which a family would be capable. To represent the systemic repertoire requires a shape, such as those in Figure 10-4. The curve represents the most extreme functioning manifest in the family for each possible variation of regime. The one point that best represents each family is the "center of mass" of its repertoire. For family A this is point X; for family B, point Y. In Figure 10-4, family A is best characterized as a closed regime, though it is capable of a limited amount of open regime functioning; the opposite is the case for family B. Both families B and C are predominantly open regimes with the same "average" style of collective functioning, but family C is more complex and has a wider range of behavioral options. Family B has a higher probability of becoming disabled than family C because of its narrower, more exaggerated repertoire as a family.

## DISABLED REGIMES

Disablement in each of the four systemic regimes can be understood from the general principles established above by integrating the contributions of other models. The discussions following also draw on the work of Leonard (1981) and Hawkins (1979), who developed self-report measures of family type and disablement.

### Disabled Closed Regimes

Closed regimes that become too highly coupled remain closed, becoming enmeshed. They cannot directly regress to become synchronous nor can they advance to become random, because both these regimes are *less* coupled. As they become enmeshed, closed regimes become rigid. Increased coupling along feedback relationships that are predominantly deviation attenuating generates rigidity in the family patterns. Only when coupling is reduced—through a breakdown from prolonged excess coupling, through systemic development, or through outside intervention—can the closed regime decay toward synchronous operation or advance toward a random regime.

When the coupling in a closed family is reduced, through breakdown or otherwise, different outcomes are possible. If the family is closer to synchrony than randomness, with members not very differentiated from each other, it will tend to decay into a synchronous regime. The relative absence of differentiation assures that, as the family slides toward disengagement, its process remains stable, leaving it rigidly disengaged. On the other hand, a more "advanced" closed regime will tend to advance toward a random regime. If its coupling becomes too low, the likely direction of disablement is to chaotic disengagement, since the higher differentiation of its members prevent it from becoming rigidly disengaged. Their maps are too different. Although this slide into a random regime may resemble "progress," it is toward a disabled form that the family drifts unless other factors favor the developmental process. Import of significant new information through therapy or other learning experiences can permit the family to move to an enabled form of random regime.

By their commitment to the active maintenance of continuity and unity, closed regimes are more likely to become too strongly coupled than too weakly coupled. Thus, for closed regimes, the most probable mode of failure is rigid enmeshment.

### Disabled Random Regimes

A random regime that becomes less coupled remains a random regime, while increases in coupling will carry it toward either more open or more closed operation, depending on whether its organization borders one or the other more closely. The typal goal of discontinuity and independence means that random regimes tend toward low coupling; their probable mode of failure is chaotic disengagement.

When coupling is increased within a random regime, if nothing else changes the tendency will be toward a disabled open or disabled closed regime, toward chaotic enmeshment or rigid disengagement. Breakdown favors regression toward the simpler system, which is closed.

The random regime favors the individual over the system, consequently, as typal goals are carried to their extremes, the system tends to be sacrificed for the survival of individuals. But process degenerates into a free-for-all in which survival of the fittest reigns. As the power struggle among individuals escalates, the system may collapse and disperse. Although some members may try to save the system, only the strongest message can be heard above the fray. Power becomes the final arbiter of disputes and, if the system is to survive at all, a new authoritarian regime is constituted.

## Disabled Open Regimes

The form of analysis employed for closed and random regimes can be extended to open and synchronous ones. Open regimes, being intrinsically highly couples, are prone to enmeshment more than disengagement. The higher level of individuation and the abundance of deviation amplifying feedback results in chaotic, rather than rigid, enmeshment. If the stress of overload continues too long, the system breaks down, decaying into a random regime.

The process may be understood as beginning with a crisis beyond the problem-solving capacity of a particular open regime. Turning to its established methods of negotiation, dialogue, and discussion, the family begins to "process" more and more. But consensus is not reached and the family spins its wheels endlessly, importing more and more information, delaying resolution indefinitely. The group process consumes ever more energy until too little is available for individuals to function as individuals. In response to this depletion of reserves and in seeking more information, the family disperses. Confusion and ambiguity reign as the family generates its own ever-shifting tide of opinion and incomplete resolution. Ultimately, individuals give up in exhaustion and renege on their commitment to the group, thus the family becomes disengaged. If the open regime more closely resembled a random one, then the chaos continues. If mutual identification dominates over differentiation and the regime more closely resembled a synchronous regime at the start, it will wind up disengaged but not chaotic.


## Disabled Synchronous Regimes

The synchronous regime is intrinsically uncoupled and therefore tends toward disengagement. Its typal goals may be said to be effortless and natural harmony among members and between system and environment. Its extremal form is rigid disengagement, constancy without resort to interactive controls, dependent solely on what is already common agreement among its members.

Dysfunctional forms of synchronous regimes may appear to be more abundant than functional ones for reasons made clear by theory. The larger the repertoire of behaviors and range of situations over which individual cognitive maps must be coincident, the more unlikely synchrony will be and the more difficult it will be to achieve. In practice, synchrony that continues over very long periods is likely to be more or less impoverished.

Confronted by a challenge beyond its coincident capabilities, the synchronous system tends to maintain the agreed upon ways that worked in the past. Its failure becomes progressive as its members labor autonomously in proven but now increasingly more limited and ineffective ways.

Eventually the system breaks down, necessitating the reinstitution of structure. Distinct and varying experiences by different individuals can interfere with synchrony and lead to the reestablishment of dialogue in an effort to restore synchrony (regression to an open regime) or to imposition of hierarchical structure. New information represents an advantage to its possessor. Whether it is shared openly to collective advantage or used for individual gain depends on the particular values coincident among members. In other words, the direction of breakdown of a synchronous regime, toward open or closed operation, should depend on how the synchrony arose.

In a way, the term "rigid" misrepresents the form of disengagement found in synchronous regimes, for the system per se does not actively sustain the rigidity, as is the case in rigidly enmeshed systems. Instead, it is the paucity of interactive structure that maintains continuity.

Disabled synchronous regimes may be most likely to be found at the extremes of the socioeconomic scale. At the one end are disabled families so impoverished, so painfully and completely preoccupied with mere existence (which, after all, must border on our shared genetic programming), that there are no significant exchanges. The family, with deadened feelings, eats its meager meal in silence, precisely as it has always before and expects to do tomorrow. Families of poverty do not necessarily or commonly exhibit this pattern, of course. The portrait is of a *disabled* poor family with an amorphous synchronous regime.

Strangely, though not at all surprising from a theoretical perspective, a similar scene may be reinacted in certain disabled upper-class families. The film, *Julia*, has a scene in which Lillian Hellman has dinner with her rich friend, Julia, and her family. The meal passes in utter silence, precisely as it has and will every evening. Not even a holiday upsets its rigid disengagement. With leaden composure, Julia ends the dinner by ritual good wishes to her unresponding grandparents. As Kantor and Lehr (1975) express it in describing the breakdown of a closed system to rigid disengagement, "affection may deteriorate to hollow echoes of true exchanges as members become slaves to a conformity of expression, both bored and boring in their stereotypic range of emotional responses" (p. 152).

SECTION

# IV

# TOOLS AND TACTICS

CHAPTER

# 11

# MEASURES AND METHODS
## Tools and Techniques for
## Family Evaluation and Intervention

It is impossible to catalog the current pharmacopoeia of family therapy techniques in a single chapter; were it possible, it would still be inappropriate in this book. While many family therapists may deal in technique per se, in the paradigmatic framework, technique does not exist apart from context. Intervention follows from evaluation, and techniques are created ad hoc or tailored to fit a particular family and their unique problems.

The family therapist does, however, need a knowledge of broad classes of tools available from which specialized implements may be forged for specific purposes. There are hardly any techniques used in any of the schools of family therapy that are, in themselves, incompatible with a paradigmatic focus. Paradoxical intention, therapeutic double binds, reframing, role reversals, art therapy, communications training, behavioral therapy, gestalt techniques like doubling or "the empty chair," psychodrama and role plays, family sculptures, family games, even hypnosis, are among the techniques that have been used by therapists working within a paradigmatic framework. What distinguishes the paradigmatic use of these is whether they are chosen to meet certain ends in relation to a family's paradigm and regime.

### STRUCTURED TECHNIQUES: COMMON ISSUES

Some techniques, however, are particularly suitable within a paradigmatic approach; these are "structured techniques" having a special affinity for or relationship with a focus on family paradigms and regimes. In general, activities or games with a task focus are better suited for assessing a family's regime, while those that are imagistic or metaphorical are better suited to gaining access to the paradigms of families. Some issues are common to almost all structured techniques, whether of the imagistic or the task-oriented variety.

## Introduction and Biasing Set

Beginning therapists may have difficulty introducing structured tasks, especially something imagistic, such as family drawing or sculpture. Often they encounter resistance to such "silly games." Keeping in mind a few points can help overcome the therapist's initial discomfort and the family's resistance.

1. All structured tasks and techniques should be introduced matter-of-factly, as if there were no question whatsoever about their appropriateness at that time or in that setting. Uncertainty will be picked up by the family. ("I don't know. Maybe you'd be willing to try drawing pictures of your family.") Problems are less likely to arise if the therapist says, "This is something we do with every family when they first start seeing us." Or, "I tell you what, we're going to make it possible for you to *show* us what it's like in the morning at home." Or, "This is a chance for you to do something together that you all can be involved in, even Bobby here. So, we have these big blocks over here. You're going to build something together and afterwards we'll all talk about what happened."

2. The task should be related to what has been happening and should have a believable purpose. ("One reason we have people *draw* what it's like in their family is that it makes it easier for everyone, even little Johnny, to get their views across." "It sounds like you three each see the family in different ways. I want you to use these pens and paper to *show* me what your perspectives are.")

3. Visual, spatial, and kinetic metaphors are common parts of everyday language. Talking about "view," "perspective," "viewpoint," "how you see it," "getting the picture," and "what it looks like to you" makes it easier for a family to relate to a visually oriented task and accept it as appropriate. In approaching a construction task or a decision-making process, the therapist can speak of "getting to do something," or "seeing you all in action." Games that are also interventions or of diagnostic value can be introduced as games, as an opportunity for the family to play together. Role playing can be talked about in terms of "as if" and "let's pretend," as a chance to "act out" or try out "what it might be like if. . . ."

The exact instructions given to family members before they begin a task are very important matters to which many therapists are not very sensitive. The instructions establish what I call a "biasing set"; they bias the individual's expectations and behavior in a particular direction. Often just a few words can make a major difference in the results. It is not so much that there is a particular "right" set of instructions. Rather, it is essential that the therapist be aware of the effect of biasing set in order to take it into account and use it strategically in evaluation and intervention.

As a rule, however, it is counterproductive to use words that imply a "testing" or "evaluation" set. ("Let's see how well you do on this." "I want to see how you really interact." "I'll be watching to see what happens and how you do.") This set only raises anxiety and may push the family toward trying to impress or put their "best foot forward."

## Time Limits

In most structured techniques in family therapy, careful use of time can be important. The inclination of many therapists is to "stay flexible" and set no time limit on tasks. This feels open, free, and flexible, and has the advantage of giving enough time for even the slowest family and slowest member to finish. On the other hand, in some tasks it may mean that everyone waits an unreasonable length of time for one person; very often this is discovered to be a typical control tactic within the family.

Setting a fixed time limit not only gives advanced justification for interrupting or hurrying someone, but it can be used the other way around: as a counteraction for premature completion. The therapist might announce that 10 minutes will be taken for drawing a "picture of what it's like in your family," and that the whole 10 minutes will be used regardless of when individuals finish. On numerous occasions family members have produced significant additions or elaborations to their drawings or constructions after "completing" them but while waiting for the time to run out. A fixed time limit also makes it easier for the therapist to plan the session and assure ample time for all agenda items.

Timing within a session can be important. If a structured task is introduced just as the family enters the room, the odds are that important issues and agenda items being brought to the session will be missed. If someone is in personal pain, is puzzled by something from the previous session, or has a bone to pick, charging ahead with a structured exercise can create very justified resentment and fracture fragile working alliances. If the therapist merely adapts to presented issues and the family's agenda, however, the session may be nearly over before the task can be introduced.

The therapist must be open to what the family brings to the session while remaining tuned in for just the right point to segue deftly into the task. ("That sounds like a real problem, Mrs. Samser. I think maybe you should *show* us just what that is like for you. I have some markers and paper here. In fact, I'd like *each* of you to draw a picture that shows what the problem in the family is like for you.")

## IMAGE AND METAPHOR

The concept of *image* in human experience has become an important focus in various fields (Boulding, 1956). Each of us carries images of our entire interpersonal world and, especially, of our families. These images are the encoded, simplified representations of our understanding of complex interpersonal realities. They are the maps by which we negotiate our way through life, and they are the screens through which we filter, sort, and categorize our experience.

Not only does each family member carry images of what their family is and ought to be, but the family as a whole has shared images of itself as an entity, its nature, goals, and orientation. If the therapist is to understand a family and intervene efficiently and effectively to enable it, these images must be made accessible and be understood.

The term *image* is an appropriate choice because it suggests a visual and spatial representation. There is no direct evidence as yet that interpersonal reality is literally stored as images, but there are suggestive clues that spatial, visual memory is especially important in interpersonal interactions. For example, the right hemisphere of the brain is more heavily involved in recognition of faces and in interpretation of expression and gesture. The ease with which most people are able to represent their family experiences in spatial terms through art and family sculpture is evidence directly relevant to family therapy.

This section deals with evaluation/intervention techniques that are designed to gain access to spatial, imagistic, metaphorical representations of family systems. Three major variants of these techniques will be explored: drawings, construction tasks, and spatializations (or "family sculptures").

### Family Drawings

There are many variants on family drawings. Most are rather informal, though some have been formalized and systematized, such as Kinetic Family Drawings (Burns & Kaufman, 1972). All have in common their basic material: drawings of a family produced in simple art media. One may think of them as part of expressive therapy, as a form of projective testing, or, as I do, merely as a means to help family members externalize their images of their family and its situation.

## CONJOINT AND CONCURRENT DRAWINGS

Family drawings are of two basic forms. A *conjoint family drawing* (Bing, 1970) is one drawing produced by the whole family working on it together. The drawing itself is often of less significance than the process by which it was produced. *Concurrent family drawings* are produced by each family member working separately.

The basic theory underlying the conjoint drawing is that, working nonverbally through the medium of the task, the family will act out and preserve on paper essential features of its patterns in process and its current disablement. The therapist watches the drawing process carefully. Videotaping the task can also be useful to both the family and the therapist. Ample time must be allowed to view the tape and to discuss emerging material.

Working in a color medium is especially important in conjoint drawings, as the contributions of each member can often be distinguished after the fact by their color. When one family studied their conjoint drawing they noticed that nearly all the changes and alterations were in blue and that no object in the drawing that stood on its own was in blue. The grown daughter who had used blue emerged as a strong Opposer who disowned her opposition to many of the family values and whose frequent passive–aggressive attempts at sabotage were ignored by the rest of the family.

Concurrent, individual family drawings have one major advantage over the conjoint form. Because each is produced independently and usually differs markedly from the others, the drawings and the ensuing discussion graphically establish an important principle. Though they are one family, there is no one "right" picture of the family. Each member "sees" the family uniquely, and each view is a valid perspective.

For this reason it is generally worthwhile for the therapist rigidly to enforce rules of silence during the drawing task and of working independently. A family's or individual's inability to comply with these rules is itself important information.

It should be apparent that the task of producing individual family drawings is an intervention operating at more than one level and in multiple dimensions. I like to introduce it in an early session, not only for its value in assessment, but also because it sets the stage for many other techniques. It lets the family know that this is not just talking therapy, that action and activity are to be expected and that images and metaphors are as important as words and ideas. It communicates to them that every member's contribution is valued and begins the process of teaching a systems view of family process by validating the multiplicity of valid perspectives that combine to make a whole.

The differences among individual perspectives in family drawings can be dramatic and the exploration of these differences can itself be productive. Peter, age 11, was one of four children in the Wayland family who drew a picture of "what it was like for him in the family." The others drew conventionalized pictures showing little differentiation among figures and little of interest. His picture showed a figure hung on a cross, with an angry crowd surrounding him. When asked about his drawing, at first he said the central figure was himself and he identified each of the other family members by name from among the "crowd." When challenged by his mother to explain it, he replied that it was a picture of "Christ, and those are all the Jews angry at him." In making this switch, he employed a style of denial and obfuscation similar to that of his mother, with whom he closely identified.

### MECHANICS AND MATERIALS

The materials needed for family drawings are few and simple, but the choice of media and methods can still be important. Although any media at hand may be used, water-based colored marking pens on large paper are preferred by most therapists. Pencils and ordinary pens leave out the dimension of color, which can be important in various ways. Wax crayons are not as vivid or quite as easy to use as markers, though they are less expensive—and I have occasionally found adults who consider crayons "for kids," but willingly use markers. Broad-tipped markers are more durable and easier for small children to use; the fine-pointed variety can also be difficult to see when drawings are displayed and discussed by the family. Solvent-based markers are to be avoided; they bleed through paper and can leave indelible marks on rugs and clothes!

Ordinary 8½- by 11-inch paper is too confining for family drawings. It forces a cramped style and leaves no room for detail or for representation of things outside the family boundary. Small paper also puts very young children who lack fine motor coordination at a greater disadvantage. Large sheets of newsprint are ideal: they are economical, and their size alone introduces an element of novelty to the task. Paper about 11 by 17 inches is the practical lower limit; larger sizes are better.

## TIME

Rarely is more than 10 or 15 minutes required for either a conjoint or simultaneous family drawing task. Generally, any one such task furnishes more than enough material for discussion and exploration to fill an entire hour or hour-and-a-half session. Unless there were very specific and overriding reasons to do so with a particular family, it would probably be an error to introduce a drawing task with less than a half hour remaining in a session.

## TALK

As a rule, family drawings are best done without talking. Drawing is, obviously, intrinsically nonverbal. It is intended to tap into preverbal or nonverbal levels of understanding, and talking is only likely to interfere with access to these levels.

In conjoint family drawings it is especially important to keep the interaction at the nonverbal level. This constraint on interaction facilitates the acting out of family rituals and stereotypic processes. Patterns of interaction become exaggerated and simplified in ways that make them stand out more clearly to the therapist as well as to the family. Nonverbal tasks are also equalizers; by disabling logic and language, family members of differing age and intelligence are given more equal and immediate access to interaction. Differences observed under these conditions are more likely to reflect personal style and position in the family rather than mere verbal facility.

## BIASING SET

As in all structured techniques, just how a drawing task is introduced can bias the outcome. For example, one might instruct family members to "draw a picture of your family" or one might say, "draw a picture that represents what it is like for you in your family." The first is much more likely than the second to leave the therapist with a series of "family portraits," drawings in which all family members are lined up in a row and drawn to approximate scale. Little of interest may be revealed in such portraits.

In the second example, the key word "represents" sets a bias toward symbolic, metaphorical imagery but does not force it. If a person then produces a "family portrait" type of drawing after those instructions, he/she may be saying something important. The therapist might ask whether it feels rather stiff and formal to the person who drew it. The phrase "what it is like for you" discourages each person trying to represent objective reality ("what it is 'really' like") and sets the precedent for validating each person's distinct perceptions of the family.

If the therapist asks for a drawing of "what it feels like in your family" attention is focused on the dimension of affect. If, instead, the therapist says "what it means to be in your family" then family meanings and boundaries have been highlighted.

Kinetic Family Drawings (Burns & Kaufman, 1972) include the instruction to draw "the family doing something" or to draw "the people in your family doing something." This puts the emphasis on action and behavior and on interrelating. It also may make it easier for some people who need something concrete for a point of departure. Note that the first "set" above establishes an implicit bias toward representing the family doing something together; the second form leaves this as a possibility but does not suggest it.

The instructions may establish a biasing set in time as well. "What it is like in your family right now" obviously focuses on the current situation. If the therapist is especially interested in the general or long-term dynamics, the instructions might refer to "what it is usually like in your family" or "how it is most of the time." Either of these last two phrases directs the family to think about pattern in process.

There is no reason why the therapist cannot use the biasing set to explore any dimension of family process or even some very specific aspect of a family's experience, though a more open-ended and non-specific set is more likely to be appropriate in early evaluation. One example of a specialized biasing set is "draw a picture of what your family would be like without Kara" (for a family dealing with a young adult leaving home).

For one couple in therapy the theme of "moving" (from house to house) emerged as having special salience. They were bright, intellec-tual, task-oriented high-achievers. The cotherapists assigned them the task of designing the floor plan of their ideal house. This very focused task of "engineering" brought out very clear differences in their per-sonal priorities, their needs for privacy, and their fantasies about the future. The object, of course, is to employ the family's meanings and issues in establishing the set.

It is important to keep track of the biasing set used if family drawings are to be interpreted later and related to other tasks assigned in the course of therapy. After a session the instructions given can be written on the back of the drawings.

## PROCESSING AND INTERPRETATION

Some family therapists, more often those trained first in individual therapy and especially those with a psychodynamic or psychoanalytic orientation, look to somewhat standardized interpretations of family drawings. Kinetic Family Drawings even have a manual for interpretation (the snake is a phallic symbol, omissions indicate denial, and so forth).

Families, too, may ask after a drawing is complete, "Okay, so what does it mean, Doc?" Indeed, resistance to doing family drawings is sometimes related to fears that such a "test" will reveal secrets about the family or the individual despite their efforts to conceal these. It can be useful to allay such fears by explaining in advance that the drawings are not some kind of projective psychological test.

As I use family drawings, I like to take all the individual drawings and spread them on the floor or tape them up on a wall for all to see. (This in itself is a metaphor.) I usually begin by asking if there is anything anyone wishes to ask about or anything they particularly notice about any of the drawings. If I am asked what something means, I turn the question around: "It's Angie's drawing, maybe you should ask her." In keeping with the theoretical and practical perspective introduced in earlier chapters, it is the individual member's and the family's private meanings and interpretations that are of greatest interest. At the same time, the family's interactions around the drawings and their significance provide a further sample of their process. Of course, the interaction itself validates their differing views and helps them to communicate and understand these.

With or without a set of standard assigned meanings, certain aspects of the drawings are important for the family therapist to note. All the following are features I have found frequently related to important family dynamics.

*Size.* The size of figures may relate to their importance to the person who drew them or to their perceived power in the family system.

*Order of Drawing.* The order in which family members are drawn is often related to their importance to the drawer. When the drawer puts himself/herself in the picture last (or not at all), it is tempting to see this as evidence of a poor self-image, but there are other possibilities. In one case a parent felt like he didn't really belong in the family. In another, a teenaged girl tried to remain invisible and avoid attracting attention to herself in many ways. I suspect that drawing oneself last, much smaller, or not at all is always significant, but other evidence is usually needed to understand its meaning to the individual and the family.

*Position.* Closeness and distance in the drawing often parallel interpersonal closeness and distance in the family. Sometimes vertical position, like size, reveals itself to be a metaphor for power. A central figure in the drawing or a figure at the edge is likely to represent a perception of that person's central or peripheral role in the family.

*Crossing Out.* One reason marking pens are preferable to pencils, even colored pencils, is that they leave a complete history of the drawing's production. Crossing out is very common and, unless you believe in psychic determinism and the continual manifestation of the unconscious mind, it is undoubtedly sometimes of no significance other than artistic. Things crossed out are still worth inquiring about. The therapist might say, "It looks like you changed your mind here." Or, "Was this someone else in the family?" When a present member has been crossed out and not redrawn, the chances are slim that it is merely a matter of aesthetics or motor ability.

## SCULPTURE AND SPATIALIZATION

Family sculpture and its variants are among the most widely known and used of structured family therapy techniques based on image and metaphor. These have in common the use of space and movement in space as a metaphor or analog of other dimensions of relationships and family process of interest to the therapist.

It will not be necessary to go into detail about the techniques and uses of family sculptures here, as there are other sources available (e.g., Constantine, 1978; Duhl *et al.*, 1973). Instead, a sampling of the array of possibilities will be selected to suggest something of the open-ended potential for the use of space and motion for metaphorical measurement and intervention with families.

### Spatialization

In spatialization, a physical dimension of space is used as a simple analog for some quantity or aspect of process of interest. For example, position along a line might represent "powerfulness" or distance from the center of the room "alienation from the family business." The basic variations are based on different ways to use physical space or draw the analogy.

In every case, it is important that the therapist carefully delineate the physical space and define the analogy or metaphor clearly. It is helpful to use chalk or string to mark out lines or boundaries on the floor. Labels lettered on paper can serve as reminders of what a position or object represents. In most cases when people have to position themselves it is best to have them do so without talking, as this helps keep people from "negotiating" or "arguing" their position. It is helpful to have people move around in the space and try out various positions and places until they find the one that "feels right." This helps avoid too much rational "figuring out" of where someone "should be."

Talking about the exercise while people are standing in position within the sculpture has many advantages. It makes everyone aware of where everyone else is "coming from." It also keeps associated feelings and images vivid. ("What does it feel like being left way out here in the cold with everyone else snuggly warm in the center?" "It feels safe. It's too hot in there." "What does that bunch up there at the other end of the power spectrum look like from here?" "It looks like Prince Machiavelli and his quisling court!")

Spatializations can be repeated many times with different biasing sets. ("Okay, now let's do it again, only this time how you would *like* things to be." "This one will be what you expect will be the case in 10 years when Shanna graduates.")

LINEAR SCULPTURE

A linear sculpture uses a simple linear representation in one dimension. Usually a line is chalked or designated on the floor and its meaning is explained. Family members are asked to walk back and forth along it to find the spot that best represents where they are in relation to what is being represented. The representation may be unipolar (e.g., "jealousness" or "quick-temperedness") or bipolar (e.g., "head-oriented vs. gut-oriented"). The therapist selects a dimension relevant to the family and its situation based on emergent themes. For example, a sculpture of "risk taking" or "orderliness" might highlight differences and clusterings in these stylistic concerns of certain families. Of course, such things may also be explored verbally, but the spatialized approach has a number of advantages. For one thing, a spatialization of power in a family is more vivid and compelling than a conversation about power. Its novelty increases the likelihood of fresh insight being generated. As a "picture" it is worth many words, is more easily remembered, and captures complex combinations of interrelationships more compactly. When a shy young woman places herself beside her gadfly mother at the "high end" of a sculpture of "risk taking" we learn something about her sense of identification with and envy of the mother who denigrates her. The sculpture helps the mother to realize that her daughter takes what are, to her, substantial risks.

Of all the linear sculptures used in family therapy, one of the most broadly useful is a "Power Line." In this sculpture, one end of the line represents "being so powerless in this family that nothing ever comes out the way you want it to" and the other end represents "being so powerful in this family that everything comes out just the way you want it to." The sculpture may be repeated with numerous variations. Each person in turn could position everyone else, showing how they perceive the whole system in terms of power. This has the special advantage of separating out process from pattern in process, allowing the least powerful to convey their impressions as vividly as the most. Differences between actual relationships in the power dimension and desired relationships can be explored. Processing can explore both the feelings that each person's position evokes and the meaning of power to each person.

MATRIX

A matrix sculpture is a representation in two dimensions of one's position with respect to two factors at once, for example, "dominant–submissive vs. affectionate–antagonistic." It is generally a bit too complicated for use in therapy, but has occasionally been useful with sophisticated families to explore two interrelated issues.

POLAR

Polar sculptures use distance in any direction from some object (the pole) to represent the factor of interest, for example, relationship to "the spiritual heart of this family." These are broadly useful to explore identification with images as well as individuals. (For example, "Grandma isn't here, but if we pretended she were sitting in that chair there, how close or distant from her would each of you feel?" Or, "Let's let this sheet of letterhead stationary represent the family business. Where are each of you in relation to that?") Several poles may be represented at once without making the sculpture unworkable. ("Here, let this hat be your job, Tom, and the pen over there is yours, Delia. Now this glove is your marriage, okay? And over here we'll put the toy car; that's for little Tom, the baby. Now, where do each of you feel you are in relation to these different parts, these different pulls, in your life? Try moving around among these objects until you find a spot that feels about right for where you are.")

Some sculptures make use of distinct regions of physical space to mean distinct things or represent different periods of time. One of the most broadly useful of these is a "developmental" sculpture, sometimes called the "Life Spaces" technique. Distinct areas of the room (perhaps marked out by string or chalk on the floor) are used to represent key developmental stages in a person's or a family's life history. These may be generally significant periods (for example, "this circle represents the period you were away at college" or "over here is the period right after you two were married") or they may be special to a particular family ("when Tommy was in jail"). A family member is invited to enter each "life space" in turn and to describe its quality, what it feels like, who are the significant people in that space and the important events taking place there. When the sculptor is ready, he/she moves on to the next "life space." The technique is a dramatic and efficient way to collect history and explore the development of relationships. It tends to be more interesting for children to participate in or to watch than are verbal methods of history taking.

## Sculptures

Family sculpture is really a more elaborate form of spatialization in which movement, expression, gesture, body position, and even objects are used in all three dimensions to represent more complex and total aspects of relationships within a family. As a rule, one person at a time is the "sculptor" who, with the help of the therapist as a "monitor" or facilitator, arranges others in a tableau representing how the sculptor sees their interrelationships. Sculpture techniques vary considerably in brevity, specificity, and focus. In general they highlight or reveal aspects of a family's regime and patterns in process. Other references should be consulted for methods and discussion of variations. Here a few somewhat neglected specialized forms will be sketched.

MINISCULPTURES

As a complete sculpture of a family by one member may take up to an hour, condensed versions can be used in evaluation or short-term therapy. In the most straightforward variant, family members take turns rapidly positioning everyone in the family into a living tableau representing how each fits in the family. For example, in 15 minutes, the Yanoffs completed the four sculptures sketched in Figure 11-1, providing an exceptionally rich picture of family relationships. Both the father, Herman, and son, Dan, saw an intense, conflicted involvement between the mother, Antonia, and daughter, Dee, with Herman making an ineffective attempt to affect their conflict. Antonia and Dee both described the central conflict as between Herman and Antonia, but where Antonia places herself in the position of the oppressed, Dee makes her the oppressor (another example of the conflict between mother and daughter). In all four sculptures, Dan is the most peripheral.

Kantor originated a crisply structured approach to rapid sculptures in which physical proximity is used to represent emotional distance, vertical position to represent power, and gesture and expression to represent other aspects of relationship. In this way power and affect are represented straightforwardly in a single sculpture, while some of the richness of meaning is also portrayed.

**FIGURE 11-1.**
Family minisculptures completed by the Yanoffs.

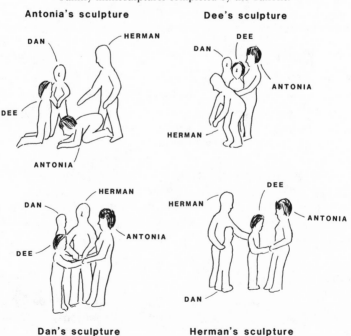

Antonia's sculpture          Dee's sculpture

Dan's sculpture          Herman's sculpture

Another variant is to use standardized postures or movements to represent a set of possible positions in the family. Each family member takes on one of a set of standard positions or roles and these are quickly combined into a tableau. Satir (1972) describes postures representing four defended styles of communication: Placating, Distracting, Blaming, Computing. The four psychopolitical positions can be represented by the spatial metaphors introduced in Chapter 7: Moving by central position, Following by facing inward nearby, Opposing by facing tangentially or outward, and Bystanding by watching from a distance. Psychopolitics can also be acted out in motion, with a Mover moving, Followers following, Opposers deflecting, and Bystanders hanging back. Yet another set of related positions/actions can be derived from the "drama triangle" of Persecuter, Victim, and Rescuer (Karpman, 1968), plus Audience.

## BOARD SCULPTURES

Sculptures and spatializations need not be carried out with people positioned around the room. The analog can be shifted to any convenient space.

> The Meyers, whose dramatic use of space was introduced in Chapter 8, were very resistant to techniques involving movement in space, even to being seated differently in the room. The therapists, being highly committed by training to sculpture and spatialization, had tried on several occasions to use conventional sculptures but had met with little success. But the Meyers loved to play board games and several of them were avid chess players, so the therapists had them all use chess pieces to represent themselves in a sculpture on a chess board. "Now" and "earlier" sculptures revealed general agreement that the son and father had become less alienated. The therapists were represented as closer in the "earlier" sculpture and as further away in the "now." In talking about the sculptures, the family discovered it was getting ready to terminate.

The Kvebaek Family Sculpture Technique (Cromwell, Fournier, & Kvebaek, 1980) is a similar standardized procedure that has been developed using small figurines and a 10 by 10 board. This approach allows the therapist to compute measures of cohesion and isolation and to make simple comparisons between families.

## SCULPTURE AS FEEDBACK

Family sculptures are most often used as assessment tools; somewhat less often they are thought of as interventions. It is also possible to use them as metaphorical feedback from the therapists to the family. An

advantage of this symbolic form of communication is that it stimulates
the family to do the work of interpreting and understanding, in contrast to a verbal summary, which can often seem predigested and not
open to interpretation. In addition, a sculpture done by the therapist
can bypass intellectual filters and communicate to a family at a nonverbal level. On some occasions, this form of feedback itself prompts
major changes in a family's relationships.

## TASKS AND GAMES

Metaphorical and imagistic elements may be present in the techniques
discussed in this section, but these tools are generally of more interest
for the process they evoke than for the product produced. They are,
therefore, often of greater use in understanding family regimes and
family process than family paradigms.

### Discussions

The least structured of structured tasks directs the family to "discuss"
or "talk about" some subject. This is so widely and informally used by
family therapists that it is rarely thought of as a technique. Nevertheless, it can be very useful to help the therapist to Bystand and get a
glimpse of something akin to the family's "normal" process. It is a
crude but effective way to break out of a pattern of communication all
too common in therapy where most of the communication is between
the therapist and each of the family members rather than within the
family. This pattern may be acceptable for eliciting information, but
does little to reveal process or make it available for manipulation.

More specialized versions may involve particular pairs or other
subsystems. A father and son might be directed to sit facing each other
in the middle of the room and talk about their careers. Any such move
can be a strong intervention, as it identifies a subsystem as a relevant
entity. In the process of highlighting the subsystem, the therapist may
metaphorize certain aspects of it, for example, having two people who
never talk directly with each other carry on a conversation seated back
to back.

Carefully circumscribed, time-limited interaction can be used for
specific purposes. For example, in many families, members have difficulty appreciating or validating each other. Either this does not
spontaneously occur or affirmation is always disqualified by a verbal
"kicker" that effectively cancels it. ("Very good report card, son. Of

course, if you had applied yourself properly you wouldn't have gotten that 'C' in math.")

In alternating pairs or on a rotating basis, each member can be told to spend a certain number of minutes (usually from one to three) saying only positive things to the other person, describing their assets and strengths or things about them that are liked and appreciated. Enforcing the use of the entire time is important, as it gets members to "dig" for positive things, rather than give up after a few quick and easy ones. The exercise can have numerous benefits, as it increases the sense of being appreciated in a family that might otherwise be cold, critical, impersonal, or unaccepting. It is also practice for future expression of validation. Furthermore, it can increase awareness of differences and help refine members' perceptions of each other.

Such narrowly focused interactions must be timed and chosen with care. In the above example, if someone absolutely *cannot* express appreciation to some others, the effect can be devastating and discouraging. The therapist must also be prepared to coach some members and to intervene to prevent the inclusion of "kickers" or other agendas.

## Decision Making

The use of family decision-making tasks has long been common in family therapy. In the prototypical task, the therapist describes a problem or situation and the family is directed to decide on a solution. A common assignment is for them to pretend they just got a hundred dollars that they must decide how to spend. Another popular variant has the family deciding what to do on their next vacation.

Experience has shown that, for some families, the amount of money is more than they can hope to have as discretionary funds or is too trivial to consider seriously. In any event, the money isn't really theirs, so it is really "let's pretend" time. Choosing a vacation can likewise be "unreal" for a family that never takes one or that always goes to their summer place in Maine.

The unreal or play-acting aspect of these assignments can be both advantageous and a drawback. In a family seriously enmeshed in rageful conflict, the game-like quality may allow them to get somewhere with the task without replicating their on-going battle. This same quality may compromise the usefulness of the task as a stimulant to process for valid assessment by the therapist.

Ideally, one would like to tailor the task to the family, using a problem that is relevant to their current situation. The presenting problem is seldom appropriate—if they could decide on a solution to it they wouldn't be in therapy—but something related to it in a serious or even humorous way may be. This increases the investment in both the decision-making or problem-solving process and the outcome, while being an intervention at another level. A family with a school-phobic child might be given the task of working out details of a new way for the kids to get to and from school. A family with a deep schism into two groups might be asked to decide how they are going to spend the time between Christmas and New Year's Day.

The therapist observes the process to identify decision-making style and clues to the family's regime, but, of course, many other things may emerge. Preferred psychopolitics often become quite apparent, and important family themes may be revealed. Out of the discussion of their winter holidays a family may show the glimmering awareness of an impending divorce, for example.

The therapist must pay close attention to the biasing set created by the instructions given to the family. "Deciding something to buy with the hundred dollars" is different than "figuring out what to do with the hundred dollars." The former assumes that spending the money is the only option and implies that only one thing can be bought. Telling a family to "agree on a vacation" pushes the family toward unanimity and may exclude the random regime's tactic of each doing their own thing.

Decision tasks are also useful for intervention and teaching, as the family can be coached through other ways of reaching a solution. This can be especially useful for helping a family to "import" a strategy of another regime, an important treatment technique to be introduced in Chapter 14.

### Construction Tasks

Construction tasks, like family drawings, have many variants. A family as a group or as individuals can be asked to construct something out of almost any material toward almost any conceivable therapeutic end. However, to avoid having to explore the full range of expressive therapies applied to family work, this section concentrates on construction tasks using building blocks.

The medium I have found most useful and versatile is a set of the large hardwood blocks commonly known as kindergarten blocks and available from school supply houses. They come in a more or less standard assortment of shapes. Similar sets of smaller, usually colored blocks are sold in most toy stores.

Block-building tasks are almost invariably collective efforts. Again, the focus is primarily on the process the task elicits rather than the product. Typically, a family is asked to build something together using the set of blocks. The task is best done entirely without talking and there is usually a time limit.

As with family drawings, the biasing set is important. Unless the therapist makes clear that the family is to build one thing together, each member may undertake a separate project even if this is not typical of their interaction. Specialized instructions can be very useful: A young couple who were living together denied that commitment was an issue for them. They were asked to build something together in which each could imagine living in a fairy-tale sense "happily ever after." Although the resulting castle-like construction was all connected, it really consisted of two distinct structures: one secure and tightly bounded, the other open and rambling. As they discussed their "home" and how they went about building it, it became clear that her paradigm was closed, his was random. What each wanted from the relationship and envisioned for the future were very different. She admitted to wanting marriage and stability; he preferred to "hang loose" and "play it by ear." They saw the struggle they experienced trying to integrate their disparate block structures as foreshadowing difficulties they would have if each tried to fit into the other's reality in marriage.

In addition to highlighting differences in preferred regime and paradigm, nonverbal block construction tasks reveal psychopolitical preferences and patterns very quickly and obviously. In fact, these tasks are probably the most efficient assessment tool for analyzing psychopolitical patterns. The person to pick up the first block and begin laying a foundation is generally the strongest and most frequent Mover. Opposers and Followers quickly reveal themselves in how they alter or elaborate the structure. Someone who hangs back to study what is being built and only adds a block or two late in the construction is often found to be a Bystander in other ways and contexts as well. Families will usually confirm the ways in which patterns of interaction revealed by the task are similar to common sequences of events in everyday life. As in conjoint drawings, videotape can be a useful tool—after an initial debriefing, the family can watch the tape and comment on what they see happening. This not only reinforces seeing the family's experience as a pattern of the whole, but it makes it easier for each member to Bystand his/her own part in the process.

To bring out important interactive patterns and psychopolitical preferences, each member's level of investment in the outcome of the task may be increased. One way this can be done is to draw on personal values. Each person can be asked to take a minute to imagine something beautiful (or important) they would want to construct with the blocks. Then they are told that it is to be a joint effort, that the group/

family can construct anything they wish, but they are to make one thing, and each participant is responsible for seeing that the end product in some way reflects the image they originally had in mind.

This, of course, is a metaphor for the duality of group and individual in family systems. It pushes the family and individual members to use their resources to strike a balance or integrate individual and group directions. This becomes a powerful diagnostic of their ability to do so and the strategies they use. It can be quite surprising how closely the construction process parallels the family process in general and reveals features of their disablement in particular. In processing the results afterwards, the compromises, sacrifices, and successes of individuals in the family can be explored.

As with all structured tasks, it is important to draw out the connections with what happens in the rest of the family's life and with their current impasse. ("Is that familiar, Jen pretty much getting her own way?" "The 'castle' kept changing, always being rearranged by someone. Is life at home anything like that?" "So, Jason concluded there wasn't any space to build in the main court there. He ended up making his own little out building. It's kinda the way you described your problems together, with him holing up in his room and never telling anybody what's happening. Is there any room for you 'in the center of things' at home, Jason?'")

The resulting structure may reveal something of the family's paradigm, but unless there is a particular biasing set the construction itself is more likely to be of transient interest and the results more variable over time. One possible biasing set to attempt to tap into collective paradigmatic images would be to "build something together in which you all could live in fantasy for a long, long time." The emphasis on fantasy is important or families will try to build some kind of scale model of an actual livable house.

## Role Playing

Role playing has many uses in evaluation and intervention. One of the most straightforward and broadly useable is to have a family role play or act out a situation instead of talking about it. Role playing specific or recurring fights can be far more useful to the therapist and the family than having them talk about these. The therapist gets to "really see what's going on." Role playing is less likely to be muddled by other levels of struggle, such as competition for who will act as the family's interpreter of disagreements, or by problems of filtering and censoring.

A situation to be acted out may be chosen because it is thematically important to the family or for its generic value. Morning rituals, dinner time, and bedtime are all productive focuses for role playing, as these are critical times of interaction for most families. Dinner times, especially, often embody in condensed form the bulk of a family's key patterns in process.

Role played sequences also afford an opportunity to intervene and bring about alternative resolutions. The new outcome may be important in itself or the role play may be primarily intended as a rehearsal for learning new behaviors. In-session role playing using new skills is especially important when family therapy takes on a communication skills focus.

Role reversal is so widely used it seldom is accorded attention or comment. It is probably the most common form of role play in family therapy, perhaps because it combines high diagnostic value with strong intervention possibilities. Although role reversal is often regarded as a "primitive" technique, it is actually quite subtly paradoxical. When the family is directed to "do the same thing, only you two switch roles," they are doing the same thing, still just "being themselves," and yet they are not. Having two people "switch roles" is often used to disrupt a stuck pattern of interaction or to help clients get a new perspective on a situation. It also gives the therapist information about flexibility, accuracy of interpersonal perceptions, and empathic abilities of the role players.

CHAPTER

# 12

# MAPMAKING, SELF-TAUGHT
## A Discipline for Mapping
## Family Systems

A map is a guide to some territory, and a family map is a guide to the family's territory. The purpose of mapping a family is to make visible and accessible the structure of the family, its basic organization. There are many ways to do this within the various schools and approaches to family therapy. The approach presented in this chapter resembles the family assessment technique of Geddes and Medway (1977), but is intended for use by the therapist. The family map facilitates gaining access to the full range and depth of data already known to the therapist, externalizing these in a manner uniquely valuable to the particular therapist making the map. This method is organized but not rigorous, drawing on intuitive, metaphorical understanding as well as an analytical knowledge.[1]

## METAPHOR AND ANALYSIS

A metaphor, as introduced in Chapter 4 and used throughout this book, is an image of a system, an image that, whether expressed visually or verbally, carries more information about the system it represents than is contained in the metaphor itself. It is the implications of the metaphorical image that, drawing on a common pool of

1. This chapter was adapted from a memorandum by the author used in the family therapy training program at Boston State Hospital (Constantine, 1976b). The technique of mapping was originally the joint product of numerous faculty members of The Center for Training in Family Therapy, and this tutorial benefited from their input. Ann Spitzer and David Kantor warrant special mention.

shared experience and understanding, carry the "extra" information. Thus a metaphor is often the most efficient way to communicate a complex notion or to describe a complex system. When the metaphor is expressed visually, additional leverage is gained because vision is a communication channel of such high capacity.

Visual metaphors for family systems also make it easier to tap into the mental images we all build and use in dealing with complex human relationships. Properly done, the process of mapping a family system gives access to much the same kind of unarticulated data that are revealed by a family sculpture (Constantine, 1978; Duhl *et al.*, 1973).

## Analytical: Structural Family Diagrams

One of the most widely used schemes for mapping family systems is the one worked out by the structural family therapists and presented by Minuchin (1974). This representational system, which I will refer to as "structural family diagrams," reflects concerns of the structural school of family therapy with subsystem boundaries and the systemic faults of enmeshment and disengagement. The basic symbols of structural family diagrams are shown in Figure 12-1. The graphics represent boundaries between subsystems and relationships between individuals. The restricted, disciplined graphics make the method easy to learn and to use. However, some aspects of the diagramming approach do not model the structural concepts very well. For example, enmeshment and disengagement are conceptualized as properties of systems, but enmeshment is diagrammed as "overinvolvement" between pairs of individuals, and disengagement is not directly represented at all. It is possible to show overly rigid boundaries, but family members may be disengaged from each other without having even clear interpersonal boundaries; such is the case in disabled synchronous families.

As the diagrams highlight relationships and subsystem boundaries, genuine systemic properties cannot be modeled directly with structural family diagrams. Possibly the most crucial omission is the important boundary between the family and its environment. Of course, nothing prevents the therapist from adding such detail to a structural diagram, nor, for that matter, from integrating the structural scheme into another one.

Structural diagrams and derivative schemes emphasize linear, analytical thinking about family systems; they do not inherently facilitate intuition and metaphor. To the extent that the scheme raises analytical questions early in the mapping process, intuitive thinking may be

**SUBSYSTEM BOUNDARIES**

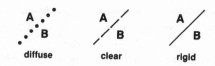

diffuse          clear          rigid

**DYADIC RELATIONSHIPS**

conflict          affiliation          overinvolvement

**TRIADIC RELATIONSHIPS**

coalition against
third party

**FIGURE 12-1.**
Structural therapy representations commonly used in mapping families.

hindered. Their formalized, logical presentation does simplify reporting and comparisons, consequently they are often preferred for publi-
cation and communication between professionals.

## Pure Metaphor: Family Drawings

At the other extreme from the discipline and logic of structural family
diagrams are family drawings. Conventionally, these are produced by
family members, separately or conjointly, usually for the purpose of
evaluation. Family drawings were explored in Chapter 11 as therapy
tools. There is no reason, however, why a therapist who has been
working with a family for a while could not produce a drawing, too.
On occasion, I have done my own drawing of how I see a family at the
same time that family members are doing their drawings. This can be
an effective intervention, but therapists must be careful that their
drawings do not become "the correct view" of the family, to be accepted on authority or challenged for whatever reason.

Free form, representational or symbolic drawings of a family can be produced by therapists for their own use in understanding the family, but these are not family maps. Ideally, family maps integrate analytical and metaphorical representation to create a good overview of the whole family territory.

## FAMILY SYSTEM MAPS

A family system map is an attempt to represent graphically a comprehensive "picture" of a family system. Ideally, every family should be mapped at least once, usually at or near the end of an initial evaluation; but any time the therapist feels lost or confused or is searching for new direction in the therapy is an appropriate time to map the family. An earlier map may simply be revised, but if much time has passed it is better to draw a map again from scratch.

For reasons I do not yet understand, therapists often find themselves reluctant or hesitant to begin a map. Even after countless successes the process can still feel strange or silly. All I can suggest is to go ahead anyway; the results will be worth it.

### How to Draw a Map

Mapping a family is an interactive process between the therapist and a piece of paper. The object is to project onto the paper a visible, compact, coherent representation of the map you already have in your mind but cannot "see." The map on the paper organizes and systematizes the data so that they make sense and form a whole. In the process, you will often be surprised by how much you knew and understood; even more importantly, you have a chance of identifying what you do *not* know about the family—missing factors are much more obvious in a picture.

In order to make it easier for the therapist to draw on both halves of the brain, integrating metaphorical and analytical models, the rule of thumb is: *Draw first, explain later.* In this way our verbal reasoning ability augments rather than inhibits intuitive exploration and does not get in the way of learning what we know but do not know we know.

Only after completing each step in drawing the map do we pause, step back, take a look at what is on the paper, and try to understand it. We try to construct a plausible explanation for each thing we have drawn. We always begin by accepting the map just as originally

constructed thus far, acting as if it were an absolutely correct representation of the family. Reasoning from that premise, we try to come up
with a logical explanation or conclusion. What could that dumbbell
shape of the family mean? What might it do to the father to be
blockaded in one corner by six females? If the whole family really were
spinning around like that, what would happen to the people inside?
The whole idea is to tap into and utilize the inherent but unarticulated
wisdom of the brain, which is always constructing its own maps of
relationships and reality.

If you have trouble beginning or get stuck later on, it is probably
because you are trying too hard to "figure it out" first. Don't think,
draw! Try transfering the marker or crayon to the other hand, especially if you are right-handed—this gives priority to control by the
subdominant hemisphere, the metaphorical, intuitive "right brain" in
normal right-handers. Put the marker on the paper and start it moving, whether or not it makes sense or seems to go in the "right
direction." Let your hand "take over" and move whatever way it
wants. The object, of course, is to gain more immediate access to the
images in the subdominant hemisphere, bypassing the normal censoring of the verbal brain.

## BOUNDARY

Draw an outline of the *shape* of the family, of its boundary. Do this
fairly rapidly and without thinking too much about what to draw.
The boundary you draw may be thick or thin, constant or varying,
broken or unbroken. The space it encloses may be large or small,
simple or complex, in one piece or more than one.

Compared with structural family diagrams, family system maps
make use of an extended and considerably more flexible scheme for
representing system and subsystem boundaries. In family system maps,
boundaries may be represented by lines of any shape, density, thickness, or form that conveys information. The concept of permeability is
retained from structural family diagrams and is represented in similar
ways by the thickness and continuity of the line, but other properties
may be conveyed that have intuitive or logical appeal in representing
the family. For example, a thick wavy line of complicated shape may
convey a relatively impermeable but complex family border, while a
heavy straight line suggests rigidity and simplicity along with impene-
trability. The shape itself may convey significant meaning, as in the
perfectionistic family whose outer boundary is represented as a leaning
square, suggesting their inability to achieve and sustain their goal of

perfect rectilinearity. Examples of maps throughout the book show something of the tremendous range of possibilities.

One at a time each member of the family system is positioned within the family space in a place that "feels right" in relation to the space and to other members. Many therapists borrow from genealogy and use squares to represent males and circles to represent females, but more information may be gained if the therapist simply uses any shape that seems appropriate at the moment. Many find they naturally employ size to represent power or influence. You should work fairly quickly and don't worry about getting just the right blob. Be sure to identify members by name and then number them in the order in which they were added to the map.

Identify and depict any clear alliances or disconnections or other interpersonal relationships within the family that seem important. Family system maps use an extended set of graphics derived from structural family diagrams. In addition to conflict, affiliation, overinvolvement, and coalitions as represented in structural family diagrams, family system maps represent other relationships using the symbols shown in Figure 12-2. These were developed over the years to represent clinically significant relationships that arise frequently enough to warrant having a common symbol. Dashed rather than solid lines between members imply that the designated relationship is covert rather than overt. The symbol for "disconnection" is used to show uninvolvement or emotional distance where graphic distance alone would not convey the lack of relationship. Often family members identify with each other whether or not they have an active or overt affiliation; this is represented by adding the mathematical symbol for "approximately equal" to the line representing the relationship. A "behavioral mapping" means that the behavior of one member has been found to "mirror" that of another, either directly or in some form of reversal; arrows added to a line suggest this relationship. The mathematical symbol $\pm$ appended to a line denotes ambivalence. Symbols may be combined as freely as needed and appropriate. Thus, two people might have a conflicted overinvolvement (Figure 12-2;j), an emotionally distant mutual identification (12-2;k), or even a covert affiliation (12-2;l).

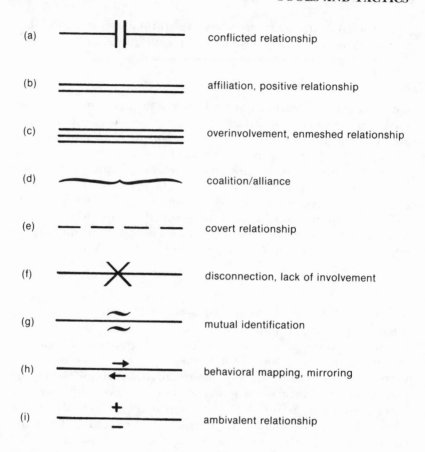

(a)                    conflicted relationship

(b)                    affiliation, positive relationship

(c)                    overinvolvement, enmeshed relationship

(d)                    coalition/alliance

(e)                    covert relationship

(f)                    disconnection, lack of involvement

(g)                    mutual identification

(h)                    behavioral mapping, mirroring

(i)                    ambivalent relationship

*EXAMPLES OF MIXED SYMBOLS*

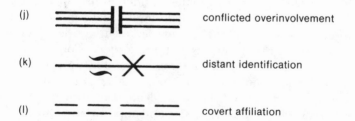

(j)                    conflicted overinvolvement

(k)                    distant identification

(l)                    covert affiliation

**FIGURE 12-2.**
Extended representations of interpersonal relationships.

The symbols of Figure 12-2 should not be taken as rigid specifications but as a flexible guideline. Using established graphics makes it easier to communicate with others and to remember what an old map meant, but the idiographs should not get in the way of freely representing the therapist's understanding of a particular family. For this reason, too, it is not necessary to specify relationships for every possible pair in the family—what stands out to the therapist is what should show on the map.

The map should also portray any subsystems with distinct functions or boundaries. As with the boundary of the whole family system, the graphic symbols developed by Minuchin are often useful and may be extended as needed in any way that has intuitive appeal (e.g., a heavy, moat-like, wavy line may completely enclose Mom, Dad, and Heir Apparent, who have a tight-knit royal subsystem from which everyone else is excluded).

### PSYCHOPOLITICS

Identify and make note of the psychopolitical preferences of each member and the particular character they bring to these psychopolitical positions (e.g., Reluctant Mover, Distant Opposer, Energetic Follower, and the like). Clearly distinguish multiple preferences from those cases that are ambiguous or on which there is insufficient data. It may be necessary to qualify positional preferences by dimensions of process (e.g., "Stephen is the chief Mover in terms of meaning, but Bystands in the family's emotional life").

### DIMENSIONAL ANALYSIS

At the bottom or to the side, list the dimensions of family process: space, time, matter, and energy; content, control, meaning, and affect. In a word or phrase or two, characterize what you know of the family's transactions and operations in each dimension. Dig for what you know, but acknowledge and note where your knowledge is incomplete. Typical questions to ask include: What is the dominant affect? How is power distributed? What characterizes the material organization? What are the family themes? How is time managed?

By identifying characteristics of the family's structures and process in all eight dimensions, the therapist is able to check how completely the family is understood. Missing or confusing data are highlighted, indicating directions for further exploration.

PARADIGM, REGIME, AND PROCESS

Another short list identifies the family's characteristics at the three levels of paradigm, regime, and process. Descriptions should be qualified briefly as needed, for example, "struggling whether to be open or closed," "borderline closed/random," or "neglectfully random." The principal direction of disablement of the family (rigid–chaotic, enmeshed–disengaged) should be identified.

QUINTESSENTIAL METAPHOR

In a single word or phrase, attempt to capture the essence of the family, an overall metaphor that conveys the basic strategy and organization of the family as a whole (e.g., "Huddled together in the center for warmth." "A giant centrifuge spinning everyone out against the walls." "The Brooklyn Zoo." "A rotten apple with a worm eating its core out").

CONNECTIONS AND CONTRADICTIONS

What kind of picture does your map form as a whole? What are the interconnections and contradictions among the parts of the map: boundaries, membership, alliances and subsystems, psychopolitics, dimensional analysis, and quintessential metaphor? How do you explain these?

Other Things to Do

1. After completing the family map, add yourself and your cotherapist to the picture. How does it change? What happens at the interface between cotherapy system and family system? How does the expanded map relate to your actual experience with the family?
2. Draw a picture of the actual physical arrangement of everyone in the therapy space on the first meeting; then draw one of their arrangement on the last meeting. How do these relate to your metaphorical map of the family?
3. Save the map and update it periodically. Are the changes due to obtaining missing data or to earlier mistakes? Is the system more enabled or merely different? Can you interpret your later experiences in working with the family in terms of what the map says of how the family operates?

4. Save all your maps. Compare different families and your experiences working with them. What have you learned about mapping? Theory? Intervention?

## MAPS IN APPLICATIONS

The principal uses of family system maps are in planning interventions and in guiding further evaluation. The map will usually highlight quite clearly those areas where important information is missing or is not really understood by the therapist. Sometimes it will be enough for the therapist to attend more closely to some aspect of family process in the next session. Other times it may be necessary to employ a specific diagnostic tool for further assessment in some area.

We learn whether the map we picked up at the local gas station is accurate by using it to get around. If it enables us to get from home to the ski lodge with a minimum of hassles, then we consider it valid. Similarly, a family sytem map is validated by successful negotiation of the territory, when movement on the map can be reflected in movement through the territory. Family maps can be independently validated by testing out an anticipated consequence of some move by the therapist. More often, the map is validated through its use in planning intervention.

Strategic use of family maps is a two-step process, like using a road map to plan a trip. First you study the map to find where you want to go and figure out how to get there. On the map you trace the route, noting steps along the way and landmarks that could be used to check your progress. Then you start driving the actual roads.

Using a family system map, the therapist first defines a desired change in terms of the map alone. The therapist plays an "as if" game in which the map is assumed to be correct and interventions are carried out on the map as if it were the family, not merely a representation of it. The "route" to more healthy functioning is traced on the map.

Consider the family mapped in Figure 12-3. The bloated blob of the eldest daughter virtually fills the center, squeezing all but a favorite aunt into a narrow neck of the family space. The family seems to subscribe to a random paradigm, but is being regulated by an ineffective closed regime with the overweight daughter in charge. Things are so "heavy" in the family, that it has lost its ability to play. Strictly in terms of the map, the desired intervention might be to enlarge the family space and move the daughter out of the center so all members can have more equal access to it. Family play and recreation are suggested as media for implementing this shift.

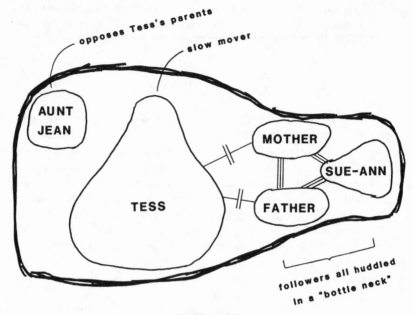

**FIGURE 12-3.**
Map of the Hurd family.

The second step is to translate the interventions on the map into interventions with the family itself. The therapist might promote an alliance between Tess and her aunt Jean, suggesting activities outside the family for the two of them. The therapist might concentrate on helping other family members to acquire confidence in asserting themselves, enhancing each other's self-esteem. The interests of each of the other family members could, in turn, become occasions for discussions and suggestions for family outings, literally expanding the family's boundaries and giving every member a chance to be center stage.

What the therapist sees as a problem and how this problem is translated into intervention will depend on the personal and professional proclivities of the therapist, but the same sequence of steps applies. The intervention is planned on the map, then translated into moves with the family. In using family maps, you can get lost in much the same way you can on an automobile trip. You could have a poor or outdated map, you might not read it correctly, or you might do a bad job of actually "navigating" on the road. If the family system map is accurate and the translation is faithful, however, the results in the family should mirror the anticipated changes in the map.

In this example, if the daughter's weight problem was indeed related to the "heaviness" of the family and to the burden of being centrally responsible within it, then as she moves toward the periphery and the center becomes more flexibly accessible, she should lose weight. If not, then the map and strategy need revision.

CHAPTER

# 13

# EVALUATION AND ASSESSMENT
## Access to Paradigm, Regime, and Process

Family evaluation and assessment, now recognized as of central importance in family therapy (Karpel & Strauss, 1983; Keeney, 1983), are
at the heart of a paradigmatic approach. As used here, family evaluation refers to the initial procedures by which the therapist finds out
what is "really" going on in a family, building the understanding
necessary for an idiographic theory, a comprehensive and comprehen-
sible map of the family system. Assessment refers to similar procedures
that, once treatment has commenced or has approached termination,
help assess what has happened, what has changed. This chapter will
expand on the general overview of evaluation introduced in Chapter 3
to consider some specific topics in greater depth and detail.

## THERAPIST STYLE AND FAMILY STYLE

Various therapies and therapists have developed distinct approaches to
family evaluation or diagnosis and assessment (Liddle, 1983). The
paradigmatic approach neither prescribes a choice from among these
variations nor formulates a new "method." Recognition of variation
in family paradigms and regimes does draw attention to the possible
significance of the "fit" between the family and the therapist's style
and approach to evaluation.

## Mover–Opposer aand Follower–Bystander

The psychopolitical model can be useful to differentiate styles by which therapists enter, gain access to, join with, and evaluate a family. There are many variations in the major schools of family therapy and even more variation among therapists, but one of the most basic distinctions can be drawn from the therapist's position in relation to the family's process.

In one style, the therapist is interested, at least initially, in the family's process as it presents itself, as undisturbed by "intervention" as possible. In this Follower–Bystander approach, the therapist's job is considered to be that of a more or less passive observer or else an outsider who "joins with" the family by adopting or "mirroring" their own style of interaction.

In the Mover–Opposer model, evaluation proceeds as a result of the therapist's probes and prods to the system, trial interventions that test the structures of the family. These probes feed information back to the therapist about rigidity or resiliency, about the nature of boundaries and coalitions, and about other features of the family's structures.

Of these two directions, the more active, provocative Mover–Opposer style is probably somewhat riskier, both in its potential for unintentioned impact on the family and for the possibility of backfiring on the therapist. The more provocatively oppositional the approach is, the greater is the risk of unnecessarily alienating or antagonizing certain families, especially those with closed or synchronous regimes. Therapists who prefer this style would argue that it is a more rapid approach to evaluation and combines intervention with evaluation.

## Technique-Oriented and Therapist-Oriented Evaluation

Evaluation may also be characterized by the extent to which it emphasizes the use of technique as opposed to the therapist's use of self. At the one end of this spectrum, the use of techniques, tests and measures, such as those described in Chapter 11, is seen as the major source of information about the family. At the other end, the therapist's personal experience of the family and use of self are the principal sources of information. The symbolic–experiential approach (Keith & Whitaker, 1981) not only eschews technique per se but argues that formal procedures of evaluation detract from the therapeutic encounter, reducing necessary spontaneity and interfering with the formation of a therapeutic relationship between therapist and clients.

Regimes and Evaluation

It has been my experience that closed regimes tend to be the easiest to evaluate because the strength of alliances, the closedness of boundaries, and the stability of interactions make them more visible and more easily described. The more inflexible a family's process is, the less behavior need be sampled to understand the patterns in process. On the other hand, closed regimes compartmentalize relationships and control access to information; they are the most prone to have "secrets" that are significant to the family process. These may complicate the process of evaluation: the pattern may be clear, but its full depth of meaning may not.

The rigidity of disabled synchronous regimes ought to make them easy to understand as well, but they are often experienced as having a vague, amorphous, or elusive quality that makes them difficult to evaluate. So many significant aspects of the family are implicit and internalized that a clear formulation can elude the therapist. Their deadness is apparent but not its dimensions or details. The therapist's experience of the family is a key piece of the evaluation and an important source of data. The best formulation in these cases may be a detailed unraveling of the impact the family has on the therapist.

The chaotic aspects of disabled random and open regimes can confuse, distract, or bedazzle the therapist. Patterns in the randomness may only become apparent to the therapist after he/she "steps back," "defocuses," or "tunes out the noise." The complexity of most open regimes may make thorough evaluation somewhat more difficult than for other regimes. Concentrating on higher levels of description, maintaining a strict sense of relevance, and dealing with the more global patterns can help the therapist manage the complexity.


Differential Diagnosis

In earlier chapters—notably Chapters 6, 8, and 10—numerous differences among family regimes were introduced and explored. Of the many distinguishing features of family regimes, a few are especially useful for "differential diagnosis."

RESPONSE TO OPPOSITION

Kantor's original formulation that family stereotypes were most clearly differentiated by their response to opposition has been established in clinical practice. How the family deals with internal opposition, dissidence, or deviance is probably the best and quickest indicator of a family's regime. In Kantor's terms, closed regimes control opposition; random regimes oppose control. At issue is not the amount of opposition, but the collective corrective response to that opposition. A disabled closed regime may be riddled with rebellion but will be hallmarked by attempts of the operative regime to control it. If attempts to control opposition fail, the closed regime tries to contain it, isolating it to limit its influence—thus prisoners and scapegoats are made. Failing in this, the closed regime moves to cut the opposer off, disowning the dissident. The effective control of opposition is essential if the closed regime is to achieve a high degree of continuity and stability.

By contrast, the random regime vigorously opposes control and thereby permits or promotes opposition. In opposing controls, the regime enhances its ability to generate variety. The opposition within random regimes is an expression of individualism and a form of differentiation, but it is not *used* by the regime except as it disables any control attempts.

The open regime is said to *enclose* opposition, embracing it actively and using it as an integral part of its search for creative consensus. Its goal of adaptability is best served by valuing opposition while channeling it toward collective enrichment. Opposition is not valued within the synchronous paradigm, but the basic strategy of the synchronous regime for dealing with opposition is to ignore, deny, avoid, or bury it. In less pure cases, the synchronous regime may deal with opposition more actively, trying to restore consentaneity by direct appeal to thought, insight, or tuition. Where the closed regime is more likely to direct its efforts to deviant behavior and action, to the synchronous regime, nonconformity in thought is most important.

The therapist must keep in mind that the family's response to internal opposition may be quite distinct from its collective response to opposition from the outside or its response to its own members' attempts to oppose outside influences. In general, response to internal opposition, oppositon by family members to defined family action, is more indicative of regime.

DECISION MAKING AND PROBLEM SOLVING

The decision-making and problem-solving styles of the four regimes are sufficiently distinctive to be valuable indicators for evaluation of regime and paradigm. Decision tasks, like those discussed in Chapter 11, usually give a sufficient sample to differentiate different styles. The card-sorting task developed by Reiss and associates (e.g., Reiss, 1981) is a standardized approach that yields quantitative scores usable for identifying a family's regime. Table 6-4 summarized key identifying features of decision making and problem solving in each regime.

### BOUNDARIES

The family's management of its external boundaries and various interfaces with the world vary by paradigm and regime. Although this is more impressionistic than decision-making style, observations about internal and external boundaries can be useful for "differential diagnosis." The most open boundaries are associated with random regimes, the least with closed regimes. Open regime boundaries are also quite open, but are managed more than those of random ones, being more selective about ingress and egress and the flow of information. Internal subsystem boundaries are likely to be the most marked in closed regimes, although disabled closed regimes often violate the expected boundaries with intrusions, enmeshments, or inappropriate alliances. Subsystems are generally less distinguished in open regimes, least of all in random ones.

## BASIC FAMILY EVALUATION PROCESS

A thorough evaluation of a family could potentially have to sort through and condense an enormous quantity or information. Most approaches to family therapy point the therapist in particular directions, highlighting the importance of certain processes and structures. The therapist may be alerted to cross-generational alliances, "triangling," "perverse cycles" of interaction, and so forth. Such formulations are not incompatible with a paradigmatic focus, which adds to them a concern with family images, structures, and style of interaction. In a paradigmatic approach, however, the therapist identifies family paradigms and regimes and seeks to understand the problem and formulations of it in terms of these.

Thus, the task of evaluation is to understand the family at three interrelated but possibly distinct levels: (1) process and behavior, (2) regime, roles, and structures, and (3) paradigm and critical images. The presenting problem, precipitating crisis, and the role of the identified patient are all placed in relation to the family's paradigmatic commitments and the regime by which it realizes or attempts to realize these images. Current functioning and family strengths may also be cast within this context. The analytical concepts of psychopolitics and process dimensions are closely related to the general formulation of family paradigms and regimes. A complete evaluation enables the therapist to understand psychopolitical preferences and structure and to analyze the family in all eight dimensions of physical and informational interaction.

## Referral and Initial Contact

Family evaluation begins even before any family member is seen by the therapist. The referral source and context is now recognized as an important part of the systemic situation confronting the therapist and a source of information about disablement (Selvini-Palazzoli, Cecchin, Prata, & Boscolo, 1980). The first phone contact or exchange of letters gives the therapist additional data about the family, the presenting problem, and member's perceptions of it (Karpel & Strauss, 1983). Even from these early points, the therapist is formulating working hypotheses about the family. While some therapists try to resist this temptation as a form of premature formulation, the practice-of-theory approach of this book and of the systemic therapists (Selvini-Palazzoli, Cecchin, Prata, & Boscolo, 1978) suggests that it is more fruitful for the therapist simply to make these early guesses explicit and testable. A note after a referral and initial phone contact might include the following:

> The Lingens [referring psychologists] are concerned that the son is drifting toward serious depression, possibly suicide. Both they and the father insist that past sexual deviance is irrelevant. Father seemed very rational and controlling over phone. Hypotheses: sexual deviance *is* important aspect of presenting problem; the Lingens are bridge into family but may have vested interest in minimizing sexual problems; father regulates access, controls information, important to form early alliance with him; probably closed regime.

A family entering therapy in serious crisis is, of course, in a different position than one with a relatively minor presenting problem or bringing in some general level of dissatisfaction with their family relationships. Possible life-threatening situations such as anorexia, suicide attempts, or domestic violence represent the most extreme cases. The therapist has an obligation to help the family deal with the crisis as rapidly and efficiently as possible; the luxury of an extensive evaluation is not available. This does not mean that therapy must proceed without any evaluation, but it does require a kind of dual focus of attention that keeps the process relevant to resolution of the crisis.

## History Taking

Therapists vary tremendously in their emphasis on family history and how much they collect from new clients. Some history in relation to the presenting problem probably has to be learned in all cases, and very few therapists would not at least try to understand the precipitating crisis in some larger context. ("What brings you to look for help now? What's different or what happened that brought this about?") History taking has an advantage in giving the therapist and family something concrete to do in the earliest parts of therapy, a routine task that is not intrinsically threatening.

### IMAGE-ORIENTED HISTORY TAKING

The facts of a family's history can sometimes be dry and the gathering of it tedious. I am inclined to exploring "history in context," that is, as it comes up more or less spontaneously in evaluation or therapy or in response to specifically focused probes. This informality risks missing important details but keeps those that do emerge relevant and in context. Most history taking deals primarily in the dimension of content whereas my initial interests are more in meaning, in what is significant to the family. This favors the use of more image-oriented history taking, such as the Life Spaces technique described in Chapter 11, rather than more fact-oriented media such as family history forms and genograms.

The "Life Line" is another technique stressing meaning and affect that can be used to gather a rapid perspective on the highlights of a person's life or a family's history. A line running the length of the room is used to represent the period of time from some point (e.g., "when you first met," "the day you were born") until the present. The one or more persons involved are told that they have a set time to walk the length of the line representing that time period. As they move "through time" they are to mention things that happened at each step, whatever they happen to think of or feel is significant. Others in the family can join at the points they entered the family and contribute what they think of as significant. Usually 5 or 10 minutes to "walk the line" is workable. This framework limits the time commitment and keeps history focused on personal perspective and events that stand out for family members. The spatial metaphor often proves helpful both in "jogging memory" and ordering events. It also helps the therapist's later recall of the relationships among events.

FAMILY GENOGRAMS

Genograms that present the multigenerational history and constituency of families are widely used by family therapists. Although they are basically oriented to facts, concrete relationships, and events, they are easily extended to tap more fully into meaning and affect. ("So, what was he like?" "How did the family take to the divorce?") As a means of getting the "big picture" they have much to offer, especially if they are extended to include "significant others" who may not have legal or blood ties with the family. If ancillary information about the people and their relationships is appended to the genogram itself, it can be an important tool for understanding key features of a family regime.

For example, the Branch family genogram in Figure 13-1 constructed by a school counselor, highlights a pronounced split in roles assigned to males and females. The family seems to be a closed regime disabled in part by an exaggerated and distorted differentiation of roles. Thematic terms are readily apparent in the capsule descriptions. Nearly all the males on both sides of the family were described as dependent or irresponsible in some sense and/or as "cruel and domineering." Only females seemed to be allowed to function effectively. The identified patient, a 9-year-old boy, was referred because of poor performance in school and incidents involving cruelty to animals.

## Current Context: Space and Time

The physical dimensions of space and time are essential aspects of family process. A complete family evaluation should help the therapist understand how the family operates in and manages itself in these dimensions.

At least one home visit as part of a family evaluation is extremely valuable, however, it is not always practical to visit some clients' homes and some therapists are uncomfortable with working outside of the office or with crossing what they consider important boundaries between therapy and family life. Karpel and Strauss (1983) have family members describe their home in considerable detail as part of family evaluation, and I have often had family members take me on an imaginary tour of their house. ("Now, let's see, over here you said was the door to the basement stairs. Why don't you take me downstairs and tell me what I'd see.")

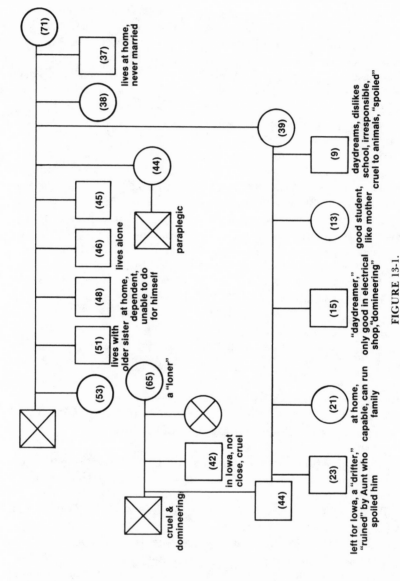

FIGURE 13-1.

Genogram of the Branch family.

lives at home,
never married

paraplegic

lives alone

lives with
older sister   at home,
dependent,
unable to do
for himself

a "loner"

cruel &
domineering

in Iowa, not
close, cruel

daydreams, dislikes
school, irresponsible,
cruel to animals, "spoiled"

good student,
like mother

"daydreamer,"
only good in electrical
shop, "domineering"

at home,
capable, can run
family

left for Iowa, a "drifter,"
"ruined" by Aunt who
spoiled him

A family's management of time is often a strong clue to their basic regime and other aspects of current functioning. I frequently ask families to pantomime or act out their typical interactions at certain key times of the day, notably morning and dinner time. Karpel and Strauss (1983) have the family describe in detail what happens during a typical day, starting with the first person to rise and running through the last to bed. The data can have dramatic implications. Compare, for example, the start of two different families' "typical" days: In one, the mother and father each get up first on alternate days to fix lunches and see their two teenagers off to school. In the other, a 12-year-old rises first to fix breakfast for herself and two younger brothers; the mother dosen't get out of bed until after the father leaves for work.

## Feedback and Contracting

The family map and formulation are the key results of a family evaluation for the therapist. Often the family may get a little out of the evaluation process, especially when the focus has been almost exclusively on evaluation and very little on intervention. In most cases, if it is at all possible and appropriate, I like to give the family some feedback on what I have learned about their family process and the problems they are experiencing; for some therapists such sharing of information is a natural and comfortable part of their therapeutic style. Some approaches and techniques of family therapy, however, may depend on the therapist keeping the formulation from the family. In my own experience it has always been possible to find a meaningful and useful way to express some of the key features of my understanding of the family to them. I try to make this part of the process of contracting for therapy. ("I think we need to contract for another 12 to 15 sessions. Getting the big teeter-totter between Mom and Donna to stop bouncing is going to take some doing. Dad has a lot of catching up to do in learning how to hang in there with Mom.")

## WHOM TO SEE: CHILDREN, PARENTS, AND OUTSIDERS

Naturally most family therapists will want to see the entire family during evaluation, but it may not always be practical to see everyone in the first session and in some cases it may be inappropriate. Whatever the commitment of the therapist to a systems view, when the presenting problem is a marital one, the therapist should consider seeing the married couple first. It is possible that some radically egalitarian random or open regimes might have little difficulty with addressing a marital problem in the presence of the entire family, but even then the therapist would want to consider whether or not to reinforce this aspect of the family's style. In the absence of strong reasons to the contrary based on a clear understanding of a family's regime, the therapist should assume that exploration of a marital problem should initially involve only the couple.

Some presenting problems and referral processes require even the systems-oriented family therapist to start by seeing an individual client alone. Whenever an individual has asked to talk with someone about a "personal problem," the therapist should begin by honoring the request and seeing the client alone initially, even when the family may be strongly implicated (Karpel & Strauss, 1983). Experience with marital therapy has shown that certain key information, such as an extramarital affair, may never surface unless the therapist sees the partners separately at least once (Constantine, 1986).

## Children in Family Evaluation

Although "family therapy" would seem to imply the inclusion of children as integral parts of the family therapy and evaluation processes, many family therapists seem to have ambivalent or conflicted feelings toward children. Karpel and Strauss (1983) even suggest that many therapists are afraid of children. At any rate, if seems true, that a great many family therapists, though they acknowledge the need to include children in family evaluations and therapy, are not sure what to *do* with the children once they are there.

Some family therapists do well with adolescents in family therapy, even with school-aged children, but are at a loss to deal with preschoolers—yet it can be productive to include even very young children in a family evaluation and in family therapy. How family members respond to and deal with the new baby is essential data. I have had children under 2 years old involved in family drawing tasks in ways that yielded important information; whether a family validates or denigrates a child's crude first efforts to express himself/ herself may reveal something of the early experience of the older children.

Family therapists can learn much from the play therapy techniques of child psychologists and psychiatrists. Story telling, puppet plays, and art therapy techniques are all effective ways for engaging children and drawing on their potential contribution to therapy. There is great potential in nonverbal techniques for interactions with very young children. I once conducted a "Boundary Sculpture" (Duhl *et al.*, 1973) with a baby only a year old.

## Significant Others

The principles of general systems theory easily carry the therapist into a more "ecological" framework in which the family is assessed in relation to its extended connections into the community and the world. It is difficult to know whether therapy can or should include some of the "significant others" in peoples lives, from distant but live-in relatives to close friends and lovers. The network approaches (e.g., Speck & Attneave, 1973) may bring in neighbors, other human services professionals, and even tradespeople in some cases. In order to know who might be relevant to understanding the family, one must have some basis for selection, which suggests starting with a smaller unit. Extended family members or significant others may join in therapy without necessarily having to be included in an evaluation.

I expand the evaluation and therapy to include others as the process itself reveals them to be significant. In one case, work with a couple revealed an on-going, openly acknowledged affair between the wife and a neighbor. Other close connections between the two families pointed to the potential gains from their inclusion in therapy. Eventually, the babysitter shared by the two families and the childrens' school principal, both connected by extramarital relations, also became part of the network in therapy. Not all therapists would be equally comfortable including extramarital lovers in marital or family therapy, but this can be a powerfully effective intervention in itself and may be especially appropriate in certain open families where there is an open marriage (Constantine, 1986).

As a rule of thumb, close relatives residing in the same community and anyone, other than an ordinary boarder, living with a family ought to be at least considered for inclusion. As a minimum, the therapist should have some knowledge from the family of the significance of these others and their relation to the family.

## CONSULTING EVALUATIONS

An evaluation at the request of another professional or agency affords some special opportunities. For one thing, this frees the therapist to concentrate on evaluation as a process in itself with less perceived pressure to intervene. Moreover, the need to report the findings to others forces a clarity of focus and an economy of expression about the family structure and dynamics that is probably worth emulating in the work we do for ourselves.


## General Family Evaluation

The Strongs were evaluated for a family service agency after Mrs. Strong, in individual therapy himself, requested help controlling her "hyperactive" son, Pete, age 8. Pete, his sister Rachel (age 10), and their mother were seen three times. An evaluation of three to four sessions usually seems to be about right for these purposes, but this may be a habit stemming from family therapy training, rather than a rational distillation of experience. In outline, these sessions were fairly typical of an initial evaluation.

### FIRST SESSION

The first session generally focuses on the current dimensions of presenting problems, moving toward a systemic focus. The therapist is interested in the general nature of the disablement and how it is sustained, the family's basic regime and paradigm, and their main assets and weaknesses as a family.

With the Strongs, an open-ended discussion about "why the family was there" quickly focused on discipline as the presenting problem. A request for what this meant in concrete terms led them into talking about their mornings, apparently times of high stress for the children as well as Mrs. Strong. Picking up on the family's themes, the therapists asked them to role play a typical morning, which they did, although all three often functioned more as "directors" than "actors." In the role play, Mrs. Strong kept hurrying the children, while making repeated demands on them to do things in one particular way. For example, she would tell Rachel that she was too slow and needed to hurry, then insist that she change her blouse so that it would match her skirt to make her look "decent." Rachel was inclined to be more passively aggressive, while Pete would struggle more openly against his mother's attempts at control. He would reject outright her choices of clothes for him and find repeated excuses to go into her bedroom. "Misbehavior" was greeted with threats of punishment if it didn't stop or with promises of gifts if it did.

The therapists then introduced a preplanned drawing task. The three separately drew pictures or how they saw their family. Mrs. Strong's was meticulously drawn; Pete said it looked like they were posing for a family portrait. His own drawing included a pile of boxes, presents from Fred, his mother's boyfriend, as he explained. Both his and Rachel's drawings included Fred, placing him with Mrs. Strong, but separated from them. The therapists, taking a cue from the family's attention to "the right and proper way," validated each drawing as "right" for the person doing it and focused attention on the differences among them.

At one of many points when Pete was energetically distracting, one of the therapists held out his hands, inviting Pete over. Pete responded with panic, "Oh, no! You're not going to hug me!" There had been no evidence of affection or validation within the family, only an abundance of criticism communicated with energy but emotional detachedness. The therapists considered Pete's apparent fear of being hugged as key.

SECOND SESSION

The next session shifted from a predominantly "present time" focus to an exploration of the roots of the current systemic disablement. The mother was led through an experience to recall salient aspects of several crucial periods in her life: growing up, single adulthood, as a couple with her first husband, as a young family with children, as a single parent before Fred came along, and after his arrival. The Life Spaces technique, described in Chapter 11, permitted a very efficient history-taking that remained focused on issues relevant to the current situation and engaged the attention of the children thoroughly.

Mrs. Strong's family of origin had rigidly defined what was right and proper, using a stick to enforce parental standards and demands energetically. Her father had little to do with the family, which, despite its high energy, tended to be emotionally cool. Mrs. Strong turned to a substantially older boyfriend for her emotional needs, eventually exchanging him for an even older man, her first husband. She married primarily because she was pregnant with Rachel, whose arrival increased her responsibilities but helped satisfy her contact needs. As the baby's needs declined, she planned the second pregnancy. From the beginning, her husband was relatively uninvolved.

THIRD SESSION

Even when the mandate is primarily to evaluate rather than intervene, it is generally appropriate to provide some feedback to the family. This process in itself usually yields further data.

By this point the essential dynamics were fairly clear and it was possible to construct a simple map of the Strong family (Figure 13-2). "The Belt" that Mrs. Strong used to discipline the children was included in this map as it had figured so prominently in discussions that it was almost like a member of the family. In effect, it was an icon for the absent father, indeed for all the men in her life.

The Strongs were clearly guided by a closed paradigm reflected in a closed regime. Their particular rigid enmeshment was characterized by high energy demands and constricted affect. The dominant affect appeared to be anger, but this was denied and rarely expressed openly. Instead, The Belt seemed to function as a symbolic repository for anger. What little affection was expressed was communicated through commodities, through gifts that were almost always tied to "good behavior." ("Fred is very affectionate with the kids. He gives them presents, like when Pete keeps his promise to do something for him.") In general, objects mediated emotions, just as they did in Mrs. Strong's original family. Physical punishment not only served to convey and enforce values, but, almost perversely, The Belt had become a symbolic substitute for affection. The children believed that both their mother and especially Fred enjoyed spanking them. Pete's nightly forays into Rachel's bed usually resulted in a spanking.

Energy was one of the family themes: Pete's "hyperactivity," Rachel's sleeplessness, their mother's complaints of not having enough energy to meet all her responsibilities. She had been driving herself to assume responsibility since she was a young teenager. The family was driven like a dynamo. In the morning, she would be tired from the day before and would stay in bed until it was too late to get everything ready except by "whipping" everyone into a frenzy. The

FIGURE 13-2.
Map of the Strong family.

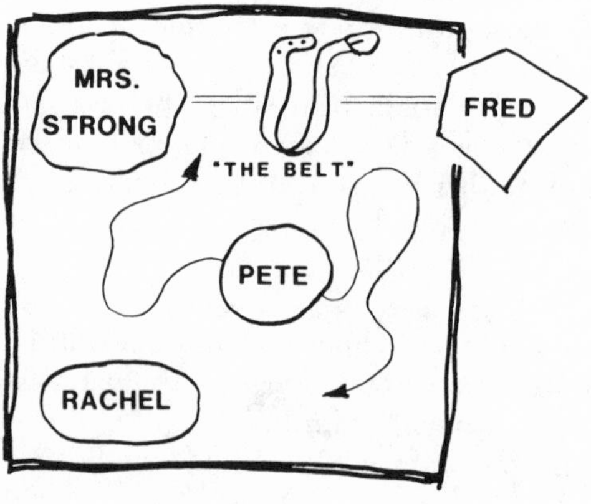

children's "uncooperativeness" justified her intrusive management and simplistic discipline, which reinforced their opposition.

The most obvious aspect of the family's operation in the dimension of meaning was Mrs. Strong's intense and pervasive attempt to regulate her children's values in even the smallest detail of dress and wording. This regulation was almost entirely negative and was returned in kind by the children who were every bit as critical and invalidating. Only one right way to see things and do things was possible. (At one point, Mrs. Strong agreed that Rachel and Pete might legitimately see things differently, but later revealed that to her this meant, "The children have different perceptions because they are children and are subjective rather than adult and objective like me.")

Power, like affect, seemed to be focused in The Belt, the ultimate expression of Mrs. Strong's attempted power. Both Rachel and Pete were locked in a struggle for control with her. Rachel's silent withdrawal appeared to be one form of opposition that her mother could not punish with The Belt; Pete's "hyperactivity" served a similar function, although he was more open in his opposition, hence more at risk. In a way that would not become clear until the third session, Pete, too, derived power from The Belt.

Feedback in metaphorical form has many advantages, particularly in closed families where it gets around normal censorship of communication without violating it. The family is free to discuss or deal with the metaphor as they are able, or to ignore it verbally and consciously altogether. Even where a metaphor is apparently ignored, however, it often seems to have some indirect and enabling impact on the family's images of itself, hence I have long made use of metaphor wherever possible.

The Strongs were therefore asked to bring in The Belt, which was given a chair of its own in the session. This triggered a highly charged exchange. Mrs. Strong expressed guilt over using The Belt and helplessness over not knowing any other way to discipline. Rachel and Pete admitted to using her guilt to try to counter her efforts at control. All three expressed a similar mixture of fear and anger concerning The Belt. They agreed on wanting to find a better way.

Based on their theory that The Belt and corporal discipline were functioning as substitutes for touch and affectionate contact in the family, the therapists had the Strongs act out a sequence they had earlier described as leading to a strapping. This time, however, Mrs. Strong had been given separate instructions to hug Rachel at the critical moment instead. Rachel started to cry and admitted that she really wanted to do what her mother was asking anyway. Mrs. Strong reported she suddenly felt calm for the first time in many months. The crucial role of The Belt was confirmed even more dramatically when Pete later squirmed out of his mother's embrace and implored her to use The Belt instead.

A brief family sculpture was used by the therapists to give more direct feedback to the family, inverting the more common use of sculpture as an exploratory technique. The therapists arranged the family in a circle, arms stiffly at the sides as in Mrs. Strong's "family portrait," not touching except for intermittent swats at each other accompanied by the repeated litany, "You're wrong."

Recommendations for long-term treatment with this family included two primary emphases derived from the evaluation. Structurally, the family needed to become less enmeshed in general but more able to communicate directly rather than through objects, especially to express affection and mutual validation. The object was to help the family to form an effective closed regime, however, not to get it to become open. To some degree the regime could be influenced directly, but its disablement was deeply rooted in critical images that Mrs. Strong was in the process of reifying once again in her relationship with Fred. He, like her father, first steady boyfriend, and husband, was another rigidly authoritarian older man who could offer little warmth but who, despite his marginal position, somehow seemed to promise her relief from the demands of her life. The still operative, ineffective patterns from her early life and the dynamics of the forming couple would be important to consider in intervening in the relationship with her children. Thus a transgenerational focus dealing with critical images and repeated patterns needed to be employed in addition to the more direct work to disengage the family and improve communication.

## Focused and Special-Purpose Family Evaluation

Consultative evaluation does not always go as smoothly as the preceding example suggests. The relationship of clients to the referral source can be a critical part of the system dynamics. It is always necessary to be flexible and adapt to client style and emergent aspects of the situation, but in the following case this need is especially highlighted.

Family evaluations conducted for another therapist or an outside agency always pose problems of translation. The needs and interests of nontherapists are often different from those of therapists, and therapists who do not have a family systems orientation may not have the same concerns as do family therapists. When there are specific questions to be answered, the entire evaluation process may have to be "customized" to address those questions in a manner that will prove ultimately useful to the user of the results. One example of such a situation is when the family therapist is called on to provide input in a child custody decision.

The more exceptional situation following illustrates not only the problems of devising a suitable evaluation sequence for answering specific questions, but the problems of interfacing with an agency unfamiliar with family systems concepts and accustomed to thinking only in terms of traditional views of the individual.

> Adam and Elaine Stevens were a recently married couple in their late 20s. They had met and married while he was on parole from a sentence for aggravated assault. As the result of an incident involving physical assault on a teenage boy known to be a homosexual prostitute, Adam was remanded to a mental health facility for evaluation to determine whether he was "sexually dangerous." He had been found to be innocent of the assault but in technical violation of the terms of his parole on earlier charges. Adam had a long history of getting into fights and brawls and had admitted to being sexually attracted to the teenager involved in the latest incident. The authorities began to be concerned about sexual violence acted out toward adolescents.
>
> The mental health agency decided that it would be important to understand the nature of the Stevens's marriage and the extent to which it might contribute to or detract from Adam's emotional stability and continued progress in individual treatment. An evaluation of the couple system was undertaken toward the specific end of providing further data on his potential sexual dangerousness and emotional stability. Two family therapists were given a week in which to complete an evaluation for that purpose.

The family therapists, faculty members of a training facility connected with the community mental health center, were able to plan and schedule three 1½-hour sessions. Because of time limitations they elected not to delve into early history, which were already detailed in the case record, but to focus on the current dynamics of the relationship. Sensing that there could be a problem of credibility of their findings, they chose to limit themselves to fairly simple evaluation procedures with substantial face validity. They set for themselves a set of target questions they wished to have answered and specific criteria by which they would judge the health (enablement) of the couple system. They felt it was a key part of their responsibility to communicate their findings effectively to colleagues who were oriented to individual therapy and had been traditionally trained.

The assessment criteria chosen by the therapists were (1) functional health: the extent to which the relationship met important needs of both partners and to which their role needs and styles were compatible; (2) flexibility: the capacity of the relationship to adapt to and survive stress and crisis and the ability of the partners to perceive and alter the patterns in their interactions if need be; (3) differentiation: their ability to establish and maintain clear interpersonal boundaries, without enmeshment or disengagement; (4) long-term stability.

In keeping with the practice of the training facility, the sessions were videotaped for review and as documentation.

> The presence of the camera and operator was upsetting to the couple, who showed considerable anxiety before ultimately stating their concerns. Without first talking to his attorney, they refused to be interviewed. Each was willing to attribute to the other the basis for refusing. The cameraman was then dismissed and the therapists continued to talk with the couple. They were aware of the pressure and the possible benefits of being seen as a couple, but were weary from the long ordeal of their crisis. Eventually they acquiesced and the therapists started to introduce the Life Spaces technique. The same pattern of refusal repeated. Not until the subject was changed did Mrs. Stevens volunteer to go first. When she finished, Mr. Stevens began without prompting.

In planning for the second interview, the therapists decided to accommodate themselves to the couple's verbal style and reduce their anxiety by sticking to a verbal format in a semistructured interview focused on certain themes, among them positive and negative experiences living together, areas of differences between them, and their sexual relationship. The latter was considered to be essential to assessing the soundness of their relationship and its relationship to his previous and possible future sexual misconduct.

The therapists felt that by the third interview the therapeutic alliance could stand up to the introduction of another structured approach, but chose the revealed-differences technique for its essentially verbal nature. Each was asked independently to complete a list of what they saw to be their own assets and liabilities and those of their partner. These lists were then discussed and compared item by item.

With their systemic view, the family therapists were more aware of certain paradoxes in the structure of the treatment and confinement situation than were others involved with the case. Several clinicians commented in committee meetings on Mr. Stevens's "inappropriately flat affect." The couple interviews revealed that he was aware of being a "model patient" who was being described as having "blunted affect." He was aware of the paradoxical bind, knowing that he was being watched carefully for signs of dangerousness. He felt the need, consequently, to modulate emotional expression, especially anger, carefully. There were independent reasons to believe that in some cases, had he expressed more anger on the ward, this would have been taken as evidencing "dangerous lack of impulse control." Most ironic was the fact that his original commitment was related to homosexual activity with a minor, yet the system forbade him conjugal visits with his wife, the one "appropriate" sexual relationship he had been able to sustain in his life.

The therapists realized that effective intervention with the couple was predicated on their evaluation becoming an effective intervention with the mental health center. They argued that the marriage needed to be recognized and supported by the system, not undermined. Responding to concerns of "the system" for treatment and of the couple for opportunities to demonstrate their responsibility and commitment, the therapists suggested that the couple be made responsible for entering on-going marital therapy, preferably with a male–female cotherapy team. They also argued that concerns with community safety were better served if provision were made for voluntary, time-limited recommitment in the future, as Adam was loathe to make a "voluntary" return to a state system that seemed bent on indefinite commitment.

## OUTCOME ASSESSMENT

Ideally, family therapy probably always includes a reassessment of the family before termination, yet in most practices this is an implicit and intuitive process if it occurs at all. An assessment at termination need not be as formal, systematic, or thorough as an initial evaluation, but it should at least be explicit.

Many of the evaluation techniques introduced here and in Chapter 11 can be used for outcome assessment, though some lend themselves better to repeated use than others. Obviously, family histories and genograms would not be taken again. Usually the same role play or decision task would not be repeated. On the other hand, family sculptures can be repeated any number of times to assess progress over the course of therapy. They reveal dramatically how members relationships and perceptions shift and can give termination a particularly graphic and memorable punctuation.

Repeating the same measure or evaluation technique is most useful because it makes comparison between "then" and "now" so easy. This may in itself account for the reluctance of some therapists to use repeated measures. Even if the therapist does not actually conduct any additional formal evaluation of outcome, redrawing the family map can be very useful, both as a final addendum to the case files and for comparison with the initial map developed by the therapist.

CHAPTER

# 14

# PRACTICE AND PARADIGM
## Principles of Paradigmatic
## Family Therapy

Having established the theoretical and pragmatic bases, it is now
possible to present a complete overview of a paradigmatic approach to
family therapy and the broad principles by which this framework can
be applied in practice. The basic assumptions that distinguish the
paradigmatic framework were introduced in Chapter 3 and are briefly
restated here:

1. Families differ from each other in the regimes by which they
   are organized and in the paradigms by which they define the
   family and through which they view the world. Many different
   regimes and paradigms can lead to successful family living.
2. Family paradigms function as points of reference for regimes
   through which overarching images are translated into family
   process.
3. Family regimes and paradigms vary widely, but within this
   variability can be identified distinct primary forms.
4. Families that are guided by different paradigms and organized
   by differing regimes will tend to have different strengths and
   weaknesses as families and to have different probable directions
   of failure.

On these four concepts, a paradigmatic approach to family therapy can be based. Family system evaluation emerges as a vehicle for
effective family therapy. A thorough evaluation includes identification
of a family's paradigm, regime, and patterns in process, plus the
interrelationships among these. It includes an understanding of the
family's problems as well as the relationship between manifest prob-

lems and the family's regime and paradigm; thus strengths and assets are identified in addition to disabled aspects of the family.

An idiographic theory specific to each unique family is developed from the family evaluation. This one-of-a-kind theory reflects the particular paradigmatic images by which a family is guided and the specific regime by which its processes are regulated; it is made explicit as an overall map of the family. Treatment is systematically guided by the map of the family, as revised and updated through the therapist's growing understanding. Intervention tactics and strategy are derived from this map based on explicit predictions of outcome. Thus theory is used interactively as a vital component of the therapy process, guiding therapy but also being guided by it, as the map is revised through feedback from its application in therapy.

The assessment of outcome in family therapy must reflect each family's goals for itself as a family, as well as the therapist's perspectives, and must always take into account what is reasonable and appropriate in terms of the family's own paradigm and regime. Therapists have an obligation to remain aware of their own personal family paradigms and the paradigmatic basis of the theories and techniques they employ and to distinguish their own paradigmatic preferences from those of the families with whom they work.

## STRATEGIC PRINCIPLES AND ISSUES

As the next chapters will detail, therapy with families of different paradigms and distinct basic organizations proceeds quite differently. Each paradigm and regime presents its own special problems and pitfalls as well as unique opportunities. However, the framework for understanding disablement developed in Chapter 10 made it clear that broad, general principles of intervention can apply across all paradigms and regimes, though, of course, these must always be sensitive to differences among individual families.

### Borrowed Strategies

One of the most basic principles of the paradigmatic approach was introduced by Kantor and Lehr (1975). In discussing disablement in each regime they noted that, to bypass or overcome an impasse, families needed to "borrow" strategies from another paradigm. The most probable mode of failure for each regime is an exaggeration of its own paradigmatic commitments; to become less stereotyped, less tied up by its own guiding images, the family needs to reach outside the confines of its usual strategies. This does not mean a change of paradigms or an abandonment of basic values. The family is helped to "borrow" strategies from another regime, enhancing its basic flexibility without denying its paradigmatic commitment.

Consider, for example, a random family chaotically disengaged, unable to resolve the crisis of a school-phobic child because everyone is too busy going off in every direction to hear the cry for help and too committed to radical independence even to consider her failure to attend school as possibly being a problem. They may need to borrow a strategy from either the closed or open paradigm to avoid escalating the situation into a more severe crisis. One person might be helped to take charge and act the part of a firm but caring parent with the child, listening to her fears and confidently supervising her going to school. This would represent one way an enabled closed regime might deal with the problem. Or the therapist might amplify the child's symptomatic statement to be dramatic enough to get all the members to sit down together and respond to the situation, drawing on an open regime strategy.

The above exemplifies a general principle for borrowing strategies from other regimes. As a rule, it is easier and more productive to borrow strategies from adjacent regimes than from the opposite regime. This general rule of thumb applies because each regime has an innate tendency to become either enmeshed (overcoupled) or disengaged (undercoupled), and because adjacent regimes have *opposite* intrinsic coupling. For example, the random regime that is ignoring the school-phobic girl is unlikely to start responding to her through a synchronous strategy of "noncommunication." They already tend to act separately and independently but lack the ability to "think in parallel" that would be necessary to implement a strategy for synchronously responding to her need. They are more likely to resist borrowing from the closed paradigm, which as a random family they actively reject, than from the open paradigm, although it is always possible to reframe a strategy within a given paradigm to make it more palatable. The therapist might look to a member who is a likely candidate for the highly involved parent and encourage him/her to act on instinct, independent of the others.

Reframing and communicating in a language that is compatible with a family's paradigm gives the therapist added leverage and increases the likelihood that a new strategy will be implemented. Thus, in a closed family with a dominating, overcontrolling mother who is invasive with her 12-year-old son, the temptation might be to get her to back off and give freer rein to a son who is entering adolescence, in short, to be more permissive. However, expressed directly, this will almost certainly be rejected. ("The problem is he's too lazy and shift-less already. I don't believe in this permissive stuff.") On the other hand, the therapist could sympathize with her being overburdened and agree with her concern that her son learn to be more responsible. ("You work so hard to teach him, but parenting is a tough job. Hard as it is on both of you, I think he needs *more* responsibility, and you have to teach him.") Disengaging the two becomes reframed as a form of engagement. ("He leans on you, takes advantages of you, and depends on *you* to check up on him all the time. You have to put more on him; be firm. Refuse to check to see if his laundry is done. Don't let him trick you into looking over his room—you'll only feel guilty and end up cleaning it yourself.")

## Axes of Intervention

Borrowing strategies from adjacent regimes usually influences the degree of coupling between members, having the effect of moving a family on the enmeshment–disengagement axis in a direction opposite to their paradigmatic tendency toward exaggeration. In the broadest strategic terms, coupling or engagement–disengagement is one of the basic structural variables through which the therapist can work. There are a number of such axes on which family paradigms and regimes are distinguished; these comprise the directions in which family move-ment may be generated. To make use of these "axes of intervention," the therapist must know the family's paradigm and its current regime and determine the direction of "error," whether it is overcoupled or undercoupled for its regime, for example. This is not enough to formulate a unique prescription for a family, but it does point out a therapeutic direction.

Table 14-1 identifies some basic axes of intervention for conduct-ing family therapy within a paradigmatic framework. These axes are dimensions on which different paradigms/regimes may be distin-guished. Although there are many such dimensions, the ones in the table lend themselves to designing interventions, choosing techniques, or planning homework in order to nudge a family in a particular direction. Interventions that promote movement along these therapeu-tic axes essentially accomplish the same thing as borrowing strategies from other regimes. Successfully importing the strategies of other regimes can also effectively move a family along some one or more of these axes.

**TABLE 14-1.**
Principal Axes of Intervention

| Axis | Direction of probable disablement | | | | Examples of intervention strategies | |
|---|---|---|---|---|---|---|
| | Closed | Random | Open | Synchronous | (To Increase) | (To Decrease) |
| Coupling (enmeshment–disengagement) | + | − | + | − | Joint activities; family discussions or meetings | Separate interests; limits on topics or time spent together |
| Expressiveness (meaning and affect) | − | + | ++ | −− | Practice communicating feelings; bypassing "taboos" | Practice calm, rational discussion; ignore or counter emotionality |
| Differentiation (individuation–identification) | − | ++ | + | −− | Promote open disagreement; underscore differences | Explore and highlight similarities; promote agreement |
| Formal structure (explicit rules and roles) | ++ | −− | + | − | Impose new rules; establish set roles and procedures | Suspend or bypass rules; divide or interchange roles |
| Hierarchy (vertical–horizontal) | ++ | −− | − | +? | Establish/support leadership; promote loyalty, dependence | Share or distribute leadership; promote equality, independence |

COUPLING: ENGAGING AND DISENGAGING

The dimension of coupling (engagement–disengagement) can be thought of as the principal axis for intervention, in part because overcoupling or undercoupling is so frequently essential for sustaining disabled processes. As closed and open regimes will tend to err in the direction of enmeshment, they have more to gain from importing random and synchronous strategies because these are inherently less coupled, less engaged. Similarly, importing either open or closed strategies into a random or synchronous regime will have the effect of increasing coupling, promoting engagement.

There are many ways in which the therapist can influence the degree of coupling in a family. Coupling can be increased by involving the family activities together, by increasing the salience of messages communicated, or by overcoming taboos or rules constricting communication, for example. Coupling might be decreased by seeing family members or subsystems separately, by getting them involved in separate outside activities, or by getting them to place strictures or limitations on communication. Such manipulations have a predictable effect on a family—moving in a direction opposite to its paradigmatic tendency, tends to counter disablement.

Families who are enmeshed or disengaged in a direction *opposite* to their paradigmatic tendencies, are not often encountered in practice. Both undercoupled open and closed families are occasionally seen. These usually present with a surface resemblance to random or synchronous regimes. History seems to be crucial in these families, as often an event or sustained crisis earlier in the family's history will be found that accounts for their disengagement. Something too "hot," dangerous, or painful can lead an open family to abandon its open communication or a closed family to give up its reliance on tradition and authority; thus, knowing the family paradigm alone is not always enough to indicate a strategic direction for therapy.

EXPRESSIVENESS–INEXPRESSIVENESS

The axis of expressiveness may be thought of as related to coupling but is also useful to consider in its own right. A family may be very invasive or intrusive (enmeshed) yet not very expressive, not disclosing their true feelings or talking about important issues. The therapy session is often a context in which family members can be led to higher levels of expressiveness. ("I want you to act out your feelings of anger in an exaggerated way." "What's some feeling that you have that you almost never express to your wife.") Excessive or untempered emotional expression between a couple can be effectively countered by calmly ignoring it while attending to and dealing with communications delivered more temperately.

In another example, the mother in a very random family would emotionally recount the graphic details of her own mother's numerous and ghastly suicide attempts. When her youngest children giggled and the middle children yawned, she would remind them, "This is serious." The laughter indicated the children's discomfort with the violence and gore, and the boredom revealed their desensitization to an oft-repeated tale. The therapist said the subject was too much for the kids and sent the younger ones from the room for the rest of the session. This very directive intervention at once validated the matter as serious but reduced the emotional involvement of the children in the mother's unresolved issues.

### DIFFERENTIATION: INDIVIDUATION-IDENTIFICATION

Differentiation of members from each other is another principal axis of intervention. Techniques for increasing differentiation can be as simple as just "underscoring" or "highlighting" every spontaneous example of differences among family members' feelings, ideas, or viewpoints (e.g., by the therapist repeating, commenting on, or playing up such differences). Conversely, the focus might be on similarities and points of agreement. More structurally, members can be helped to differentiate by steering them toward different interests or by encouraging disagreements. Of the four regimes, random regimes are likely to represent the highest levels of differentiation and synchronous ones the lowest.

### STRUCTURES: FORMALITY-INFORMALITY

Random and synchronous regimes usually exhibit the least amount of formal or explicit structures as represented by stated rules, procedures, and set roles or relationships. Introducing formality and "official" roles or responsibilities into such systems tends to move them in a direction opposite to their paradigmatic tendencies. Closed families usually exhibit the most formal structure, hence reducing it by undermining, suspending, or softening the rules or by blurring or modifying the roles will move it away from its paradigmatic tendency toward excess structure.

It is possible to frame such moves in ways more or less compatible with a family's regime. For example, structure might be introduced into a random regime by having members draw household duty assignments for each day out of a hat. A closed family might agree to "suspend the rules about curfew temporarily while we try to work out some rules that can be made to stick," especially if the therapist asks the recognized family leader for permission.

HIERARCHY: VERTICAL-HORIZONTAL

The hierarchical aspects of a regime are a special case of family structures. The therapist moves a closed family in a direction away from its paradigmatic tendencies of exaggeration by "leveling" operations so as to distribute power or status more evenly. ("Dad, I know she is only fifteen, but I want you to put Pinky, or should I say, Virginia, in charge of the weekend trip.") An open family caught in an excessive and insensitive egalitarianism might be induced to incorporate hierarchy by having them rotate the leadership of family meetings, having each family member rank order the others on leadership ability, then posting the combined rankings, thereby identifying a clear "leader among leaders."


## Progress and Paradigm: Termination Criteria

As paradigms define the special concerns and goals of families, attention to paradigm leads to taking these into account in assessing progress and outcome in therapy. Therapists sensitive to paradigmatic issues consider not only assessment from their own more general, global perspective, but also from the perspective of the family's own goals. Neither can take absolute precedence over the other, as the therapist is in a special position of knowledge as Bystander to the family process, but the family is in a better position to know and define its goals as a family.

One of the problems with broad, universal criteria for family health, such as those discussed by Curran (1983), is that these do not take into account paradigmatic differences. While it may be hard to quarrel with such bromides as "good communication" and "sharing time," even these are subject to great variability across paradigms. Communication may be the *sine qua non* of open regimes, but it is practically the *bête noire* of synchronous ones. An unsophisticated or indiscriminant emphasis on it could even enhance family enmeshment in a disabled closed regime. Moreover, substantial shared time as a whole family cannot be expected of even a well-functioning random regime.

Thus the goals of therapy and the criteria for progress and outcome need to be tailored to each particular family, not only to its presenting problems, but to its paradigm and regime. In a family with a strong commitment to a random paradigm, it is unrealistic to try to get the parents to take clear and consistent charge of the children or to expect to get everyone to invest substantial time in collective problem solving. These goals, even if desirable and appropriate in some situations, must be balanced against the counterpull of the family's random paradigm. At best one can hope for some small progress in that direction.

This is no less true when a family comes in with stated goals running against their own paradigm and the established regime. For example, a strongly synchronous family, with an extraordinarily consistent commitment to agreement and being alike, entered family therapy with the stated desire of "learning to communicate better" and, as the parents put it, "for the kids to share more openly with us." As the family was very disengaged and quite deadened, this defined an appropriate direction for them to move. Authentic communication was very difficult for them, however, as what they really sought was confirmation and reinforcement of consentaneity, rather than communication to explore or understand differences. As long as what was shared confirmed consentaneity, it was accepted, otherwise, nobody wanted to hear it. The therapists' goals for this family in terms of the extent and depth of communication were necessarily more modest than they would be for a family with a genuine commitment to an open paradigm.

## FROM MAP TO INTERVENTION

The family map, as developed from family evaluation, is the embodiment of a therapist's idiographic theory of a particular family. As such, it plays a central role in a paradigmatic approach to family therapy. Having formulated the theory, the therapist does not merely stick it in a file drawer for reference when someday writing a book, but uses it actively in therapy. It is tested, used to generate interventions, periodically revised, and used to assess progress.

### The Therapeutic Experiment

The purpose of the therapeutic experiment is to test some critical portion of an idiographic theory of a particular family. It is usually a small-scale intervention which is planned on the basis of a family map from which clear-cut predictions can be made. It is, of course, not a "scientific" experiment, but a therapeutic one, meaning it can never be carefully controlled or completely unambiguous. This also means that the experiment as therapy and its impact on the family are at least as important as the confirmation or disconfirmationn of the therapist's theories.

> The Kaisers were referred for therapy by a physician who had been asked to treat 8-year-old Markie for "hyperactivity." In the office, Dick (age 38), Dency (age 34), and their daughter Cynthia sat in a perfect triangle with their chairs as far apart as the room allowed. Cynthia was a quiet teenager who said she was "14½." Diana (age 5) sat restlessly with Markie on the couch. As soon as therapy began, she and Markie moved to the center of the room and started to tussle.
>
> Markie was referred to as "the trouble," but the family did not resist shifting the focus elsewhere. Dency, studying her hands with a look of depression, announced that "life is empty" for her and that there was "nothing, really" between her and Dick. He seemed to agree by his silence. She described him as "logical, always logical," in a tone that made this a deep fault. He was, throughout, cool and detached, occasionally punctuating his statements with a short, nervous laugh. Cynthia, answering questions in an almost inaudible voice, said she, too, felt empty. Diana and Markie seemed to have most of the energy, but even Markie appeared to draw his from the sparks Diana triggered off.

After the first session, the therapist drew up the map in Figure 14-1. In retrospect, the evidence suggests that his was a disabled synchronous family: except for the youngest members, they were well into rigid disengagement. But the synchronous family had not been conceptualized at the time. The therapist's theory of the family was that Diana was the only effective Mover and that she was supplying most of the energy and "life" of the family—even Markie was mostly a conduit for her verve. Her 5-year-old zest could not yet be swamped or lost in the family's deadness. On the the other hand, she seemed stuck in a position that would eventually drain her.

Consistent with the developmental psychopolitics model introduced in Chapter 9, an experiment was planned for the next session. The therapist drew Diana aside and asked her to just watch with him. The rest of the family was told to continue with what they were talking about, which had concerned the behavior of the youngest children. To engage her in Bystanding, the therapist told her they were going to play a game; they were going to try to figure out what was happening in her family and why. The two of them withdrew to one side of the room where they whispered quietly about what they saw.

There was not much to watch. For an excruciatingly long 3½ minutes, the rest of the family, "hyperactive" Markie included, sat in utterly rigid silence. This is a highly unusual outcome, as few families can sustain silence for even a fraction of that time when they know

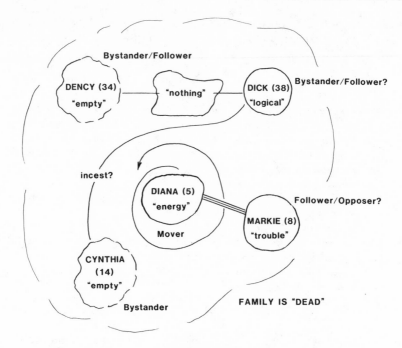

**FIGURE 14-1.**
Map of the Kaiser family drawn after first session.

they are "supposed" to be talking. At long last Dick spoke. Looking around at the others, he said, "Well, what do you think we should say?"

The basic assumptions of the map were dramatically confirmed in this spatial metaphor. Diana was the only member of the family who could Move effectively, and she was virtually the sole source of energy and life in the family. When she was taken out of the center, it died. In the interaction that followed, psychopolitical preferences became clarified, showing Dick to be another Bystander/Follower and Markie to be a Follower/Opposer by preference.

It was concluded that the burden placed on Diana was too much for someone her age and that some "action" between the parents needed to be stirred up, bringing them into the center. This strategy could not be carried very far by the therapist, however, because after a few sessions Dency acted out the family's image by attempting suicide. The attempt was entirely consistent with the family's disengagement and with the pervasive sense of nothingness, as it was carried out in a drunken stupor while the kids were playing and studying quietly in other parts of the house. At that point Dency seemed to feel more connected with the therapist, whom she called just before slashing her wrists, than with her family. The attempt failed, but it did bring the focus in a dramatic way onto the couple and their relationship, leading to some good work in therapy.

It is not unusual for Bystanders to translate family images into metaphors in action, so the therapist should have been alert to this possibility. In this family, however, there were three possible candidates, although hindsight suggests Dency to be the most likely to attempt suicide at that time.

### Deriving Intervention Tactics from Family Maps

Any "therapeutic experiment" is also an intervention. In the example above, the family was strongly affected by the temporary peripheralizing of their daughter; at the same time, she began to learn a new game, "waiting and watching." However, during most of any therapeutic process, the focus is primarily on intervention and only secondarily on "experimentation." Each intervention derived from an explicit family map nevertheless affords an opportunity to test and revise the map. This is a major reason for making predictions of outcome explicit and defining them in terms that can be interpreted both concretely and theoretically.

The Waylands were a closed family with synchronous overtones. They were sullenly enmeshed, lost, confused, and ineffective. They talked a great deal but were generally bewildered and wildly inaccurate in their perceptions of each other. They claimed and expected complete agreement but had little understanding of each other or what was happening to them. Their manner of communicating almost always seemed to result in confusion, ambiguity, and distortion. The map in Figure 14-2 portrays Mrs. Wayland in the position of "switchboard operator." All communication with outside agencies was carried out by her. Family members seldom talked with each other directly; most messages went through her. Even in family meetings, she would "interpret" what one person said to another. The most striking aspect of her fulfillment of this function was that she invariably garbled the message, delivering a confused, contradictory translation, effectively blocking any real understanding.

While this behavior clearly served a function in the family, it also appeared to be a pervasive aspect of Mrs. Wayland's functioning in the world in general. Blocking her from "facilitating" communication and interpreting for others had an almost immediate effect on the

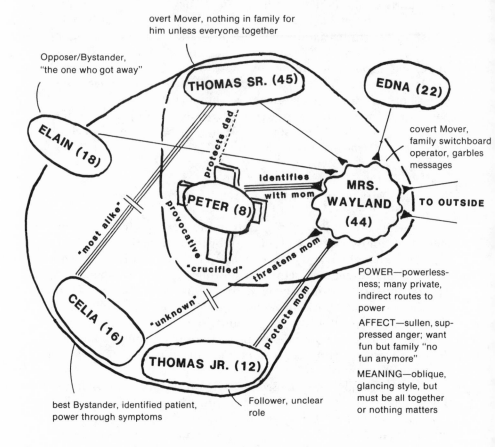

**FIGURE 14-2.**
Therapist's map of the Wayland family.

clarity of communication in the family. The main purpose of this move was not to test the map, but the outcome did confirm the therapists' view of the family. The long-term strategy suggested by the map was to strengthen and capitalize on the family's ability to interact without her so that it became less dependent on her as intermediary, although her own style of communicating did not vary.

### Basing Strategy on Family Maps

As seen above, long-term treatment strategy may also be derived from family maps by focusing attention on more global features of the map and objectives of and for the family as represented in the map.

The Turans were referred for therapy on behalf of their son Jerry (age 19) who had dropped out of college and was "doing nothing." They were referred by a team of prominent psychologists who knew the family personally and concurred with the family's assessment that Jerry was in serious emotional difficulties. The referral was made to the family therapists in part because of their reputation for tolerance and ability to deal with "deviant" sexual lifestyles. The Turans were a family that had been involved in incestuous "sex education" with their children. Although the incest had stopped, Bo Turan and his second wife, Gertie, were active "swingers" who engaged in sexual mate-swapping.

From the beginning, the therapists wanted to deal with the complete family. The first session included Bo and Gertie, Bo's ex-wife Kitty, and their four children, Dave (age 25), Dana (age 22), Tammy (age 16), and Jerry. The family turned out to be extremely enmeshed and highly conflicted, but Jerry's difficulties over direction in life were quickly revealed as a distraction from the family's more serious and more pervasive difficulties. Bo and Jerry were locked in a struggle in which the harder and more "logically" Bo pushed Jerry into "doing something with his life," the more irrational and passively resistant Jerry became. It quickly became clear that, under Bo's persistent dominance, therapy could not easily be shifted from this focus.

Bo, who tended to dominate the entire family network, was still locked in a struggle with his ex-wife. Besides the conflicts with Jerry and Kitty, intensely negative relationships between Bo and Jerry's girlfriend, Eve, and with Margaret, married to his son Dave, also became apparent, though these latter people were not in the first session. In contrast with Jerry, Dave was a driving young businessman with his own store, the son who could do no wrong. He had been born with a relatively minor congenital deformity but had been always pushed by Bo "so that he doesn't see himself as crippled and fail because of his handicap." Dana, the oldest daughter, was Father's pet, anxious and unwilling to differ with him.

After a second session the therapists constructed the map shown in Figure 14-3. This map makes clear that the parents had effectively divided up the kids and that there really were two distinct but tightly enmeshed families involved. The dimensional analysis is also summarized in Figure 14-3. The values of the two systems reflected their architects: although both were closed in somes areas, overall, the Bo–Gertie family was a rigidly enmeshed closed regime, while the Kitty family was a somewhat neglectful random one. The most dramatic dimensional feature of the family was its preoccupation with power and its tendency to confuse other dimensions with power. Thus Bo said, "it's not control, it's love." Dominance was used to obtain sex and sex became a bid for power. The enmeshment between the ex-spouses was partly sustained by his insistence on reviewing and ap-

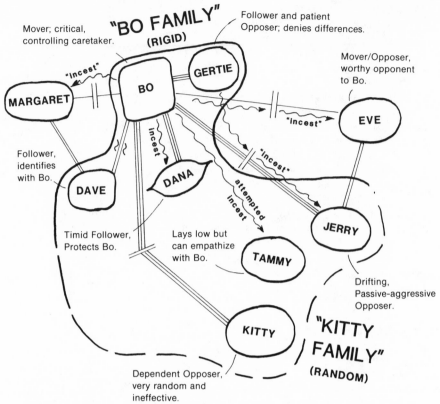

**FIGURE 14-3.**
Map of the two Turan families.

POWER—Preoccupied with power, Bo central but denies, "It's love, not control." Eve bids openly for power.

MEANING—"Must do best, help each other out." Really two enmeshed families with differing but equally rigid sexual values.

AFFECT—Controlled; suppressed anger, pain, and hurt; sex and love confused with power and control.

proving her every expenditure and her willingness to remain financially dependent on him. Thus he used money as an excuse to continue to try and control her while she used it as a way to continue to oppose him without disengaging.

To decrease the enmeshment between the two subsystems, the therapists planned to draw increasing attention to "the two families" and their very different ways of operating. Eventually, this became a convincing rationale for seeing the families separately. This met with

Bo's approval, because he wanted Kitty to "grow up" and be "straightened out," too. She agreed readily, in part because she wanted to protect her "remaining" children from Bo's influence.

The full dimensions of the incest involvements were not known to the therapist at the start of therapy. Their referral source had told them that Bo had "initiated" his oldest daughter at the age of 12, that several years later, Gertie had seduced her stepson, Jerry, and that his girlfriend, Eve, had told the authorities. Incestuous relations had stopped by the time therapy began.

The family was certainly rife with serious issues. The past incest relationships were obviously related to current problems but they were also a "red herring" that was too hot for the family to handle. One side of the family, the Bo–Gertie group, did not want to talk about the incest under any circumstances. They, especially Bo and Dana, felt there was no point in talking about it; it was a dead issue, unrelated to their current distress. On the other side, Kitty, always the outspoken critic of everything Bo and Gertie did, wanted to talk of nothing else, seeing all problems and subsequent evils to have been caused by the abomination of incest. Each side tried to get the therapists to declare allegiance, defending the incest as harmless or denouncing it as evil.

Although Jerry was far from being a contented, well-adjusted young man, the therapists judged him not to be in serious difficulty at that time. He conveyed the impression of some latent potential for self-destructiveness, but this did not come across as an imminent threat.

The therapists concluded that their first maneuver must be to reduce the conflicted enmeshment between father and son, encourage differentiation, and redirect attention away from the identified patient. The father conveyed the implied but clear message that he would not permit attention to be diverted from what he thought was important, the implicit threat being withdrawal from therapy. The strategy chosen was to agree with him overtly, insisting on making a referral for individual therapy for Jerry, thus removing this as legitimate issue within the family therapy. Jerry recognized this as a way to get out from under his father's thumb. He was encouraged to tell Bo that he was "working on it in therapy" whenever pressure began to be applied. This helped disengage father and son, giving Jerry outside resources on which to build independence. This was also a conservative strategy in relationship to Jerry's low self-esteem and potential self-destructiveness. (Several years later when he developed suicidal ideation, he was aided by the precedent of his earlier experience and reentered therapy.)

A central strategic decision was to bypass the incest issue altogether. The family map suggested a close relationship between the incest and the most intensely enmeshed or conflicted relationships, thus indicating an alternative framework in which to operate. In response to the family's stated concerns about "problems communicating" the therapists agreed to help them learn to communicate better, thereby indirectly helping Jerry. Of course, what Bo meant by better communicating was being more persuasive with his son and ex-wife, thus the family therapy held an implicit promise of some payoff for him. Part of the treatment strategy involved training in communication skills (Miller, Nunnally, & Wackman, 1975), at one level responding to the family's stated agenda, while at another level creating opportunities for assertive differentiation.

Jerry's girlfriend, Eve, figured so prominently in discussions that the therapists felt that she might hold some kind of key to the situation. This was confirmed when they proposed including her in sessions, which the family vehemently rejected, insisting that she was "not family" and had nothing to contribute. The therapists decided that including her in therapy was an appropriate long-term objective and they made it a "background theme" to work toward this end.

This tactical decision converged with the major strategic decision (to ignore the incest issues) when Eve finally did join one session, a 5-hour marathon. Having identified the dimension of control as a critical component of the family's disablement, in the middle of the session the therapists introduced a linear sculpture of power (the "Power Line" described in Chapter 11). As soon as they explained what the family would be doing, Dana became physically ill. As denial of her anxiety was also important to her, she recovered enough to participate after sympathetic support from the therapists about how "scary" the sculpture must be.

In the sculpture, nearly everyone clustered toward the more powerless end of the line. They also all tended to see themselves as less powerful than others saw them, although Bo was recognized by everyone as being the most powerful in the family. Jerry, the identified patient, placed himself in the least powerful position. Finally, as the implications were being discussed, his girlfriend made her move and passed Bo up, declaring herself to be more powerful than he; the others agreed. The therapists expressed wonderment over Eve's great power and asked what it was all about.

The cat, then, was out of the bag. Incest and power were isomorphic. Incest was Bo's expression of dominance and the dark secret by which he maintained power over each member of the younger generation, keeping them in ignorant isolation from each other. For some there was the inchoate threat of what had not yet happened; for others, the private shame and confusion over what had taken place. But Eve's

power stemmed from her willingness to reveal the incest, thus cancel-
ing Bo's power. For the first time the dimensions of the problem began
to be revealed and the whole family started to get some perspective
on it.

In that session it became apparent that no one in the family,
except Bo, had been fully aware of the scope of the problems. Bo had
strictly controlled communication. He had a "special and private"
relationship with each one, thus keeping them ignorant of the other
relationships. Then Bo and Gertie had tried to engage Eve in a sexual
triad. Although Eve had already had sex with Bo, she balked at this
and subsequently went to the police. (Because of her long-term involvement with Jerry, the relationship between her and his father must
also be regarded as incest, symbolically if not actually.)

It was now clear that an important factor in the family disablement was the disabled sibling subsystem (Bank & Kahn, 1982). The
boundary between it and the parental systems needed to be further
reinforced, and the brothers and sisters needed to become more engaged with each other as adults and more mutually supportive. In
view of their ages as adults or near-adults, it was deemed appropriate
to see them as a group. The therapists began to see this group separately, including Dave's wife, Margaret. Drawing on the family map,
the therapists now suspected that there had also been sexual involvement between Bo and his daughter-in-law. The first session with the
siblings revealed this relationship and established the basis for new
understanding between the alienated brothers and more mutual support among all of them.


## THE PARADIGMATIC BASIS OF THERAPY

Therapy itself is guided by paradigms and the therapeutic system
established in the consultation room has its own regime. Some therapists operate on a distinctly closed model: The therapist is an expert
with special knowledge not shared and generally not to be shared with
clients. The therapist is in a position of authority, power, and responsibility in relation to the family. Control over the process must be
maintained. In some cases, the therapist "works magic" or "prescribes
cures" for the family, trading on powers invested by the family.

Other therapists work according to a more random paradigm,
seeing therapy as a process of exploration and unfolding in which
clients and therapists participate primarily as persons mutually experiencing each other. This here-and-now interaction is seen as therapeutic, often as liberating the inherent and unique healing potential

of each person and family. Such therapists may be inclined to "wing it," responding to the moment-to-moment revelation of process, and disinclined to conduct evaluations or plan strategy.

Therapists who work within an open therapeutic regime are likely to stress communication and "working on" problems, to use some of the style and tactics of both closed and random approaches, but with a commitment to openness, to the sharing of special knowledge.

The theories that therapists espouse and the regime they promote in the office need not necessarily coincide. The therapist who works in a very closed style may subscribe to a very here-and-now, communications-oriented theory. The therapist with a highly structured theory focused on the past and how it is continued into the future might work in a very open style.

There is no research on how therapist paradigms and family paradigms interact, and clinical insight in this area is scant. A few general working principles have been recognized, however, and some special rules of thumb have been formulated.

## Entry and Access

As a rule, access to a family and its engagement in the therapy process is facilitated by operating in a style consistent with, or at least not inconsistent with, a family's paradigm and regime. This compatibility assists what Minuchin (1974) refers to as "joining." One tries to meet the family "on familiar ground." The therapist who starts off by sitting a closed family down and trying to get them to "open up" or the therapist who "clamps down" on an open family, calling for discipline and control by the parents, are both risking alienating the family, compromising their effectiveness as therapists, or driving the family out of therapy altogether. Therapists whose practice is carefully circumscribed ethnically, geographically, and socioeconomically may have less to worry about in treating all families alike on first approach, but other therapists may find it worthwhile thinking in terms of how their own paradigms are reflected in their first approach to families.

One may be able to go only so far in meeting families "where they are" without risking being disingenuous or compromising one's own basic commitments. There may also be practical limitations. I cannot redecorate and rearrange, my office for each new client, though I know that its "casual eclecticism" sometimes puts off people in closed and synchronous families, while its work-oriented accoutrements (shelves and shelves of books, a word processor) do not impress the more random ones.

### The Wizard of Oz and Open Paradigms Therapy

The open paradigm, with its inclusive orientation drawing on and synthesizing features of both random and closed paradigms, may have some advantages as a paradigm for therapy. However, this may just be my own open paradigmatic bias showing. I see the job of the therapist to be to remain flexible and be prepared to do whatever works, to be creative or dogmatic as fits the situation, to work paradoxical magic, to talk things out, or to get down on the floor and play games, even, on occasion, to just sit in silent empathy.

Two things distinguish this style from being flavorlessly eclectic. First, there is the commitment that perfuses this book to having technique, style, and strategy in therapy be responsive to each family, interventions proceeding *from* understanding. Being prepared to do whatever works does not mean haphazardly sorting through techniques, trying them all until something happens. It means having a large toolkit from which to select the most effective tool for a particular job. (Of course, these are clearly open paradigm images.) Sometimes one must be willing to be inventive and off-the-wall, other times may require one to stick doggedly to a single routine.

The second feature of my particular favorite realization of the open paradigm is wizardry. I have always liked the kind in "The Wizard of Oz." That wizard was ultimately exposed to be just another hapless human being; how he worked his "magic" was revealed. His final wizardry, wonderfully paradoxical magic that it was, was done unconcealed—that he told his clients that he was no magician and the magic lay already realized within them did not prevent it from working.

I myself am uncomfortable leaving clients mystified, thinking one thing happened to them when it was really something else. Whenever possible, I prefer that they become reenabled *and* know how it happened, so I try to find some way to share what I know with a family. I look on this as part of a commitment to primary prevention, giving them insight and tools so that the next time they may not need me.

Certain schools of thought in family therapy regard insight as irrelevant or even sometimes counterproductive. It is argued that knowledge of how they themselves work and insight into their disablement becomes part of the perverse family process sustaining the disablement. There can be truth in this, indeed anything may be used to sustain disablement, just as a knowledge of good parenting skills can be used destructively in a seriously disturbed family. However, there is also a self-serving component to this position on the part of the therapists. It keeps families dependent on therapists for "working the magic," suitably in awe in many cases, and in any event maintains the status differential between therapists and clients. Not sharing their insights with families preserves the therapists' monopoly.

Of course, it is also argued that some of what "we" know can't be communicated to "them"; it's too complicated. There is a grain of truth in this but not so large it need clog the channels altogether. Most of what we know or think we know about families today is really quite primitive and can be made a lot simpler than we make it when we are talking to each other. Consider this example.

> The therapist asks a mother if she knows what happened, why things are better and have settled down at home. She says she thinks that her boy is growing up and that the "talking to" he got from the therapist "straight-ened him out." The therapist says, "I see it a little differently. You know what I think happened? In a way, you were being too good as a mother. You all were being too good at what you do as a family, just too much the McGregors." The parents laugh knowingly. "The harder you tried to be a good mother and watch over Billy and teach him how to do things, the less he needed to do anything himself, the more resentful he got of you. In a way, you needed to become a worse mother, more like Mrs. Kettle down the block. Sometimes we need to borrow the way other families do things. Like borrowing a lawnmower from a neighbor. We can give it back when we're through. In the meantime, the lawn gets mowed. I kinda tricked you into borrowing the Kettle's lawnmower." More laughter, and giggles from Billy. "In the future, when the weeds get out of hand, you might want to borrow their hedge trimmers."

## THE LONG HAUL IN FAMILY THERAPY

Much of family therapy is, and is intended to be, short term. The structural, strategic, and problem-solving approaches all emphasize efficiency and economy of treatment. Much of the literature of family therapy deals with quick, clever interventions intended to "get them back out the door" as soon as possible. Other approaches with this emphasis include intensive, marathon formats and time-limited or symptom-focused contracts. Family therapy has always been proud to claim efficiency among its major advantages as a treatment modality. For the most part, this is all laudable; certainly, clients need not and should not be encouraged to draw out or become dependent on ther-apy. But one of the results is that relatively little attention has been paid to what happens in extended family therapy, issues that arise when therapy moves beyond crisis and presenting problems, beyond the point where the family is "working" again. These issues are certainly not confined within the paradigmatic framework, but the framework does have something to offer in clarifying them.

It is possible to define a hierarchy of family therapy priorities. Starting with a family in crisis—and to some degree all families entering therapy are in crisis, however small it may seem—the first order of business or highest concern is crisis resolution. No system can sustain a chronic crisis state without potentially disastrous consequences. The family needs to use, resolve, move beyond the immediate crisis. The presenting problem may not have the same dimensions as the precipitating crisis. If it does not, it warrants separate attention.

A great deal of family therapy stops at crisis resolution and/or symptom relief relating to the presenting problem. It may stop with these not only because some therapies and therapists choose to stop there, but because many families do. Once relief begins to be felt, the motivation for therapy diminishes significantly.

The paradigmatic framework pushes for at least one step more: reenablement of the family's regime. This may coincide with crisis resolution and solution of the presenting problem, but it need not. A family may be out of crisis and symptom-free without being any more enabled than when they entered family therapy. Outside pressures or precipitating factors may have abated or the family may have adopted a less painful but just as ineffective stuck mode of operation. Leaving the family as an enabled version of itself should be the minimum goal of therapy.

Beyond that minimum is a concern for the family's future. Ideally we would like to prevent some as yet unencountered problems from disabling the family again. We would like to help families become more robust and resilient, better able to meet and surmount the exigencies of family life in today's world. We are interested in prevention not just treatment.

Once more, the paradigmatic goals of families suggest directions, as these in all cases extend beyond immediate concerns, guiding the family over time. Thus each family paradigm includes within it a formulation of a family's unrealized potential. Preventive work with families can thus be directed toward helping each family to acutalize its unique potential as a family.

## The Next Vulnerable Structure

Even as the family is ushered out the door after their "final" session, we are almost always aware of lurking problems, hidden weaknesses, traps waiting to be sprung to catch the family again. Often we have quite specific predictions about what symptoms are likely to show up in the future, who is the next candidate for identified patient.

In the structural–analytic approach, Kantor (1980, 1983) introduces the concept of the "next most vulnerable structure." The next most vulnerable structure is like the weak link in the family chain. It is the person, relationship, or family strategy that seems most likely to break down or run into difficulty in the future.

When a family chooses to continue in therapy beyond problem resolution and reenablement to work on preventing future disablement, the family map, as updated to that point in therapy, often points directly to the next vulnerable feature. In the Wayland family introduced earlier in this chapter (and in Chapter 11 concerning family drawings), 11-year-old Paul was clearly the most likely next candidate for identified patient. His family drawing of himself as a crucified Christ amidst an angry mob conveys the painfulness of his position being stuck in the middle. With the older children leaving home, he will be left behind in a more difficult and confusing position with his mother and father. (Although this concern was expressed to the Waylands, they did not stay in therapy. Within a year, they had moved away and follow-up was not possible.)

## Reiterative Exploration of Critical Images

Family therapists who are used to time-limited therapy employing sharply focused interventions are sometimes at a loss for what to do when faced with the prospect of long-term work with a family. At the end of a 10 or 15-session contract, most issues have been covered, but experience has shown that certain ones can be productively worked again and again without depleting the soil.

The critical images around which family paradigms are organized are examples of such fertile ground. Individuals carry critical identity images (Kantor, 1980, 1983) with them into the formation of a new family, and certain key experiences and events in this family become images that form the core of the family's identity. These images are so central and important for understanding the family's way of looking at and operating in the world that they warrant exploration in depth. Moreover, critical identity images are so rich and well articulated, so ramified throughout a family's organization and process, that a single investigation can hardly exhaust its resources.

For example, in one family, the adoption of a child several years earlier had become a developmental crisis around which the family organized itself ever since. The child's arrival challenged the family's prior images of itself as a smoothly integrated system. The parents were used to their children living up to unstated expectations, but this child, whose papers declared her to be an 8 year old, was actually 12 and violated expectations incontrovertably. Each time it came into focus, new dimensions of this crisis became apparent.

The imagistic tools introduced in Chapter 11 can all be brought to bear on critical images, each in turn giving a slightly different perspective on the same theme. A critical image like the one described above can be discussed, the events surrounding it can be acted out in role play, the family "before" and "after" can be sculpted or portrayed in family drawings. With each reiterative exploration, the family gains perspective on its own "programming" and gains control over the role these images may play in their future experience.

## Family of Origin

Another productive route for longer term therapy is to delve into the families of origin of the parents, perhaps involving these families in therapy. This, of course, is a primary emphasis of some therapists and therapies, while in the more strategic, problem-solving approaches it may scarcely be considered.

In some families the transgenerational issues are more prominent than others. Some current disablement may be largely reflective of unresolved conflicts and developmental crises from the parents' families, while in other families, present problems are more clearly contemporary. The paradigmatic framework offers another focus for investigations into transgenerational issues, exploring similarities and differences in family paradigm and regime. Transgenerational issues will be considered in more detail in Chapter 20.

## Therapy as Education

Even in the most mystifying or manipulative of therapies, there is a certain amount of education taking place. The family is learning something about families and family therapy. In the early stages of therapy the presenting problem and precipitating crisis loom larger; relieving stress and reenabling the system take priority. When therapy continues long enough new opportunities open for the therapist to function more as a teacher than as a mechanic, manipulator, or magician.

The object of therapy as education is prevention, to reduce the future risk of the family needing therapy again. The therapist is working toward a family that is not just "unstuck" but that is richer and more flexible as a family, hence less likely to get stuck in the future. For example, given more knowledge of basic human develop-ment, many families would be better prepared for the many transitions that growing up and growing older bring. On their own, families are unlikely to push for this—once things "get better" they are ready to move on.

Skill building can be an important part of therapy or a follow-up to it. Therapists should become familiar with enrichment techniques, communication skills (e.g., Miller *et al.*, 1975), parenting methods (e.g., Gordon, 1970, 1976), and the available resources for teaching these.

Of all things a family might need to know about itself to function more successfully and to avoid future disablement, the most critical is to understand its own paradigm and its particular disabling tenden-cies. This may be likened to an individual becoming aware that he has weak ligaments in one knee so he can strengthen the muscles around the knee and find ways to avoid stressing it improperly. Knowledge of weakness is strength.

For example, an open family that understands the tendency for open regimes to become chaotically enmeshed has an awareness that can function like an alarm or early warning system. Adding this small, but important refinement to its usual strategies increases the chance of somebody saying, "Hey, I think we're really getting caught up in this. We sound all confused and we're getting nowhere. Why don't we all sleep on it, and mull it over on our own for a while. The problem will still be here; we can always come back to it."

Families can be helped to understand the basic legitimacy of their choices of family lifestyle and yet be aware of how every such choice is double-edged, that nothing comes without price. This knowlege gives them a chance of heading off disabling patterns before they become entrenched or escalated beyond their abilities to influence. This knowl-edge carries no guarantee, but it does make the odds a little better.

## Pitfalls of Long-Term Therapy

Some families change more slowly than others; some therapists go for "deeper" or more pervasive change; and some families face more difficult circumstances. A family with a history of multiple incest, plagued by repeated suicide attempts, and operating on the bare edge of subsistence is not in the same position as a financially solid family with a child who has trouble sleeping. For whatever reasons, family therapy sometimes stretches from a handful of visits into months or even years. There are special pitfalls and problems as well as special obligations for the therapist when family therapy becomes long term.

MAINTENANCE THERAPY, DEPENDENCY, AND RESCUING

Although therapy involves change, families do not necessarily want it; more often than not they want restoration of some prior status quo. Therapists, however, usually judge therapy by progress and change. Nevertheless, sometimes therapy bogs down, and it seems that the very best efforts of the therapist are needed just to keep the family on an even keel. Though therapists' ideal may be to work themselves out of a job, sometimes this seems unattainable.

To draw a parallel, in rehabilitation work, the best that can ever be achieved in some cases is employment in a sheltered workshop. Some maintenance or institutional supports are necessary as the "least restrictive alternative." Some families may *need* the structured support of on-going family therapy, although these families and this kind of work have received little attention in the literature.

The problem is how to tell whether the therapist has been inducted into the family system, is promoting dependency, or is involved in legitimate long-term family therapy. The solution, of course, is to turn to a Bystander, a supervisor or consultant who is outside the immediate system and can help the therapist get perspective. As regular supervisors or peer groups are also vulnerable to becoming part of the stuck process, it may be worthwhile to bring in a consultant at intervals in any long-term case.

Nearly all therapists are vulnerable to rescue fantasies; if they weren't they probably would have gone into another field. The impulse to rescue a family member or even an entire family may come at any time, but the very early and very late phases of therapy are particular temptations. The family that cannot, will not, or does not change may prompt the therapist to want to "at least save somebody." Fortunately, this urge can have its functional sides and can be turned to positive uses.

In the Turans, whose children were all grown or nearly grown, the father and his second wife were deeply and rigidly enmeshed, wholly uncommitted to change and relatively uncommitted to therapy. They wanted to see others change. Their subsystem seemed beyond reach, yet its effects on the next generation were clearly destructive. The urge to "save the children" suggested a strategy to reduce the coupling between generations and strengthen the sibling subsystem.

Therapy concentrated on helping the offspring gain independence and see their primary support as coming from their siblings. Their age suggested this approach as appropriate and workable. Ultimately the couple system was little affected by therapy but became more isolated from the rest of the family. The couple left therapy, apparently contented with their little island.

### THE THERAPIST AS FAMILY MEMBER

Families do not always stay in therapy because they haven't changed or because they're dependent on the therapist; neither is on-going therapy necessarily an opportunity for sound preventive work. Sometimes families stay because they like therapy, it's familiar, fun, and comfortable. The therapist becomes another family member with whom they get together for a family activity. This is a form of *induction*, where the therapist is drawn into playing a part in the system. In this case, the system may not be disabled and the induction may not be bad for either the family or the therapist, but it might be better and more honest to terminate therapy and become friends. The lack of crises or serious issues is a good clue that induction may have taken place, especially when the therapist really likes the family, misses them when they are away, and looks forward to their weekly visits. In this case, the following resolution can be posed: "What if therapy stopped and we got together over lunch (or at the tennis courts, etc.) instead?" The therapist's and the family's reactions are generally quite telling.

# FAMILY THERAPY
# BY THE PARADIGM

CHAPTER

# 15

# STABILITY THROUGH TRADITION
## Closed Families and Family Therapy

Knowing that a family operates by a closed regime and is guided by a closed paradigm is not enough to formulate a "prescription" for a treatment strategy, much less specific techniques. The best that can be said is that this perspective highlights certain issues that are either more or less likely to be relevant in closed families than in the other primary forms. This chapter (and succeeding chapters on other types of families) cannot be a "how to" guide, but it can point out potentially important issues and directions for working with one class of families.

It is likely that closed families constitute the greatest share of the caseload of most family therapists. The majority of case reports that have entered the literature describe families guided by closed paradigms, most of them with closed regimes. Some schools of therapy are founded on assumptions that favor closed regimes or effectively recognize only the closed paradigm for families. Because there has been so much said before about this paradigm and the treatment of families with closed regimes, this chapter will be kept brief.

## DYSFUNCTIONAL DYNAMICS IN CLOSED REGIMES

Although each disabled closed regime may vary, there are certain patterns of dysfunction particularly common to closed regimes. The most probable overall pattern is, of course, one that demonstrates rigid enmeshment, inflexibility of interaction sustained by overinvolvement.

## Rigid Roles

The closed paradigm assumes fairly strict differentiation of complementary roles, and closed regimes usually delineate roles quite sharply along general lines—such as age, sex, and generation—and between specific people. This division of labor is normal to closed regimes; in disabled closed regimes it may be carried to rigid and ridiculous extremes. A husband may have *all* the contact with the outside world and do almost nothing at home, while his wife is an agoraphobic recluse whose life is bounded by the walls of the house. Or the family may strictly divide up characteristics between two children. This one is bright, that one dull; the one is musical, the other can't carry a tune; he likes blue, she hates it; his room is a trash heap, hers is immaculate.

The sharp role divisions in families are reinforced by labeling and by family sanctions. Eric knows he is "The Slob." The family "reminds" Bobbi of her expected role: "You don't have to go caroling with us, Bobbi. We know you're not musically minded." If members depart from their assignments, they are subjected to pressure to get "back on the track," even if they go off in a supposedly "good" direction. "What, Eric cleaned his room? I can't believe it! He must have gotten Bobbi to do it for him. Don't worry, he'll mess it up again in no time."

### THE PARENTALIZED CHILD[1]

The notion of "parentalized child" as pathology, of a "parental" role as inappropriate for a child, is in some respects itself a closed paradigm construct. It assumes the necessity of a family hierarchy and "division of labor" that may not hold under random and open paradigms. From a strictly systems theory point of view, any fixed, inflexible role assignment implies limitations in a family's interpersonal repertoire and reduced adaptability to varying contingencies. In random or open regimes, this criteria applies universally: anyone stuck in a parental role may be a manifestation of some disablement in the system. In the closed paradigm, on the other hand, the parental role is assumed to "belong" to the parents.

In random or open regimes, the parental role may be assumed by anyone and may shift from moment to moment; but in closed regimes,

---

1. An accepted and widely used neologism, "parentalize" derives from the adjective "parental" by analogy to the derivation of the still-older "infantilize" from "infantile." There is no justification for introducing yet another neologism, certainly not the dysphonic linguistic violence of "parentify," which some writers have taken to using.

roles are more permanently assigned to role incumbents. The parental role in the closed regime is thus more likely to become a more or less fixed burden for the parentalized child. The parentalized child is also problematic for a closed family because this particular assignment of roles violates the hierarchical assumptions of the closed paradigm, creating a tension between expected image and actual structure.


## Rigid Alliances

Like role assignments, alliances in closed regimes are prone to be less fluid than those in random or open ones. In disabled random and synchronous regimes, the scattered independence and emphases on equalness work against alliance formation, while in disabled open regimes the enmeshment of the total family in endless negotiation inhibits separate alliances. However, fairly rigid alliances are completely compatible with disabled closed regimes.

The most visible aspect of a rigid alliance is the collaboration of the two people it joins; but any fixed alliance is an alliance *against* someone else and thus involves three parties. Alliances should be distinguished from "identifications." The identification is not "against" another member, but rather implies a mapping from the behavior and functioning of one member to that of another. In the Waylands introduced in the previous chapter, Peter was strongly identified with his mother, as the map in Figure 14-2 indicated, but he was not in an alliance with her. Indeed, his efforts to protect his father were, if anything, an alliance against her. An identification is based on perceived or desired similarity, but an alliance may involve members who are very dissimilar. Identifications within a family may offer the therapist clues to when one member, often a child, may be acting out a "script" for someone else or repeating a multigenerational pattern. In the case of the Waylands, the identification suggested Peter's vulnerability, given his mother's poor level of functioning.


### CROSS-GENERATIONAL ALLIANCES

The generational boundary between parents and offspring is important for effective governance within a closed regime. A stable alliance between a child and one parent violates this boundary and interferes with the "normal" functioning of parental authority. The fact that such an alliance is often *against* the other parent or another adult makes it even more problematic.

## Intrusion and Confusion

Disabled closed regimes tend toward enmeshment, which means they are characterized by excessive coupling between components. This may be manifest in many ways. One common example is parental intrusiveness, where one or both parents is excessively involved with the children, monitoring them more closely then necessary and attempting to regulate them too broadly. This phenomenon is often described in terms of diffuse, excessively permeable boundaries, however, in the view developed in Chapter 10, the permeability of the boundaries is not at issue. Indeed, many children under these circumstances fight hard to maintain their boundaries; the work the parents put into being invasive also testifies to the intact nature of the interpersonal boundaries. What is more significant in the family's disablement is the excess coupling, that may take place across boundaries of varying permeability.

The phenomena of cross-generational alliances and parentalized children are often similarly described as examples of role confusion or of diffuse boundaries. On close examination, however, the roles of allied parties and parentalized children are no less well defined than any other family roles. The boundary between the other children and the parental subsystems consisting of 14-year-old Cary and her mother is apt to be quite clear if not rigid. The fact that this is not the subsystems the therapist expects to see or the one prescribed by the closed paradigm does not mean that roles are less clear or interpersonal boundaries any less closed than in a "normal" enabled closed regime.

## Identified Patients

In keeping with its strong differentiation of roles, the closed regime often singles out one clear "identified patient" more sharply than do other regimes. The identified patient is used by the family to sustain its process and to resist change. An asthmatic child, for example, became the center of family activity, keeping his mother busy with appointments, medication, and cleaning while his father worked overtime to pay the medical bills. Thus mother and father had neither time nor energy for each other and thereby avoided dealing with the hidden issues threatening the stability of their marriage.

## Scapegoating

A family scapegoat is an extreme form of the identified patient. Because it places the family above the individual, the closed regime is somewhat more likely than other regimes to allow a member to become a scapegoat. As the scapegoat allows the family to function and resist change, the basic commitments of the closed paradigms are not violated. A scapegoat must be distinguished from a family member who simply gets left out or short-changed, which may occur in any regime. The scapegoat's role is essential to the family—the success and happiness of the whole are made possible by the scapegoat's misery. The scapegoat is the symbolic repository of the sins and suffering of the rest of the family; through its sacrifice the others are enabled.[2]

The scapegoat becomes the "enemy within." It "embodies" badness or sickness or deviance and therefore suffers as the rest of the family lays claim to health and goodness and normality. This stark splitting of roles is more compatible with closed than with other regimes. It would be more difficult for the others to sustain a process of scapegoating while remaining true to their paradigms.

The family caught in this process needs its scapegoat to blame, to channel their guilt, to deflect their energies, to avoid self-awareness, and so forth. This double-edged function of the scapegoat needs to be kept in mind as the therapist attempts to imbalance the system and decrease the scapegoating.

Candidates for the role of scapegoat often seem to be selected for their difference or deviance, which is increased or exaggerated by the scapegoating process. Strong Opposers are the most likely to be scapegoated by closed regimes.

### Process Dimensions

Dimensional crossing appears to be fairly common in disabled closed regimes. A dimensional crossing involves the use of transactions in one dimension of family process to gain access to the functional targets of another, or one dimension serving as a substitute for another, or a confusion of two dimensions. The Turans introduced in Chapter 14 were a closed family in which feelings were avoided or expressed with careful modulation by all but one member, the somewhat infantilized first wife, Kitty. Material exchanges, in the form of gifts and money, and sexual relations were virtually the only tokens of expression, but

---

2. Nowhere is the function of the scapegoat made more painfully clear than in Ursula K. LeGuin's frighteningly insightful short story, "The Ones Who Walked Away from Omelas" (*The Wind's Twelve Quarters*, Harper & Row, 1975). In Omelas, the town's true happiness rests on the tragic imprisonment of a single child. Knowing of the child's misery on their behalf spurs the townsfolk to live life well and to the fullest. The child's pain and their pleasure are recognized as unavoidably reciprocal. The title refers to the few who walk away from this complementary utopia.

both sex and money were used by Bo and his second wife, Gertie, to control and to bid for power. Thus affect and control were crossed. Interventions were called for to clarify this "misuse" and facilitate clear, distinct communication in each dimension.

In keeping with their reliance on role differentiation, closed regimes often have some degree of "specialization" in certain dimensions by particular members. In disabled regimes this division of labor can be extreme. One daughter might be known as "the emotional one," loud and histrionic, while another is "the quiet intellectual," incapable of expressing any affect. Relationships may also be dimensionally specialized, as with a father and his only daughter who share neither knowledge (content) nor personal meaning, their transactions being limited to emotional extremes of affection and anger mixed with a covert struggle for power.

The therapist should be alert to the relationship between dimensional specialization and the family's disablement. Certainly there are legitimate individual variations in propensities to transact in certain dimensions. Some people seem to be constitutionally more emotionally expressive than others; some friendships are more specifically tied to shared images than shared feelings. Often, however, the dimensional specialization is isomorphic to other manifestations of disablement, as in the Turan family, where the closed subfamily headed by Bo and Gertie, two specialists in power, had all the "achievers," and the random one, headed by the expressive but emotionally immature Kitty, seemed locked into failure.

In disabled closed families such isomorphisms may be abundant, possibly an inclination related to their leanings toward simple, stable structures. Any level of the isomorphism is a possible lever for change, and successful intervention at one level is usually reflected in change at another. If one tactic is blocked, the therapist can turn to an isomorphic feature of the family—or, for maximal impact, the therapist can operate at more than one level at once.

The careful regulation of affect in closed families often prompts therapists to encourage its freer expression. This impulse is not entirely inappropriate. Where unexpressed or carefully modulated feelings are characteristic, as they often are in typical American closed families, opening up affect can have the paradoxical effect of *decreasing* enmeshment. For example, in one family, the coldly controlling manipulations of a powerful father kept his eldest son locked in a perpetual struggle for power. The father seemed bitter and disappointed with his son, as with himself, but never admitted this, always delivering his critical condemnation of his son in a calculated and detached manner. His anger was drawn out by the therapist "coaching" him and acting as a "double," expressing his buried feelings.

Eventually he blew up at his son, and, as he ranted on about all his disappointments in the boy, began to cry over his own perceived failures. The son found even his father's open anger easier to take than the coldly detached criticism. He was able to sympathize with and reassure his father concerning his sense of failure. Eventually, he stopped struggling for a position of power he had come to see as empty.

## Family Secrets

Secrets are common in closed regimes, as they are compatible with the paradigmatic commitment to control information and to limit dissemination. Only a synchronous regime, with its noncommunicative style, is as likely to have secrets. Family secrets may be known only to an individual and kept from the rest of the family, may be shared among members of some subsystem but kept from the rest of the family, or may be shared by the entire family but kept from the outside world. Secrets constitute and reinforce boundaries. For example, in the Turans, introduced in Chapter 14, Bo kept his incestuous relationships with some of his children secret from the rest of the family but also kept each of them from being aware of the others. Thus the rest of the family was closed out from aspects of the incestuous subsystem. Equally important, the boundaries between the children, who were unaware of each other's knowledge and relationship, were also reinforced. Sharing a secret has the added effect of reinforcing alliances among the "insiders."

Secrets may or may not play a significant role in family disablement. To varying degrees, secrets add to distortion and mystification in the meaning dimension and almost invariably elevate anxiety within a family. For the therapist who becomes aware of or suspects the existence of family secrets, the question of disclosure is raised. Karpel and Strauss (1983), who analyze the issue of family secrets in some detail, distinguish things that are legitimately private from those that are secret. The key question concerns the relevance of the information for those who are unaware of it. Bo and Gertie's sexual involvement with certain family members was not a legitimately private matter because it was of profound relevance for the entire family.

Both the revelation of family secrets and their continuation have consequences for the family and for the therapy process. Who discloses the secret, how, and when, all require careful consideration. Although Karpel and Strauss do not mention paradigmatic considerations, they do suggest being empathetic with both the secret holders and those who are unaware. The fact that closed regimes are tolerant of secrets should be kept in mind by the therapist. This means that private matters or secrets not strongly related to therapeutic goals may be left alone. It also means that disclosure of secrets involved in disablement may be strongly indicated, as this can have a major unbalancing impact on the family.

## EVALUATION OF CLOSED REGIMES

The closed paradigm has at its core a hierarchical model of relationships in which roles are strongly differentiated and boundaries are important. The therapist always has the choice of challenging these notions or the structures in which they are reflected or of operating in congruence with them. There is, naturally, no right answer for all closed families and all situations; indeed, there is probably no "right" answer even for one particular family in a specific situation. What is important is for the therapist to be cognizant of the probable effects of different approaches and to choose among them deliberately.

### Entry and Engagement

The style of the therapist's entry into the system can be more of an issue for closed regimes than for other families, especially when the family's incentives for entering into therapy are marginal. The closed family more closely regulates and patrols its boundaries than other families. It is quicker to reject or eject undesirable intruders as well as to withdraw from threatening encounters. The more rigidly closed the system, the more criteria it may have by which the therapist will be judged, for example. In the extreme, as in the case of working with an evangelical fundamentalist family, the therapist who does not conform precisely with the family's definition of a proper counselor or advisor may be rejected outright or may not be able to do effective therapy at all.

It is not necessary for the therapist to espouse the same beliefs as the family or to work always in an appropriately authoritative style, but the family will be checking to see whether the therapist is aware of their values and is prepared to acknowledge and respect these. A capacity for respect is more important than agreement. In many cases it can be a disadvantage for the therapist to agree explicitly with presented family values or to start off by stating his/her own position, as either may commit the therapist unwittingly in a family struggle or may prematurely "freeze" the family's concept of the therapist.

In keeping with their preference for role differentiation, closed regimes usually have a "gatekeeper" who "runs interference" for the family and determines who is admitted and when. This role may or may not be filled by the same person who serves as "spokesperson" for the family. The first person to contact the therapist might have been the family gatekeeper or the family spokesperson or merely a family "errand boy/girl." It can be important for the therapist to identify the gatekeeper and understand the ritual necessary for admission. Bypassing this person, failure to get their approval, inadequate attention, or failure to build a good working alliance may lead to the therapist being rejected and the family being pulled from therapy.

Unless it is carefully or coincidentally tuned to the closed regime's style, a Mover–Opposer approach to entry and evaluation is less likely to succeed with a closed regime than a Bystander–Follower one. However, the closed regime is likely to respond positively to the therapist who firmly but gently takes charge and conveys a sense of authority and confidence. The closed paradigm recognizes and values the role of expert, and closed families are frequently looking for a "good advisor" who will "tell them what to do" or a "good doctor" who will "cure them."

### Evaluation Technique

The full range of verbal, nonverbal, informal, and structured techniques of evaluation have been used effectively with closed families. If there are any precautions to take into account, these would have to do with the mode of introduction and interpretation. The conventional, traditional orientation of most closed families may make them resistant to nonverbal and imagistic techniques unless they are carefully introduced in a nonthreatening way. Premature interpretation to the family or feedback from evaluation may be of limited value, may induce a family to leave therapy by being too "on target," or may simply be incorporated into their stuck regime. Owing to their rigid enmeshment, the chances of family insight becoming a further mechanism of disablement is somewhat higher in closed regimes than others.

## TREATMENT OF CLOSED REGIMES

Because of the belief that human relationships are intrinsically hierarchical, closed families will tend to see the therapist as an expert or authority figure who is in a position of power. Therapists can capitalize on this perception and use the attributed influence to lever the family more or less directly into a more enabled position. Direct prescription, with or without paradoxical intention, is consistent with this aspect of the closed paradigm. The "doctor" gives the family a "prescription" that "cures" it; or, the "counselor" "advises" the family so that they "get better."

In general, the structural and paradoxical techniques of the "systemic," structural, strategic, and problem-solving schools of family therapy are congruent with the closed paradigm. The intervention is something done *by* the therapist *to* the family. The family is not usually told, even after the fact, what therapy was all about or what, from the therapist's viewpoint, "really" happened. The process and structure of therapy reinforce the one-up position of the therapist and a "magical" or "medical" interpretation of therapy from the family's perspective. They do not know that there is really no "Greek chorus" (Papp, 1980) behind the one-way mirror and after they leave therapy they are unlikely to understand what happened to them. Systemic, structural, and strategic manipulations probably reflect, to some extent, their evolution within practices dealing largely with closed families, hence they are likely to be effective approaches to family therapy with closed families.

## Closed Families and Change

It is important to keep in mind when working with closed families that the closed paradigm represents a family commitment to resisting change. The therapist knows that change is necessary for the family to become reenabled, but direct appeals and pressure are unlikely to precipitate it. General appeals to "trying something new," "changing and growing," "learning how to be a better family," besides being too unfocused, are likely only to sponsor resistance.

The morphostatic tendencies of closed families probably account for a good share of the development, rapid dissemination, and wide use of paradoxical techniques. These use the family's resistance to its own ultimate advantage.

Working in the therapist's favor is the fact that closed regimes depend on careful boundary regulation and a certain amount of isolation to resist change. Information must be channeled, limited, and regulated. The very process of therapy can interfere with this, especially when the therapist uses the setting to import new information into the system in ways that in themselves bypass censorship and depart from assigned channels. Just talking about something in a new way does not get new information into a family; however, because it is a living system, novel, focused information that actually enters the family will slowly but almost inexorably promote change and evolution of the system.

## Reframing within the Paradigm

Therapists often find themselves fighting against a family's paradigm, an uphill battle if ever there was one. It is always possible to reframe an intended change into terms consistent with a family's own paradigm. Not only is this likely to make needed adaptation easier, but it is more respectful of a family's own values.

Consider, for example, an overstressed closed family with a rebellious teenaged boy. The 17-year-old son has been "running around"; he stays out late or even all night without telling his parents where he is going, has been falling behind in school, and repeatedly forgets his household responsibilities. The parents respond to his rebellion by clamping down on him. They set curfews that are ignored, lose sleep waiting for him to come in and then order punishment that cannot be enforced. They constantly monitor his activities, checking up on his homework, talking with teachers in classes where he is having difficulty, calling his friends to verify his whereabouts. He responds to these "intrusions" by escalating the rebellion, which generates still stronger and more futile attempts to control him.

The therapist may see the son's behavior as exaggerated but rooted in age-appropriate attempts to differentiate and separate from the family. The therapist, who probably grew up in a closed family, may even identify with the son's frustrated attempts to gain independence. Siding openly with the son in any direct way is obviously one way to become part of the problem and may lead to the family leaving therapy. For that matter, simply taking the opposite tack and helping the parents to "control" their son would also reinforce the same feedback loop. On the other hand, attempts to get the parents to "let go" and ease up on their son are likely to be perceived as promoting lax, "permissive" child rearing, which runs counter to the family paradigm.

What must always be kept in mind is that every family paradigm has enabled versions. For this case, the therapist must remember that enabled closed families do deal successfully with adolescent differentiation and separation. The closed paradigm recognizes the need for children to grow up, leave home, and found families of their own. In enabled closed families, the parents use their position of authority to regulate graded increases in privilege and responsibility. Effective parents will use feedback from their youngsters as a guide, but will create the structures and set the changing limits themselves.

In the example here, the job of the therapist is to use the language and images of the closed paradigm to help the family become an enabled, rather than disabled closed family. The therapist identifies with the authority structure of the family—which means forming an alliance with the parents, not against them—while conveying to the son the essential benevolence of this move. (In a sense, the quintessential metaphor for an enabled closed regime is a "benevolent dictatorship.")

"I can see that you try really hard as parents, yet Joe just seems to get more and more frustrated. You have been very responsible and work very hard. You know that it's a tough world out there. Joe doesn't seem to know this yet. He doesn't seem to have learned how to take care of himself and be on his own yet." (*Joe protests, thus signaling that he's been "hooked" by the therapist.*) "It's up to you to teach him, to see that he learns what it's really like out there."

"But we've tried, we've tried everything. We talk to him and talk to him and he never learns."

"Maybe he just can't learn that way. Maybe he's one of those kids who has to learn the hard way." (*Dad agrees, "That's him!"*) "Well, we all know parents sometimes have to take charge and do tough things for their kids. I know you've really tried, but it sounds like you really are going to have to make things tougher for Joe. Maybe you have to do the really hard thing and push him out, give him a taste of what it's like to be out there, with no one to nag him about his homework or to wait up for him Saturday nights, or to gather up his laundry when he doesn't put it in the hamper."

The therapist, in the name of authority and responsibility, is moving toward a more flexible regime. Appeals are made to vital images within the closed paradigm ("tough world out there," "take charge and do tough things for their kids"). Often there is historical material on which to draw for support. In this example, the father had left home at age 16 to get a job and support himself. He was proud of his early self-reliance but wanted to "make things easier" for his kids. The therapist suggests that, "many kids today have really had it soft," and supports the parents in not insulating their son from the consequences of his behavior.

For an intervention like this to work, the therapist must take into account the entire structure of the system maintaining the disablement, in particular, the gains obtained from the disabled structure. If nothing is offered in return, changes are likely to be sabotaged. For the son, a real increase in responsibility must be coupled with increased independence and freedom from intrusion. Mother "needs to be needed," and it will not be easy to get her to stop picking up after her son, gathering his laundry, and so forth. Yet it is important that she do so, not only because of the impact on her son, but because her sacrifice is part of how she justifies controlling intrusion. ("After all I've done for him, I have a right to know who he's going out with.") The father, who like so many fathers in closed families, is relatively inaccessible to everyone, may be drawn in by putting him in charge of "protecting his wife from her own goodheartedness." His job is to distract her from "taking care" of her son by spending time with her doing something they enjoy. In this way, the marital dyad is reinforced while the intergenerational boundaries are clarified. Finally, the oppositional tendencies of the son are capitalized upon by the therapist who challenges him by implying some doubt or concern about his ability to handle the responsibility of being a grown-up.

# 16

# VARIETY THROUGH INNOVATION
## Random Families and Family Therapy

The random paradigm represents commitment to change and variety through creative individuality. In enabled random regimes, cooperative family activity occurs spontaneously. Individual autonomy does not prevent members from spontaneous responsiveness to the needs and interests of others. In disabled random regimes, these mechanisms have broken down or become dysfunctional so that the family fails to function in any effective coordinated way on its own behalf as a family. At the same time, the needs and interests of individual members are lost in the welter of competing bids for independence and self-gratification.

## EVALUATION OF DISABLEMENT IN RANDOM REGIMES

Disabled random regimes are distinguished by their chaotic disengagement, an exaggeration of the innate tendencies of random regimes. In the extremes of chaotic disengagement, family members scatter to pursue personal interests and meet their independent needs outside the family. What remains of the family's interior may be a battlefield where members compete as individuals for the scarce collective resources remaining. In this chaos, the needy cries for help for the individual are lost; to be heard or seen at all, symptomatic behavior may have to be extreme or may have to attract the attention of the outside community.

A disabled random regime does not necessarily reflect the presence of an underlying random paradigm. It is a fairly safe working hypothesis to assume that a closed regime implies the presence of a closed paradigm, but disabled random regimes can originate in numerous ways. Dysfunctional random process may reflect parental abdication or irresponsibility without commitment to broader aspects of a random paradigm. It can come about as the result of a never-resolved, continuing struggle between competing paradigms, especially between closed and random paradigms. (Such mixed cases will be discussed in Chapter 19.)

### Advanced Disablement in Random Regimes

Random regimes that have been chronically or repeatedly in crisis can reach a stage of disablement that is clearly chaotic but that may appear to have some features of enmeshment rather than disengagement. The struggle they become locked into is a highly competitive fight for survival, with "everyone for oneself." Frequent bickering and spontaneous eruptions of angry, hostile arguing are characteristic of this phase. Playful sparring, which may be common in more enabled random regimes, often degenerates into purposeless fights that may become loud or even violent. The fights may be marked by pronounced blaming and defensiveness, which family members argue are "necessary for survival in this family." The fights can be seen to have little to do with attempts at problem resolution except as each member battles for a separate piece of the lean collective pie.

The open-regime struggles that this battle seems to parallel may also often be marked by anger and blaming, but are more pronounced as endless unsuccessful attempts for *joint* resolution. The random regime in an advanced stage of disablement is more caught up in cutthroat competition than by the complexities of consensus.

Fierce competition is fueled by the propensities of individuals in random regimes to scatter and meet their needs independently whenever spontaneous group process fails to satisfy them. Thus the system becomes in danger of flying apart, being sacrificed to individual initiative and autonomy. Internally, the runaway random regime becomes a dangerous and chaotic jungle where the emotional rule becomes one of "survival of the fittest."

If the disabled random regime is to continue to exist as a family, engagement must be reinitiated and structure reimposed. The atmosphere of individual competition makes the regime ripe for the initiation of an authoritarian structure by the strongest competitor, whoever is strong enough to clamp down on the system and impose order. Thus, as follows from the general model introduced in Chapter 10, the random regime "collapses" into a simple, possibly quite primitive, closed regime.

The seriously disabled random regime is sometimes held together by little more than its symptoms, which represent some very tenuous and implicit "glue."

> The Whalens were a chaotic and neglectful family in which every member had a serious weight problem. Overweight was almost the only thing family members had in common; they even thought of themselves as a "fat family." Overeating fit well into their disabled regime. Each member responded to the perceived scarcity or emotional and other resources by turning to the immediate, strictly personal gratification obtained from food. Fat also helped each member to feel personally protected and invulnerable. Thus overeating compensated, in part, for the emotional starvation of the family.

### Symptoms and Identified Patients

A person who tends to remain stuck in a position of opposition can be frustrating to work with, although certain therapists love them. A whole family of strong Opposers can be a real problem. Members of a disabled random regime are often experienced by outsiders and outside institutions as rebellious, obstructionistic, and provocative. They may be described as impulsive, overaggressive, egocentric, or even narcissistic. Especially in a late stage of disablement, individuals may have learned to act in completely self-serving and opportunistic ways. The hostile competition and negativism of the family's very disabled process matches with a general attitude of cynicism and distrust. In identified patients, especially adolescents, this may lead to depression, isolation, and self-defeating behaviors or to rebellious acting out and delinquency (Costell & Reiss, 1982; Voiland, 1962).

In the disabled random regime, creative individuality and mild counterdependent tendencies may be escalated into a general disregard for authority, an investment in deviancy for its own sake, and insensitivity to the consequences of antisocial behavior. Nonconformity becomes an end in itself.

The disabled random regime is likely to be at serious odds with the larger community. Voiland (1962) called this type of family the "unsocial family," defined by one or more of several marked tendencies: (1) a lack of any need to *resolve* problems or to take social demands and the requirements of reality into consideration, (2) some level of deviance constituting an "offense against the culture," and (3) individual inabilities to care for oneself, endangering oneself or others.

Parents in these families may actively reject all parental responsibilities or they may passively abdicate as parents. Thus these families
often come to the attention of social service agencies for neglect.
Parenting is often erratic and inconsistent in style, tending to be overly
lax or permissive. As parents and children vie on equal terms for
limited emotional resources, fighting may sporadically escalate into
violence or abuse. Intense rivalry among siblings may be further fueled
by parental inconsistency, which can take the form of strong favorit-
ism toward certain children or rejection of others.


## INTERVENTION IN RANDOM REGIMES

Although random families may be less familiar to many family therapists, work with them follows the same general principles as with
other families. The overall strategy is one that moves the family in a
direction opposite to its paradigmatic tendency for exaggeration, to a
less extreme and more enabled version of itself. The therapist remains
aware of the family's paradigm in order to select consciously between
moves that reinforce or counter the family's paradigmatic tendencies.


### Entry and Engagement

The therapist can join and gain access to a random family by mirroring their random style, participating in the informal, freewheeling,
and spontaneously creative process of random regimes. Depending on
the particular family, teasing, good-natured bantor, jokes and puns,
and other playful exchanges are likely to engage the family. Random
regimes tend to respond well to play, and techniques based on play,
like therapeutic games, expressive techniques, and role playing, are
among the most effective joining maneuvers. Approaches that permit
and validate individual expression and creativity (like individual family drawings) are the most congruent with the random style.

For the seriously disabled random family, interventions that generate opportunities for family fun and recreation may be especially
important. The Whalen family, for example, had almost no source of
pleasure other than eating. The competitive struggle in which they
were locked blocked any capacity for spontaneous play. Teaching
them to have fun together was a key element of the treatment strategy.

In the process of joining with the family, the therapist may
intentionally mirror only selected, usually enabled, aspects of the
family or may use approaches that subtly pressure the family in a

direction the therapist wants to help them move. For example, as disabled random families are generally chaotically disengaged, a conjoint family drawing task might be used. This is a metaphor for creative family cooperation and establishes an opportunity to experience, however briefly, a positive, whole-family interaction.

Therapists who do not "go with the flow" and respond with their own creative or whimsical contributions may find it more difficult to join with random families and to get them engaged in therapy. Therapists whose style is more closed or open supply disabled random regimes with important tools and models for countering their centrifugal tendencies, but these same therapists may be seen as uptight, demanding, or authoritarian, triggering further rebellion and increased chaos. These therapists may have to work especially hard to join with the family by building unique, separate alliances with each family member.

Random families' attendance in therapy sessions may be sporadic even when they are fully engaged in the therapy process; who is present may fluctuate from week to week. This must be recognized as an expected manifestation of family style and not necessarily a form of "resistance" at all. Having new and interesting things for the family to do in therapy promotes engagement and regular attendance. Tasks and games as interventions fulfill this function and provide an excuse for imposing rational structure and conveying the possible benefits of structure.

Often the main dimension for engagement of random families in therapy is meaning. A sense of "family," of shared values and common commitment to a joint image, is especially important for random families, which may lack the *structures* of commitment that in open and closed regimes promote collective processes and mutual identification. This identification with a common paradigm or set of family images is often lacking or impaired in disabled random regimes. Echoing and selectively reinforcing the family's self-image is both a joining maneuver and an intervention to reenable the family in many cases.

## Structure and Chaos

The chaos of the disabled random regime may attract the attention of the family therapist more readily than its disengagement. Therapists, especially those who have difficulty dealing with high energy and disorder, are often inclined to try immediately to impose order and structure in a fairly direct way.

Disconnectedness and chaotic process conspire in the family's disablement, as both contribute to their inability to respond to each other and to their difficulty in generating even brief, spontaneous cooperation. Imposed structure that does not meaningfully "reconnect" the family is not likely to be very effective. Family members need to be able to hear and attend to each other to be able to help each other and cooperate spontaneously. Reconnecting members and reenabling their creative responsiveness to each other will reduce their chaotic dispersal, thus reengagement is usually the priority.

It is useful to keep the enabled random regime in mind and to think in terms of interventions that promote movement toward that model. Kantor and Lehr (1975) introduced the distinction between creative randomness and chaotic randomness. Families guided by a random paradigm may differ considerably in the extent to which the "creative" and "disordered" components seem manifest. It is even possible (though not common), for a random family to have a neat and carefully arranged home environment, their random paradigm reflected predominantly through creativity in the arrangement of the environment. One successful family of this sort had remodeled their house to reflect their randomness in the unusual juxtaposition of odd spaces, cozy little conversation nooks tucked under stairs, a hanging loft reached by a rope ladder, and unusual interior decorating employing an eclectic variety of art objects and crafts—yet every object was in its place, conveying a sense of "planned disarray."

Such an upper-class ideal may not be appropriate or achievable for all families. All *enabled* random regimes, however, tend to be more creative than chaotic, though these may still be more "random" and unpredictable than would suit the therapist's personal preferences. The aim of therapy is, then, to free the family's innate creative potentials rather than to clamp down on its chaos.

The oppositional tendencies so apparent in random regimes while often frustrating to family therapists, are easily used in therapy. The more stuck in Opposing family members are, the more readily any form of "reverse psychology" can be made to work. Under these circumstances, "prescribing the symptom" can be very effective, especially if it is directed toward the most oppositional members.


## Borrowed Strategies

The most promising strategies to borrow are those that promote connectedness. Because the therapist also wants to liberate the family's spontaneous creativity, strategies borrowed from open regimes may

have a slight edge over ones from closed. In part it depends on the
severity of the disablement; in the most severe cases, some imposed
structure is the first priority to keep the family from completely disin-
tegrating.

The strategies to be borrowed from open or closed regimes can be
reframed to make them compatible with the values and priorities of
the random paradigm. For example, enhancing connectedness
through better communication can be reframed in personal, individualistic terms. ("You seem to be struggling, each of you, to get what you
need. You each seem to have some difficulties getting your own messages across, which keeps you dependent on each other." "You are a
very creative group of people but do not seem to be able to communicate your individual creativity very well." "I think each of you would
be able to be more creative if you could use each other's ideas to
stimulate your own thoughts, but you seem to have some trouble
hearing what others have to say.")

Closed regime strategies may be more appropriate for random
regimes in late stages of disablement. The therapist can help establish
enabled elements of a closed regime, especially where parental neglect
of younger children is involved, but this is not likely to be an easy or
straightforward task. The therapist should evaluate the various com-
petitors and assist the family in selecting the most promising candidate for leadership in a new regime, even if temporary.

In some cases neither parent is suitable or capable in the short
run, and the therapist may be faced with the unexpected possibility of
supporting the parentalization of one of the children. If this is already
a symptom of the family disablement, the therapist would be prescribing the symptom. This has been productively combined with a creative
injunction in which the inadequate parents are directed to learn how
to parent from the parentalized child. ("We're going to have to do
something unusual and creative here. Jessie seems to be such a good
parent that you two could learn a few things from her before you can
really get this family in shape. For now, she's in charge of teaching
you how to deal with the littler kids. And you are to listen to her and
watch carefully what she is doing.") This highlights and legitimizes
the already operative structure but marks it as a temporary expedient.
At the same time, the parentalized child's role has been subtly but
importantly modified from being in charge of the other children to
being in charge of teaching her parents how to be in charge. The
"leveling" of status between parents and children in this case is congruent with the random regime's "equalitarianism." A move toward
engagement has also been created between the parents and the parentalized child (who is often very isolated). Both the parents and child in
this situation need strong support from the therapist.

Random regimes approach problem solving with a high tolerance for ambiguity and little need to reach closure. Under normal circumstances, this allows them to leave differences unresolved and to accept separate, independent solutions to their problems. When disabled, random regimes can benefit from borrowing problem solving strategies of closed or open regimes, either of which stresses the need for closure. Of the two, the open strategy may be the easier to "import" as it, too, accepts and thrives on creativity and diversity. The family may have to be pushed to persevere and resolve problems. The therapist can frame the open consensual decision-making style in terms largely compatible with the random paradigm. ("This can be quite a fun challenge to see how creative you all can be solving this problem." "You need to find some really creative combination that will allow each of you to get what you really want for yourself.")

### Support and Positive Experience

Members of disabled random families usually do not experience much support from each other, and often, because of their deviant, self-defeating, or antisocial behaviors outside the family, get little real support elsewhere as well. Supportiveness directed at the individual is congruent with the random paradigm's priorities and can begin to reduce the neediness of family members. Unless it is carefully modeled or maneuvered by therapists, support is not likely to become generalized into mutual support within the family. Some form of individual supportive therapy as a prelude to family therapy may be useful, as achievement-sensitive families (disabled random regimes) have been reported to have difficulty in treatment that emphasizes openness and trust (Costell & Reiss, 1982).

In more seriously disabled cases, positive, supportive exchanges within the family are so rare that even the smallest experience can begin to counter the cycle of distrust and competition. These are best carried out during therapy sessions under close supervision rather than being given as "homework," which is likely to be sabotaged. Cooperative (rather than competitive) games can be useful "play therapy," as many of these families have forgotten their playfulness.

### Family Therapy with a Random Regime

In the following example, a family with a consistently random style was helped over a 2-year period to borrow strategies from other regimes and become a more enabled random system.

Naomi Brenner, age 38, was a single parent living on welfare with her two children, David, age 14, and Robin, age 12. While in college, she had been active in the counterculture and had married a farm labor movement activist. They shared an ethic of freedom and radical independence and a lifestyle that creatively took advantage of "The System." After the children were born, he left for parts unknown.

Naomi started therapy because of conflicts with her son who was having difficulty in school. She deliberately sought out a therapist who was also identified with counterculture lifestyles. As a mother, she wavered erratically between invasive overcontrolling and complete laxity. While she prized her own independence and privacy highly, she was often insensitive to the boundaries of others, treating the entire apartment, including her children's bedrooms, as if it were hers, for example. Interaction among the three of them involved a great deal of mutual opposition. David would actively resist Naomi's erratic control and invasion until he got really angry. He would then act out, by taking his mother's car for a joy ride, in one case. (This was an exquisitely precise oppositional response involving separation, self-gratification, violation of community rules, and reciprocal invasion of his mother's domain.) Robin was more quietly independent, more passively uncooperative.

The first meeting was in the therapist's office, but the family had so much difficulty being together in the car on the way to therapy that subsequent sessions were conducted in their apartment. In this case, home-based sessions were an important accommodation to the family's style as well as a source of useful data. The apartment, four similar small rooms opening off a central living room, was filled with myriad objects scattered and piled everywhere, miscellany collected by Naomi who foraged at rummage sales and scavenged discards. She freelanced as a graphic designer but did not report the extra income to welfare agencies. The walls were papered with sketches and designs, hers as well as the children's. The family was quite egalitarian even if not very cooperative. All three dressed similarly in an early 1970s "hippy" style. Naomi would sometimes strike up an independent friendship with one of her children's friends as though she were "one of the gang."

The family managed time as well as space randomly: they were informal about starting therapy sessions, had difficulty ending on time, and occasionally one of them would even walk out early. The boundaries of the therapy were not always very clear. Naomi would sometimes seek out additional counseling by letter or over the phone and once offered to trade an hour of career counseling (which she also did as a sideline) for an hour of family therapy.

Family drawings done in an early session (see Figure 16-1) reflected the Brenners' creative self-expression and suggested not only the antagonistic competition between mother and son, but also the

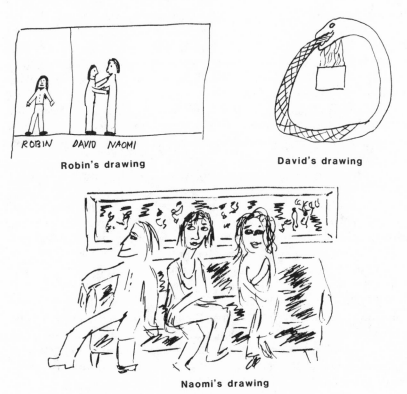

Robin's drawing                              David's drawing

Naomi's drawing

**FIGURE 16-1.**
Family drawings by members of the Brenner family.

isolation of the daughter. Robin remained withdrawn until the therapist, noting her impatience with the therapy, put her in charge of keeping track of the time. This gave her an easy responsibility and involved her without requiring her to *be* involved; it also gave the job of managing time back to the family.

The overall therapeutic strategy was to engage the family with each other in some ways, especially those of mutual support, while disengaging them in other more conflicted areas, thus helping them develop a more enabled style of randomness. In part this required helping the mother become more fully autonomous and therefore more respectful of David and Robin's autonomy. Formulated developmentally, she was being helped to learn to be an effective Mover–Bystander rather than an Opposer and ineffective Mover. To the mother, the autonomy issue was framed by the therapist as getting her kids to cause her less trouble and be more responsible; to the kids it was framed in terms of getting more of what they wanted and freeing themselves of pressures from Naomi. For example, the kids wanted a Christmas tree but Naomi claimed the hassle and expense were too much. The kids were encouraged to find their own solution, which they did, using money from their allowances to buy a small tree and decorations, getting a friend to ferry it home by car, and putting it up on their own. They were pleased with themselves and Naomi was delighted. (Though nominally Jewish, the family was not religious. Consistent with its regime, it borrowed ethnic referents freely and rather indiscriminately.)

With the help of Robin, who was often the family's best Bystander, Naomi gained increasing perspective on their actual working and learned how to Bystand some herself. Robin, on the other hand, was helped to be more assertive and to Oppose more effectively and directly. David began to be able to Move with greater autonomy and clarity without depending so much on Opposing to get his needs met. Eventually he entered private school through a grant from the state and did better than ever before.

The family was encouraged to use inventiveness to find creative solutions to their problems. When David complained that his mother kept going into his room when he wasn't there, the therapist suggested he put a lock on the door. But progress was slow, and one day when Naomi thought she needed something from his room, she was equally creative and broke the lock.

A breakthrough of another sort occurred when the therapist told them, with evident frustration, that what they lived in wasn't a home; it was more like a boarding house. At that point, they began to see the apartment as a space they shared, like roommates. They started to cooperate in the cooking and other household responsibilities, seeing these as appropriate for roommates. In other words, they were helped to formulate a conception of their random style that legitimized cooperation and organization, enabling them to import closed and open strategies. They remained predominantly a random family, but one equipped with a wider repertoire.

# ADAPTABILITY THROUGH NEGOTIATION
## Open Families and Family Therapy

Family therapy has often advocated or promoted a paradigm for family life that it has not actually understood very well. In some cases the bias toward the open paradigm have been quite clear and explicit (Constantine, 1977a; McGinnis & Ayres, 1976; Satir, 1972), but, more broadly, the preferences are implicit. In reviewing typal theories of family, Leonard (1981) found that nearly three-quarters of the widely used models equated healthy family functioning with open regimes or failed to recognize any disabled form of an open regime.

The potential shortcomings, limitations, and weaknesses of open family systems have been poorly understood. Because prevailing models in the family field appear to promote or even idealize open families, a detailed analysis of disabled open regimes is justified. To the extent that the "promotional" efforts of the family field succeed, it could become even more important for clinicians to understand open family disablement.

## EVALUATION AND ACCESS TO OPEN FAMILIES

Clinical experience with open families is still somewhat limited. They do not typically show up at clinics, and when they do, they may often be misdiagnosed or misunderstood. Their flexibility and continuous

Portions of this chapter are reprinted by permission from L. L. Constantine, Dysfunction and failure in open family systems: II. Clinical issues, *Journal of Marital and Family Therapy*, 1984, *10*, 1–17.

adaptive search for solutions meeting individual and family needs may make them somewhat less prone to becoming disabled in the first place. So-called pseudo-open families, whose limited resources as open families make them more vulnerable, are major exceptions. In general, they are special cases requiring special treatment and will be considered separately below.

The likelihood of open families seeking professional help when they do become disabled is still unknown. On the one hand, such families have an open, permeable boundary and characteristically solve problems through active exploration of external resources, seeking information and guidance from the environment. On the other hand, their problem-solving orientation itself, coupled with a strong sense of self-sufficiency, may keep them trying to solve their own problems without outside help. Because they become chaotically *enmeshed* as they become increasingly disabled, the inward-turning tendency is exacerbated. This would suggest that an open family that is not disabled or whose disability is mild or in an early stage would be more likely to seek professional help than a family that is in serious trouble.

Costell and Reiss (1982) reported that "environment-sensitive" (open) families with an adolescent in an inpatient family treatment setting had the least severe problems and were good candidates for quick and effective therapy. My clinical experience is consistent with this; for whatever reasons, open families seen in therapy have tended to be less disabled than typical random and closed families seen in the same practices. Open families may even seek therapy more as an enrichment experience than in resolution of serious difficulties. However, after prolonged, severe disablement, when the open system has begun to dissolve, its members turn outward to renew their individual resources. Clinicians may thus see decaying open families as the result of individuals seeking help. Individually oriented clinicians, rather than marital and family therapists, may therefore be more likely to see this "fall-out" from disabled open regimes.

### Criteria for Differential Diagnosis

Clinical assessment that distinguishes disabled open regimes from other disabled families is important because treatment approaches and goals can differ substantially. For clinical purposes, a family can be diagnosed as a disabled open regime if its manifest values are approximately those of the open paradigm and if its process can be characterized as tending toward *chaotic* enmeshment. Not only its egalitarian value structure, but the intense, volatile, strongly ambivalent character of its overinvolvement are essential for distinguishing the disabled open regime from a disabled closed one, which tends toward *rigid* enmeshment.

Several criteria are key for recognizing disabled open regimes. The diagnosis of chaotic enmeshment is based on evidence of continuing, seemingly endless, intensely emotional negotiation without resolution, characterized by high levels of ambivalence and confusion. It is distinguished from the rigid enmeshment of a disabled closed regime by its overwhelming rather than stultifying quality and the tendency for participants to become exhausted rather than frustrated by constriction.

Less enabled open regimes, with their probable surplus of Movers, can be considerably better at starting things than finishing them. The surplus of initiative-taking in the open regime coupled with its commitment to resolving problems can lead to a phenomenon that might be called the "pending project syndrome." Open families, particularly as they become more disabled, are likely to have longstanding unresolved problems as well as numerous incomplete projects. The open regime does not simply abandon or give up on these, as a random system might do when it moves on to something else, but considers them to warrant continued attention and effort.

Experience shows that the most crucial general indicator of a family's regime is its orientation toward disagreement and dissidence. While the closed regime strives to eliminate most disagreement and all real dissidence, and the random regime tolerates but mostly ignores both, the open paradigm values and includes disagreement and dissidence by drawing on them for the vitality of its problem-solving processes.

Another valuable clinical marker is the expression of anger, which in the open paradigm is accepted as legitimate, normal, even as evidence of authenticity. ("Come on, don't pussyfoot around. You're angry. Why don't you really show it?") Less universally, there is also a tolerant, somewhat permissive approach to sexual–erotic expression. Commonly some sort of explicitly stated single standard of behavior is maintained for children and adults as well as males and females. Open regimes are most sharply distinguished from random regimes in their orientation to problem solving in the face of strong differences. The open regime is strongly committed to working out a mutual concensus, while the random regime practices relativism and is content to leave "each to their own opinion." This, of course, protects the random regime from the dangers of chaotic enmeshment, but leaves it vulnerable to becoming disengaged.

## Composite Clinical Picture

From clinical experience and the various empirical and theoretical models introduced in Chapter 10, it is possible to construct a detailed clinical composite of the disabled open regime family. Olson and colleagues' theoretical integration (1979) furnished the critically important concept of chaotic enmeshment, although the corresponding clinical picture was sketchy. Chaotically enmeshed systems were described as having nontraditional or no leadership, lax discipline, implicit and dramatically shifting rules that are capriciously or arbitrarily enforced, with endless negotiation yet poor problem solving. Couples characterized as "conflict-habituated" (Cuber & Harroff, 1955) represent a chaotically enmeshed marital system.

The environment-sensitive (open) family (Klein & Hill, 1979; Reiss, 1971, 1981) believes the environment is masterable and trustworthy, a belief essential for its commitment to consensual problem solving and "win-win" solutions. Believing that creative, open, consensual process must eventually succeed enables the family to persist and thus fulfill its own belief. But this is also a hook on which the open regime may be caught when it faces a problem that is actually intractable given its resources or when it is dependent for cues from an environment that is not essentially trustworthy. Because it is invested in closure and can tolerate ambiguous, inconclusive situations, the open regime persists despite the impediments, gathering and processing information, exploring possible approaches and solutions, only to heighten ambiguity and uncertainty.

## Symptomatic Behaviors

Specific symptomatic aspects of the chaotically enmeshed process in disabled open regimes are most likely to be manifest in three areas: stress-related symptoms, aggression, and sexual acting out.

### STRESS-RELATED SYMPTOMS

A full understanding of individual symptomatology in relation to disabled open regimes must await further analysis and additional clinical data; however, it is possible to make some reasonable conjectures not incompatible with previous work. Based on Kantor and Lehr's and Voiland's descriptions, stress-related symptoms in both children and adults can be expected, including such stress-related and stress-exacerbated diseases as asthma, dermatitis, ulcers, and colitis.

Children, having fewer psychological resources and fewer options for exit or outside renewal, may be more likely than adults to become identified patients under the high-tension conditions of chaotic enmeshment. The emphasis of the open regime on early self-reliance and acquisition of interpersonal problem-solving skills means a disabled open regime may overstress children (de Lissovoy, 1977). For the same reasons, however, such children may escape detection, appearing to outsiders to be just well-socialized high-achievers. Children may reflect family enmeshment in having restricted friendships and limited social contacts; the intense chaotic aspect may be reflected in aggressive, violent, and/or overly erotic behavior.

### AGGRESSIVE SYMPTOMS

Legitimized expression of anger and other "negative" affect, in the crucible of emotion-dominated chaotic enmeshment, can escalate into outbreaks of exaggerated aggression and even violence. Angry outbursts, screaming arguments, attempts to physically restrain a family member from quitting prematurely, and the like may become increasingly common as the family becomes more disabled. Episodic outbreaks of actual violence may occur but are not likely to become routine, owing to the chaotic nature of the family's process. Carry-over into school, the workplace, and other external settings, however, may become the basis of referrals for therapy. As the mapping established in Chapter 7 would suggest, Blaming, the more defended or exaggerated form of Moving, can be expected to increase with growing disablement in open regimes.

### SEXUAL SYMPTOMS

Voiland (1962) noted a connection between "egotistical" families and "sexual deviance." Analogous to the eruption of excessive aggression or violence, the open paradigm's ethic of openness and tolerance in sexual matters can, in disabled families, become exaggerated into dysfunctional forms of sexual behavior.

Not all couples in open families will have nonexclusive sexual relationships, but sexually open marriage (O'Neill & O'Neill, 1972) is closely related conceptually with the premises of open families (Constantine, 1977a). It has long been understood that extramarital relations are not intrinsically unhealthy and do not necessarily evidence pathology in a relationship (Ellis, 1969; Meyers & Leggitt, 1975). The same applies to open marriage and comarital sexual relations (Constantine, Constantine, & Edelman, 1972). Open marriage values have been found to be positively related with marital satisfaction and adjustment (Wachowiak & Bragg, 1980). In disabled open regimes, as described by Voiland, however, open relationships can become "perverted" so that talking about sexual relations with others or encouraging affairs becomes a substitute for intimate sexual relations between the partners.

Voiland found eroticized overinvolvement in "egotistical" families, suggesting a potential for incest in extremely disabled open regimes. Overt incest, where it materializes, will generally differ markedly from familiar patterns of incest in closed regimes. In the typology of Summit and Kryso (1978), father–daughter incest, clinically the most significant form, typically involves a rigid pattern of collaboration involving both parents. In the "imperious" variant, incest is simply part of a broader pattern of authoritarian domination by the father who is overprotective and controlling. In "true endogamous incest," the father is inhibited, overconventional, and rigidly devoted to a traditional male family role. These most common patterns seem to describe disabled closed regimes; none is compatible with even a failed open regime. More likely is "ideological sexual contact" wherein incest is an extension of an ideology of sexual freedom and openness. In this pattern, casual nudity, early "sex education," and eroticized affection are part of the family's value system and may lead to inappropriate sexual expression between parents and children or between siblings. These are an exaggeration of both the egalitarian ethic and the affective openness of open regimes.

This does not mean that incest, in any form, will necessarily occur in disabled open regimes; the therapist need not mount a "pathology hunt" for incest in every chaotically enmeshed family. It may be useful, however, to remember that patterns in incest vary, and therefore the cues the therapist relies upon must be adjusted to the particular vulnerability of the family in treatment.

## INTERVENTION STRATEGY

Because the disabled open regime is typically intense and emotionally volatile, constantly shifting among ambiguous foci, the therapist may be tempted to deal directly with the chaos: to clamp down on the family, impose rules and order, and bring the process under control. But the disabled open regime is enmeshed as well as chaotic; the chaos is generated by the enmeshment and not vice versa. To bring the family back to a more moderate mode of operation, therapy must initially induce some degree of disengagement. There is no formula for bringing this about; interventions must fit the particular family. As they become more disengaged, however, exhausting negotiations should taper off, and individuals will be freed to recover and restore their personal resources.

If the family is not simply to reenter the same infinite loop that disabled them before, therapy must also assure that important aspects of the context change before they become more engaged again. Skill building and reframing the manifest problem are both appropriate.

Open regimes are unique in that they explicitly examine and negotiate their own structure (Constantine, 1977a). Explicit metacommunication about the on-going process is normal to the family; in disablement, the metatalk can become part of the enmeshed process itself rather than a mechanism for leaving the loop (Harris & Berlin, 1982). These characteristics can be exploited in therapy.

For example, a temporary ban on talk about process, limiting interactions to concrete, pragmatic aspects of their manifest problems, simplifies family interactions and reduces demands on overtaxed resources. It also appeals to the open paradigm commitment to efficacy and pragmatism. The family must, however, be presented with a temporary expedient lest it be perceived as a violation of their paradigm. Relationship issues are, in effect, tabled, to be returned to at a later time.

With less disabled open regimes, therapy can take advantage of the family's conceptual sophistication, eagerness to import new data, and tendency to "process" everything. Simple, direct reports of the therapist's understanding of the family's structure and the factors in its current disablement have a good chance of being effective, much more so than with any other type of family.

A family therapy trainee was treating an egalitarian single-parent family with three school-age children, each also seeing separate individual caseworkers. As the family left the clinic one week, the mother complained about how difficult it was to coordinate appointments. The therapist remarked that, at least, it kept them from spending all their time together, loading everything onto each other. In the next session the family announced their conclusion that the therapist was wrong; they had been using much of their time together dealing with issues raised in individual therapy, pitting one interpretation against another. Having diagnosed their enmeshment, they decided to continue the separate therapies as private sources of outside renewal.

Even a casual disclosure or mere hint from therapists may be taken in, processed through the family's highly verbal mill, and incorporated into its own self-directed change process. Even without explicit in-

structions from therapists, open families are apt to use the time between sessions more productively than other families.

However, even when significantly disabled, open regimes may
work against the use of paradoxical techniques of all kinds, but especially those most closely dependent on outright deception in order to
work. The family is likely to see through the manipulation, defeating
the intervention and perhaps even rejecting the therapist. Certain
paradoxical techniques, such as reframing, can be used provided they
can be "delivered" with a sense of wry humor and even self-mockery
that "exposes" the paradox and lets the family know the therapist is
aware that it, too, is "in on the secret."

Approaches based on education and training are appropriate for
moderately disabled open regimes, including families that have already negotiated past crisis to become, once more, "flexibly connected" (Olson *et al.*, 1979). The content of skill development for open
regimes is discussed in the next section.

### Pseudo-Open Regimes

The pseudo-open family is a mixed system in which there is a pronounced incongruency between what the family says it wants to be and
the means by which it tries to achieve this. It may be guided by an open
paradigm but regulated by another regime; it may use the structures
and processes of an open regime, while being covertly guided by a
commitment to another paradigm; it may be a family whose stated
goals or values are "open," but whose actual operation is not.

A pseudo-open family most often has an essentially closed regime;
under the initiative of one or some of its members, or in response to
outside influences, it has attempted to "become open." Unfortunately,
the old hierarchy is still actually in place and its members remain the
basically cooperative (or uncooperative) followers they always were.
The result is a sham, a parody in which consensual problem solving is
reduced to an empty exercise. The family cannot deal with real dissent;
its members know this but cannot admit it because their rhetoric is
that of the open paradigm. This version of pseudomutuality leaves a
family paying much of the "overhead" of an open regime without
getting the benefits of the open, adaptive process. It is at risk for many
of the same kinds of failures as a genuinely open regime, but has more
limited resources.

Pseudo-open families present a dilemma for the therapist. The
family is, in one sense, an open regime, while in another sense it is not
open at all. Is the therapist to assist in reenabling the family as an open

regime, consistent with its stated values, or as another type, consistent with its actual behaviors and present capabilities? Aside from ethical issues, there are substantial practical differences in the two directions. Unfortunately, the therapist does not have the luxury of going along with what the family wants or manifests, for it is, in fact, presenting a double message. Therapeutic choices that enhance one direction at the expense of another cannot be avoided.

To help the pseudo-open (operationally closed) regime evolve into an enabled open one requires two things from therapy. First, en route to a full-fledged open regime, the family needs a period of individuation that will generate a more random process (consistent with the morphogenetic sequence introduced in Chapter 9). In effect, the therapy spreads protective wings around the family, reassuring them that the chaos and divergence they are going through are necessary and useful to realizing their goals. Therapy provides a temporary, artificial boundary to counter the centrifugal forces that will threaten to pull the family apart. Generous hand-holding and reassurance give the family a substitute cohesion and the encouragement to keep evolving toward more differentiated reintegration.

Secondly, the family must learn new communication and decision-making skills needed for sustaining an enabled open regime. These skills include: enhanced self-awareness, active or empathic listening, assertive self-expression, no-lose (win–win) problem solving, and consensual decision making. The content of most of these areas is well developed in various "enrichment" and "enhancement" programs, notably, couples communication (Miller *et al.*, 1975) and parent effectiveness (Gordon, 1970, 1976). For the open family, communications skills usually directed at couples are extended to include children, and negotiation skills first elaborated as parenting techniques are generalized to relationships among adults. A growing literature on consensual processes in small groups (Avery, Auvine, Streibel, & Weiss, 1981; Fisher & Ury, 1981) is also a useful resource.

For the family to become reenabled as a *closed* regime, the approach is, of course, entirely different. Therapy must address the family's unrealistic image of itself as an open regime and support the "open" and honest establishment of an effective closed regime. The intergenerational boundary is deliberately enhanced and clarified, for example. Pseudo-open families, because of their token resources as open regimes, are more likely than open ones to be seen already in collapse or moving toward disengagement, rather than in chaotic enmeshment. In such cases, reengagement, promoting "togetherness" around a traditional family model, is doubly functional if therapy is to promote the family's closed rather than open elements.

A priest and cotherapist were called in by the Irish Catholic father of a large family. As janitor at a progressive school he had overheard enough "new ideas" to convince him that his family should be more sharing, involved, and democratic. When the therapists arrived, they were asked to help persuade three older teenagers to stay for the session. The older kids stood in the doorway for the entire hour while three younger children reluctantly sat at the kitchen table with the parents. The father wanted to call the shots for change; the others were quite content with things as they were. With three kids already "on the way out" and three more closely behind, the family was well into disengagement. The father wanted his wife to support him in the decision to become more open, but certainly did not want *her* to become more independent and differentiated. The therapists concluded it was probably too late for the changes the father wanted and helped him appraise his situation more realistically.

The choice of one strategic direction or another is not simple; it involves ethics as well as pragmatics. The matter of values cannot be avoided in family therapy (Trotzer, 1981). Therapists must be clear about their own values, even if the family is not. An important consideration is the therapist's assessment of the likelihood a family will remain in therapy long enough to complete the difficult process of developing a functional open regime. If this process is truncated, the family may be left more disabled than ever, but clinically less accessible. In some cases, the manifest values of the family are superficially open, but the more deeply held images are more congruent with random or closed paradigms. In such cases, the going may be easier when the direction is compatible with the deeper values. It can also be argued that this is more respectful of the family's values.

## TREATMENT OF A DISABLED OPEN REGIME

An example illustrates how aspects of disablement in an open regime may be manifest and how understanding the open paradigm can shape the therapeutic process.

The Dorrs initially sought therapy because of the elective mutism of their 5-year-old son, Adam. Jan and Dan, married about 6 years (Jan for the second time), also had a younger son, Aron, not quite 2. They considered themselves to have a sexually open marriage that was basically sound and had selected the therapists based on a reputation for tolerance toward unconventional lifestyles. Dan, an assistant professor at a local college, and Jan, who did occasional freelance writing for a local newspaper, both had degrees in art history.

Except for Adam, who could already read and write but spoke only in a whisper and only to his father, the family was highly verbal and committed to talking things out together rationally. Adam communicated his anger and frustration very successfully, nonetheless, striking another child in the waiting room before the first session, throwing coffee on one of the therapists, and later trying to pull down curtains in the office. The parents were ineffective in setting limits verbally. During a family drawing task, Aron completed not only his own drawing but kept embellishing his mother's. Her repeated protests were sincere but weak.

The first assessment session revealed a family with a strong commitment to individuality and collaborative problem solving. They were activists, involved in the peace movement, community affairs, and the arts. In view of the family norms, Adam's symptomatic behavior could hardly be more precisely targeted. Those norms, together with the couple's sometime sexually open relationship, suggested open paradigm values.

In action, however, things were different. Attempts to define or initiate joint action were abundant, but these were generally ineffective. In its own metaphorical terms, the family was "always moving" (and, geographically, soon to move again), but lacked direction. Except for Aron, whose provocative mixture of affection and aggression was especially effective on Jan, family members seemed unable to get what they wanted from each other. Though intensely involved, they remained uncoordinated. The family appeared to be a system standing near the borderline between a random and open regime, perhaps slightly over the fence into open, but clearly disabled and lacking in critical capacities for managing an open family regime.

Parental overinvolvement, uncharacteristic of disabled random regimes but typical in disabled open ones, was split between the parents. Jan's involvement with Aron was intensely ambivalent. A weak and ineffective Mover, her frequent efforts to assert herself were often thwarted by Aron's aggressive "affection." Adam's whispered alliance kept his father engaged and separated both somewhat from the maelstrom between mother and younger son.

The therapeutic strategy was, therefore, to disengage the family structurally in terms of parent–child relations while simultaneously building the basis for more successful intimacy between the parents. Benign neglect toward Adam's behavior was considered therapeutic, especially as the focus on him tended to corner him into the symptomatic role. The couple were seen for a period without the boys, allegedly to work in a less chaotic setting on what they as parents could do to help Adam. A principal focus of these sessions was actually to enhance differentiation, helping them to become more aware of personal boundaries, to clarify, and, finally, to sustain their differences instead of falling into obfuscation or flight to protect their boundaries.

As suggested in Figure 17-1, therapy initially nudged the family toward becoming more random before again becoming more open.

While committed to individuality and to sharing differences, the actual prospect frightened Jan and Dan. Dan dealt with escalating disagreement by escape; Jan would become increasingly muddled and ambiguous. An uncertain and fuzzy illusion of agreement was sustained along with a myth about their ability to talk things out. Homework and tasks were assigned that eroded the illusion while creating opportunities for learning assertiveness toward each other. Boundary sculptures (Constantine, 1978; Duhl et al., 1973) were employed to explore differences in their presentations of self and interpersonal style.

Once the parents were able to clarify their own interpersonal boundaries, the children were reintroduced into the therapy using another drawing task. Generalizing the learning within the adult subsystem to include the children at this point was in keeping with the family's norms as an open regime. Eventually, Adam was able to say that, though it had started somewhat as a game, he felt he had become trapped in his mute role at the learning center he attended. Jan was charged with organizing a school visit and a meeting between the therapists, Adam's teacher, and the school psychologist. The teacher

**FIGURE 17-1.**
Progress of Dorr family regime through course of therapy.

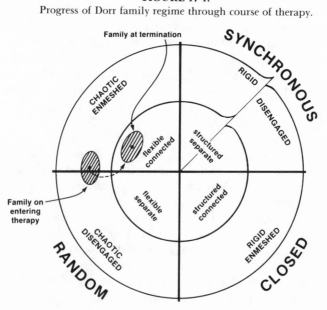

was encouraged to express her concern for Adam through simple support and affection, rather than constant attempts at drawing him into conversations that only helped maintain Adam's "distinction." Adam's tape recording of lessons for other students and acting in rehearsed plays were created as devices to ease the transition to full verbal involvement.

As the family became more effective and better able to listen, Adam was able to speak more freely about his thoughts and feelings. They moved to another state where further work with a special needs teacher completed Adam's return to normal speech.

Two years later, the therapists were able to make the follow-up visit. In the meantime, besides coping with the move and overcoming Adam's mutism, the family had dealt with the death of Jan's father. Guided by their experience during therapy dealing with an earlier death, the family was able to share its grief openly. Nevertheless, at first Dan and Jan were inclined only to tell the children that their grandfather had died in an accident; but ever-perceptive Adam somehow figured out his grandfather was shot in a random street crime, thus giving the whole family the chance to explore their values as pacifists, their sense of justice and fairness, and their anger at senseless violence.

Before the therapists arrived, Adam expressed some anxiety that they would see him only as "that 'dumb' little boy." They did not, of course, and the follow-up made clear that the family had continued to evolve as an open regime, coping with adversity, increasing its ability to sustain disagreement and intimacy, and extending itself again into the community.

Of course, effective therapy with the Dorrs could have been conducted without benefit of any perspective incorporating a model of open regime disablement. On the other hand, the efficiency with which this model highlights therapeutic direction is valuable; certain therapeutic "digressions" may thus be avoided.

If a closed paradigm had been used as the standard of reference, the Dorrs would have been considered a seriously disordered family. Inadequate parental discipline and marital sexual "misconduct" would be counted among their liabilities. Yet imposed order would not only trigger strong resistance, it would violate the family's own values. To teach the parents to become effective within a traditional model of parental control and limit-setting would likely have needed a very prolonged effort, and the incongruence between values and behaviors would be likely to generate chronic strain.

A diagnosis of "disabled random," that is, of chaotic disengagement, would have led to strategies promoting engagement. The chaotic aspects of a disabled random regime reflect the lack of connection and engagement of its members. The random family as an entity becomes in danger of being sacrificed to the pursuit of separate individual interests. This was clearly not the case with the Dorrs. In chaotic disengagement, bringing members together into greater contact or involvement creates the opportunity for joint enterprise and of itself becomes a form of collective process. Therapy that moved the Dorrs in such a direction would have had a high probability of increasing the degree of disorder and heightening the pressures sustaining symptomatic behavior.

# 18

# HARMONY THROUGH IDENTIFICATION
## Synchronous Families and Family Therapy

The synchronous regime may be the most puzzling form of human organization, and, to many people, the synchronous paradigm is an elusive concept. Is there really such a thing as synchrony? What is it, and what does it mean to the family professional? The difficulty of the notions of synchronous regulation and a synchronous worldview justify starting with a thorough reconsideration of the paradigmatic basis of synchrony. By no means have all the theoretical issues been worked out or the practical problems thoroughly explored.

## THE SYNCHRONOUS PARADIGM, PARADOX, AND REALITY

The synchronous paradigm begins with an intrinsically paradoxical orientation to time. The closed paradigm is oriented to continuing the past into the future, the random paradigm to change in the present, and the open paradigm to the integration of past and present into the future. These are all active processes reflected in the feedback communication mechanisms by which each corresponding regime maintains its paradigmatic commitment. The synchronous paradigm is the anti-

Portions of this chapter are reprinted by permission from L. L. Constantine and J. T. Israel, The family void: Treatment and theoretical aspects of the synchronous family pattern. *Family Process*, 1985, *24*, 525–547.

synthesis of continuity and discontinuity, the opposite of the inclusive "pantemporal" orientation of the open paradigm. Its orientation to time is to stand apart from it; the synchronous paradigm is therefore said to be "atemporal." It is not committed to continuity in time but to timelessness itself. This viewpoint may itself be viewed as utopian or unreal, but real families with this enduring sense of changelessness, of apartness from time, have been described (Beavers, 1976; Liedloff, 1975).

A related paradox of the synchronous paradigm inheres to its overarching commitment to harmony itself, to harmony without process, and to agreement based on consentaneity and identification. Realization of this ideal would require a system regulated without processes of adjustment, compensation, or negotiation, a system with enduring agreement not dependent on communication. It is thus paradoxically commited to agreement and mutual identification but not to the processes by which these are normally reached. Through an essential identity of individual viewpoints the synchronous paradigm is also able to deny conflict as well as the need to resolve conflict, whether among individuals or between individuals and the collectivity.

All forms of the synchronous paradigm thus partake of a utopian, mystical, or perfectionistic quality (Stafford, 1979), a worldview that unavoidably involves idealism, naiveté, myth, or mystification. The paradoxes and contradictions that seem to make the synchronous paradigm so difficult to comprehend are in the nature of the model and worldview.

The synchronous regime depends for its regulation upon the identity of individual "programming," on a sense of mutual identification or consentience that does not rest on communication but on inner agreement. This is often perceived as impossibly idealistic and utopian or else as profoundly dysfunctional, as "dystopian." The concept of synchronous operation has been challenged as a theoretical construct and the existence of synchronous regimes in practice has been questioned. Taken as a whole, however, the clinical record and the combined models of numerous theorists and researchers argues for the importance of the notion of a synchronous paradigm and regime and the value of distinguishing these from their closest parallels.

Perhaps the strongest argument for the theoretical significance of the synchronous regime and paradigm is that synchrony completes the mappings among systemic models, individual behavior, and group dynamics in a way that is consistent and makes sense. This mapping juxtaposes group process based on "prior programming" and mutual identification (without communication) with Bystanding and neutrality toward process; with detached, superreasonable communication and bland, hypernormal behavior; and with the pastimes of early group formation and the universal issues of group termination.

The theoretical argument for synchronous regimes is bolstered by various researches and theoretical formulations. Reiss's (1971) consensual experience model includes distance-sensitive families, a class of families that is found to exhibit clinical characteristics that are, in most respects, what would be predicted from the synchronous paradigm. Olson's (1983; Olson *et al.*, 1979) circumplex model incorporates the disabled extreme of rigid disengagement, a condition that becomes understandable as the dysfunctional exaggeration of a synchronous regime. In Voiland's (1962) analysis of family casework records, both "inadequate families" and "perfectionistic families" have some characteristics of disabled synchronous regimes as derived from theoretical argument, although the "perfectionistic" type is the more consistent.

The concept of synchronous organization is not, then, unprecedented; many of the characteristics of synchronous regimes have been recognized by various observers for some time. The conceptualization of synchronous regimes as a distinct mode of systemic regulation is original, however. It is this conceptualization that enables us to integrate clinical experience with disparate descriptions in the literature to form a useful composite.

## FORMS OF SYNCHRONY

The paradigmatic map of family regimes includes a "discontinuity" in the upper right quadrant that suggests that synchronous regimes may take on two forms, markedly different in certain observable characteristics. The underlying distinction between these two variants is in complexity. The simpler, more entropic system is "understructured," lacking in feedback regulation, of course, but also with limited consentaneity or overlap in individual cognitive maps. The more complex, more negentropic form has substantial coincidence of cognitive maps and may even be thought of as "overstructured" by these identities. The more primitive variant is termed an "amorphous" synchronous regime, and the highly structured variant a "perfectionistic" synchronous regime. There can be said to be a discontinuity between these two variants that is isomorphic to the discontinuity in the group dynamics model explored in Chapter 9. The amorphous synchronous regime is "underdeveloped" and the perfectionistic synchronous regime is "overdeveloped." The underlying basis of these two variants is identical, however, and both will tend toward similar exaggerated extremes of rigidity and isolation.

To many observers, the absence of structures, especially hierarchical ones, is automatically equated with chaos, even when actual day-to-day process may be rigidly predictable. The amorphous synchronous regime, which lacks both the expected internal structures and readily apparent mutual identification with common values, has been described as chaotic, but there are inherent contradictions in such descriptions. For example, Beavers (1976) describes "the most seriously disturbed or *chaotic* families" (emphasis added) as "timeless, repetitive in interaction" with "little change in the family world" (p. 49). They cling together in "an amorphous ego mass," (i.e., with little differentiation or individuation). Instead of "goal-directed, active negotiation," the family relies on fantasy and "studied unawareness." There seems little doubt that these are disabled synchronous regimes. The families are said to fail to help children learn autonomous action or develop clear boundaries of self. They behave as if "closeness is found by thinking and feeling just like one another."

Contradiction and paradox are the norm under the synchronous paradigm, but clinicians need to be careful to distinguish truly chaotic process from the simple absence of apparent regulating structures. The former is more likely to typify disabled operation in random or open regimes, while the latter characterizes synchronous regimes. Amorphous synchronous regimes are likely to present as neglectful but docile and compliant, definitely not actively antisocial. They look outside for rules and definitions of acceptable behavior.

## SYNCHRONY, CHANGE, AND DIFFERENTIATION

Disabled synchronous regimes employ a variety of strategies to maintain synchrony or the appearance of synchrony in the face of change or differentiation between members. The maintenance of synchrony at the expense of necessary communication, reality testing, and effective coping is at the heart of the disablement of synchronous regimes. The paradigmatic commitment becomes more important than the actual issues of the real world itself. To be true to its paradigm of harmonious identification, the disabled synchronous regime must obscure or deny differences and change and must do so without communicating. It is axiomatic that one cannot not communicate; not surprisingly, then, the strategies of attempted noncommunication introduced in Chapter 5 abound in seriously disabled synchronous regimes. Less seriously disabled synchronous families resort to strategies that restrict or markedly reduce significant communication.

Beavers (1976) catalogued strategies used by severely disturbed "amorphous" families to avoid acknowledging change and difference. The majority of these are uniquely suited to synchronous regimes. Most are compatible with a preference for the detachedness or neutrality of Bystanding (or its simulacrum) or with highly defended forms of Opposing. Among them are (1) the excessive use of questions rather than statements; (2) unresponsiveness, allowing the communications of others to fall flat, thus introducing subtle sanctions that control without taking responsibility; (3) distracting, being evasive and making unexpected shifts in meaning, thus deflecting and obscuring differences without directly exposing the Opposer; (4) sarcasm, ridicule, and disguised hostility that are controlling but, through slippery language, discourage counterattacks; (5) "mind reading," speaking for other members or depending on others to present one's views; (6) close mutual monitoring, almost automatically "checking each other out" nonverbally, thus making sure that answers do not betray obvious differences.

## Timelessness

An outstanding and distinctive feature of the synchronous paradigm is the atemporal orientation, the antisynthesis of the inclusive, pantemporal orientation of the open paradigm. Synchronous regimes as implemented in real families have a common tendency to ignore or deny the passage of time. Beavers (1976) describes severely disturbed, "amorphous" families as "extremely reluctant to acknowledge the passage of time," using a variety of unrealistic methods to "obscure the evidences of change" (p. 75). Their interaction is "stereotyped, repetitive, and devoid of any real encounter." A dream-like or mythic quality of enduring timelessness prevails.

## The Function of Mystification

Whether amorphous or perfectionistic, disabled synchronous regimes are often found to depend on some form of mystical or utopian thought for a point of reference. Several writers have described amorphous families as manifesting "magical" thinking and a naive faith that everything magically works out, even when their own experience contradicts this. Perfectionistic families are more likely to present a utopian faith in calm rationality or "correctness," or a belief that "rightminded people" or "right thinking" will inevitably or ultimately triumph.

Mystification and fantasy can play an important function in seriously disabled synchronous regimes. As the family mystifies its members and substitutes fantasy for reality, it maintains the appearance of synchrony without actively countering differentiation or dissent. Family myths simply overlay or replace reality-based descriptions of family events and processes. Change and differences are "magically" eliminated by a shared myth, without resort to argument, persuasion, authority, or chance. The shared myth is itself a form of synchronous thought, and thus, through sacrificing its links to reality, the family preserves its synchrony.

## DISABLED SYNCHRONOUS REGIMES

Recognition of synchronous regimes and families guided by a synchronous paradigm is made simpler by certain marked characteristics of such families when they become disabled. The rigid disengagement into which they are prone to lapse is the most significant evidence. It is often experienced as a quality of "deadness," a pronounced ennui pervading the family.

### Rigid Disengagement

To understand synchrony, it is useful to keep in mind that the synchronous paradigm is the antithesis of the open paradigm—what the one is, the other is not. While the open regime risks overloading its children by deluging them with data, the synchronous one risks undernourishing its children from a shortage of essential communication, most especially affect. Neither open nor synchronous regimes are predestined to failure, of course, and when they succeed and are enabled, each will strike a balance in all essential matters. When they fail, they will fail in essentially opposite ways.

While open regimes become too hot as they become more disabled, the synchronous regime becomes too cold. With increasing disablement, the open regime will process more and more: the synchronous, less and less. The synchronous regime, faced with growing evidence of essential disagreement between the parents or the essential failure to socialize children into harmonious patterns, turns more and more to mechanisms of denial. Differences must, of course, be denied, but the core of essential values and expectations must also be denied, because to verbalize this core is to expose it to scrutiny, making visible any discrepancies in behavior. The appearance of synchrony would thereby be lost.

Active denial itself is a form of dissent and a manifestation, however minor, of friction, so the family maintains its integrity as a synchronous regime by learning to avoid areas of proven or potential conflict altogether. Unless underlying problems are resolved, this constriction of communication can become chronic and progressive. Slowly but surely the family is dying; eventually nothing will be shared and nothing will happen. Its commitment to the synchronous paradigm is its last reference point for coordination, and the family becomes rigidly disengaged. They do not necessarily stop speaking to each other—although speech may be more limited than in other families—but in their commitment to the appearance of normality and unity, their conversations become overconventionalized. Nothing of importance is said, and, as a family, they are dead.

The condition of rigid disengagement can be baffling to the family therapist. The family may confirm and acknowledge the chronic and invariant nature of their problem. The therapist can see the stereotypy of behavior, the invariant repetition of interactions, and can experience their rigidity when the family is probed and prodded to change; but there is little sense of active resistance. There seems to be no particular "homeostatic" action to account for their being so stuck. There is no ossified authority, or closely monitored restrictiveness. Change doesn't happen, but not because it is sabotaged or opposed in any discernible way. The vectors of change lose their force, go nowhere, seemingly absorbed like sound in an anechoic chamber. The therapist who is used to working with family homeostasis, especially one adept at therapeutic paradox and the leverage of prescribed symptoms, will find the rigidly disengaged family frustratingly elusive.

The paradigmatic model of this book clearly points out the strategic direction for work with a disabled synchronous family: reengagement. Something needs to start happening. The family's heart needs to be restarted. However, therapists must avoid getting into a position where they are the ones making things happen. The family can function as an almost infinite sink, absorbing the energy of the therapist during sessions without ever becoming reactivated.

### Clinical Indicators

Responding to the deadness of a disabled synchronous regime, therapists are apt to feel the need to energize and revitalize the family, to "get things going" and restore it to vitality. The family, however, can function like a therapeutic "black hole," swallowing without visible effect the most potent and energetic interventions. The subjective experience of the therapist may thus be one of the strongest indicators of an exaggerated synchronous regime. Since the synchronous paradigm is committed to perfection, the vulnerable therapist may easily be caught in powerful but unstated demands to cure the family and restore an effective synchrony. Not all therapists will be equally sensitive to this pull, but many will and may thus become inducted into the family's disabled process, to become trapped by the implicit message that nothing is good enough, that nothing short of the most brilliant therapeutic razzle-dazzle will suffice to recharge the family. The therapist who ignores flagging energy and valiantly searches for the "right" intervention has the opportunity to experience the sense of doom such families can elicit in the "inadequate" child who never quite catches on to the family's expectations. The therapist who withdraws in resignation, earlier or later, is then thoroughly inducted into the family's rigidly disengaged regime.

Above all, the synchronous family values harmony, getting along, and smooth running. This is ultimately of greater importance to the family than other goals that the therapist may want to see gain ascendancy. There may even be one or more members who want "more communication" or "more sharing," but attempts at authenticity are generally weak or are quickly swamped by discounting and disaffirmation. The family may acknowledge that they have their share of disagreements, get upset, and express anger, but role-play demonstrations or detailed discussions of past instances will reveal these to be emotionally controlled, muted, or supremely rational encounters.

DEATH AND DEADNESS

Not only is a quality of deadness diagnostic of disabled synchronous regimes, but synchronous families may have a special thematic investment in death. The magical timelessness of the synchronous paradigm denies the inevitability of death. The death of a family member is a loss that can only be denied at the peril of the death of the family in some important sense. Once again we see the how the synchronous family may become caught in its own paradoxes: in avoiding dealing with death, it dies as a family. Or the deadness of the family may be acted out in the suicide or attempted suicide of one member, as in the Kaiser family introduced in Chapter 14.

> The Ridges, a decidedly unlively family who seemed to have great difficulty sharing anything, entered therapy with an extraordinary "secret": Gerri Ridge was dying at the age of 43. Three years earlier she had been diagnosed as having a rare, invariably fatal disease and was then given about 6 years to live. Eventually the subject of illness and health came up in therapy and the truth was revealed. She and husband George thought

they had discussed her disease, though not her dying, with their four nearly grown children; the children didn't remember.

It is also possible that the failure to deal with death or to grieve the loss of a family member can contribute to establishing a disabled synchronous regime. One single-parent family espoused generally open values but seemed to function at the borderline between open and synchronous operation. Their failure to resolve fully the loss of the mother's sister, who had done most of the parenting, seemed to push them into a bland disengagement. The mother, who had been fairly uninvolved before her sister's death, ended up quietly stumbling along as a parent.

IMPLICIT COMMUNICATION

Many synchronous families manifest an underlying belief that wants, wishes, and feelings should not have to be explicitly stated, certainly not spelled out in detail. Other family members should "just know" what someone wants, thinks, or feels. Feelings, especially, are not to be expressed directly. This value itself may only be expressed as an implicit metacommunication associated with numerous specific statements, e.g., "He already knows how I feel; there's no need to tell him I love him." Parents may be particularly reluctant to admit to having expectations for their children and will avoid communicating any clear and specific demands. Should children ask for directions, they are likely to be told, "You know right from wrong. I'm sure you know the right thing to do. I trust you to do what's right." This conveys very strong expectations that only very specific behaviors are acceptable or desired, yet nothing is revealed of the actual standards and criteria being invoked. The child must already know or deduce intuitively what the expectations are.

Consonant with its reliance on programs held in common by its members, the synchronous family calls upon various forms of "mind reading" as a substitute for ordinary communication. It is very common for family members to speak for each other or to introduce each other's contribution. ("She feels threatened." "He has something to say.") This kind of "mind reading" is familiar to any family therapist, but in the case of the synchronous family, not only is projective communication more frequent, it often proves, in an unusual number of instances, to be surprisingly accurate.

IDENTITY THEMES AND BOUNDARIES

"Difference" and "sameness" are both thematic and problematic within synchronous families. There are likely to be frequent references to being alike or being different, to agreement and disagreement, but considerable difficulty sustaining examination of either side of these issues.

These concerns are important not only because the synchronous regime depends on coincidence of mental maps for its continued coordination, but because similarity and difference are the principal elements by which it defines its boundaries. The synchronous paradigm, recall, does not ultimately define boundaries in conventional spatial terms. In effect, the synchronous family says, "If you are one of us, you think like us, and see things the way we do." The converse, that someone who does not think like others in the family is not "really" one of the family, may be left unstated, but it is always clearly implied. This distinction can be a source of great anxiety for children who are struggling with issues of belonging or differentiation. The child who has yet to figure out the family's definitions or expectations or the child who is trying to differentiate from the family is vulnerable. The paradigm implies that to see things differently is equivalent to not being a member of the family.

DIMENSIONAL FOCUS

Synchronous regimes generally seem to be caught up in *content*, sometimes almost to the exclusion of other dimensions. The absence or extreme attenuation of affect and the confusion or obfuscation of meaning in disabled synchronous regimes contribute to this focus on content. The therapist's attempts to clarify meaning are likely to be thwarted by mystification and distraction. Feelings are seldom expressed directly in words, and nonverbal expressions of feeling are denied, censored, or censured by others. Attempts to get at feelings are often met by explanations or reasons for behavior. Prompted to express their feelings, family members often substitute other material that is labeled as a feeling. ("I feel that he is wrong about what occurred that night.") Feelings are often depersonalized. (Talking about his evident pain in reaction to rejection by his son, a father says, "The feeling is one of being misunderstood.") Disabled synchronous families may be only slightly more at ease in the dimension of meaning.

A markedly reserved, "dry" emotional climate may show up either in synchronous regimes or in closed regimes where the traditional norms are of emotional control. Extreme detachment or extremely flat affect is more characteristic of synchronous regimes, however. This is consonant with the detachment from reality characterizing disabled synchronous regimes, a detachment that is ironic in view of the veneration of literal content by these families—it matches well with the superreasonable "computing" of disabled Bystanding.

## The Relationship between Closed and Synchronous Regimes

The closed and synchronous regimes, in adjacent quadrants of the paradigmatic map, share certain characteristics. Compared with random and open regimes, both are more stable over time and are distinguished by lower degrees of individuation or differentiation among members. Although both paradigms address continuity and consentaneity, in the closed paradigm the commitment to continuity entails a need for conformity, while in the synchronous paradigm the reverse is true: the commitment to harmony entails a requirement for invariability. The commitment to continuity of the closed paradigm is more active than the timeless orientation of the synchronous paradigm. The closed regime uses explicit authority and corrective communications to sustain stability dynamically, while the synchronous regime uses implicit authority and the absence of communication to avoid change. It must be kept in mind that chronically disabled closed families are prone to decay or collapse to synchronous operation.

Earlier descriptions of family types tended to lump synchronous and closed families together into a single category of rigid, homeostatic families without distinguishing the markedly different mechanisms by which these families sustain regularities in process. Beavers (1976), however, clearly differentiated amorphous, understructured families (quite consistently described in synchronous terms) from rigid and overstructured families, which were argued to be more highly developed.[1]

## Clinical Access to Synchronous Families

An outstanding feature of many synchronous families, especially the perfectionistic variant, is their apparent normality, their bland ordinariness. The personal style most compatible with this paradigm

1. Beavers (1976) also places these and a third type on a developmental continuum in order of increasing complexity, from amorphous, through rigid, to balanced. By Beavers's original descriptions these are, respectively, amorphous synchronous, closed, and the closed–random transitional form known as the "democratic family" that will be described in Chapter 19. This ordering is consistent with the developmental model introduced in Chapter 9. Beavers failed to recognize enabled forms of the first two categories, however, and thereby conflated system negentropy with degree of functioning or enablement, from "severely disturbed" through "midrange" to " healthy."

is superreasonableness or hypernormality. The effectively socialized member is likely to be quiet, cooperative, easy going, and fairly likeable. Even the members of severely disabled synchronous families may be socially successful and effective in the outside world. More often than not they will not fit into conventional diagnoses of psychopathology. As a family, they may appear almost boringly normal unless scrutinized quite closely.

In view of their smooth exterior and quietly reasonable inner workings, one wonders how such families would ever be seen in family therapy. Indeed, the rigidly disengaged family is likely to wither away quietly or to sustain its funereal interaction indefinitely without reaching any crisis in functioning that brings them to the attention of the helping professions.

An exogenous crisis or intervention is one possible precipitating agent. Synchronous regimes have little if any access to *resources of differentiation,* that is, those based on the separate identity and unique experiences of individual members. The rigidly disengaged family with its severely limited interactive ability is also handicapped in being able to use its shared resources. Thus, such a system is surprisingly easy to overload.

Death, an accident or health crisis, a grown child leaving home, or other normal developmental crises are likely to exceed such a family's coping abilities. Young adults, especially prior to forming their own families, may bring their families of origin into therapy.

Early work at the Kaiser–Permanente Clinic (Leary, 1957) suggested that individuals whose interpersonal style is adjustment through hypernormality may be especially prone to psychosomatic complaints, and, while denying personal problems, may find their way into the mental health system by referrals from doctors for psychosomatic or physically related problems.

By contrast to perfectionistic families, the amorphous variant may be characterized by serious individual problems. Families with diagnosed schizophrenic members are often found to be synchronous regimes caught in processes of mystification and mythologized interaction (Beavers, 1976).


Entry and Engagement

Synchronous families, even those that continue for some time in therapy, seldom seem to be very committed to it. In keeping with their paradigmatic investment in uncommitted appraisal and their general tendency toward disengagement, they do not become intensely involved in therapy. In workshops, the most frequent question raised about working with synchronous families is how to get them *engaged* with the therapist and therapy. Therapists report feeling as if such families will terminate at any moment; the clients seem to put very little into therapy and get little out. The threat of premature termination may hang like a pall over the entire therapy.

Recognizing this common tendency of synchronous families can be helpful in keeping the therapist from becoming too off-balanced by it. Working under a renewable contract for a set number of sessions may be useful, as such families respond well to implied responsibility and are unlikely to pull out before the specified sessions are completed.

Gaining entry to a synchronous regime can be difficult. To join with the family in a manner consistent with its paradigm would require demonstrating essential agreement with the family, participating in its "group think." An active, engaging, expressive family therapist is at odds with the family's basic style of interaction. While countering the family's disabled detachment may be indicated or even necessary, this may tend to work against formation of any therapeutic alliance in the short run.

### Process and Progress

In contrast to the open regime, which embraces and deliberately chooses change, the synchronous regime denies change in its paradigmatic commitment to "timelessness." This quality of timelessness has a peculiar impact on therapy.

The family is likely to deny that there is any special significance to their entering therapy at a particular time. The presenting problem is often described as permanent, without beginning. ("It's always been that way with the kids. As long as we can remember we couldn't pry it out of them.") The significance of possible precipitating events is denied.

In keeping with its paradigm, the synchronous family screens out or denies all change, including therapeutic change. Therapists may find themselves in a peculiar position when they are successful in helping a synchronous family change. The changes may be quite evident, even remarkable, as seen by an outsider, yet the family will discount or deny that anything has happened. ("What do you mean we're talking more? We've always talked." "There isn't any real change; it's still business as usual.") Therapists may find themselves in the awkward position of trying to convince a changed family that change has occurred.

Therapists who feel compelled to convince the family and who depend on the family's affirmation for validation are, of course, often trapped by families that withold confirmation. It is not uncommon for families to recognize change but to attribute it to causes other than therapy, consequently, good therapists learn not to depend on clients for validation, but to consider change itself a measure of successful outcome. The synchronous family can be considerably more frustrating because the therapist is left with no outside criteria.

Resistance in synchronous regimes is more often passive than active. It is commom for family members to be "unable" to take on an assigned role or to try out a new behavior. Assignments between sessions are seldom carried out; they "forget" or "just can't find the time" to carry out instructions. "Homework" involving the whole family or more than one person is seldom completed, as family members are typically scattered and have may have little contact during the week.

Carry-over from interactions in therapy sessions is minimal. In sharp contrast to open regimes, which spontaneously discuss and explore anything and everything that happens in therapy, synchronous regimes act almost as if therapy were not taking place. Even dramatic encounters or surprising disclosures may go undiscussed between sessions.


## SYNCHRONY AND PARADOX

To appreciate fully the clinical issues of the synchronous family, the therapist must keep in mind the paradoxical nature of synchrony. Paradox is intrinsic to the definition of synchrony. The paradoxes of "coordination without process" are reflected in very real, sometimes poignant ways in families guided by the synchronous paradigm. The impact of these paradoxes on children may be especially powerful.


### Perfection and Synchrony

In Voiland's casework model the family conforming most closely to the synchronous paradigm was the "perfectionistic family." Perfectionism may not be the most central defining feature of synchronous families, but it is an aspect with many important clinical implications. The investment in perfection may be thought of as one familial way of reflecting the utopian, transcendent aspects of synchrony.

The synchronous family does not exactly *seek* perfection; more accurately put, the synchronous family wants to *be* perfect. In contrast to the open family, improvement and "progress" are of little interest to the synchronous family. They want to "be there," to bypass the process altogether. In family therapy, this contributes to an inability to perceive progress or to appreciate change when it becomes evident (which may contribute to the therapist's sense of inadequacy and even feeling the need to persuade the family that they have changed.)

Perfectionism is, of course, not limited to synchronous families, but synchronous families, even those more superficially amorphous, are almost invariably perfectionistic. Their perfectionist is often implicit, and may even be denied if the subject is raised, nevertheless, the need to be perfect is communicated with great force to children. If anything, it appears that a lack of communication is often the very mechanism by which perfectionism is communicated by parents to their children.

The restricted communication of the synchronous regime leaves little room for praise and none for enthusiasm. Children of synchronous families may speak of feeling that nothing they did was ever good enough, yet expectations were never directly stated. They sensed an unspoken standard of performance and behavior against which they were measured, but they were never able to deduce and emulate it well enough to be rewarded. The sparse and neutral messages of their parents were like a vacuum drawing another generation into the pursuit of perfection in the hopeless hope of finally winning parental approval. Such parents are seldom aware of witholding affirmation, and in many cases the children will be unaware of it also until, as young adults, they look back on an emotional desert. In some families, dry and dispassionate appraisal by a superreasonable parent only adds to the apparent demands for perfection. Points of "rational and objective criticism," although delivered without rancor or malice, nevertheless may be experienced by the children as barbed and critical, while calm and objective appraisal of merits rings hollow and empty.

It is part of the synchronous family's preoccupation with perfection that precise standards of performance should not have to be made explicit, that expectations need not be articulated because they are already "understood." One "just knows" these things; the "right way" or the "best way" is obvious. To have to state standards and expectations is, it seems, an acknowledgment of imperfection, a demonstration of the lack of synchrony in family member's understanding.

The child is inducted into the synchronous regime by a rather subtle, almost devious mechanism. To fit in, children must understand the parts they are being asked to play in the family and the standards to which they are to conform, yet these are not—indeed,

cannot—be discussed or communicated openly. The child must, therefore, become a skilled observer and deduce from indirect cues and signs
what the family's images and values are. In short, the child is drawn to
the position of Bystander.

The "good child" in a synchronous regime is the one who, by
watching carefully and by knowing the family and how it operates,
knows just when to help without having to offer or even to be asked. In
this way, the family's perfect harmony is confirmed.

### Individuation

The synchronous paradigm affirms individuality in apparent contradiction to its basic premise. On closer examination, however, this is
found to be very different from the sense of individuality affirmed by
the random and open paradigms, which are themselves quite distinct.
In the random paradigm, individuality means being unique, different.
The open paradigm emphasizes inner directedness, the strength to
hold one's own in negotiation.

The synchronous paradigm values the separate, detached individuality of the Bystander. The synchronous regime, however, depends
for its coordination on members who basically think alike; thus it
wants its members to arrive at the same conclusions but to reach them
independently. At its core, the paradigm reveals a passionate belief in
some one, ultimate, real, universal, transcendent, or best way of seeing
things.

The synchronous paradigm thus affirms that there are many
paths to truth with but one destination. The parents in synchronous
families will often state that they want their children to be independent and to find their own ways, but the children report being more
aware of the unspoken message that the way they must find must be
"the right one" or they will never be accepted by their parents.

The child must not merely Follow, however, for to do so violates
another of the basic tenets of the family's charter. In the synchronous
paradigm, Following is problematical, therefore compliance is an
unacceptable strategy. The child who takes the "easy" way and Follows, must deny it, claiming independent choice. The child who
Opposes must not appear to do so, consequently the defended form,
Distracting, is common. To satisfy the requirements of the family
fully, children must willingly and independently reach the one acceptable but never stated conclusion.

The threat this poses to the child in a synchronous family may be
exceptionally potent because of the way such families define their

boundaries. To be "in," one must share the vision; if you do not, then even if you stay around, you are really "out." The implied penalty is, in effect, "excommunication" (paradoxical pun intended).

In disabled synchronous families, the child so excluded may repeatedly ask, "But what do you want from me?" The reply is typically "Nothing. We just want you to be yourself." This response implies universal acceptance, and that is part of the necessary fiction of the disabled synchronous regime. The detached neutrality of the Bystander permits a kind of universal, unconditonal love, genuine even if not especially warm. In the enabled synchronous regime this is genuine enough to leave room for some individual divergence from family norms and for family imperfection. In the disabled synchronous regime, the need to sustain the appearance of synchrony prevails. The parents have difficulty communicating their dissatisfaction to the children, as this exposes essential disharmony and may generate more.

To define one particular, most deviant child as "not one of us" is therefore a conservative strategy, in one stroke excising the greatest source of disunity and serving as an example for the remaining children. The example not only defines the threat more clearly, but gives the remaining children a better picture of the unarticulated demands. What they must *not* do is thereby evident.

In disabled synchronous regimes, the commitment to harmony becomes transmuted into a commitment to avoid all conflict, which results in attempts to minimize confrontation and, finally, communication. Both the denial and the silence pose central difficulties for the children in these regimes. What the child needs to know, to have confirmed, and to talk about is precisely what is avoided and denied. The child is left without tools.

## TREATMENT OF DISABLED SYNCHRONOUS FAMILIES

The Ridges were a socially successful, upper middle-class Catholic family who entered family therapy on behalf of their 21-year-old adopted daughter, Su-Li, a Cambodian refugee.[2] Individual therapy had found her deeply entangled by an acute sense of not belonging in her family and a correspondingly intense need to be accepted by them. She was haunted by a past she had disowned. Her father, George, was a hard-driving, successful businessman, always reasonable and cool but

---

2. Costell and Reiss (1982) noted that among adolescents and their families in treatment, the greatest number of adoptees were from distance-sensitive families. Adoption may pose an exceptional challenge to the distance-sensitive/synchronous family.

often dispassionately critical. His wife, Gerri, was acknowledged by the others to be the family leader, although George frequently spoke on her behalf or prompted her. Older brother, Steve (age 22), was considered, especially by his father, to be irresponsible and direction-less, drifting into failure, while younger brother, Dean (age 19), a pre-med student, was the apple of his parents' eyes. Laura (age 15) was the quiet and compliant younger daughter who had considerable diffi-culty differing with her parents.

The family was rigidly disengaged. Communication strategies to sustain the impression of synchrony were abundant. Statements were often couched in vague or neutral terms; assertive positions were avoided. ("Well, it was okay, I guess. I don't know." "What should I say?") Members would look around to each other for cues or for help when asked a question. Almost any disclosure was greeted by pro-longed silence, discouraging further disclosure. George expected the kids to know when he needed help at home and to pitch in without being asked. He would often speak for Gerri or prompt her. ("I think you have some things to say about that." "She probably should talk for herself. But let me say that she is pretty upset.") In one structured exercise, Dean declined to express any positive feelings toward Su-Li because "she already knows." The family was and had always been generally cool and unexpressive; Gerri admitted to hardly ever having hugged her children.

The following exchange not only illustrates the tendency of fam-ily members to speak for each other but shows a unique "communica-tion" strategy the family had developed. When one person was unable to recall and describe a pleasant event from childhood, someone else supplied, "What about the time with the apple tree?" This was greeted by a chorus of "Oh yeah!" and "I remember that, sure. The tree." By *referring* to events rather than talking about them or describing them they created opportunities for confirming consentaneity without risk-ing possible exposure of different memories or interpretations.

As is not uncommon for synchronous regimes, the family had major developmental failures to deal with.

> The adoption of Su-Li had created the first major developmental crisis for the family; it had remained unresolved for 9 years. The relief agency through which Su-Li was placed had assured the Ridges that they would be adopting a young child. However, her papers had been mixed up or falsified at some point, and instead of a child of 7 or 8, the Ridges suddenly found themselves with a young lady of 12, nearly the age of their oldest boy. Synchronous families can be expected to have some difficulty dealing with the changes of growing up; the Ridges got it all at once. In a sense, they never forgave Su-Li for being older than she was supposed to be.

Furthermore, whereas the family was founded on similarity and agreement, Su-Li looked different, talked different, and had already been thoroughly socialized to different norms of behavior and emotional expression. Not only did she not fit in, but there was little chance that she could be made to fit in within the time remaining.

The family claimed allegiance to independent thought but thrived on confirming their essential similarity. Su-Li had become caught between competing demands: on the one hand, to be herself and disclose what she really thought and felt; and, on the other, to be one of the Ridges, to be like the rest of them. She protected herself by closing off her Cambodian past and increasingly withholding her real feelings. This confounded her isolation and contributed to the family mystification of her place in it. ("Of course she is really a member of the family, just as much as anyone else. She just doesn't feel like she belongs. She never shares things with us like the other kids. But she's really the same.")

In family therapy her dilemma was made poignantly, paradoxically clear when she tearfully asked her parents to tell her what they wanted from her. Her mother answered, "We don't want anything from you. We just want you to be yourself, just like everyone else in this family."

Even when other children shared her perceptions of the family or empathized with her, they were reluctant to acknowledge this as it risked defining them, too, as "outsiders." Thus the sibling subsystem was also disabled. Though Steve and Su-Li were both seen as "nonconformists" who were "always in trouble," they were unaware of their similarities or common experiences. Similarities and possible alliances between Su-Li and anyone else had to be denied. In one case, when both Steve and Su-Li said almost identical things to their father, George was unable to comprehend her message and could not see that they were expressing similar thoughts.

The chessboard family sculptures completed by the family in the first session manifested features of the synchronous regime. George placed the pieces as in Figure 18-1, describing this arrangement as "the others are spaced evenly around me," despite the obvious disparities. Gerri's sculpture had everyone else in the family in a perfect line behind her. Su-Li, after having great difficulty with the task, perfunctorily arranged them about the same as her father had, saying that it didn't really mean anything to her anyway.

The family's deadness was related to another unresolved developmental crisis. Three years earlier Gerri had been given 6 years to live. With only 3 yet to go, the family had still not talked about her dying. Gerri was, on the one hand, a major force for change in the family, wanting to have more real intimacy and sharing with her family. Yet,

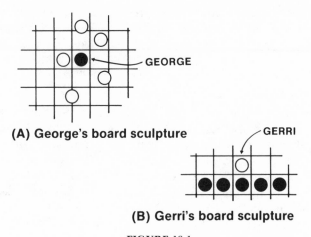

**(A) George's board sculpture**

**(B) Gerri's board sculpture**

**FIGURE 18-1.**
Sculptures done on a chessboard by members of the Ridge family.

fearing the outcome of confrontation, she also longed for a lost sense of harmony in the family. An attempt in one session to bring her and Su-Li into a face-to-face encounter as adults ended in Gerri's abruptly sitting down in silence. George started the next session by announcing that Gerri was just about ready to pull out of therapy.

In fact, even after 10 sessions, the family seemed almost indifferent to continuing in therapy. Though by then they had begun for the first time to talk about Gerri's dying and had had several significant encounters, they denied that anything was different or that anything important had happened. Once the therapists recognized this detachment and denial of change as symptomatic of a synchronous regime, they became less concerned about it.

The therapists drew the map shown in Figure 18-2 and selected a two-step strategy. Before helping the family deal more fully with her dying, Gerri was to be temporarily taken "out of the center." She was a key to engagement of the family but was feeling threatened. Her concerns about death, even before openly stated, her deep ambivalence over change and authentic communication, and her unusual alliance with George all tended to dominate family process. She was therefore told she was "off the hook." As a major concern of hers was the disconnection from Su-Li, the therapists felt that dealing with differentiation of her children was appropriate. Su-Li could only be truly accepted into the family as it could become aware of and acknowledge her difference. Real alliances and mutual identifications, which always imply differences, were to be underscored, and the disengaged sibling subsystem was to be strengthened and reenabled.

The therapists concluded that strategies borrowed from closed or random regimes could not help the family deal with its unresolved developmental crises *and* remain true to its paradigmatic commitment as a synchronous family. A new, enabled synchrony could only be established by temporarily resorting to open regime methods to deal with Su-Li's integration into and differentiation from the family and with Gerri's impending death. This conflict and the need to sacrifice some safety and tranquility in the short run for greater consentience in the long run was spelled out for the family, leaving the choice to proceed to them. (Characteristically, they never announced any clear decision, but merely kept coming to therapy.)

The therapists selectively reinforced certain subsystems that had enhanced opportunities for real communication. For example, since Dean identified with the parents and emulated his achievement-

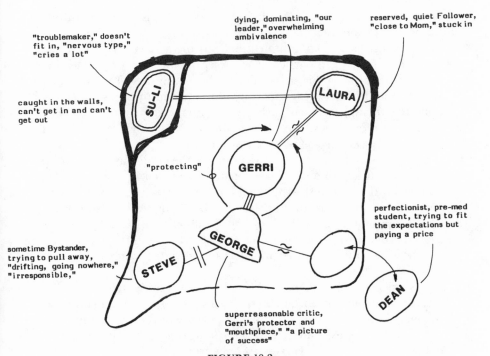

**FIGURE 18-2.**
Family system map of the Ridge family.

oriented father, he and his parents were directed to discuss "careers and future plans," a recurrent family issue differentiating him from Steve; the others watched from behind a one-way mirror. The rest of the "younger generation" then discussed "unstated parental expectations" while Dean and the parents watched. In this way, the sibling subsystem heard implicit expectations made explicit while the parents heard about the impact of implicit demands on their children.

Separating the family with the mirror resulted in more energetic, focused, and meaningful interaction than when the whole family was together. Such techniques seem to have a particularly strong impact on synchronous families, perhaps because splitting the family disrupts synchrony, while coached observation helps members become more effective Bystanders on their own family process. The techniques are essentially "compliance-based" symbolic enactments rather than paradoxical uses of a therapeutic team and one-way mirror (Papp, 1980). The focus on the improvement of sibling relationships, an important but often neglected aspect of family work (Bank & Kahn, 1982), is especially appropriate with synchronous families, where issues of differentiation may be hidden under a heavy gloss of automatic identification without appreciation of real differences. Underscoring differences between Dean and Steve helped build a basis for real mutual support, for example.

Not just lack of communication, but the avoidance of pain and "negative" feelings in particular was keeping the family from dealing with its painful problems. Among other things, Su-Li had never talked about her early years in Cambodia. In a multipurpose intervention, the therapists asked each person in the family to share one painful memory from before he or she was 12, which for Su-Li, of course, meant before she was part of the family.

The session became a turning point for the family, as Su-Li ended up talking at length about her growing up, which had been riddled with painful memories. At the end, both Gerri and she spoke of the sense of calm and warmth they felt. The following session was opened by George and Gerri telling of the Cambodian dinner Su-Li had cooked for them in her apartment. The whole family was clearly "celebrating" their renewed understanding and pleasure with each other.

Gerri continued to have difficulties concerning her sense that everything depended on her, that she was the only one pushing for change. She would push for change, especially improved communication, until it seemed imminent, then she would pull away, even running out of one session. Her behavior expressed the family's intensifying ambivalence about change. She was tired of always having to push and did not want to be "different," either in wanting change or by becoming the focus of important work. She would vacillate between insisting that nothing was happening and reluctantly acknowledging small progress limited to Wednesday evenings (when the family met for therapy).

The therapists "sided" with her, saying the family would have to meet more often, outside of therapy. They put Laura, the youngest, in charge of the first such meeting, giving her an explicit set of instructions for a structured exercise and a mandate to "push" the others as much as needed. For the first time, the family followed through on a homework assignment, not only doing the exercise but continuing on their own initiative to deal effectively with some difficult issues.

At the next therapy session, Gerri startled everyone by admitting that she "really was impressed by the remarkable strides they had *all* made." In truth, even as they celebrated their progress, they continued to employ synchronous tactics to protect the restored consentience they valued so much. They had reached this point of acknowledged change not by becoming an open system but by borrowing some of its strategies; it was this enrichment of their repertoire that had helped them to become more enabled as a synchronous regime.

CHAPTER

# 19

# ADJUSTMENT THROUGH ACCOMMODATION
## Mixed Regimes and Competing Paradigms

In real families, paradigm, regime, and process often do not match perfectly. A family may have inherited strong images of ideal family life that they are ill-equipped to implement. From grandparents they may have retained a clear picture of a close-knit and smoothly functioning closed family, yet have never worked out the new strategies needed to implement this ideal in the bustling and competitive urban scene in which they live. Or the model they seek to emulate and by which they judge themselves as a family may be completely new, but the only strategies and structures they know are left over from the parents' families of origin. It is not easy to find a single, nonpejorative word to describe these many situations in which action, structure, and image are imperfectly aligned. The term "incommensurate system" will be used, as it denotes the lack of a "common measure" for the levels of the system without implying that this is necessarily undesirable or dysfunctional.

The assortative mating schemes of a complex modern society do not insure that the family's "architects" have the same or even similar family paradigms in mind when they set out to build a family. It is not uncommon for two or more images to be in competition within a family. Each may be reflected in distinct dimensions of family process or hold sway with certain members. Divorce can create boundaries and distance that make possible the clearer emergence of competing paradigms in "binuclear" families (Ahrons, 1979), and remarriages generate many new opportunities for families with fully developed but distinct styles to attempt to blend together. Whether the family remains locked in paradigmatic competition or forms some hybrid image from its paradigmatic roots, the result can be called a "compound system."

The four primary paradigms represent polar points in a continuum of possible models and worldviews; the shades of grey in between are also possible and realizable in families. "Compromise systems" are families that seem to balance between paradigmatic commitments or remain poised at the borderline between distinct styles.

Several distinct complications are thus introduced to be explored in this chapter: "incommensurate systems" having an imperfect alignment between paradigm, regime, and process; "compound systems" guided by distinct, multiple paradigms; and "compromise systems" blending adjacent paradigms and regimes.

## INCOMMENSURATE FAMILY SYSTEMS

Probably most families through some greater or lesser portion of their life cycle are "incommensurate systems," lacking a "common measure" of their paradigm, regime, and process. These may be conceptualized as in Figure 19-1, as "misalignments" between levels of description of the family. In the example, a family with an open-to-synchronous image of family is coordinated by a mostly random regime and experiences random process. A family with a clear and unambiguous common commitment to a closed ideal may, thus, go through periods of greater randomness or openness without ever modifying or compromising its paradigm. Its structures may break down and decay or fall into disuse, to be replaced by others that may or may not align with its family paradigm.

Such incommensurabilities are not uncomon and are not, in themselves, dysfunctional. The pseudo-open family, discussed in Chapter 17, is a common example in which regime and paradigm are not aligned. Although incommensurate systems are not necessarily disabled, it does take extra energy to sustain process that does not fit well with a family's regime, and there is an unavoidable and chronic tension when a family wants to be something it is not. Acting as an overarching guide to shape family life, the paradigm defines a set of congruent regimes and related family interactions that will take the least energy to sustain at some given level of functioning. In the very large universe of possible families, those whose paradigm, regime, and process are closely aligned represent configurations of lower energy demand. In effect, a particular paradigm creates a "pull" toward certain concrete structures and day-to-day dynamics. The stereotyped cases of families whose paradigm, regime, and process are "pure and

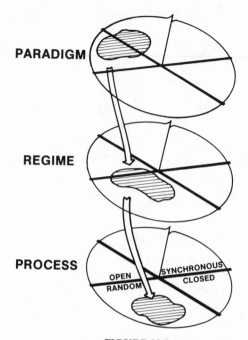

**PARADIGM**

**REGIME**

**PROCESS**

OPEN    SYNCHRONOUS
RANDOM    CLOSED

**FIGURE 19-1.**
Representation of "incommensurability" of paradigm, regime, and process in a family.

simple," all fitting well together, represent local "energy minima." Other combinations that are similar but less closely matched across levels will take slightly more energy to maintain. The greater the disparities between paradigm, regime, and process, the more family energy will be used up.

It is tempting to consider this energy "wasted," but it must be kept in mind that this is the extra work that a particular family must do in order to maintain its unique combination of image, structure, and action. Only if some aspects of one or more of these were to change would the energy demand change.

The energy invested in sustaining incommensurate elements among the three levels becomes important if the family system is disabled or in danger of becoming disabled. The extra resources consumed in sustaining the incongruencies may make the difference between a family besting its problems or being bested by them. Clinically, this means that incommensurable aspects, though not themselves a form of disablement or signs of dysfunction, must be attended to as possibly compounding family difficulties.

## COMPROMISE FAMILY SYSTEMS

Families that "sit on the border" between adjacent quadrants attempt a balance or blend between two paradigms. This compromise is itself a paradigmatic commitment and may be an important part of the family's image of itself. One family, for example, was particularly proud of their ability to "walk the fine line" between an ordered but unexciting life and one more chaotic but also more exciting, that is, between a closed regime and a random one. The contributing adjacent paradigms are not necessarily carried by different people; most commonly the admixture is reflected in the images of most or all family members. Some border cases seem to be "easier" than others, namely those that do not juxtapose antithetical paradigms.

A compromise paradigm or regime is one possible resolution to competing paradigms in a family, the compromise blends elements of what would otherwise be competing paradigms and regimes into a new entity in which the distinct character of the original images and structures become submerged. By contrast, the "compound" family system retains the competing images and structures as distinct and recognizable features of the family. Figure 19-2 represents the four compromise regimes/paradigms.

### The Closed-Random Compromise

The closed-random compromise family system is attractive for many of the same reasons that draw people to the open paradigm. Such a family promises some of the benefits of both, adding flexibility and independence to stability and cohesion. It differs from the open family both in how it formulates the nature of the combination of closed and random and the methods by which it envisions or attempts achieving these. Whereas the open paradigm is a commitment to a synthesis, that is, an entirely new model and method of realizing the model, the closed-random compromise, as the term suggests, attempts to hover in balance between competing pulls. Perhaps the key feature distinguishing them from open families, which in some respects they resemble, is their investment in and willingness to compromise rather than being committed to negotiating to unanimous consensus and the complete synthesis of individual and group interests.

Like open families, these compromise families are likely to hold frequent or regular family meetings, but these are more likely to be based on democratic process and parliamentary models than on consensual decision making and "win-win" problem solving. The dis-

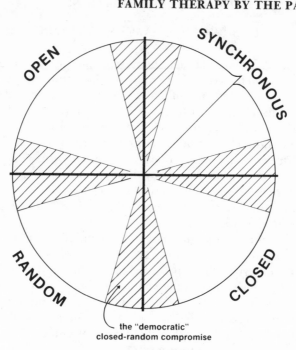

the "democratic"
closed-random compromise

**FIGURE 19-2.**
Compromise regimes/paradigms.

tinction between compromise and democratic process, on the one hand, and consensus and negotiated problem solving, on the other, is an important one, though it is a difficult one for some people to understand. In a compromise, neither party to a negotiation gets what they were after, but rather something in between that may or may not meet their needs. If Mom wants to go to Bar Harbor and Dad wants to go to Key West, they can compromise by spending a week in Washington, D.C. If the reason behind each original choice was a desire for restful quiet "away from civilization," neither "wins" in the compromise. Open regime negotiation seeks to uncover the underlying issues and find a creative synthesis that meets everyone's needs. Dad may have spoken for Key West because he wants to go fishing with his brother who lives in Miami. A suitable synthesis might have the brother join them all in Bar Harbor. The democratic process of vote-taking in families has related side effects. One can only vote for or against what has been proposed. In most cases, a minority must accede to the wishes of the majority, even if these reflect nothing of minority interests.

Parents in such "democratic" families want to "allow for" individuality, "give a certain amount of freedom" to children, yet "set clear guidelines and limits." In these aspects they are similar to parents in the best functioning of closed families. Like their counterparts in random families these parents want to foster creativity and believe that the unique and special potential of each individual should be allowed to flower to its fullest.

The family process is an on-going balancing act between order and disarray, between togetherness and independent activity, between autonomy and loyalty. These remain in competition because the family's paradigm does not include the image of these as reconcilable dualities, but rather sees them as polar opposites. The compromise regime does not incorporate mechanisms by which they can be reconciled, since it is based on unintegrated borrowings from closed and random regimes.

The American ideal of "the democratic family" and a great deal of the popular literature on parenting and childrearing reflects this compromise paradigm (e.g., Dreikurs, 1964). The common tendency to see parenting as being on a continuum from permissiveness to restrictiveness with a "healthy compromise" in the middle is evidence of the significance of this borderline construction of family reality.

Families based on the closed–random compromise can be enabled at the cost of the energy needed to succeed in the never-ending balancing act, resisting the pull to either side. In a sense, these families are in an unstable or metastable position with a pronounced tendency to drift too far in one direction or the other before corrective action restores the balance. Thus they may enter therapy with pronouncedly random or closed process incommensurate with their compromise regime. A substantial drift toward randomness is not easily countered by a "democratic" regime. As the random regime is also next in the morphogenic sequence, randomness that is problematic for the family is somewhat more likely to be presented by the family. Parents from these families may present themselves as "progressive parents" whose kids "went too far," for example.

It is appropriate to borrow strategies of the regime away from which the family has drifted, but the therapist should not miss the possibility of borrowing open regime strategies, which can be quite easy for the family to incorporate. This will not make the family an open regime but may make it a compromise system with new tools to help in its balancing act.

## The Open–Synchronous Compromise

The family on the borderline between open and synchronous paradigms/regimes is committed to another sort of balancing act. The balance it attempts to strike and maintain is not between extremes in levels of certain process variables, such as, closeness or orderliness, but in the nature of process itself. The open–synchronous compromise balances between the open regime propensity to overprocess and the synchronous regime's tendency to process too little. It wavers between regulation by communication and regulation without communication (by identification). The compromise paradigm is one that balances a commitment to the dynamic intimacy, reality testing, and active problem solving of the open model and a commitment to the harmonious and perfect identification of synchrony.

Families guided by this paradigm are liable to drift toward too little or too much communication, toward unnecessary "checking out" or toward unwarranted assumptions of agreement. The dance between these is illustrated in the following dialogue, which occurred while I was revising this chapter. I went into the kitchen to get some coffee and chat about the open–synchronous compromise.

> JOAN: While you're out here, could we . . .
> LARRY: Yeah. The tree.
> JOAN: (simultaneously) The tree.
> LARRY: Let's go check out things to put it on.
> JOAN: I suppose I'll need my boots.
> LARRY: We're just going downstairs.
> (We go down to look for boards on which to set the Christmas tree. Finding nothing suitable, Joan suggests a wash tub stored out in our shed.)
> LARRY: Good idea.
> JOAN: I thought that's what you meant originally. I'll have to get my boots on.
> LARRY: You knew what I knew even before I knew I knew it.
> JOAN: Yeah, I just had to check it out.

The position of the open–synchronous compromise (see Figure 19-2) corresponds to that of Mover–Bystander in the map of individual behaviors, suggesting the potential power of this compromise. Such families represent maximally internalized locus of control. The particular effectiveness of the compromise comes at the cost of the balancing act and at the risk of drifting too far in either direction. If families on this border come into therapy, they are somewhat more likely to resemble synchronous regimes than disabled open ones, as the drift toward disengagement (too little checking out) is not intrinsically self-corrective. This drift is also in the direction of morphogenetic evolution outlined in Chapter 9.

## The Open–Random Compromise

The compromise represented by the border between random and open quadrants is similar to that between open and synchronous in that it represents a choice between "working things out" and "letting it happen." The resulting process is much more variable and disordered, however. As the family leans to one side of the balancing act, they strive to negotiate to consensus, often with somewhat undeveloped skills and overdeveloped senses of autonomy. To the other side, they let everyone do their own thing, trusting to creative coincidence to bring about desired group ends. The family is incompletely committed to working things out collectively and may be unsure whether that approach can work, yet they are not satisfied with merely letting things happen. This keeps them in tension between competing methods of coping.

In general, however, there is considerable compatibility between these adjacent paradigms, especially as the open paradigm recognizes the random regime as a subset contributing to its synthesis. Thus the tolerance of open regimes for random subsystems and for members committed to the random paradigm may be quite high.

Such families are almost certain to present with symptoms of chaos rather than rigidity, but may not be clearly overcoupled or undercoupled and are quite likely to fluctuate between enmeshment and disengagement. Their lack of order is essentially compatible with either of their paradigmatic leanings.

## The Closed–Synchronous Compromise

Families on the borderline between closed and synchronous quadrants appear to be quite common. In most respects there is an essential compatibility between closed and synchronous ideals—either kind of family is likely to be quiet, conventional, and stable. Both are likely to employ static, external points of reference for their values. The competing forces that are compromised in the borderline case are togetherness and separateness. The closed paradigm favors warm, "close" families, while the synchronous paradigm sponsors cool compatibility and quiet separateness. Although both may put a premium on agreement, they differ in how this is to be achieved: the closed paradigm advocates that conformity be taught, imposed, or handed down by an active process of imprinting and regulation that the synchronous paradigm abrogates.

Exactly the opposite of families on the open–random border, these familes are almost certain to be rigid in disablement but may not be clearly enmeshed or disengaged. In the family adrift on the synchronous side, the amorphous lack of formal structure and active processes of control may sometimes suggest disorder to the therapist, but process itself will nonetheless be quite repetitive and predictable.

## COMPOUND FAMILY SYSTEMS

A compound family system results when two (or occasionally more) paradigms within a family are not blended together or do not fuse into a compromise but remain as competing images. They vie as points of reference for the design of structures and regulation of process, or they guide distinct and recognizable subsystems within a family. Compound regimes arise when two systems are joined, as in a reconstituted family, or when a single system divides itself into subsystems with different regimes. This division may occur because of exogenous factors, such as prolonged separation, but far more often reflects preexisting competing images of family. Under the influence of competing paradigms, distinct subsystems develop. It is quite common for two people to marry who have very different views of how a family should be organized and operate.

Compound regimes are often identifiable by the presence of distinguishable subsystems. Family systems whose regimes appear to be a homogeneous blend of the characteristics of different regimes are more often found to be transitional forms, compromise families on the borderline between adjacent regimes.

There is a clear and usually easily identifiable cost in terms of energy needed to maintain compound family systems. When the struggle between competing images is unresolved and on-going, the cost is obviously the investment the family makes in the struggle. Even when distinct subsystems derive, each owing allegiance to separate images, energy is consumed in maintaining the interface between subsystems, whether this is lost in "friction" or consumed in maintaining elaborate bridges and borders.

> At a professional conference, one marriage and family counselor described his family as basically closed, while his own leanings were toward open systems. He said, for example, that his family had already put up its traditional Halloween decorations by the first of October and, not wanting these to be seen at the wrong time, discouraged him from inviting friends and colleagues over. And how did he deal with all this? "I travel a lot," he said. The energy cost in this case could be easily identified and even measured in terms of jet fuel, hotel bookings, and time spent in preparation and travel, for example.

## Formation of Compound Family Systems

Pairings that result in families with competing paradigms are common. Couples are drawn into such relationships by a general tension of approach–avoidance toward a model that is opposite to their own or by a specific need to complete something missing in their own family experience.

The compound family systems most frequently encountered in clinical practice are those between closed and random. When someone with a closed worldview marries someone with a random orientation, there are several common outcomes: they eventually break up; they have children and subdivide into two essentially independent families under the same roof; or they continue to drive each other crazy year in and year out. The formation of a compromise regime is also possible but seems to be rare unless the differences between the original paradigms were minimal. The closed and random regimes are, however, antithetical and, in their purer forms, highly incompatible. The success of a subdivided family hinges on the ability to develop strategies that minimize the interfaces between the incompatible subsystems. The more contact and interaction between the random regime and the closed one, the more friction and conflict there is likely to be.

What would ever bring a person from a closed family with a closed worldview to marry one from a random one? The dynamics of this union are illustrated by the following case example.

Marya and Adam share an Irish Catholic background, but while she attended a Catholic college, he joined the Navy to see the world. Adam took some college courses while based in San Diego, but when his tour of duty was over, opted for more travel and adventure by becoming a flight steward for an international airline. He lived alone and stayed alone whenever he stopped over in a distant city. He kept his relationships casual and varied until he met Marya, just after a turbulent holiday in Bombay during which he was stoned on hash most of the time. He had stretched himself as thinly as he could and was looking for something stable to which he could tether his restless spirit. Marya, who had led a somewhat cloistered life in college, was attracted by Adam's colorful style and, sensing his need, saw the chance to take care of Adam and protect him from his wilder impulses. She figured that their common ethnic origins meant they had similar basic values and that they could settle down into a stable family life spiced up occasionally by Adam's adventurousness. Each at that time in life needed the other as a counterbalance. The problems arose because at the deepest level they had little in common in how they saw the world. Not even their family backgrounds were actually similar. Her family were devout, solid, hardworking citizens; his came from Irish revolutionaries and writers who drank and brawled their way through life.

The intrinsic dilemma that each paradigm is "incomplete" in some sense provides the basis for the attraction across paradigmatic lines. Children from closed families may grow up with a longing for freedom and adventure, those from random ones having a sense of missing stability and security. The offspring of open families may develop a yearning for tranquility, while those from synchronous ones may seek intimacy and involvement.

The differences in paradigms need not even be very great. For example, one woman who grew up in a family that was a somewhat neglectful, amorphous variant of a synchronous regime married a man whose family had a more rigid, perfection-oriented closed–synchronous regime. She saw his family as caring and invested in a way that hers was not, while hers suggested to him a freedom and flexibility lacking in his. Though both paradigms were synchronous and the family they formed together was also synchronous, tension between agreement-oriented perfectionism and the values of autonomous responsibility and self-discovery were greatly elevated in this family.


## Competing Paradigms in Compound Family Systems

Tension between competing paradigms is not normally manifest in a straightforward way as conflict at a basic level. More often it results in more superficial but pervasive tensions or chronic fights consisting of repetitions of standard disagreements that are never resolved and that proceed almost identically on such reiteration. The real unresolved struggle is too basic and fundamental for the couple to acknowledge. In such cases, if the couple is to establish a more adaptive, enabled regime, family therapy must make them aware of the underlying conflict of images and create opportunities to explore other options and possible resolutions. They usually fear the dissolution of the relationship or the sacrifice of one partner's paradigm to the other, but these are not the only possibilities. Other options for mixing and matching elements of their images can be facilitated by the therapist.

In this search for options, understanding the basis for the attraction across paradigms is important. The search to replace or compensate for something missing from one's childhood can be abandoned for more gratifying endeavors in adulthood. The potency of images of loss or deprivation can thus be reduced, leading to easier compromise and synthesis in developing a joint family style.

The therapist who wants to work within a paradigmatic framework must keep in mind each of the competing paradigms in a compound family and be prepared to respect these as part of the family's paradigmatic commitment. On the one hand, this complicates therapy, creating the potential for divided loyalties or the therapist's triangulation into the paradigmatic struggle. On the other hand, a multiplicity of paradigms opens up a richer repertoire for the construction of an enabled family regime.

A real dilemma for the therapist is created when the conflict in paradigms is between generations. Children are increasingly subject to autonomous sources of socialization beyond the control of parents and are being presented images of family that may be at substantial odds with those of their parents. With growing frequency, children, even at a fairly young age, are placed in a position to form well-articulated family paradigms that diverge considerably from their parents' paradigms. On one side of the dilemma is the fact that the parents may be in or attempting to maintain positions of power in the family and are, in many cases, the "paying customers" for therapy services. On the other side is often the therapist's awareness that the paradigmatic preferences manifest in the younger generation may be desirable counterparts to the disabled regime operating within the family.

It is not easy to offer help consistent with competing paradigms. The therapist's internal dilemma mirrors the struggle in which the family is caught, and it may be useful to keep this sympathetic idea in mind. At the heart, the problem is not much different than the task of importing strategies borrowed from another regime. The kind of creative reframing introduced in preceding chapters to assist the import of borrowed strategies can be employed to bridge the gap between competing factions in a single family, making each more palatable to the other and suggesting possibilities for creative synthesis.


## Blended Families and Mixed Regimes

Blended or remarriage families commonly involve competing paradigms or incommensurate regimes. In fact, one particular pattern has been seen repeatedly in family therapy. This pattern arises when remarriage takes place after an extended period as a single-parent family. Usually, the new partner is a single adult without children.

Many single-parent families evolve from closed into more random or open regimes out of necessity. The economic and practical demands of heading a household and parenting alone are very substantial. The newly divorced parent often cannot provide as close continual supervision as before and must depend on more mature and responsible behavior from children. In this way a more cooperative or permissive household becomes established. The children as a group, but older ones especially, may become "parentalized," taking on more "adult" responsibilities and even providing the single parent with a certain amount of emotional nurturing.

This more egalitarian pattern is a practical response of the family to changed circumstances and is usually a sign of successful adaptation rather than a form of dysfunction. It commonly takes place at the level of regime and process without a corresponding paradigm shift, although adaptation in paradigm may sometimes follow. When the single parent is a woman, as is more often the case today, the shift in regimes is even more likely. Male single parents as a group enjoy considerable economic advantages over female single parents, which often translates into more free energy for parenting responsibilities. In many cases, the economic advantage can enable the single father to hire additional household help. Added to the economic disadvantage for many women is the fact that the normative closed regime is traditionally male headed. This can make it doubly difficult for a woman alone to take on the full content of the role. She may have little experience with certain facets of the role, such as that of "stern disciplinarian," and may even have already showed a preference for more lenient parenting.

The real difficulty begins when a new partner enters the system. In the most common situation, the new husband or partner imports a closed paradigm and attempts to restore a closed regime. Often he is eager to prove himself as a parent but has little or no experience. He wants to "become a father to the kids" as well as a husband to their mother. The random-to-open behavior he sees from the children strikes him as disorderly and disrespectful. In some cases he may be aided by the mother in his attempts to impose order, but in others she may be more neutral. Open paradigmatic conflict between the adults is the exception because at this stage in the relationship the single parent is usually reluctant to escalate conflict of any kind, so the conflict tends to be concentrated between the stepfather and his stepchildren. Adolescents especially will vigorously resist the loss of the freedom and mutual respect they had experienced with their mother.

Amy, age 36, became a single parent after her first husband, a college teacher, left her for a younger woman. Several years later she married John, age 31, a hard-working electronics technician who was also studying in night school. While Amy came from a large, loose-knit family, John, who had not been previously married, was an only child whose parents had been strict and overinvolved. John and Amy soon had a baby, a girl, who joined Amy's six children by her first marriage: two boys, ages 16 and 15, and four girls, ages 14, 12, 9, and 4. Their referral for therapy came from a family service agency as a result of John's difficulty with

Sean, the second oldest. Sean was described as "passive but disobedient," always "hanging around" and "never doing what he was told."

The therapist began the first session of a brief-therapy contract by asking each person to introduce some other member of the family, saying something about what that person was like. The children eagerly participated and introduced each other with considerable affection and perceptiveness. No one introduced John. After talking about the youngest as "a good baby who isn't any trouble," he went on to describe himself as "stern, less permissive" than Amy. He felt it was his job to "straighten out" the kids and often had to "step on them." When all were asked to do drawings of the family, both parents portrayed everyone doing separate activities. Nine-year-old Debbie prominently signed her drawing with her full name, which, of course, meant her original last name. Although two of the children identified John as Rudolph, his actual first name, which he never used, none of the drawings excluded him or set him apart completely. Possibly the most telling drawing was Debbie's: she showed her stepfather as one of the kids.

Except for John, who anxiously and somewhat ineptly tried to run things and get everyone to shape up, the family turned out to be random-to-open in most respects—more random in how they managed their time but markedly open in their verbal communication. John's style was in sharp contrast with the rest of the family's; while they tended to be personal and direct in their communication, he objectified everything. ("A parent expects cooperation." "One gets tired.") While the general conversation was generously sprinkled with talk of fun, friendship, and other positive references, John only complained.

The kind of all-controlling parenting John had received in his family was his only model, and his lack of experience with children was evident. (John would follow 15-year-old Sean around, angrily exhorting him to take more responsibility.) Yet he felt a need to prove himself in his new role and be accepted by the children. The harder he tried, the more tired and frustrated he became, which prompted him to demand more from them, as he felt it was their uncooperativeness that caused trouble. Amy expressed some support of John's closed images when he asked for it, but did not seem as concerned about many of the things that upset him. Except for Sean, who was a somewhat passive-aggressive Opposer, the kids tried to give John the benefit of the doubt. They would, however, stand firm when they strongly disagreed with him.

The therapist made two interventions that had a major impact on the family. Most of one session was spent exploring John's growing up and contrasting it with Amy's and with the experience of the kids. As he began to open up and talk personally about his past, the children responded positively. They seemed to appreciate getting to know him for the first time and, now that they could understand "where he was coming from," began to communicate more warmth toward him. This in itself lessened his need to prove himself by being a "good" parent. Picking up on his theme of what hard work parenting was for him, the therapist also gave him permission not to work so hard, stressing that it would take time to learn how to deal with each of so many children and suggesting that maybe with such a large family he might have to slow down to keep from becoming completely exhausted.

The therapist's strategy did not deal directly with the conflict of paradigms, but rather enabled the family to use its own resources and natural tendencies to deal with the problem. The rapidity of change probably owed most to the strength and adaptability of the sibling system. Evidence suggests that they functioned with their mother as a system on the verge of an open regime. For example, the family had generally dealt with most problems by resolving them on an ad hoc, one-to-one basis. The notion of all getting together for family therapy meetings struck them as both novel and attractive; soon they were having family meetings outside of therapy.

SECTION

# VI

## SPECIAL ISSUES

CHAPTER

# 20

# GENERATION ON GENERATION
## Children and Parents in Family Therapy

It has long been abundantly clear that problems in families may be passed from generation to generation, that children may echo the unresolved issues of their parents who, in turn, carry the patterns of their own upbringing into their new families. The way that patterns in systems are replicated or not replicated from generation to generation has been a focus of family therapy from its beginnings. As the latest recipients of a family legacy and often the most overtly symptomatic members, children may have special roles in family therapy. The purpose here is not to treat on transgenerational issues exhaustively, but to consider highlights from a paradigmatic point of view.

### CHILDREN IN FAMILY THERAPY

As each regime is characterized by different styles of parenting, each paradigm sees children differently. These differences need to be taken into account when working with different kinds of families. Families come into therapy with attitudes about the place of children in the family and their role in therapy. Closed families, for example, frequently try to exclude certain children or even all children from therapy. ("I really think Chrissie is too young for this sort of thing." "We left Paul home. He's a good boy. Eddie is really the problem." "I don't see why we should bring in the kids, this problem really is just between us.")

Systems-oriented therapists usually want to see the whole family at least once; many work almost exclusively with the entire family unit. Efforts to bring this about are likely to be more successful when congruent with the family's paradigm. ("I can see you are a really close family so its fitting that we see all five of you together." "You and Eddie are going to need all the help you can get. Paul could be a real asset with something valuable to contribute.")

### Entry Style and the Role of Children

Family therapists usually claim to want the full attention and active participation of children in therapy. They will argue that the family is a system with all members—parents *and* children—as collaborators in its process. They will say that they want children to contribute to therapy and communicate openly, that what the children have to say is just as important as what the parents say. Yet, therapists often act and conduct therapy in ways that undermine their stated goals.

When talking with children, most adults use different intonation and inflection than used with other adults. The younger the child is, the more pronounced the differences are likely to be. The use of this distinct voice is nearly universal and generally unconscious. Even among family therapists it is common, although they are often unaware of the change in voice until confronted by recorded evidence.

Subject matter as well as style usually differentiate adult–adult exchanges from adult–child ones. Adults may be addressed by title or proper first name, while children are addressed by diminutives or nicknames. ("Hello, Mr. Garin, Mrs. Garin. Oh, this is your daughter Susan? Hi, Susie.") On first meeting, children are asked how old they are or where they are in school. Adults are asked "what they do."

These distinctions reinforce traditional or expected role differences, no less than when a therapist reinforces sex-role stereotypes by asking the husband what his work is but not the wife. In just the first few words, therapists who use a distinct voice and content to address children underscore that they know who is a child and who is not and that different relationships are anticipated.

Children are used to these differences in speech style. Thus the therapist who switches to a "talking-with-kids" voice is also communicating that the therapy setting is like anywhere else, that the name of the game is "business as usual." In fact, unintentionally, though often rather blatantly, therapists communicate to children that therapy is "grown-up stuff." ("Jennifer, please sit quietly. Your mother and I are talking about important things.") It should not be surprising, then, if children subsequently become bored with therapy, lapsing into uninvolvement or becoming disruptive. After all, the therapist has established that therapy is "standard operating procedure" where children are less important than adults. In some cases, even experienced "family" therapists may actually be quite condescending with children without being aware of it.

One can, however, in the first minutes or even seconds, help define therapy as "something different," a context in which children are involved and in which their contribution is truly valued. Children, especially those from closed families, are often intrigued, sometimes even registering mild surprise at merely being greeted in the same normal tone of voice as were their parents. If the therapist is careful not to change inflection or to reflect status in opening questions, this tells the children that therapy is something special and begins to build therapeutic alliances. In therapy, as in other settings, children generally respond with interest and greater candor to any adult who clearly addresses them and regards them as persons.

The therapy itself comprises a temporary regime. The paradigm by which the process is designed can be chosen by the therapist. If one favors an open communication model for therapy itself, one can actively set up an egalitarian structure, for example. Parents often introduce their children and tell their ages or say something about each one. ("This is Marshall; he's a good boy." "And that's Penny; she's 11.") This might be met with an "equalizer." (Pointing to mother, "And, Marshall, who is this? What is she like?" "And Dad, how old are you?") These often provoke laughter and have the effect of defining all participants as of equal interest and importance to the family therapist.

Actively promoting an egalitarian regime within therapy is basically congruent with open or random paradigms and does not seem to seriously challenge synchronous families. It can be a strong challenge to the closed paradigm, but closed families generally see the therapy setting as "outside," where different rules may operate anyway. Therapists, after all, are not "ordinary" and are not expected to behave in ordinary ways. Thus the tendency of this sort of leveling is to create an isolated regime within therapy that may operate by its own distinct rules.

The therapist committed to a closed paradigm for therapy would not be expected to make any leveling moves of this type, but would rather reinforce conventional role and class distinctions. Introducing oneself by title ("I'm Doctor Weisenberg.") would reinforce an hierarchical model. This, in turn, might inhibit joining with a random or open family, but would help to put most closed families at ease.

## Participation by Children

It is not necessary to see all family members at all times to do family therapy. One can even do systems-oriented family therapy with only individual interviews. What makes it family therapy and systems-oriented is the therapist's veiwpoint, the constant awareness of the systemic context and the attention to information about the functioning of the larger systems of which the client is a member. Of course, this is harder to do when all information flowing from and into the family is channeled through a single representative. The therapist is handicapped by the lack of direct observation and by a paucity of viewpoints.

In most cases, however, it is assumed that family therapy involves the "whole family," at least at some point, therefore, family therapy almost inevitably involves children. The index patient, more often than not, is a child. The role of children and of child–parent relationships in family problems is at the heart of much family therapy literature.

Many family therapists, surprisingly, do not work well with children in families, especially younger children. Some may even start out seeing the whole family, but quickly conclude that, at the heart, the problem is a marital conflict and requires couple therapy. Of course, sometimes this is a valid formulation and isolating the couple system may be a useful intervention. The practice is suspect when it becomes almost the universal diagnosis and treatment.

Even among those who do work with entire families, what passes for family therapy is sometimes better described as couple therapy or individual interviewing in the presence of the children. I have suggested to trainees a quick subjective test for this possibility. Any time the therapist experiences children as a distraction or feels the impulse to try to "keep them busy" while the therapy goes on, there is a good chance that what is happening is "adult therapy with children present." For trainees, especially, but for some experienced family therapists as well, a big part of the difficulty is being stuck in "talk therapy." When this is clearly "grown-up" talk and about big, complicated problems, younger children readily become lost and disinterested.

The use of expressive and nonverbal techniques bypasses many of these problems. Aside from the rationale for their use in general, these techniques are equalizers, permitting even very young children to be active, valuable participants. The approach need not be elaborate, nor highly structured; just a readiness to have people "show," "do," and "act out" things can be a powerful tool to engage children. ("So when your Dad comes to take you for the weekend he gets very angry at Mom. Can you show us how he looks when he's so angry, how does he act? And how do you look?") Role playing and role reversals can be done with any child old enough to understand "let's pretend." After taking part in such a "game" children are much more interested in talking about it than they are about more abstract or remote things. ("What was happening with you, Wendy? What were you feeling, right then? I'd be kinda scared myself.")

With family drawings, generally even the youngest child can be involved in the task. ("Yes, I know Tess is only two, but she seems to be an important part of the family who has a lot to say. Yes, I heard you scream all the way in here, Tess. Here, you take a crayon, too. What color would you like?") How the family deals with the limited motor skills of the "baby of the family" is important data, as is the "interpretation" they give to his "production." ("I think Mikey has the right idea. Our family is a mess!") As pointed out in Chapter 12, the *process* by which drawings or constructions are produced can be even more important than the product.

> In the first session, the Dorrs were asked to do individual drawings of their family. Both brothers were given their own paper and choice of crayons. When the 2 year old finished his own "drawing," he started scribbling over his mother's. She protested, pleading with him and weakly pushing him away, but she was ineffective in protecting her own boundaries. This transaction proved to be very significant as a metaphor for their relationship and an indicator of the ambiguity of her boundaries. It was repeated on other occasions in somewhat less dramatic form.

Expressive and nonverbal techniques are not only great "equalizers" but good "disequilibrators" that can help to loosen up a family. The ability of the family to "play" and their willingness to try something new are important indicators of flexibility and may suggest the direction therapy might take. Trying to get everyone down on the floor in a joint block-building task is a multilevel assessment and intervention tool as well as a technique for engaging children. This is very different from keeping younger children busy playing with blocks while the older members take part in the "real therapy."

Merely having children present, even if bored or busy playing, is not without value, however. Children pick up and understand much more from others' conversations than adults think they do. One should not assume that a child not involved in a conversation didn't hear it. A spontaneous remark much later in therapy often reveals that the child understood perfectly well what was going on.

## Movement and Setting

The setting of therapy can have even more impact on children than on adults. One therapist told me of the tribulations of working with a father and his hyperkinetic son; it turned out they were meeting in a tiny cubicle barely big enough for three chairs. Even when the room is ample, it is remarkable how static much family therapy is; so many videotapes of therapy reveal hour after hour of people sitting in a circle or semicircle, talking and talking. The fact that young children may have difficulty sitting in one place for an hour at a time is no problem for the therapist who *moves* and who uses space and movement as an integral part of the therapy process. This does not require doing family sculptures in every session, but rather a sensitivity to spatial metaphor and a commitment to using it as a tool. ("So, where would you like to sit, since you seem so uncomfortable next to your brother?" "While you're trying to talk with your son, why don't you sit facing him. And, Marta, here, come sit next to me, out of the line of fire." "Well, Cyndi and Dad seem rather cozy over there. You don't seem to approve, Mom. How would you like them to sit?")

## Mixed Metaphors

It may be particularly poignant when therapy uncovers a real mismatch between a child's paradigmatic preferences and the parents'. Children generally do not have fully developed family paradigms for themselves; more often these resemble their family's. This is not necessarily always the case, however. Television and the cinema expose children to alternative paradigms that may be made very attractive. The media also expose the hidden workings of families. For example, in a sitcom about a closed family, the camera follows the parents into the kitchen where they fight behind the childrens' backs or figure out how to manipulate them into some task. Children see these "behind the scenes" glimpses into family workings and often generalize, correctly or not, about their own families.

In a culture where children are increasingly the importers of social innovations, it can happen that an evolving paradigm will pit child against parent in a difficult struggle over core images. The ethical and practical problems of dealing with competing paradigms, as discussed in Chapter 19, may be complicated by great differences in power. The axiom that the therapist respect the client family's paradigm is little help. Who is the client? In most cases, the parents are, of course, the "paying customers." They are also adults. Are these overriding considerations? How much weight should be given to the desires of a school-aged child?

## TRANSGENERATIONAL ISSUES

The framework for analysis of family process, regime, and paradigm can be shifted to ever-larger scales of time. Eventually the therapist reaches the level of patterns that carry over entire lifetimes and even span generations. At one of the highest levels of analysis are found not just general images of families and family life, but elaborate "scripts" that may describe and seem to program entire life stories. It is useful to think of these programs as being like the script for a play. The script specifies the setting and the kind of story it will be: drawing room comedy, dramatic tragedy, romantic fairy tale, success story, or whatever. The plot or sequence of events and the part each actor is to play in completing it are also specified.

As experienced clinicians are well aware, the transmission of a family script can generate striking and dramatic degrees of replication. Consider the following example.

A bright, strong-willed young woman, the oldest daughter of a family living in the farm country of the Midwest near the beginning of this century, is swept off her feet by the handsome and charming fiddler who plays at barn dances around the area. They marry and she immediately gets pregnant and bears a daughter. The troubled marriage ultimately ends in permanent separation. The young mother never divorces or remarries, but supports herself and her daughter as a schoolteacher. The daughter is also bright; with her mother's help and urging, she finishes high school at 16 and then enters a teacher's college. While there, she meets a dancer from a musical theater production playing in the area. With him she has her first sexual experience and becomes pregnant. Her father, who still lives in the area, coerces the man into marrying her, then tells him to get out of town. The dancer disappears and the marriage is annulled.

The young woman herself bears a daughter, whom she also raises alone until she remarries when the child is eight. As a teenager, this daughter also engages in unprotected sex but luckily does not become pregnant. Eventually she falls in love with a jazz musician who plays in the area. They decide to marry, but 4 days before the wedding it is discovered that he is really a "con artist" who is still married to another woman. He is told to get out of town by the would-be bride's brother. In a few years she does marry but has difficulty becoming pregnant. Eventually she bears three children. Not until her oldest, a daughter, is a teenager does she complete her training as a special needs teacher at the same college her mother attended.

This example clearly illustrates a dramatic theme that is repeated, but with growing variation. Through three generations, firstborn daughters fall for the charming artist, but in each succeeding generation there are gradual transformations. The marriage in the first generation ends in separation but is never formally terminated; in the next, the first marriage is annulled and a second marriage follows only after many years; in the third generation, the first wedding is cancelled and a second follows after only a couple of years. The grandmother worked as a teacher; the mother trained as a teacher but never taught, though she worked nearly all her life; the daughter trained in a related field of education, but never worked outside the home. It is appealing to interpret this as successive generations moderating the influence of a powerful script.

Transgenerational patterns may be simpler but no less powerful. In one family, a genealogist in the current generation studied letters, diaries, and other family documents to add to the memories of living relatives and uncovered a four-generation pattern. In each generation, the rebellious oldest child developed an intensely conflicted relationship with the opposite-sex parent, leaving home at an early age. In several generations, the teenager and the parent did not speak to each other for many years. Although the sex of the oldest child alternated from generation to generation, the pattern continued.

## Induction of Children into Family Scripts

Although scripts "belong" to the family and the entire family collaborates in passing them on, they are really targeted toward individuals, because individuals must act the parts in the drama. It has been my clinical experience that oldest children are subject to the most intense processes of induction into family scripts. The firstborn experiences some period as the sole object of parental action. Moreover, the inexperience of new parents makes them more likely to fall back on patterns modeled by their own parents, on older and less flexible behaviors, and on unconscious or unarticulated models of family.

The timing of family problems can be a clue to the induction of family members into multigeneration patterns. In the case of the Kaiser family, discussed in Chapter 14, Cynthia introduced herself as "14½ years old," the kind of fine distinction teenagers seldom make. The family history revealed the following related background. Dency Kaiser's father died when she was 15, the oldest of four children. She met, Dick, her husband-to-be, a year later. He was 20, but was really more interested in her younger sister who was then 14½. More or less by default, as they describe it, he ended up with Dency. She left home to get married at 18, saying that there was "nothing further" for her at home.

In family therapy, Cynthia remained distant from both her mother and father, but often closely mirrored her father's style and actions. She felt there was little for her in the family and figured she would get out as soon as she could. How soon was that? "When I turn 18." Thus, when Dency Kaiser's daughter becomes the same age as her younger sister was when Dency originally left home, Dency starts to leave home again (first by a suicide attempt, then by an emotional divorce). Two mappings are immediately apparent, one suggested by the similarity of position in the family and Cynthia's stated intention to leave at the same age as her mother did. This would imply Cynthia's induction into the same role as her mother did. The other mapping is between Cynthia and her mother's younger sister. The therapist was thus alerted to the possible threat of incest between Cynthia and her father, but it appeared that Dick, consistent with *his* "programming," had "settled for" his wife.

Many things can moderate the transmission of scripts or interfere with their exact replication. A role may call for a very specific "actor" or very specific action: a girl, for instance, to become pregnant out of wedlock. A family may have more or fewer children or experience radically different life events than in a previous generation.

More generally, although highly programmed behavior can be functional in specific circumstances, it is, almost by definition, not adaptive. A family that gains in flexibility and decreases its reliance on behaviors set by previous generations reduces the potency of family scripts. Replication becomes less exact with each generation that becomes healthier and more aware of its own programming. This is, of course, one of the functions of family therapy, to relieve succeeding generations from having to act out the scripts of their predecessors. To the extent that family therapy or any other learning experience increases the adaptability of family behavior and its responsiveness to actual circumstances, the transmission of family scripts to the next generation will be reduced.

## Pairing and Psychopolitics

There appears to be a pronounced tendency for family systems to carry over individual psychopolitical preferences and collective strategic sequences into successive generations (Constantine, 1975). People seem to seek out and remain in situations with "familiar" psychopolitics, where there is a degree of psychopolitical "fit" that permits them to take on preferred positions and to play out familiar sequences. For example, a woman who grew up consistently Opposed by her younger brother married a somewhat immature man who was a strong and persistent Opposer. They had an intense and involving relationship though it often appeared to be highly conflictual.

Pairings giving rise to new families may, as in the example above, continue psychopolitical patterns familiar from childhood, they may replicate parental patterns, or they may fulfill elements missing from early family experience. The function and nature of the pattern may be different for the two partners. A man might be trying for a marriage like his parents had and, consciously or not, might seek out a woman who, like his mother, was striving to become an effective Mover. The woman he marries may see in him reminders of the eager Following she experienced from her younger brother.

The search to complete something missing from childhood is very widespread in all dimensions or aspects of family relations. Some people from successful closed families that effectively limited opposition within the family are drawn to Opposers, for example. Because of the relationship between regime and psychopolitics, this search often pairs partners with different paradigms.

Preparing a family genogram with reference to psychopolitics can reveal important transgenerational patterns. In Figure 20-1, mappings between partners in successive generations repeat a theme and significant variations over three generations of marriages. The variations were large enough so that, by the third generation, seeds of major incompatibility were sown, almost forcing major readjustments. This prevented continuing the dysfunctional pattern of the previous generation.

## Regime and Transgenerational Patterns

Just as disabled patterns may be passed from generation to generation or may be discontinued, family regimes may or may not replicate themselves. In general, however, success seems to breed success and enabled regimes tend to induce children to create similar regimes for themselves. If anecdotal clinical material can be trusted, disabled regimes have a somewhat greater likelihood of inducing the next generation to want to "do things differently." Often this may take the form of an overreaction, a swing to a disabled extreme in an antithetical regime. Thus the young woman who grew up in a chaotically enmeshed family longs for the harmonious calm she never had and tries

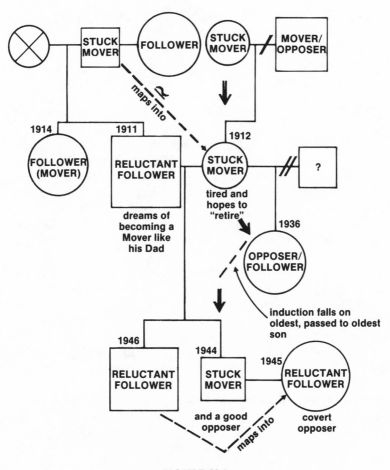

**FIGURE 20-1.**
Transgenerational transmission of psychopolitical preferences.

to establish a home more like a monastery, or the children of an ideologically committed but emotionally neglectful family of Marxists raise their children in a strictly religious and materialistic style.

When a regime is formed out of reaction against a parental regime, the new family architects are attempting to establish structures with which they have little or no experience. This can lead to numerous problems, creating easily disabled regimes. Parental behavior may be stereotyped or exaggerated, as with the "preacher's kids" who rebel against their strict background by becoming extremely permissive and inept parents, or, unable to effect the needed behaviors, they might instead adopt a pseudo-open regime in which a closed regime is cloaked in a thin veneer of openness.

On the more optimistic side, family lines do sometimes make successful transitions from one regime to another between generations. The resulting systems still bear signs of their more distant history, however. To take my own family as an example, although it was founded from the start by our clear commitment to an open paradigm, it nevertheless bears the clear traces of Joan's and my families of origin. Hers was mostly closed, but undermined by covert opposition and some open rebellion. Mine had always seemed to me to be quite closed, partly because of my father's recurrent appeals to authoritarian and traditional values. In fact, owing to rampant, strong-willed opposition and strivings for autonomy, its regime was much more random than closed. His appeals were really symptoms of the incommensurability between the regime of the family and the paradigm he inherited but couldn't practice.

Now, by successive approximations to some of the collaborative ideals to which we aspire, we approach being a "mostly open" regime. However, we are usually less organized than we wish to be. The chaos can build up until, in a mad scramble we "clean up for company" or get reorganized to hold a workshop. To be effective as a group, we have to resist a family tendency to drift toward a comfortable anarchy or to slide into some form of "parallel play" with all of us going our merry individual ways. Our daughters will tell you if you ask them, that the closed bits also creep in now and then, usually when we think some work really "has to" be done. At least that's what they tell us, rather openly, I would say.

CHAPTER

# 21

# YOU AND YOURS
## The Self in Family Therapy

The systematic approach to theory in therapy outlined in this book should never work against the therapist's use of self in therapy. However it is conceptualized, family therapy engages the family therapist as a person in a real encounter with other persons seeking help. As this last chapter is also the most concerned with "personal" issues, it is appropriate that it deal with a potpourri of things of personal interest to me.

## THE THERAPIST IN THE THERAPY PROCESS

The therapist as a Bystander to a family's process incorporates the intrinsic paradox of Bystanding. The Bystander is outside of the action yet not outside, detached yet involved, perhaps uncommitted but never truly neutral. The therapist and the family together are, unavoidably, a system governed by the same principles of circular causality as any human system. The therapist cannot ever purely observe, for the therapist is always *participant* observer. Neither can the therapist ever simply intervene in any pure sense, for this implies leverage or manipulation from a position apart from the family that does not exist. This paradox of reciprocal determinism forms the basis of the "new epistemology" or "cybernetics of cybernetics" in family therapy (Keeney & Ross, 1983). The therapist is affected by the family and becomes some part of their process. The intent of the therapist may be reframed as one of remaining enabled and playing an enabling part in the family–family therapist system.

## The Use of Feelings

The therapist's own emotional experiences are an important ingredient of the family therapy process. It is useful to think of the therapist's feelings as additional material—about the family, the therapist, and the process—to be used in whatever way is likely to lead to more effective therapy. This commits the therapist neither to exposing inner experience, sharing feelings "up front," nor to suppressing them, but leaves him/her free to do with them what seems most useful at the time. Using feelings this way draws not only on experience with a particular family, but on the therapist's own history and knowledge of personal reactions.

For example, while still in training I learned that I start feeling anxious or somewhat scared in situations where my actions have backed someone else into a corner or pressured them too much. I have no idea how idiosyncratic this response is, but for me, when it does on occasion arise in doing therapy, I immediately start thinking of who else in the room might be getting anxious, who might be feeling pushed into a corner, and what might be happening to make them feel that way. This has proven to be a dependable gauge for recognizing when I have inadvertently moved too fast.

Feelings are responses; they come from somewhere. In using one's own feelings in therapy it is productive to keep in mind that feelings can generate insights about three different things: the family, the therapist, and the process of therapy. For example, I once found myself feeling defeated, incompetent, and discouraged in working with a particular family. The first question I asked was, "What does this tell me about *the family*? What might they be doing to make me feel this way?" They were a family that never validated good performance, one in which the parents seemed incapable of being satisfied with what their children did. I wondered whether that was what it felt like to be in that family. In fact, it turned out that everyone, parents and offspring alike, felt defeated, incompetent, and discouraged. At one level, I was picking up on the family's dominant affect.

Some therapists would stop there, having accounted for the feelings in terms of the family. But the second question concerned *me*: "What do these feelings have to do with *me* and what's happening with me?" This family was one of the first families I had seen after an hiatus in my private practice. I was concerned about my own competence, wondering about how rusty I might have become. I realized this made me very sensitive to their lack of progress and the sense of defeat they conveyed. By extending my examination beyond the family, I became aware of how my own issues were becoming entangled with theirs.

Stopping there would have been a mistake, too. The next question I ask myself is, "What do these feelings tell me about what is happening *between* the family and me, in the therapy itself?" The truth was that therapy wasn't going particularly well at that point. The fact that the therapy process seemed to evoke the same sort of feelings as the family experienced in its process suggested that therapy was, in part, replicating the family's modus operandi and suggested that a different tack be taken in therapy.

## Stuck Points in Therapy

Feeling "stuck" is the nemesis of family therapists and one of the strongest and most frustrating feelings one can have. There are many variations of "stuck" feelings and how they may be described by therapists: feeling lost, confused, blocked, incapacitated, overwhelmed, trapped, "knotted up," and so forth. These all describe the experience of being unable to know what to do or unable to do anything. Like any feelings in therapy, they are just more data about the family, the therapist, and the process. But often the therapist may be unable to use these feelings until he/she becomes unstuck.

Therapy tactics used with stuck families can also be used to unstick the therapist–family system. Two of these, part of the training tradition of the Boston Family Institute and Boston State Hospital, have proven very useful over the years. The first uses a spatial metaphor: since the therapist is stuck, the first task is to get moving, literally. As soon as he/she becomes aware of feeling stuck the therapist should stand up and move to another place in the room, preferably to the periphery, taking the therapist "out of" the process to where it will be easier to Bystand.

Many therapists consider this silly, but those who have tried it find that it almost always works. In physically moving, the therapist is no longer literally stuck. The act of moving itself disrupts the process, and Bystanding from another position in the room often gives a different perspective on what is going on. Becoming a Bystander also often frees the therapist from a disabling sense of pressure to "do something" or "come up with something." It can be combined with another tactic: labeling the process. The therapist says, "I feel stuck. I'm lost. I don't know what to do." In announcing this, the therapist has worked an exquisite paradox, since the announcement is really "something to do" demonstrating he/she does know. The injunction is all the more potent if the therapist then stands and moves to the periphery. The effect can be remarkably freeing for the therapist and for the family.

## Induction and Countertransference

Therapists are inducted into a family system when they begin to play a substantial part in the family regime, thereby helping to sustain disablement or being prevented from facilitating reenablement. The therapist is no longer a Bystander to the family's process but is completely *in* it. For this reason it can be especially difficult for therapists to recognize their own induction into a family except in retrospect.

Some family therapists use the terms induction and countertransference interchangeably, but these actually identify distinct processes. Countertransference involves, by its narrowest definition, the therapist's emotional reactions to a family, in the broadest sense, all the therapist's own issues as these are evoked or brought into play by the experience with the family. Thus induction is a systemic process, and countertransference a "psychological" one. Induction almost invariably depends on countertransference, but countertransference does not necessarily lead to induction. A therapist may be less effective working with a certain family because of what it evokes in him/her and yet still not become a part of the family system.

Some families are more able or prone to inducting therapists and other outsiders into their process than are others. In general, however, the most important factor is the therapist. Almost without exception, the therapist is found to have been "hooked" by a personal issue or vulnerability. For example, a young black therapist who was keenly aware of the peripheral role black males often play in their families worked with one family having an absent father. Very soon he was acting as a substitute father, fulfilling many functions of his idealized picture of the "involved" black male head-of-household.

Induction can be very subtle, but there are clues to be picked up by an aware therapist. One male trainee presented for supervision his work with a 36-year-old single father and his 10-year-old son. The therapist saw the father, Barry, as an ineffective parent who needed to be firmer and clearer with his son, Devon. Aware of the close proximity and possible enmeshed role of the extended family, the therapist scheduled a session in the home of Barry's parents. At this session, Devon seemed lost between the adults on one side and a group of mostly preschool grandchildren on the other. The therapist suggested that Barry teach his son how to be a leader with the younger children. This was enthusiastically seconded by the other adults, especially Barry's parents, who saw this as just what was needed.

The supervision group reminded the therapist that Barry, who was the oldest of six, had been a parentalized child. This role had been reinforced by his own father, who was also named Barry and was also apparently ineffective as a parent. In effect, the therapist was directing the father to teach his son a parentalized role with his cousins, thus continuing a family pattern into a third generation. The therapist was actually acting as the agent of transmission of this pattern. The family's enthusiasm for the intervention, to be expected under the circumstances, was a clue pointing to possible induction. This therapist, proud of his own success as a father and with an apparent preference for the closed paradigm, seemed to have a particular affinity for parenting issues and for helping parents "take charge."

Consultants, supervisors, and other Bystanders are generally in the best position to recognize induction, but there are clues for the therapist, also. Awareness of one's own "hooks" can help to avoid induction and can draw attention to situations in which this is a possibility. Pronounced enthusiasm, engagement, and responsiveness from a family coupled with a general lack of change should suggest the possibility that interventions are reinforcing the status quo.

A strong awareness of each family's style and the relationship of their regime to their current disablement can be helpful. One family arrived for a session in an unusually happy mood, smiling over some recent events. After sharing these briefly, they lapsed into more characteristic silence. The therapists asked them what they wanted to work on and gently prodded them into "working." The family left with glum expressions, in sharp contrast to their arrival. The therapists felt somewhat defeated but used their sense of failure to explore what had happened in relation to the family's style of operating. They realized that the family had come in "celebrating their progress," something unusual, and difficult for them to sustain. The work-oriented focus of the session had played into their tendency to attend to their own inadequacies rather than their strengths. As a result, the therapists made "celebrations" the theme of the next session, planning it as a celebration of the family's progress and an exploration of ways of celebrating.

The complete family map is often an effective tool for recognizing induction and pointing the way out of it. The map can highlight ways in which the therapists behavior or experiences parallel those of family members or mirror family process in some dimension. Placing oneself on the map helps to visualize a process of overidentification or being

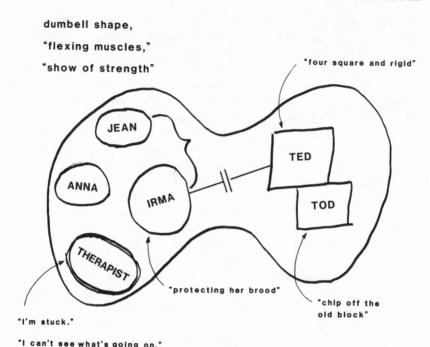

dumbell shape,

"flexing muscles,"

"show of strength"

"four square and rigid"

JEAN

TED

ANNA

IRMA

TOD

THERAPIST

"protecting her brood"

"chip off the
old block"

"I'm stuck."

"I can't see what's going on."

**FIGURE 21-1.**
Therapist in a stuck position within the family map.

caught in a disabled positon. For example, one therapist visualized her
place in the family as in Figure 21-1. In such a position, she would be
unable to move or see much of what was going on. Her "hook" was a
tendency to identify with the mother, whom she saw as an oppressed
female. The therapist had become, in effect, another daughter. The
map suggested that, to get free of induction, she needed to enter the
family from "another direction." Taking a strongly unbalancing
stance, the therapist began to build an alliance with the father, empa-
thizing and being supportive of him in areas other than the conflict
with his wife. In effect, she reentered from the right side of the map,
but without severing her connection with the mother. The family
almost immediately began to progress in therapy.

## COTHERAPY AND COTHERAPISTS

As the cotherapy team is itself a system, cotherapy can be approached
from a paradigmatic perspective. The cotherapy system establishes its

own patterns in process and, over time, mechanisms that sustain these patterns. Cotherapy teams may actually be more prone to becoming inducted than are therapists working alone. The cotherapy system often begins to mirror processes in the family. It also seems easier for cotherapists to become aware of induction, so for both of these reasons I encourage family therapy trainees to do cotherapy with other trainees. Cotherapy seems to give more opportunities to experience what it is like being sucked in *and* what it is like pulling back out.

### Developing the Cotherapy Team

Establishing a comfortable and functional joint style for therapists who are committed to distinct paradigms can be no less a problem for cotherapists than it is for a couple who will form a family. Some of the same techniques for intervention can apply.

A form of family sculpture has proven to be immensely useful in building cotherapy teams and clarifying cotherapy relationships. In this technique, known as "Negotiating the Space," an area is marked out to represent the working relationship of the cotherapists. The task is for the two of them to negotiate, nonverbally, a way for both of them to share the space comfortably. An area of 50 to 100 square feet is customary; the exact size or shape is not critical, but it is important that it not encompass the entire room. The enclosed space represents the cotherapists' working relationship, outside its boundaries are the other aspects of their lives and whatever other relationships they may have. Stepping into the marked area represents entering into the part of their lives bounded by their working relationship. As a rule, the negotiation is carried out with the help of a Bystander who reminds them of the spatial metaphor and who serves as timekeeper. A set 10 minutes, all of which must be used, has proven to be almost ideal. The Bystander directs them each to enter the space whenever they are ready, then, without talking, to explore it and work out ways of sharing it that are comfortable to both." Afterwards, the Bystander may give feedback and facilitate discussion.

In this nonverbal exercise, the therapists are dynamically sculpting their cotherapy relationship. Issues pertaining to power, status, intimacy, speed and timing, style of entry and approach are all made visible as the relationship is acted out. The exercise helps draw out the fit and mismatches between the therapists that will influence their joint style and effectiveness as a team.

Many therapists have found this technique to be so useful and powerful that they would not start a new cotherapy relationship without it. In one case, a family therapist was called in as a consulting cotherapist almost at the last minute. She insisted on "negotiating the space," which left only 1 minute for the two of them to plan the session. Her cotherapist said, "Hey, look, we've got it worked out now. We can wing it." The session went without a hitch.

## Cotherapy Relationships

Prior or outside relationships between cotherapists inevitably color their working relationship, regardless of how professional they are in trying to maintain clear distinctions. When one therapist is in a position of power or authority over the other, considerable energy may be needed to sustain a cotherapy relationship that does not reflect their hierarchical relationship outside of therapy. Common examples are teacher and student, therapist and supervisor, or even therapists of greatly different levels of experience. Similar influences may arise from differing professional affiliations or disciplines that have, by tradition, a hierarchical relationship, for example, a psychiatric nurse working with a psychiatrist. In all such situations it is harder to establish a truly open cotherapy system because of the status and power issues that carry over into the working relationship.

Often the "junior" cotherapist feels keenly aware of being judged or evaluated by the senior partner. This factor, which may be salient in other cotherapy contexts as well, can create various problems. The junior partner may feel pressure to "perform" or the need to impress the senior partner. Not only can these pressures inhibit good performance, but efforts to impress or to "perform" may themselves be cause for downgrading. An egalitarian, collaborative relationship between colleagues and a hierarchical official relationship are competitive models for the cotherapy team. A cotherapy system that tries to maintain that it can be both at once is, like the pseudo-open family it resembles, disadvantaged. To a certain degree it is a denial of reality when the supervisor of a student therapist says, "Look, Tim, while we're in there, I'm not your boss. We're equals."

## The Cosupervisor Concept

There are many ways for cotherapists to work. They can "double team" to increase their impact. One can attend to certain dimensions to which the other may be less sensitive. They can alternate or interlace interventions. They can exemplify behavior in an enabled relationship. One of the greatest things cotherapists can do for each other is to help keep the other from getting stuck. This suggests an answer to the frequent question of what the inactive or less active therapist should be doing while the other is "working with the family." The most important job for the Bystanding therapist is to watch the one thing that the other therapist cannot: namely, the system of family-plus-therapist.

In a sense, then, each cotherapist is acting as a supervisor while the other is working more actively. When the "supervising" therapist sees the therapist–family system getting stuck, he/she makes a move to "unstick" it. Usually this amounts to switching places: reaching in to pull out the partner, then jumping over the fence to enter the fray.

### Sex, Marriage, and Cotherapy

Many times it has been said that a good cotherapy relationship is like a good marriage. Cotherapy can be very demanding and, at its best, can be immensely rewarding and often very intimate. While some cotherapists are fairly casual in their work relationship or maintain a "strictly business" orientation, many become quite close and committed to their best cotherapy partners. In more cases than the family therapy field might want to acknowledge in public, cotherapists have become not only friends but lovers.

The issue is not whether such relationships are good or bad, but how they effect or enter into the process of therapy. Many married couples also do cotherapy together with greater or lesser success. Whether cotherapists are friends, spouses, or lovers, their relationship outside of therapy may enter into the processes within therapy and influence their effectiveness. It can be crucial for supervisors to know of or at least have some inkling of when cotherapists are involved in more than just a work relationship.

For example, in one case I supervised, the therapist kept shifting attention to his clients' extramarital activities, glossing over important presenting problems. The couple did have a sexually open marriage, but the pattern of their outside relationships did not seem to be closely connected to the way in which they were replicating the power struggle in which both sets of their own parents had been locked. Nevertheless, the therapist kept zeroing in on the open marriage in what seemed to be a very judgmental, even somewhat angry, manner. When he was asked whether he had any personal experiences with affairs, his denial was unconvincing. Eventually he acknowledged an intensely conflicted affair with his cotherapist on another case, a relationship that they were keeping secret from both their spouses. Only after he acknowledged the affair could he deal with how envious he was of the apparent ease with which his clients managed to be honest with each other about their outside relationships.

Married cotherapists may also bring relationship issues into the therapy they conduct. Paradigmatic considerations, once again, are important. Couples with a closed regime are often better at compartmentalizing their relationships, seeing marriage and work relationships as two separate parts of their lives. Open regime couples are apt to draw less distinct boundaries and to see things as interrelated. Of course, their need to resolve issues keeps them hanging in there to work it all out before therapy starts. On many occasions Joan and I have hassled through some problem between us on our way to doing cotherapy at a client's home. (And, I suppose, if a married couple with a random regime were to do cotherapy, they would not feel the need to work things out but would probably each do their own thing as therapists, too.)

## PERSONAL PARADIGM AND PERSONAL EXPERIENCE

Detailed knowledge of one's own personal family paradigm and the structures and strategies of one's own family are powerful tools for therapy. The most important reason to become aware of our personal paradigms is to remain cognizant in all the therapy we do of the intrinsic biases in the worldview represented by our own paradigms. Without this perspective, we have little hope of compensating for seeing "pathology" in what are only paradigmatic differences.

> One guidance counselor became alarmed upon meeting the family of a teenager who, after years of being considered to be the school's mathematics star, had begun "doing poorly" in high school. Despite an IQ of 139, his grades in academic subjects were dropping lower and lower. Against the counselor's advise, he wanted to take only art electives. He was also making a nuisance of himself by trying to spend every spare minute in the art room or in the metals shop "making things." The family home was extremely messy and the home visit so chaotic that the counselor almost ran from the meeting. He made a quick referral to a psychologist who did family therapy. The psychologist, however, found them to be a very creative, artistic family who basically needed little more than reassurance that they were not crazy, that it was "okay to be random." After talking with the boy about the expectations of outside systems, the psychologist suggested a change of schools. In a heavily art-oriented program, his academic performance improved almost immediately.

To take a personal example, my open paradigm can lead me to see *not* talking about problems as a problem in itself. I remind myself that secrets are not necessarily dysfunctional or that having taboos on some subject matter is not always disabling.

The other side of this coin is that a full awareness of personal paradigm makes it easier for the therapist to share the special perspective such a paradigm offers or to lend strategies to those families that can benefit from borrowing them. For instance, many families, not only those entering family therapy, are plagued by bedtime hassles and late-night power struggles between children and parents. In my family, our children have always determined their own bedtimes and respected the limits of our willingness as parents to be "on call" in the late evening. We have our own "open family" rationale for the strategy by which we have almost completely avoided such difficulties. The open paradigm arguments—equality of rights, mutual respect of personal boundaries, responsibility for self, opportunities for learning about one's own needs—are not of much value or interest to families with alternative paradigms, but the strategy can be. By clearly distinguishing the paradigmatic values from the tactical realization in a family regime, the therapist makes it easier for other families to make what use they can of things from the therapist's family experience. Numerous closed and random families have been helped to get out of escalating conflict by adopting some variant of an open regime bedtime policy, eliminating what often turned out to be a "manufactured conflict." Without my personal experience with my own two kids and another who lived with our family for a couple of years, I don't think I could have been as effective in helping families who could benefit from such a new strategy.


## Personal Experience

Therapists will differ in the extent that they will use personal experience in conducting therapy. As my own style is one of an open paradigm, I tend to draw on personal family experiences a fair amount. Briefly running through the times I remember referring to personal experiences while doing family therapy, I find some patterns. Most often the intent has been to build bridges or facilitate identification. ("Of course, Mrs. Baldwin, I remember when my older daughter was that age.") I am also likely to tell personal anecdotes when the situation seems to call for a concrete and convincing example of some *other* way a family might do something. I try to be sure that the purpose is not to show the family "how they ought to be" but to help them become aware of their paradigmatic commitments and their "family style," to begin to see the range of possibilities this entails, and to think in terms of the options open to them in the whole array of structures and strategies. A personal example is often cogent where a general "explanation" would not be. ("Well, you know, I think families have a lot of different ways of handling that. In our family, hitting is just not okay, though it is all right to tell each other off. Then again, that might not work for the family who lives next door.")

In a similar vein, I have often drawn on my own growing-up and efforts to understand and transcend my own "programming." I try to convey some sense that I know personally how hard the long struggle is but that it can be worthwhile to see it through. In particular, I want to get across the message that people don't have to remain forever programmed by their past failures or their parents' choices, that just because certain things are part of their background doesn't mean they can't make new choices for themselves and their children. My own view is that to overcome past "programming" requires awareness of the programs and of the range of options among which one can choose.

And, of course, I learn much of this from my clients, from sharing in a part of their family experience, as I hope this book attests.

# REFERENCES

Ahrons, C. R. The binuclear family: Two households, one family. *Alternative Lifestyles*, 1979, *2*, 499–515.

Aponte, H., & Hoffman, L. The open door: A structural approach to a family with an anorectic child. *Family Process*, 1973, *12*, 1–14.

Argyris, C., & Schön, D. A. *Theory in practice: Increasing professional effectiveness.* San Francisco: Jossey-Bass, 1974.

Avery, M., Auvine, B., Streibel, B., & Weiss, L. *Building united judgment: A handbook for consensual decision making.* Madison, Wisc.: Center for Conflict Resolution, 1981.

Bandler, R., & Grinder, J. *The structure of magic, I: A book about language and therapy.* Palo Alto: Science & Behavior, 1975.

Bank, S. P., & Kahn, M. D. *The sibling bond.* New York: Basic Books, 1982.

Bateson, G. The cybernetics of self. *Psychiatry*, 1971, *34*, 1–18.

Bateson, G. *Steps to an ecology of mind.* New York: Ballantine, 1972.

Beavers, W. R. A theoretical basis for family evaluation. In J. M. Lewis, W. R. Beavers, J. T. Gossett, & V. A. Phillips (Eds.), *No single thread.* New York: Brunner/ Mazel, 1976.

Beavers, W. R. A systems model of family for family therapists. *Journal of Marital and Family Therapy*, 1981, *7*, 299–308.

Benjamin, L. S. Structural analysis of social behavior. *Psychological Review*, 1974, *81*(3), 392–425.

Berne, E. *The structure and dynamics of organizations and groups.* New York: Grove, 1963.

Berne, E. *Games people play.* New York: Grove, 1964.

Bing, E. The conjoint family drawing. *Family Process*, 1970, *9*, 173–194.

Bloom, B. L. Factor analysis of self-report measures of family functioning. *Family Process*, 1985, *24*, 225–240.

Borneman, E. Progress in empirical research on children's sexuality. *SIECUS Report*, 1983, *11*(2), 1–5.

Boulding, K. *The image.* Ann Arbor: University of Michigan Press, 1956.

Bryson, C. H. *A study of the relationship of self-description and family dysfunction.* Unpublished master's thesis, Georgia State University, 1978.

Buckley, W. *Sociology and modern systems theory.* Englewood Cliffs, N.J.: Prentice-Hall, 1967.

Burns, R. C., & Kaufman, S. H. *Action, styles, and symbols in kinetic family drawings.* New York: Brunner/Mazel, 1972.

Camp, H. Structural family therapy: An outsider's perspective. *Family Process*, 1973, *12*, 269–278.

Conant, R. C. Communication without a channel. *International Journal of General Systems*, 1979, *5*, 93–98.

Constantine, L. L. *Transmission of pattern in family process: A transgenerational model of psychopolitics.* Paper presented at the Theory Construction and Research Methodology Workshop, National Council on Family Relations annual meeting, Salt Lake City, Utah, August 1975.

Constantine, L. L. *The psychopolitics of family life.* Paper presented at the Colloquium on Changing Family Dynamics, University of Windsor, Ontario, February 1976. (a)

Constantine, L. L. Designed experience: A multiple goal-directed training program in family therapy. *Family Process*, 1976, *15*(4), 373–387. (b)

Constantine, L. L. Open family: A lifestyle for kids and other people. *The Family Coordinator*, 1977, *26*, 113–130. (a)

Constantine, L. L. *Notes on a unified systems theory of human process.* Paper presented at the University of Minnesota, Department of Family Social Science, October 1977. (b)

Constantine, L. L. Family sculpture and relationship mapping techniques. *Journal of Marriage and Family Counseling*, 1978, *4*, 13–23.

Constantine, L. L. *Uncinate processes in large-scale integration of theory: The case of unified process theory.* Paper presented at the Theory and Methodology Workshop, National Council on Family Relations, Portland, Oregon, October 1980. (a)

Constantine, L. L. Interpersonal behaviour in families: Research on the theoretical relationship of two models. *Australian Journal of Family Therapy*, 1980, *1*, 9–16. (b)

Constantine, L. L. Dysfunction and failure in open family systems: I. Application of a unified theory. *Journal of Marriage and the Family*, 1983, *45*, 725–738.

Constantine, L. L. Dysfunction and failure in open family systems: II. Clinical issues. *Journal of Marital and Family Therapy*, 1984, *10*, 1–17. (a)

Constantine, L. L. Alternative theory and utopian models. *Alternative Lifestyles*, 1984, *6*, 186–208. (b)

Constantine, L. L. *Psychopolitical analysis: A coding manual.* Fitchburg, Mass.: Adolescent & Family Institute, 1984. (c)

Constantine, L. L. Jealousy and extramarital relations. In N. S. Jacobson & A. S. Gurman (Eds.), *Clinical handbook of marital therapy.* New York: Guilford, 1986.

Constantine, L. L., Constantine, J. M., & Edelman, S. K. Counseling implications of comarital and multilateral relations. *Family Coordinator*, 1972, *21*, 267–273.

Constantine, L. L., & Israel, J. T. The family void: Treatment and theoretical aspects of the synchronous family paradigm. *Family Process*, 1985, *24*, 525–547.

Costell, R. M., & Reiss, D. The family meets the hospital: Clinical presentation of a laboratory-based family typology. *Archives of General Psychiatry*, 1982, *39*, 433–438.

Covey, L. P., & Tannen, E. R. *Applying Kantor and Lehr's four-player family interaction: A pilot study comparing normal and schizopresent families.* Unpublished master's thesis, Boston University, School of Social Work, 1976.

Cromwell, R., Fournier, D., & Kvebaek, D. *The Kvebaek family sculpture technique.* Jonesboro, Tenn.: Pilgrimage Press, 1980.

Cronen, V. E., Johnson, K. M., & Lannamann, J. W. Paradoxes, double-binds, and reflexive loops: An alternative theoretical perspective. *Family Process*, 1982, *21*, 91–112.

Cuber, J., & Harroff, P. *The significant Americans: A study of sexual behavior among the affluent.* New York: Appleton-Century, 1955.

Curran, D. *Traits of a healthy family.* Minneapolis: Winston, 1983.

de Lissovoy, V. Open family: Ask the kid who owns one—comments on Constantine. *The Family Coordinator,* 1977, *26*, 122–126.

DeMause, L. The evolution of childhood. *Journal of Psychohistory,* 1974, *1*, 503–575.

Dreikurs, R. *Children: The challenge.* New York: Hawthorn, 1964.

Duhl, F., Kantor, D., & Duhl, B. Learning, space and action in family therapy. In D. Block (Ed.), *Techniques of family psychotherapy.* New York: Grune & Stratton, 1973.

Ellis, A. Healthy and disturbed reasons for having extramarital sex. In G. Neubeck (Ed.), *Extramarital relations.* Englewood Cliffs, N.J.: Prentice-Hall, 1969.

Ellis, A., & Grieger, R. (Eds.). *Handbook of rational-emotive therapy.* New York: Springer, 1977.

Erikson, E. H. *Childhood and society.* New York: Norton, 1950.

Ernst, F. H. The OK corral: Grid for get on with. *Transactional Analysis Journal,* 1971, *1*(4).

Evison, R., & Horobin, R. *Handbook of co-counseling.* Sheffield, England: Co-Counseling Phoenix, 1982.

Fisher, R., & Ury, W. *Getting to yes: Negotiating agreement without giving in.* Boston: Houghton Mifflin, 1981.

Fisher, B. L., Giblin, P. R., & Hoopes, M. H. Healthy family functioning: What therapists say and what families want. *Journal of Marriage and Family Therapy,* 1982, *8*, 273–284.

Fromm, E. *Escape from freedom.* New York: Avon, 1965.

Geddes, M., & Medway, J. The symbolic drawing of the family life space. *Family Process,* 1977, *16*, 219–228.

Gergen, K. *Toward transformation in social knowledge.* New York: Springer-Verlag, 1982.

Glansdorff, P., & Prigogine, I. *Thermodynamic theory of structure, stability, and fluctuations.* New York: Wiley-Interscience, 1971.

Gordon, T. *Parent effectiveness training.* New York: Wyden, 1970.

Gordon, T. *P.E.T. in action.* New York: Wyden, 1976.

Habermas, J. *Theory and practice.* Boston: Beacon, 1974.

Haley, J. *Problem-solving therapy.* San Francisco: Jossey-Bass, 1976.

Harris, L., & Berlin, D. *Metatheoretical considerations for family therapy.* Paper presented at the Theory Construction and Research Methodology Workshop, National Council on Family Relations, Washington, D.C., October 1982.

Hartmann, E. L. *The functions of sleep.* New Haven: Yale University Press, 1973.

Hawkins, J. L. *Description, development, and distinction of Kantor and Lehr's three family type theory.* Unpublished manuscript, University of Minnesota, Department of Family Social Science, 1979.

Hofstadter, D. R. *Gödel, Escher, Bach: An eternal golden braid.* New York: Basic Books, 1979.

Howells, J. G. *Principles of family psychiatry.* New York: Brunner/Mazel, 1975.

Jantsch, E. *Design for evolution: Self-organization and planning in the life of human systems.* New York: Braziller, 1975.

Kantor, D. Critical identity image. In J. K. Pearce & L. J. Friedman (Eds.), *Family therapy: Combining psychodynamic and family systems approaches.* New York: Grune & Stratton, 1980.

Kantor, D. The structural–analytic approach to the treatment of family developmental crisis. In H. A. Liddle (Ed.), *Clinical implications of the family life cycle.* Rockville, Md.: Aspen, 1983.

Kantor, D., & Lehr, W. *Inside the family: Toward a theory of family process.* San Francisco: Jossey–Bass, 1975.

Kantor, D., & Neal, J. H. Integrative shifts for the theory and practice of family systems therapy. *Family Process,* 1985, *24,* 13–30.

Kantor, D., & Vickers, M. I. Divorce along the family life cycle. In H. A. Liddle (Ed.), *Clinical implications of the family life cycle.* Rockville, Md.: Aspen, 1983.

Karpel, M. A., & Strauss, E. S. *Family evaluation.* New York: Gardner, 1983.

Karpman, S. Fairy tales and script drama analysis. *Transactional Analysis Bulletin,* 1968, *7,* 39–43.

Keeney, B. P. (Ed.). *Diagnosis and assessment in family therapy.* Rockville, Md.: Aspen, 1983.

Keeney, B. P., & Ross, J. M. Cybernetics of brief therapy. *Journal of Marital and Family Therapy,* 1983, *9,* 375–382.

Keith, D., & Whitaker, C. Symbolic–experiential family therapy. In A. Gurman & D. Kniskern (Eds.), *Handbook of family therapy.* New York: Brunner/Mazel, 1981.

Klein, D. M., & Hill, R. Determinants of family problem-solving effectiveness. In W. R. Burr, R. Hill, F. I. Nye, & I. L. Reiss (Eds.), *Contemporary theories of the family.* New York: Macmillan, 1979.

Koch, A. Y., & Hattem, D. M. *Operationalizing psychopolitical role flexibility: A method for observing Kantor and Lehr's player parts.* Unpublished manuscript, Texas Tech University, 1983.

L'Abate, L. *Understanding and helping the individual in the family.* New York: Grune & Stratton, 1976.

Lacoursiere, R. *The life cycle of groups: Group development stage theory.* New York: Human Sciences, 1980.

Lane, M. *Introduction to structuralism.* New York: Basic Books, 1970.

Laszlo, E. *The systems view of the world.* New York: Braziller, 1972.

Lazarus, R. S. On the primacy of cognition. *American Psychologist,* 1984, *39*(2), 124–129.

Leary, T. *Interpersonal diagnosis of personality.* New York: Ronald, 1957.

Lefcourt, H. M. (Ed.). *Locus of control: Current trends in theory and research.* Hillsdale, N.J.: Erlbaum, 1976.

Leonard, A. S. *Kantor and Lehr's family type theory: Towards a diagnostic instrument for family therapy.* Unpublished master's thesis, The Hebrew University of Jerusalem, 1981.

Levenson, E. A. *The fallacy of understanding.* New York: Basic Books, 1972.

Liddle, H. A. Diagnosis and assessment in family therapy. In B. P. Keeney (Eds.), *Diagnosis and assessment in family therapy.* Rockville, Md.: Aspen, 1983.

Liedloff, J. *The continuum concept.* London: Duckworth, 1975.

Lorr, M., & McNair, D. M. Expansion of the interpersonal behavior circle. *Journal of Personality and Social Psychology,* 1965, *2,* 823–830.

Mahoney, M. J. Psychotherapy and the structure of personal revolutions. In M. J. Mahoney (Ed.), *Psychotherapy process.* New York: Plenum, 1980.

McGinnis, T. C., & Ayer, J. U. *Open family living.* Garden City, N.Y.: Doubleday, 1976.

McGoldrick, M., Giordano, J., & Pearce, J. (Eds.). *Ethnicity and family therapy*. New York: Guilford, 1983.

Meyers, L., & Leggitt, H. *Adultery and other private matters*. Chicago: Nelson Hall, 1975.

Miller, J. G. *Living systems*. New York: McGraw-Hill, 1978.

Miller, S., Nunnally, E. W., & Wackman, D. S. *Alive and aware*. Minneapolis: Interpersonal Communication Programs, 1975.

Minuchin, S. *Families and family therapy*. Cambridge, Mass.: Harvard University Press, 1974.

Nugent, M. D. *Updating Leary's wheel: A new instrument with new uses*. Paper presented at the American Association of Marriage and Family Counselors multiregional meeting, San Diego, April 1978.

Nugent, M. D., Rouanzoin, C. C., Asmann, B. D., & Lighty, L. *The psychopolitics of therapeutic interaction*. Paper presented at the National Council on Family Relations annual meeting, New York, October 1976.

Olson, D. E. Circumplex model of marital and family systems: VI. Theoretical update. *Family Process*, 1983, *22*, 69–83.

Olson, D., McCubbin, H., Barnes, H., Larson, A., Maxen, M., & Wilson, M. *Families: What makes them work?* Beverly Hills: Sage, 1983.

Olson, D. E., Sprenkle, D. H., & Russell, C. S., Circumplex model of marital and family systems: I. Cohesion and adaptability dimensions, family types, and clinical applications. *Family Process*, 1979, *18*, 3–29.

O'Neill, G., & O'Neill, N. *Open marriage*. New York: Evans, 1972.

Ornstein, R. E. *The psychology of consciousness*. San Francisco: Freeman, 1972.

Paolucci, B., & Bubolz, M. *Toward a critical theory of the family*. Paper presented at the Theory Construction and Research Methods Workshop, National Council on Family Relations annual meeting, Portland, Oregon, October 1980.

Papp, P. The Greek chorus and other techniques of family therapy. *Family Process*, 1980, *19*, 3–12.

Prigogine, I. *Non-equilibrium thermodynamics, variational techniques, and stability*. Chicago: University of Chicago Press, 1965.

Reiss, D. Varieties of consensual experience: I. Relating family interaction to individual thinking. *Family Process*, 1971, *10*, 1–28.

Reiss, D. *The family's construction of reality*. Cambridge, Mass.: Harvard University Press, 1981.

Riekehof, L. L. *The joy of signing*. Springfield, MO.: Gospel Publishing, 1978.

Satir, V. *Peoplemaking*. Palo Alto: Science & Behavior, 1972.

Selvini-Palazzoli, M., Cecchin, G., Prata, G., & Boscolo, L. *Paradox and counterparadox*. New York: Aronson, 1978.

Selvini-Palazzoli, M., Cecchin, G., Prata, G., & Boscolo, L. The problem of the referring person. *Journal of Marital and Family Therapy*, 1980, *6*, 3–9.

Sigafoos, A., Reiss, D., Rich, J., & Douglas, E. Pragmatics in the measurement of family functioning. *Family Process*, 1985, *24*, 189–202.

Skynner, A. C. R. *Systems of family and marital psychotherapy*. New York: Brunner/Mazel, 1976.

Sluzki, C. E. Process, structure, and world views: Toward an integration of systemic models in family therapy. *Family Process*, 1983, *22*, 469–476.

Speck, R., & Attneave, C. *Family networks*. New York: Pantheon, 1973.

Spencer Brown, G. *Laws of form*. New York: Julian Press, 1972.

Stafford, R. H. *Family systems theory: Theological and pastoral applications*. Unpublished master's thesis, General Theological Seminary, 1979.

Stern, G. B. *People in context: Measuring person–environment congruence in education and industry.* New York: Wiley, 1970.

Stierlin, H. *Separating parents and adolescents.* New York: Quadrangle, 1972.

Summit, R., & Kryso, J. Sexual abuse of children: A clinical spectrum. *American Journal of Orthopsychiatry,* 1978, *48,* 237–251.

Sweeney, D. R., Tinling, D. C., & Schmale, A. H., Jr. Dimensions of affective expression in four expressive modes. *Behavioral Science,* 1970, *15*(5), 393–407.

Triandis, H. C. Some universals of social behavior. *Personality and Social Psychology Bulletin,* 1978, *4*(1), 1–16.

Trotzer, J. P. The centrality of values in families and family therapy. *International Journal of Family Therapy,* 1981, *3,* 42–55.

Tuckman, B. W. Developmental sequence in small groups. *Psychological Bulletin,* 1965, *63,* 384–399.

Tuckman, B. W., & Jensen, M. W. Stages of small group development revisited. *Group & Organization Studies,* 1977, *2,* 419–427.

Varela, F. J. A calculus for self-reference. *International Journal of General Systems,* 1975, *2,* 5–24.

Voiland, A. L. *Family casework diagnosis.* New York: Columbia University Press, 1962.

von Bertalanffy, L. *General system theory.* New York: Braziller, 1968.

Wachowiak, D., & Bragg, H. Open marriage and marital adjustment. *Journal of Marriage and the Family,* 1980, *42,* 57–82.

Watzlawick, P., Beavin, J. H., & Jackson, D. D. *Pragmatics of human communication.* New York: Norton, 1967.

Weinberg, G. M. *Introduction to general systems thinking.* New York: Wiley-Interscience, 1975.

Weiner, M., & Mehrabian, A. *Language within language: Immediacy, a channel in verbal communication.* New York: Appleton, 1968.

Wertheim, E. S. Family unit therapy and the science and typology of family systems. *Family Process,* 1973, *12,* 361–377.

Wiggins, J. S. A psychological taxonomy of trait-descriptive terms: The interpersonal domain. *Journal of Personality and Social Psychology,* 1979, *46,* 395–412.

Wiggins, J. S. Circumplex models of interpersonal behavior. In L. Wheeler (Ed.), *Review of personality and social psychology* (Vol. 1). Beverly Hills: Sage, 1980.

Wylie, P. *The magic animal.* New York: Doubleday, 1968.

Zajonc, R. B. On the primacy of affect. *American Psychologist,* 1984, *39*(2), 117–123.

Zuk, G. H. Value systems and psychopathology in family therapy. *International Journal of Family Therapy,* 1979, *1,* 133–151.

# INDEX